Developments
in Latin American
political economy

MANCHESTER
UNIVERSITY PRESS

Developments in Latin American political economy

States, markets and actors

edited by
JULIA BUXTON
AND NICOLA PHILLIPS

Manchester University Press
Manchester and New York

distributed exclusively in the USA by St. Martin's Press

Published by Manchester University Press
Oxford Road, Manchester M13 9NR, UK
and Room 400, 175 Fifth Avenue, New York, NY 10010, USA
http://www.man.ac.uk/mup

Distributed exclusively in the USA by
St. Martin's Press, Inc., 175 Fifth Avenue, New York, NY 10010, USA

Distributed exclusively in Canada by
UBC Press, University of British Columbia, 6344 Memorial Road,
Vancouver, BC, Canada V6T 1Z2

British Library Cataloguing-in-Publication Data
A catalogue record for this book is available from the British Library

Library of Congress Cataloging-in-Publication Data applied for

ISBN 0 7190 5458 3 hardback
      0 7190 5459 1 paperback

First published 1999

06 05 04 03 02 01 00 99   10 9 8 7 6 5 4 3 2 1

Typeset in Sabon with Syntax
by Northern Phototypesetting Co. Ltd, Bolton
Printed in Great Britain
by Bookcraft (Bath) Ltd, Midsomer Norton

Contents

List of tables   *page* vi
List of contributors   vii
List of abbreviations   x

Introduction   *Nicola Phillips and Julia Buxton*   1

Part I States and markets

1   A trip to the market: the impact of neoliberalism in Latin
    America   *Duncan Green*   13

2   Institutions and democratic consolidation in Latin America
    George Philip   33

3   Electoral and party politics   *Daniel Hellinger*   49

4   Global and regional linkages   *Nicola Phillips*   72

Part II Traditional and emerging actors

5   The military in Latin America: defining the road ahead
    Craig L. Arceneaux   93

6   Guerrilla movements   *Peter Calvert*   112

7   NGOs and the retreat of the state: the hidden dangers
    Laura Tedesco   131

8   The human rights movement and democratisation
    Alexandra Barahona de Brito   146

9   Women and politics   *Fiona Macaulay*   168

10 The environmental agenda: accountability for sustainability
    Jonathan R. Barton   186

Appendix: Virtual Latin America   205
Select bibliography   211
Index   229

Tables

1.1   Latin America: key economic indicators   *page* 30

4.1   Mercosur: timetable for tariff reductions   79

4.2   Mercosur trade   80

4.3   Evolution of the structure of Mercosur world exports   81

5.1   Military expenditures of selected Latin American countries   95

5.2   The 20 largest Latin American militaries and force distribution   99

9.1   Women in elected office in Latin America   173

List of contributors

Craig Arceneaux is Lecturer in Politics at the University of California, Riverside, US. He received his Ph.D. in Political Science from the University of California, Riverside. His research interests in Latin American politics include civil–military relations, democratisation and institutional change. He has presented several conference papers on these topics and has published work in the *Journal of Political and Military Sociology, Bulletin of Latin American Research* and *Comparative Political Studies.*

Alexandra Barahona de Brito is an Associate Researcher with the Instituto de Estudos Estratégicos e Internacionais (IEEI), Lisbon, Portugal, and has worked also at the Institute of European–Latin American Relations (IRELA) in Madrid. She has published a book on the politics of transition and human rights, *Human Rights and Democratisation in Latin America: Uruguay and Chile* (1997). Other recent publications include 'The Politics of Human Rights in Democratic Brazil: "A Lei Não Pega"' (co-authored with Francisco Panizza), in *Democratisation*, 'Promoting Democracy in Cuba? The European Union and Helms Burton', in Francisco León, *et al.* (eds), *Integración económica y democratización: América Latina y Cuba* (1998); and 'The European Union and the Mercosur: The Promotion of Democracy and Human Rights', in Alexandra Barahona de Brito, *et al., Beyond Trade: Relations between the European Union and the Mercosur* (1997). She is currently co-editing a book, *The Politics of Memory: The Decades of Transitional Truth and Justice*, on how countries in Africa, Europe and Latin America have dealt with the legacy of human rights violations in the transition to democracy. She is a member of the Editorial Board of the *Journal of Interamerican Studies and World Affairs.*

Jonathan Barton is Senior Research Associate in the School for Development Studies, University of East Anglia, UK. He has worked on political geography issues in Chile and Latin America more generally, leading to the publication of *A Political Geography of Latin America* (1997). He is currently pursuing interests in the political economy of environmental policy, such as the impact of environmental regulations on industrial production and trade, and the barriers to the introduction of environmental technologies and environmental management. He has recently conducted research for the European Commission on the iron and steel industry and environmental issues in Western and Eastern Europe, Korea and Brazil.

Julia Buxton has recently completed a doctoral thesis on the Venezuelan party system 1989–93 at the London School of Economics and works as a consultant on Venezuelan politics and economics. She is a lecturer in the Department of Social Science at Kingston University. Publications include *The Contemporary History Handbook* (ed., 1995) and 'Venezuela, Degenerative Democracy' in

Democratization: The Resilience of Democracy (forthcoming).

Peter Calvert is Professor of Comparative and International Politics at the University of Southampton, UK, and holds a Ph.D. from the University of Cambridge. He is a specialist in the politics and international relations of the Western hemisphere with a particular interest currently in environmental issues and was a delegate to the Earth Summit in Rio de Janeiro in 1992. Among his recent publications are *Latin America in the Twentieth Century* (with Susan Calvert, 2nd edn, 1993), *An Introduction to Comparative Politics* (1993), *The International Politics of Latin America* (1994) and *Politics and Society in the Third World* (with Susan Calvert, 1996).

Duncan Green is a Policy Analyst at CAFOD, the Catholic aid agency for England and Wales. He has written widely on Latin American society and economy. His previous books include *Hidden Lives: Voices of Children in Latin America and the Caribbean* (1998); *Faces of Latin America* (1991) and *Silent Revolution: The Rise of Market Economics in Latin America* (1995).

Daniel Hellinger is Professor of Political Science at Webster University, St Louis, US, and holds a Ph.D. from Rutgers University, US. He is author of *Venezuela, Tarnished Democracy* (1991) and co-author of *The Democratic Facade*, a critical examination of US politics; he is a participating editor for *Latin American Perspectives*, for which he recently edited a special edition on 'Post Bonanza Venezuela', and is a regular contributor to the *St. Louis Journalism Review*. He has published several articles on the international political economy of minerals and is presently completing research on post-Pinochet copper policy in Chile.

Fiona Macaulay is a Research Associate in the Centre for Cross-Cultural Research on Women at Queen Elizabeth House, University of Oxford, UK. She has a Doctorate in politics from St Antony's College, Oxford and her main research interests are gender policy, political parties and local government in Latin America, and contemporary politics, social issues and human rights in Brazil. Her doctoral thesis *Gender Politics in Brazil and Chile: The Role of Parties in Local and National Policy-making* will be published in 1999. Recent publications include 'Localities of Power: Gender, Parties and Democracy in Brazil and Chile', in Haleh Afshar, ed., *Empowering Women: Illustrations from the Third World* (1998) and 'Governing for Everyone: The Workers' Party Administration in São Paulo 1989–1992', *Bulletin of Latin American Research*, 15:2, 1996.

George Philip is Reader in Comparative and Latin American Politics at the London School of Economics and Political Science, UK. Recent articles focus on 'The New Populism in Spanish South America' (*Government and Opposition*), the concept of good governance, and neoliberalism and democracy. Other publications include *The Presidency in Mexican Politics* (1992) and *The Military in*

South American Politics (1985). He is currently researching the issue of presidentialism in Latin America.

Nicola Phillips is Lecturer in Politics and International Studies at the University of Warwick, UK. She received her Ph.D. from the London School of Economics, and her research interests focus principally on international political economy with a particular application to the Latin American region. She has written various papers and book chapters on globalisation and the state in Latin America, the impact of the global crisis on regionalism in South America, and East Asian and Latin American perspectives on the global economic crisis. She is author of 'The Future Political Economy of Latin America', in Richard Stubbs and Geoffrey R. D. Underhill, *Political Economy and the Changing Global Order* (second edition, forthcoming 1999), and her forthcoming book is entitled *State Power and Global Change in Latin America*.

Laura Tedesco is Lecturer in Politics in the School of Development Studies, University of East Anglia, UK. She previously worked in the Centro de Investigaciones Europeo-Latinoamericanas, EURAL, Buenos Aires, and received her Ph.D. from Warwick University. She has written on Argentina's foreign policy, the military and democratisation and economic restructuring in Argentina. Her forthcoming book is entitled *Democracy in Argentina: Hope and Disillusion*.

Abbreviations

AD	Acción Democrática (Democratic Action, Venezuela)
AD	Alianza Democrática (Democratic Alliance, Colombia)
AI	Amnesty International
AIP	Apparel Industry Partnership
AMDH	Academia Mexicana de Derechos Humanos (Mexican Academy for Human Rights)
AMNLAE	Asociación de Mujeres Nicaraguenses Luisa Amanda Espinoza (Luisa Amanda Espinoza Association of Nicaraguan Women)
ANAPO	Alianza Nacional Popular (Popular National Alliance, Colombia)
AP	Acción Popular (Popular Action, Peru)
APEC	Asia-Pacific Economic Cooperation Conference
APRA	Alianza Popular Revolucionaria Americana (American Popular Revolutionary Alliance)
ARENA	Alianza Republicana Nacional (National Republican Alliance, El Salvador)
BINGO	big NGO
CACM	Central American Common Market
CAFOD	Catholic Fund for Overseas Development
CAJ	Comisión Andina de Juristas (Andean Jurists' Commission)
Caricom	Caribbean Community
CD	Convergencia Democrática (Democratic Convergence, Colombia)
CEAS	Comisión Episcopal de Acción Social (Episcopal Commission for Social Action, Peru)
CEDAW	Convention on the Elimination of all Forms of Discrimination Against Women
CEPAL	Comisión Económica para América Latina (UN Economic Commission for Latin America and the Caribbean) *see also* ECLAC
CET	common external tariff
CIA	(US) Central Intelligence Agency
CNGSB	Coordinación Nacional Guerrillera Simón Bolívar (Simón Bolívar Guerrilla Coordinating Board, Colombia)
CODELCO	Corporación del Cobre (Chile)
COMECON	Council for Mutual Economic Assistance
CONAVIGUA	Coordinadera Nacional de Viudas de Guatemala (National Coordination of Guatemalan Widows of Political Violence)
CONEP	Consejo Nacional Protestante (National Protestant Council, Peru)

COPEI	Comité de Organización Política Electoral Independiente (Committee for Independent Political Electoral Organisation, Venezuela)
CPC	Comisión Parlamentaria Conjunta del Mercosur (United Parliamentary Commission of Mercosur)
CUT	Central Unica de Trabalhadores (Brazil)
DONGO	donor-organised NGO
EC	European Community
ECLAC	UN Economic Commission for Latin America and the Caribbean *see also* CEPAL
ECOSOC	Economic and Social Council
ELN	Ejército de Liberación Nacional (National Liberation Army, Colombia)
ENGO	environmental NGO
EP	European Parliament
EPL	Ejército Popular de Liberación (National Liberation Army, Colombia)
EPL	Esperanza, Paz y Libertad (Hope, Peace and Liberty, Colombia)
EPR	Ejército Popular Revolucionario (People's Revolutionary Party, Mexico)
EU	European Union
EZLN	Ejército Zapatista de Liberación Nacional (Zapatista National Liberation Army, Mexico)
FARC	Fuerzas Armadas Revolucionarias de Colombia (Revolutionary Armed Forces of Colombia)
FDI	foreign direct investment
FDN	Fuerza Democrática Nicaraguense (Nicaraguan Democratic Force)
FEDEFAM	Federación Latinoamericana de Familiares de Detenidos Desaparecidos (Federation of the Families of Disappeared Prisoners)
FMLN	Frente Farabundo Martí de Liberación Nacional (Farabundo Martí Front for National Liberation, El Salvador)
fob	free on board
FREPASO	Frente para el País Solidario (Front for the Solidarity of the Country, Argentina)
FSLN	Frente Sandinista de Liberación Nacional (Sandinista Front for National Liberation, Nicaragua)
FTA	free trade area
FTAA	Free Trade Area of the Americas
GDP	gross domestic product
GNP	gross national product
GONGO	government-organised NGO
GPP	Guerra Popular Prolongada (Prolonged Popular War, Nicaragua)

GRO	grassroots organisation
HDI	human development index
HRO	human rights non-governmental organisation
HRW	Human Rights Watch
ICCPR	International Covenant on Civil and Political Rights
ICJ	International Commission of Jurists
IDB	Inter-American Development Bank
IFC	International Finance Corporation
ILO	International Labour Organization
IMF	International Monetary Fund
INGO	international non-governmental organisation
ISI	import-substituting industrialisation
LAFTA	Latin American Free Trade Area
LAIA	Latin American Integration Association
M-19	Movimiento de 19 Abril (19 April Movement, Colombia)
MAS	Movimiento al Socialismo (Movement towards Socialism, Venezuela)
Mercosur	Mercado Común del Sur (Southern Common Market)
MINUGUA	UN Verification Mission
MNC	multinational corporation
MNMMR	Movimiento Nacional de Meninos e Meninas da Rua (National Street Children's Movement, Brazil)
MNR	Movimiento Nacional Revolucionario (National Revolutionary Party, Bolivia)
MRTA	Movimiento Revolucionario Túpac Amaru (Túpac Amaru Revolutionary Movement, Peru)
NAFTA	North American Free Trade Agreement
NATO	North Atlantic Treaty Organization
NCO	non-commissioned officer
NED	National Endowment for Democracy (USA)
NEIO	New International Economic Order
NEM	new economic model
NGO	non-governmental organisation
NNGO	northern NGO
NSD	national security doctrine
NSDD	National Security Division Directive (USA)
OAS	Organization of American States
OECD	Organization for Economic Cooperation and Development
PAN	Partido para Acción Nacional (National Action Party, Mexico)
PCC	Partido Comunista de Cuba (Communist Party of Cuba)
PCP	Partido Comunista Peruana (Peruvian Communist Party)
PCP–SL	Partido Comunista del Perú–Sendero Luminoso (Communist Party of Peru – Shining Path)

PdVSA	Petróleos de Venezuela (Venezuelan state oil company)
PEMEX	Petróleos de Mexico (Mexican oil company)
PLI	Partido Liberal Independiente (Independent Liberal Party, Nicaragua)
PMDB	Partido do Movimiento Democratico Brasileiro (Brazilian Democratic Movement Party)
PN	Partido Nacionalista (Nationalist Party, Chile)
PPD	Partido para la Democracia (Party for Democracy, Chile)
PPF	Partido Peronista Femenino (Peronist Women's Party, Argentina)
PPT	Patria para Todos (Homeland for All, Venezuela)
PRD	Partido Democrático Revolucionario (Democratic Revolutionary Party, Mexico)
PRI	Partido Revolucionario Institucional (Revolutionary Institutional Party, Mexico)
PRN	Renovación Nacionalista (National Renovation Party, Chile)
PRT	Partido Revolucionario de Trabajadores (Revolutionary Workers' Party, Colombia)
PS	Partido Socialista (Socialist Party, Chile)
PSR	Partido Socialista Revolucionario (Revolutionary Socialist Party, Peru)
PT	Partido dos Trabalhadores (Workers' Party, Brazil)
PTB	Partido dos Trabalhadores Brasileiros (Brazilian Workers' Party)
SAFTA	South American Free Trade Area
SERNAM	Servicio Nacional de la Mujer (National Women's Service, Chile)
SERPAJ	Servicio de Paz y Justicia (Peace and Justice Service)
SIE	Servicio de Inteligencia del Ejército (Army Intelligence Service, Peru)
SL	Sendero Luminoso (Shining Path, Peru)
SNGO	southern NGO
UCR	Unión Cívica Radical (Radical Party, Argentina)
UDI	Unión Democrática Independiente (Independent Democratic Union, Chile)
UN	United Nations
UNAM	Universidad Autónoma de México (Autonomous University of Mexico)
UNCED	UN Conference on Environment and Development
UNCTAD	UN Conference on Trade and Development
UNO	Unión Nacional Opositora (National Opposition Union, Nicaragua)
UNTAC	UN Transitional Authority for Cambodia
UP	Union Patriótico (Patriotic Union, Colombia)

URNG	Unidad Revolucionaria Nacional de Guatemala (Guatemalan National Revolutionary Unity)
USACDA	US Arms Control and Disarmament Agency
USAID	US Agency for Internationonal Development
USCC	US Catholic Conference
VAT	value added tax
WCC	World Council of Churches
WGIP	UN Working Group on Indigenous Populations
WHO	World Health Organisation
WOLA	Washington Office on Latin America
WTO	World Trade Organization

Introduction

NICOLA PHILLIPS
AND JULIA BUXTON

Since the mid-1980s, throughout the Latin American region, with the exception of Cuba, democratic politics and neoliberal economics have become the norm. The pattern of political and economic ungovernability of the post-war period, marked by military coups, civil wars, economic collapse and governmental incompetence, has been replaced with a degree of stability and dynamism as a result of extensive political and economic reform. The patterns of contemporary change in Latin America have their roots in a unique combination of domestic and international change. At the national level, the pattern of political and economic ungovernability that characterised the region throughout the post-war period has been replaced by new forms of stability based on democratic political systems and market economics. This shift can be traced to a process of rethinking based largely on the experience of economic crisis and hyperinflation in the 1980s and the legacy of military dictatorship. The direction of the reform process undoubtedly was influenced by international currents, in the shape of a new consensus on economic orthodoxy and the spread of democracy globally. Increasingly, in order to participate effectively on the international stage, countries were obliged, to a greater or lesser extent, to conform with this global spread of a certain set of ideas on politics, governance and markets. As such, reform and change in Latin America are informed by the 'globalisation' of both economic activity and political ideas.

All this is fairly commonplace, but it is often misconstrued to mean that Latin American (and other) countries have adopted the new policy consensus unquestioningly, and that 'development' can now truly be seen as a mechanistic and linear process, uncannily in line with the predictions of the modernisation theorists of the 1960s. The central contention of this project is that the current context of neoliberal and democratic consolidation, contrary to some prevalent opinion and rhetoric, does not constitute the Latin American version of the 'end of history' hypothesis. The transition to democracy and economic neoliberalism has happened, but in many ways we are now seeing the emergence of a genuine debate, at both state and societal levels, on the political and economic models that governments implemented. The implementation or 'transition' phase of economic and political reform has given way to a second, 'consolidation' phase, which generates completely new sets of issues, pressures and priorities. It is precisely in this consolidation phase of change that national-level variables become pivotal, as governments and societal actors confront the task of adapting the political and economic orientation to specific demands and necessities.

In the economic sphere, the emergence of serious social problems with neoliberalism, for example, has prompted a significant questioning of the ways in which the overall orientation can be maintained but tailored to avoid its visible shortcomings. Although the benefits of neoliberalism were clear in terms of international acceptance, financial flows and inflation figures, reforms were slow in generating the expected results in terms of growth, stability and employment indicators at the domestic level.[1] These concerns define the agenda of the 'second generation' of structural reforms, which in the economic policy arena involve such issues as labour flexibilisation. In other words, the elimination of hyperinflation and the stabilisation of the macroeconomic environment have now given way to an agenda which has significant repercussions on sections of society, and it is in this area that the real debate, and perhaps the real challenges, lie.

It is perhaps partly as a result of these trends in the trajectory of neoliberal economic reform that we are beginning to talk of the 're-politicisation' of Latin America. For much of the first part of the 1990s, civil society was almost entirely demobilised throughout the region as a result of hyperinflation, political crisis and the installation of neopopulist, quasi-authoritarian governments, such as those of Menem in Argentina, Fujimori in Peru and, arguably for a short period in 1994, Caldera in Venezuela. Such governments instituted highly presidentialist, centralised and exclusionary political regimes, which were marked by frequent recourse to presidential veto and decree powers, constitutional manipulation and corruption.[2] Although such 'democraduras' (which can be translated perhaps as 'democratorships') conform to the formal, electoral requirements of 'democracy', they fall short of the participatory and representative qualities of an open political system, and reinforce the marginalisation of societal and popular interests from the arena of domestic political activity.

This societal demobilisation certainly allowed for the reform process to progress more smoothly and more quickly than otherwise might have been the case. The consensus necessary for the economic reform agenda was constructed on the basis of a state–business alliance in which the private sector and the holders of capital (foreign and domestic) were drawn into an alliance with the reforming elites in government. The resulting coalitions represented an alliance of the holders of political power and the holders of economic power in Latin

American countries. Both as a result of the nature of neoliberal reform, then, and as a result of the changes generated world-wide by the forces of globalisation, political power in Latin America was restructured in ways that privileged business and financial agents over labour and other societal interests. As the more deleterious elements of the economic restructuring became apparent, the consensus generated by the acquiescence of civil societies and the dominance of business, financial and government elites started to become increasingly hard to maintain.

In this way, the marginalisation of participatory democracy is beginning now to give way to increased demands and pressures on the system for the democratisation of politics, particularly in terms of levels of participation and representation. Although democracy does not appear to be under threat, the sort of 'neoliberal democracy' established in Latin America depended (and still depends) on a close collaboration between the state and business sectors for its survival.[3] Although it is still far from clear that this collaboration is in fact disintegrating the state–business nexus appears to be coming under pressure from *outside* the neoliberal coalition. Both previously excluded or marginalised societal actors and external actors, such as the multilateral development banks, are pressing for an expansion of the agenda and a widening of participation in the debate. The context of the second generation reforms, therefore, is one of an increased focus, at elite and popular levels, on issues of accountability and transparency, judicial reform, corruption, human rights and the continuing reform of the state. These are the issues which are encapsulated in the new focus on 'governance' of domestic groups and development banks.[4]

The resurgence of politics in Latin America has been accompanied by an upsurge in levels of popular mobilisation. Although this does not resemble the violent forms of protest such as the so-called IMF riots in the late 1980s and early 1990s[5], it is nevertheless notable that societal actors are once again mobilising around various issues. In Argentina in recent years the 'provincial crisis' subsumed a variety of discontents, exacerbated by incidents of police brutality and growing levels of student protest. At the same time, the *carpa blanca* (white tent) of the teachers' strike erected opposite the congress building stands as a challenge to the dominant neoliberal consensus and the political complacency of government elites. The Zapatista uprising in the southern Mexican state of Chiapas similarly raises issues of both political and economic inclusion or exclusion. The stubborn persistence of violent terrorist activity in countries such as Peru, Guatemala and Colombia raises important questions that cannot be answered if one subscribes to the 'end of history' idea. In other words, popular mobilisation, both peaceful and violent, remains a crucial part of political life in Latin American countries, and fits in with questions about democracy, market economics and the future agenda of Latin American political economy.

The resuscitation of popular participation in politics – perhaps the 're-politicisation of politics' – has been both sparked and reinforced by the emergence of a range of new, non-traditional actors in the political process. This is the result of shifts at both the international and domestic levels. For years international political economists and others have been drawing attention to the transnationalisation of economic and political activity, which has picked up genuine impetus with the onslaught of globalisation. The importance of an emerging transnational civil society, composed of non-governmental organisations (NGOs) and interest groups, transnational social movements and other such formations, is currently an area of huge empirical importance and enormous academic attention.[6] There is a growing body of opinion which stresses the importance of an active and 'empowered' civil society for achieving development and democratisation.[7]

With economic and political opening at both the national and the global levels, the possibilities for these groups to function and exert influence has increased very significantly. Until recently in Latin America, the development of native civil society had lagged behind the development of transnational groups. Perhaps in something of a demonstration effect, but also as a result of recent domestic change, however, this is changing. The possibility for Latin American groups to cooperate with the larger transnational networks has facilitated the development of both. The range of issues thrown to the fore by economic globalisation and neoliberalism, such as poverty, environmental degradation and income inequality, similarly have generated a host of new interest groups concerned with issues such as women's rights, environmental protection, the rights of indigenous peoples, the new human rights agenda, and so on. Despite the hitherto centralised nature of Latin American democracies, the possibilities for participation have increased, and certainly the development of this kind of civil society is having the complementary effect of pressing for further political opening and increased possibilities for participation and debate.

What we see in Latin America in the late 1990s, therefore, is an agenda characterised both by new issues and new players. The development of new actors and the shifting policy agenda as we move beyond the world of transitions are pushing Latin American countries towards a completely new set of challenges. The traditional examples of both – democracy, stability, development, policy, the military, the state, etc. – have been pushed into a fundamental redefinition of their roles and capabilities which has changed the political and economic landscape in the region, as well as its interaction with the global arena. It is important not to overestimate the challenge to the state represented by the diversification of actors, or the challenge to the dominant economic orientation of the debate currently surrounding it. The state remains entrenched at the eye of the storm, and both the political process and the reform agenda remain dominated by the state machinery and government elites. In addition, the state is the principal player in the new international and regional context of politics and development. Similarly, the debate on economic policy is premised largely on an acceptance of the overall orientation. Therefore, our analysis needs to emphasise 'new' actors and issue-areas without losing sight of those institutional and societal structures which remain pivotal to the processes of political and economic change.

Furthermore, in conjunction with the changes noted above, we are seeing a process of a diversification of the levels on which political and economic activity is conducted. Activity and trends at the national level interact with and are propelled by change at the international or global level, particularly with regard to the processes of globalisation and regionalisation. The formation of regional blocs such as the Mercado Común del Sur (Mercosur, Southern Common Market) and the North American Free Trade Agreement (NAFTA) have generated a regionalisation of economic activity which is accompanied by a significantly regional dimension to political change. What seems to be clear is that, in Latin America and throughout the world, political economy is becoming internationalised, along with states and societies. There is a situation, qualitatively new in Latin America, in which the interests of the state are seen to coincide and intersect with the 'interests' of the international economy, and in which the national interests (however defined) are intricately linked to the dynamics currently underway at the global and regional levels.

The aim of the present volume, therefore, is to capture the changing reality of Latin American political economy, and to examine the changes in the composition of the political arena, the changing nature of the economic, social and political policy agendas, and the diversification of levels at which political and economic activity is conducted. The chapters fit with the overall aim of reassessing the dominant trends, actors and issues in the region as a whole, and in individual countries, in the post-transition period.[8] In other words, the chapters are consciously forward-looking, addressing the concepts and themes which are currently decisive, and are likely to be of central importance in the short and medium terms.

The volume collects together a group of authors of different backgrounds and persuasions, in the interests of producing a wide range of opinions, arguments and positions which reflect the nature of contemporary debates in the study of Latin America. As a result, the volume provides a wide-ranging overview of the issues and themes, and an introduction to Latin American political economy that exposes the reader to a variety of positions and approaches to the subject matter. The book constitutes a thematic introduction to Latin American political economy, concentrating in the first part on the evolution of economic policy and political systems, and in the second on the development of traditional and non-traditional actors in the political processes of the region and of individual countries.[9]

The organisation of the volume

The first part of the volume concentrates on the development of Latin American political and economic systems, focusing on the interaction between states and markets. Duncan Green's chapter on neoliberalism looks beyond the initial implementation of reform in order to focus on the contemporary trends in economic policy and performance, and the social manifestations of these processes. He pays particular attention to the problems that have come to light since the initial design of neoliberal restructuring programmes, and argues that the long-awaited 'trickle-down' effect that underpinned early confidence about neoliberal reform has still not arrived for the majority of the populations. His chapter raises important questions about how these bottlenecks can be resolved. If neoliberalism is here to stay, how can governments maintain the overall orientation while providing basic services, wealth and well-being to the population?

George Philip's chapter on the evolution of political systems in Latin America ties issues of democracy, institutional development and governance in with analysis of neoliberalism and economic performance. His chapter is in this way an examination of the relationship between states and markets, or politics and economics, in the context of political development. He argues that 'it is both possible and necessary to develop professional state institutions if democracy is to work well in Latin America', but demonstrates that at the same time institution-building depends on a degree of economic success. In this way, the tasks of democratic and economic consolidation in Latin America are bound to each other in complex and fundamental ways. Like Duncan Green, he similarly draws attention to the dangers of inequality and the same delay in the 'trickle-down' for the continued survival and/or stability of political systems.

Daniel Hellinger gives more substance to a key feature of these political systems with an analysis of the evolution of electoral and party politics. His chapter also picks up the themes introduced in the first two chapters, and returns to the perennial equation in Latin American political economy between economic and political collapse: to abandon neoliberalism would likely involve democratic breakdown, even at this juncture of consolidation. According to Hellinger, 'populist and leftist criticism of neoliberalism is tempered by knowledge that economic crisis and political polarisation were forerunners of democratic collapse'. Although the status quo might well be maintained, this is a shaky basis for the institutionalisation of elections and hence the consolidation of political democracy. In other words, there needs to be a much closer correlation, and moreover a greater public perception of the correlation, between the well-being of the electorate and the electoral process itself.

Hellinger's chapter focuses on the ways in which the neoliberal wave in Latin America has affected the role of parties in linking states and societies to each other through the electoral process. Along with the re-politicisation process mentioned above and the diversification of actors in the political process, in many countries opposition movements which offer serious alternatives to the dominant political trends of the 1990s have redefined themselves, or emerged for the first time. Much opposition is focused on the democratisation of the state and the development of a more inclusionary style of politics, and also on the ways of 'humanising' neoliberalism without abandoning the neoliberal course. Trends in party systems are diverse, ranging from the crisis of populist parties to the development of 'new left' parties. The turning point for Latin American party systems, and the crisis of party politics, has been matched around the world, perhaps adding a new slant on our argument that the globalisation of economic activity is equally a globalisation of political activity. Trends in Latin American political economy do not exist in isolation.

These international and regional linkages are explored in Nicola Phillips's chapter. She argues that political and economic change in Latin America has been reinforced by processes of international change, globalisation and region-alisation, and that reform at the domestic level has been 'locked in' by sets of international commitments and obligations into which Latin American govern-ments have entered. Although the neoliberal orientation has become well estab-lished in Latin America, however, there is a danger in assuming too great a degree of uniformity between countries either in their approaches to economic reform and the internationalisation of the economy, or in their responses to the challenges presented by integration at the global and regional levels. The chap-ter analyses in particular the development of South American regionalism, and its future trajectory both in terms of the projected Free Trade Area of the Amer-icas (FTAA) and the problems for deepening sub-regional integration. The final parts of the chapter look at the implications for political organisation and democratic government of the internationalisation of political and economic activity. In many ways the real debates are only just beginning, but look certain to be of an inclusionary nature, incorporating a range of new actors as well as more traditional state and societal interests.

The second part of the volume addresses in this context the changing nature of traditional actors and the emergence of new non-state actors in Latin Amer-ica. One of the most obvious of the former is the military, which formerly exer-cised an extensive veto power over the political process throughout the region. Craig Arceneaux looks at the ways in which the role of the military is being redefined from both inside the institution itself and as a result of 'external' change. He highlights the differences between national militaries and illustrates the distribution of military power in the Latin American region. Changes in the nature of the military and its activities, and consequently its place in the polit-ical arena, can be traced to a conjunction of international factors (such as the end of the Cold War and shifts in foreign policy interests) and domestic processes (such as democratisation and economic restructuring). As a result, Latin American militaries are described by Arceneaux as having reached a crit-ical turning point.

Just as the post-war period in Latin America was characterised by high lev-els of military intervention and activism, the political landscape was also char-acterised by high levels of terrorist and guerrilla violence, ranging from Sendero Luminoso (SL, Shining Path) in Peru to drugs-related violence in Colombia and revolutionary action in Central America and Cuba. Peter

Calvert's chapter addresses the ways in which contemporary currents of change (domestic and international) have redefined both the environment and the activities of such groups, offering detailed case studies of various countries. It seems clear in Latin America that violent protest in the 1990s has links with processes of neoliberal reform and the style of political system established with democratisation. In addition, the narcotics problem has not disappeared, and drugs-related violence continues to be a headache for a number of governments. Although the strength of most groups has diminished in the 1990s, their impact on politics, in terms of government legitimacy, stability and influence on the policy process, remains visible and important.

The following chapters in this section focus on non-traditional actors in Latin American political economy. Laura Tedesco looks at the emergence of NGOs in Latin America in the context of the redefinition of the state and the rethinking of development. She argues that the development of these forms of civil society have acted to compensate the shortcomings of the state, to the extent that the state has ceased to be responsible for the provision of basic rights. This 'NGO-isation' of development politics in this way has come to act as a cover for the inadequacies of the neoliberal state and for the huge gap left by the retreat of the state in favour of market solutions to development problems.

Alexandra Barahona de Brito's chapter looks more specifically at the human rights movement in Latin America, placing particular emphasis on both the development of human rights groups and the ways in which the human rights agenda has expanded in recent years to cover non-traditional areas such as the rights of gays and lesbians, women, and indigenous peoples. Again, recent trends are linked to developments at both the national and international levels. The partnerships established by the Latin American human rights movement with international groups and international institutions, for example, were as fundamental as the working relationship established with the domestic state and domestic groups of various colours. The activism of the human rights movement currently engages with the processes of democratisation (in the sense of consolidating and redefining democracy) in encouraging a more open and inclusionary style of politics and government, but at the same time generates a new set of demands and pressures which governments are constrained to address in the context of political and economic reform.

Fiona Macaulay picks up on one of the themes mentioned by Barahona de Brito, and gives further substance to the issue of women's groups in the region. The development of a 'gender agenda' is an important component of the context of both neoliberalism and the types of political democracy established in the region. The chapter demonstrates the ways in which women are now collectively active in both the formal and informal spheres of politics, and a crucial part of the resurgent pressures for full citizenship, contestation and genuine participatory democracy. The case of women's groups is also an excellent example of grassroots activism and lobbying, rather than a part of the top-down, elite-led process of reform of which the mainstream restructuring effort was an example. However, she argues that the 'logic' of economic globalisation presents a set of apparently intractable obstacles, generated mainly by changes in the global and national workplace, poverty issues, employment trends and government policies. In this sense, the economic trajectory of Latin American countries may be seen as at odds with the political demands for inclusion and 'gender awareness', and hence a major challenge for women's groups in the future.

Jonathan Barton, finally, looks at the development of the environmental agenda in the region, and links the growing salience of environmental issues with neoliberal economic restructuring, the processes of globalisation and regionalisation at the international level, and the emergence of new domestic and transnational actors. With the emphasis on competitiveness in a globalising international economy, the incentives for producers and firms to invest in environmental technology are likely to be fairly low, particularly in regions like Latin America. Although the private sector must shoulder most of the responsibility for environmentally damaging activities, the impacts of degradation are felt principally by the urban poor. As such, the environmental agenda is a fundamentally political issue, both at the national level and in more global terms. Similarly, the removal of the state from its former position as economic manager as a result of market reforms, as well as the centrality of the private sector in the new economic model, have meant that the state's ability to enforce environmental regulations has been eroded. This has generated something of a 'power gap', where there is no obvious actor or sector capable of pursuing the environmental agenda with any significant influence or resources.

The development of non-state interests in the environmental issue area, most notably NGOs and pressure groups, is an important response to the inadequacy of the public sphere and the apparent indifference of political parties. Their activities increasingly define the environmental agenda, reinforcing the notion that sustainable development depends on commitment and concerted action among a number of actors at a variety of levels. These observations coincide with the major analytical and empirical premises of this book. The future of Latin American political economy is likely to depend on a fundamental reaccommodation of the relationship between states and markets, between the national and international levels of activity, between traditional and non-traditional actors, and between established and emerging issue areas.

Notes

1 G. Casaburi and D. Tussie, 'Strengthening the Role of Civil Society in Local and Global Governance: The Looming Reform Agenda of Multilateral Development Banks', Series on Governance and the New Lending Strategies of the Multilateral Development Banks, Some Research Questions, Working Paper no. (Buenos Aires, FLACSO, December 1997), p. 3.

2 Recent examples of literature on these issues include S. Mainwaring and M. Soberg Shugart (eds.), *Presidentalism and Democracy in Latin America* (Cambridge, Cambridge University

Press, 1997); A. Knight, 'Populism and Neo-Populism in Latin America, Especially Mexico', *Journal of Latin American Studies*, 30 (1998); G. Philip, 'The New Populism in Spanish South America', *Government and Opposition*, 33:1 (Winter 1998); G. Ducatenzeiler and P. Oxhorn, 'Democracia, autoritarismo y el problema de la gobernabilidad en América Latina', *Desarrollo Económico*, 34:133 (April–June 1994); R. Gargarella, 'Recientes reformas constitucionales en América Latina: Una primera aproximación', *Desarrollo Económico*, 36:144 (January–March 1997); L. Manzetti and C. H. Blake, 'Market Reforms and Corruption in Latin America: New Means for Old Ways', *Review of International Political Economy*, 3:4 (Winter 1996).

3   J. Grugel, 'State and Business in Neo-Liberal Democracies in Latin America', *Global Society*, 12:2 (1998), p. 223.

4   For an elaboration of the 'governance' agenda, see World Bank, *Governance and Development* (Washington DC, World Bank, 1992). For an 'in-house' analysis of the reasons for the poor results of recent Bank programmes and the reorientation of Bank practices as a result, see R. Picciotto and R. Weaving, 'Un nuevo ciclo de los proyectos en el Banco Mundial', *Finanzas Desarrollo*, (Washington, DC, World Bank, December 1994). Also see P. J. Nelson, 'Transparencia, fiscalización y participación: La implementación de los nuevos mandatos en el Banco Mundial y el Banco Interamericano de Desarrollo', Serie de Documentos e Informes de Investigación no. 199 (Buenos Aires, FLACSO June 1996); D. Tussie, 'Argentina's Big Bang Reform: The Interplay of MDBs and Domestic Actors' (mimeo, Buenos Aires, October 1997); D. Gillies, 'Human Rights, Democracy and Good Governance: Stretching the World Bank's Policy Frontiers', in J. M. Griesgraber and B. G. Gunter (eds.), *The World Bank: Lending on a Global Scale* (London and Chicago, Pluto, 1996).

5   For an analysis of these see D. Green, *Silent Revolution: The Rise of Market Economics in Latin America* (London, Cassell and Latin America Bureau, 1995), esp. pp. 165–72.

6   For an excellent recent contribution to this literature, see M. E. Keck and K. Sikkink, *Activists Beyond Borders: Advocacy Networks in International Politics* (Ithaca, Cornell University Press, 1998).

7   See World Bank, *World Development Report 1997: The State in a Changing World* (New York, Oxford University Press, 1997). For an application of these ideas, see J. Pearce, 'From Civil War to "Civil Society": Has the End of the Cold War Brought Peace to Central America?', *International Affairs* 74:3 (1998) and 'Building Civil Society from the Outside: The Problematic Democratisation of Central America', *Global Society*,12:2 (1998).

8   For another recent contribution to these debates, see D. A. Chalmers *et al.*, *The New Politics of Inequality in Latin America: Rethinking Participation and Representation* (Oxford, Oxford University Press, 1997).

9   J. Buxton and N. Phillips (eds), *Case Studies in Latin American Political Economy* (Manchester, Manchester University Press, 1999) gives greater empirical substance to the main ideas and arguments outlined in this volume through a collection of detailed analyses of individual cases.

Part I

STATES AND MARKETS

A trip to the market:
the impact of neoliberalism in Latin America

DUNCAN GREEN

Since 1982 Latin America has seen a process of intense market reforms. Since the onset of the debt crisis, marked by the Mexican default of August 1982, a combination of influences has transformed Latin American economies in a 'silent revolution' affecting every corner of the continent and its half-billion citizens. This chapter explores the causes of the continent's abrupt change of economic direction, the economic and social impact of economic reform and the region's process of integration into the global economy.

The forces driving market reforms include both domestic and external pressures. Domestically the debt crisis which struck Latin America in 1982 was a sign of the exhaustion of the previous model of import substitution which, while it had led to the successful industrialisation of the larger economies, bequeathed a legacy of under-investment, inefficient industry reliant on high levels of state protection, and deep social and economic inequality. In the 1970s Latin American governments had postponed the inevitable adjustment by indulging in an unprecedented borrowing spree. When the influx of hard currency came to an end, the region was forced to adjust at a time of global recession. Within the political and economic elite, the travails of import substitution had led to an increased questioning of its assumptions and policies, notably its heavy reliance on the state and state-owned enterprises in managing the economy, its emphasis on producing for the domestic market, and the relatively low priority given to exports. The first signs of the impending triumph of the neoliberals came in Chile, where shortly after the coup of 1973 brought a military regime to power, led by General Augusto Pinochet, a team of economic technocrats known as the Chicago Boys took over the reins of the economy and instituted one of the most violent market transformations of recent times.

Internationally, debt crisis began at the high point of the neoliberal assault on Keynesianism, marked by the elections of Margaret Thatcher in 1979 and Ronald Reagan in 1980, and the collapse of the French Socialist government's attempt to reflate the economy following François Mitterrand's election in 1981. Latin America's crippling shortage of foreign exchange forced government after government to turn to the International Monetary Fund (IMF) for relief, placing unprecedented power in the Fund's hands, which it used to implement a rapid neoliberal market reform programme across the region. The programme has broadly consisted of three stages. The first involves an initial period of stabilisation, since the neoliberals see inflation as the greatest obstacle to growth. During this phase, economic policy consists of little more than severe austerity, with public sector spending cuts and sharp increases in interest rates. These are designed both to reduce domestic demand, and therefore inflation, and to reduce demand for imports, enabling countries to build up a trade surplus with which to meet debt service obligations. This is followed by a broader process of structural adjustment to implant a functioning market economy in the country by 'getting the prices right', removing artificial distortions such as price controls or trade tariffs, and allowing the unregulated market to determine the most efficient allocation of resources.

Because of its role in distorting prices and generally interfering with the free operation of the market, the state is seen as part of the problem, not part of the solution; the economy has to be restructured to reduce the state's role and unleash the private sector. This means privatising state firms and the broader deregulation of trade, finance and investment. Deregulation should also remove 'structural rigidities' in the labour market. In practice this means cutting labour costs by making it easier to hire and fire employees, restricting trade union activities and encouraging greater labour 'flexibility' through short-term contracts and subcontracting.

Like stabilisation, structural adjustment involves eliminating government spending deficits, which are seen as inflationary, but adjustment differs in that it more frequently involves closing the deficit by enhancing revenue as well as cutting spending. This is usually achieved by a mixture of income from privatisation and raising sales taxes such as value added tax (VAT). The ultimate aim of structural adjustment is to enable a country to move to a third stage of export-led growth. The government should give priority to exports, encouraging the private sector to diversify and find new markets for its products. This sometimes involves suppressing domestic demand (which diverts goods away from exports to local consumption). Removing all trade barriers (on both imports and exports) will, argue the neoliberals, ensure that resources are allocated efficiently, and that exports are made more competitive because their producers will be able to cut costs by importing the cheapest inputs available, whether fertilisers and pesticides for agro-exports or manufactured inputs for industry. The search for export-led growth generally means encouraging foreign investors to bring in new technology and capital, requiring further deregulation in these areas.

Reality has, needless to say, been rather more messy than such neat generalisations. The three phases have often overlapped, with differences over the sequencing of different reforms provoking lively debates among economists. No one country has implemented the full neoliberal recipe; for example, several supposedly exemplary neoliberal regimes have clung on to lucrative and strategically important state enterprises in copper (Chile) and oil (Mexico and Venezuela). Several of the most successful countries have mixed orthodox neoliberal adjustment with heterodox government controls; Mexico set wages and prices in its successful adjustment programme in the late 1980s, while Brazil, Mexico and Argentina have all deliberately kept the exchange rate overvalued at different points in the 1990s in order to bring down inflation, flouting the IMF's emphasis on 'getting the prices right'.

Particularly interesting comparisons can be made between Chile and Colombia, perhaps the region's two most successful economies between 1982 and 1998. Under both General Pinochet and Presidents Aylwin and Frei, Chile implemented almost the full neoliberal programme, while the Colombian government pursued a far more cautious form of deregulation, eschewing the latest economic fashions just as it had in refusing to become over-indebted during the 1970s. (Colombia was the only major Latin American economy to escape the debt crisis and the attentions of the IMF during the 1980s.) Chile's abrupt changes of policy under General Pinochet produced the region's wildest booms and busts, while Colombia experienced a decade of sustained, if unspectacular, growth as its Latin American neighbours were disintegrating around it. Despite such regional variations, however, all Latin America's governments have, since 1982, and particularly in the 1990s, signed up for at least part of the menu of economic reforms which has become known as the 'Washington Consensus'.

Economic impact of structural adjustment in the 1980s

The initial impact of stabilisation programmes in the early 1980s was the region's most severe recession since the Second World War, as imports were slashed and the resulting trade surplus used to repay debt service obligations. By the time the trade balance swung back into the red in 1992, Latin America had generated a total trade surplus of $242.9 billion.[1] Almost all of this promptly left the region in debt service payments. The transfer of wealth from the poor countries of Latin America to the institutions of the First World went on until 1991, a net flow of $218.6 billion,[2] or $534 for every man, woman and child in the continent. Even debt service payments on this scale failed to keep up with the interest falling due, and the region's total external debt rose steadily throughout the decade from $220 billion in 1980 to $447 billion in 1990. By 1997 Latin America's total external debt had reached $645 billion.[3] However, booming exports meant that the debt service ratio of debt repayments to export income fell steadily from a peak of 39 per cent in 1982–83 to just 14.4 per cent by 1997.[4]

The extraction of wealth from Latin America in the 1980s left a large hole in the economy, in the form of an investment collapse. Governments forced to adopt austerity measures found it less politically costly to cut public investment than to sack employees in the middle of a recession (although many did that as well), while the private sector was deterred from investing both by the impossibility of borrowing abroad and the recession and high interest rates at home, as governments lifted interest rates to fight inflation. Foreign investors also took fright. Bank loans dried up and annual foreign direct investment fell from $8 billion in 1981 to $3 billion in 1983.[5] Across the region, gross domestic investment (which includes both local and foreign investment) collapsed from $213 billion in 1980 to just $136 billion in 1983.[6] Throughout the mid-1980s, investment continued to languish well below its 1980 figure, becoming, in the words of the Inter-American Development Bank (IDB), 'the great casualty of the debt crisis'.[7] In practice, the investment slump created a backlog of what became known as the 'social debt' – a disintegrating education and health service, and an economy dogged by crumbling infrastructure, potholed roads, intermittent electricity supplies and millions of families without access to drinking water or mains drainage.

The mid-1980s saw a number of so-called 'heterodox' stabilisation programmes in countries such as Mexico, Peru, Argentina and Brazil, as governments sought less damaging alternatives to the standard IMF stabilisation packages. These used temporary government freezes on wages, prices and exchange rates and the introduction of a series of new currencies to symbolise a new start and to break 'inflationary expectations', whereby producers and employers constantly raise prices and wages in a self-fulfilling inflationary spiral. Heterodox programmes are designed to give the economy a cooling-off period while the government takes steps to remedy the underlying causes of inflation, such as the orthodox measure of cutting the fiscal deficit (hence the 'heterodox' nature of the formula).

Such programmes showed mixed results in achieving stabilisation, registering a significant success in Mexico in 1988. But in the best-known cases, the *Austral* plan in Argentina (June 1985), the *Cruzado* plan in Brazil (February 1986) and the *Inti* plan in Peru (July 1985), the governments failed to deal with their spending deficits and merely succeeded in temporarily suppressing inflation through price controls. When the controls were finally removed, the underlying imbalances drove inflation even higher than before the programmes were introduced. The failure of the heterodox plans appeared to leave the neoliberal programme in a dominant position: governments and political parties of all persuasions accepted the need for a market-led approach to policy formation and more active engagement with the global economy and foreign investment. The collapse of Eastern European statist systems in the late 1980s and early 1990s merely served to strengthen such beliefs. By the early 1990s, neoliberalism was the only game in town.

Latin America in the 1990s

According to the world's financial press, Latin America in the 1990s was a success story. The evidence for this is patchy. The most convincing achievement of the 'silent revolution' was on inflation. Although the initial impact of stabilisation programmes was to increase inflation, by 1997, the region's average inflation level had fallen to 10.5 per cent, the lowest for 50 years. The most startling success story of the decade was Brazil, where Finance Minister (and later President) Fernando Henrique Cardoso's *Real* Plan cut inflation in Latin America's largest economy from 2,500 per cent in 1993 to 4 per cent in 1997.[8] The region's performance on growth was less impressive. After a deep recession in the early 1980s, and stagnation in the latter part of the decade, the region returned to moderate growth in the 1990s, averaging 3.5 per cent between 1991 and 1997.[9] However, this was only 1.8 per cent once population growth was taken into account, well short of the region's performance in previous decades, or of other middle-income developing countries in Asia (at least until the Asian currency crisis of 1997).

The underlying reason for favourable media coverage of Latin America's economic performance was that investor confidence in the region had returned, encouraged by the announcement in March 1989 of the 'Brady Plan', proposed by US Treasury Secretary Nicholas Brady, consisting of a series of debt reduction measures. A Brady Plan deal came to be seen, like an IMF Stand-by Arrangement,[10] as a bill of good economic health, opening the door to foreign investment which played a dominant role in the region's recovery after 1990. After squeezing nearly $220 billion out of Latin America between 1982 and 1990, the international capital markets suddenly began pouring money into the region, and by 1991 the capital tide had turned. Debt service payments came to $31 billion that year, but capital inflows more than doubled in one year, leaving a net inflow of $4 billion. The net inflow then rose to $31 billion in 1993, before falling back sharply as part of the Mexican crash of December 1994. By 1997, net inflows had recovered to an estimated $26 billion.[11]

Stock markets sprang up around the continent to absorb the incoming dollars, turning extraordinary profits (except during the Mexican crash of early 1995) and becoming an essential part of international fund managers' portfolios. One of the fastest growing sources of capital has been government bonds, sold abroad by the larger Latin American countries. Income from bonds shot up from less than $1 billion in 1989 to reach a record $54 billion in 1997, as bond issues recovered swiftly from the jolt delivered by Mexico's crash in 1995. The big countries took the lion's share; Mexico, Brazil, Argentina and Venezuela accounted for 90 per cent of bond sales in 1997.[12]

Foreign direct investment (FDI) expanded steadily from $6.7 billion in 1990 to reach $44 billion in 1997.[13] In the initial stages, much of this investment was the result of the region's privatisation programme, inaugurated in the late 1980s, and was confined to the larger economies. Such FDI initially brought fewer social benefits as it only represented a transfer of ownership, rather than new investment, and was often accompanied by job losses as privatised companies shed labour either in the run up to, or immediately after, the sell-off. However, according to the Comisión Económica para América Latina (CEPAL, the UN Economic Commission for Latin America and the Caribbean), the mid-1990s saw a greater range of countries benefiting from foreign investment, and by then, privatisation accounted for only 30 per cent of the total influx, suggesting the FDI was starting to play a more productive role in creating new jobs.[14] Although the new influx of foreign investment was greeted with fanfares in the world's financial press, it did little to solve Latin America's long-term economic Achilles heel – low savings and investment rates. Gross fixed investment in 1996 came to just 20.7 per cent of gross domestic product (GDP), a figure unaltered for most of the previous 15 years. This compared to 27.6 per cent in 1980, the year before the start of the debt crisis, and was well short of the investment rates in the successful economies of East and South-East Asia.[15] Furthermore, in foreign investment more than in most other areas, there is no such thing as a free lunch. Latin America's profits and dividend payments to parent companies outside the region rose inexorably from $7 billion in 1990 to $16 billion in 1996, becoming a serious drain on the economy.[16] Between 1991 and 1997, profit repayments rose from 4.1 per cent of GDP to 6.1 per cent.[17.]

Privatisation became a crucial, if unsustainable, source of government revenue in the 1990s. The growing fiscal crisis of the state sector, provoked by both foreign and domestic debt payments, forced governments to increase revenue or cut expenditure; privatisation achieved both, shedding loss-making companies while raising substantial amounts of cash. In Argentina, President Carlos Menem's privatisation programme raised $9.8 billion in cash, and enabled the government to cut a further $15.6 billion off its foreign debt between 1989 and 1993 as transnational corporations bought up debt paper and swapped it for a stake in the newly privatised companies.[18] In Mexico, privatisation raised a total of $13.7 billion in 1990–91, providing just under a tenth of government revenues.[19] Between 1990 and 1996, the total value of Latin American privatisations came to $73 billion. By the mid-1990s, Mexico and Argentina had little left to sell, while Brazil was just beginning its programme, and looked set to dominate sell-offs for the rest of the decade. The main privatisations took place in electricity generation, telecoms and oil and gas. Government concessions to the private sector to build infrastructure such as airports and seaports also became an increasingly important source of revenue.[20]

For some countries, the renewed capital influx also helped to ease the pain (and political cost) of economic stabilisation. In the early 1980s, stabilising countries had both to reduce inflation and generate a massive trade surplus with which to keep up their debt service. The only means to achieve this double objective was to inflict a huge recession at home. After the late 1980s, there was another option, as foreign capital came to provide a cushion against the worst effects of adjustment. Latecomers to stabilisation, such as Argentina's Menem and Brazil's Cardoso, found themselves able to control inflation without the same degree of austerity, by using capital inflows to keep up debt repayments. Large capital inflows also led to overvalued currencies, which help suppress inflation by holding down import prices. The effects were spectacular: Argentina's inflation fell from 4,923 per cent in 1989 to 18 per cent three years later,[21] and within months of the adjustment package, the economy moved smoothly into four years of record-breaking growth – over 6 per cent in every year from 1991 to 1994.[22]

The cost of this strategy was a loss of export competitiveness and an ensuing trade deficit, which could only be covered by capital inflows, as long as they lasted. The Mexican crash of early 1995 graphically demonstrated what happens when dollar inflows stop. On 20 December 1994, the Mexican government finally responded to a year of disastrous political and economic news which had alarmed investors already concerned about the country's overvalued currency and escalating trade deficit. Mexico's reserves had fallen from $30 billion in February to just $5 billion, and its government was in danger of defaulting on debt repayments in a repeat of the 1982 crash which precipitated the region's debt crisis. In the end, an unprecedented $50 billion bail-out coordinated by Washington prevented collapse, but in return Mexico was forced to abandon the end of this 'easy option' of foreign investment-driven stabilisation, announcing an austerity package on 9 March 1995 which raised taxes, cut public spending, floated the interest rate and relied on rocketing interest rates to control inflation. The results were predictably catastrophic as growth ground to a halt, a wave of bankruptcies ensued and an estimated 1.2 million jobs were lost by the end of May.[23] In what became known as the 'Tequila effect', investor fears spread to other 'emerging markets', particularly Argentina, which was also forced into a severe austerity package to replace its previous 'easy option' of exchange-rate-based stabilisation. Mexico's economy shrank by 7 per cent in 1995, while Argentina's fell by 5 per cent. However, the harsh economic medicine appeared to cure the hangover, as both returned to strong growth the following year.

Overall, the region has only mixed results to show for 16 years of painful reform. Inflation has been defeated – the major gain in the process – but growth is fitful, investment and savings remain low, and such limited gains have only been achieved at a profound social cost, discussed below.

Latin America's integration into the global economy

The speed with which Latin America became integrated with the global economy over the course of the silent revolution was truly remarkable. Latin America's courtship of global capital markets was a whirlwind affair. The spread of regional stock markets, privatisation programmes, bank deregulation, bond issues, and the growing number of Latin American companies whose shares trade on the stock exchanges of New York and London greatly increased the region's openness to international capital flows. Although this provided Latin America with much-needed capital, it made the region vulnerable to external shocks by increasing the impact of any sudden withdrawal of foreign capital. Such a withdrawal precipitated devastating recessions in Mexico and Argentina in 1995, and forced the Brazilian government into a painful austerity pro-. gramme in late 1997. Observers such as CEPAL continued to stress the need for Latin America to increase its savings rate, thereby reducing its dependence on foreign capital flows. They also pointed to the dangers of excessive deregulation, which led to a rash of banking crises in countries such as Mexico and Venezuela, as poorly supervised banks were allowed to pile up bad debts. Bailing out such crashes was a costly business: the Venezuelan crisis of 1994 cost the government 13 per cent of GDP, while in Mexico in 1995, the bill came to 8.5 per cent of GDP.[24]

Booming trade bound the region ever more tightly to the world economy. From the mid-1980s, exports rose much faster than the economy as a whole, doubling in value between 1990 and 1997 to reach $326 billion.[25] New primary products, such as fresh fruit and vegetables, mining and manufactured goods produced in cheap labour assembly plants, or *maquiladoras*, led the growth in exports, along with the boom in intra-regional trade, especially within the Mercosur countries. All countries increased their exports of low-tech manufactured goods such as furniture or footwear, but only the largest economies moved into high-tech exports such as cars, steel or electronics.[26] Imports rose even faster than exports, as Latin America became increasingly oriented towards trade with the rest of the world, leaving behind import substitution's emphasis on production for the domestic market. Exports (rather than consumption or investment, which both lagged behind) became the driving force behind economic growth in the 1990s.

From the late 1980s, under pressure from the international financial institutions, Latin America began to liberalise imports at a breakneck rate, despite the lack of any reciprocal opening from US or European governments. In all the major economies, maximum import tariffs which had typically exceeded 100 per cent were reduced to 35 per cent or less. Between 1989 and the end of 1992, Argentina's average tariff fell from 39 per cent to 15 per cent, Colombia's from 44 per cent to 12 per cent and Peru's from 66 per cent to 18 per cent.[27] Neoliberals argue that liberalising imports improves economic efficiency and benefits everyone. Local factories can import the best available machinery and other inputs to improve their productivity, while consumers can shop around, rather than be forced to buy shoddy, home-produced goods. Competition from abroad will force local factories either to close, or to improve their products until they become competitive with other countries' goods, paving the way for increased manufactured exports. In practice, import liberalisation unleashed a consumer boom, as Latin Americans flocked to snap up imported goods at bargain prices, with a drastic impact on the region's trade balance. In the early 1990s, Mexico and Argentina ran up huge trade deficits as import bills rocketed – in Argentina imports quintupled between 1990 and 1994.[28] Import liberalisation and an overvalued exchange rate were the underlying reasons for the crashes in both countries in 1995.

Two respected Latin American economists, Ricardo Ffrench-Davis and Manuel Agosín,[29] have laid out some clear conditions for successful trade reform: the value created by new activities must exceed that lost due to the number of factories destroyed by competition from cheap imports; export industries must be sufficiently linked to the rest of the national economy to spread the benefits of improved exports throughout the country; and increased competitiveness must be achieved by continuous gains in productivity rather than through low wages or ever-greater subsidies or tax breaks. The authors do not believe these conditions were met in the recent Latin American trade reforms and point out numerous serious failings:

- countries unilaterally opened up their economies in a protectionist and stagnant world economy, allowing other regions to increase their imports to Latin America without having to reciprocate by buying the region's exports;
- countries liberalised far too rapidly, not allowing local firms sufficient time to make the necessary changes and investments to adapt to the new rules and improve their productivity before the import floodgates opened. This wiped out numerous potentially competitive companies in a wholly avoidable manner;
- Latin American countries fell back into relying on their static comparative advantage, which led them to concentrate their efforts in the least dynamic areas of the world economy, such as commodity exports;
- the deregulation of Latin America's financial markets and influx of foreign capital, which coincided with trade liberalisation, led to overvalued exchange rates and high interest rates (set by governments to attract foreign currency). Overvalued currencies made the region's exports less competitive, while high interest rates discouraged exporters from borrowing to invest in increasing production.

Regional integration

An important aspect of the new emphasis on trade was the burgeoning number of free trade agreements (FTAs) between Latin American countries (numbering 36 bilateral or multilateral agreements by 1997),[30] and between Latin America and other regions (see Chapter 4). Best known was the North American Free Trade Agreement (NAFTA) between Mexico, Canada and the United States, which came into force in 1994. Different kinds of free trade agreement had contradictory effects on the Latin American economies. FTAs such as NAFTA with more industrialised, advanced nations served to increase Latin America's reliance on its traditional 'comparative advantage' of raw materials, commodities and goods produced with cheap labour. Intra-regional trade, on the other hand, tended to include a higher proportion of manufactured goods, and so had a more positive effect in developing local industry. By 1994, intra-regional trade accounted for 19 per cent of the total. The most dynamic sub-region was the Mercosur FTA, comprising Argentina, Brazil, Uruguay and Paraguay. Mercosur members' trade with each other shot up from $7 billion in 1992 to $17 billion in 1996, accounting for 23 per cent of all trade.[31]

In 1994, the North American and Latin American leaders announced their intention to negotiate a 'Free Trade Area of the Americas' (FTAA) covering the whole hemisphere, by the year 2005. However, by early 1998, the process had become bogged down through President Clinton's inability to win approval from Congress for a 'fast-track' procedure which was seen as the only feasible means of carrying through the negotiations. Instead, Latin American governments, especially those of the Mercosur, continued to make the running on regional integration, notably by incorporating Bolivia and Chile into the Mercosur's free trade area.[32] The Mercosur also began talks with the Andean Community on a similar arrangement.

The social impact of neoliberalism

Throughout the region, after decades in which the percentage of Latin Americans living in poverty had been falling (though not their actual number), poverty is once again on the rise. Between 1980 and 1994, CEPAL reported that 75 million new names had joined the grim roll-call of the poor, leaving 39 per cent of the population, 209 million people, living in poverty. Almost half of them were indigent, barely existing on an income of less than $1 a day.[33] Shrinking wages and rising prices for food and other essentials increased unemployment or 'underemployment' and collapsing government services: the human cost mounted inexorably throughout the silent revolution, exacting a toll of hunger, disease and despair. According to the director of the United Nations (UN) International Fund for Agricultural Development, 'chronic and persistent hunger' weakened and killed 40,000 people a day. Some 55 million people suffered from undernourishment in the region, while the mortality rate due to 'chronic non-infectious diseases' typical of malnutrition doubled.[34] Neglected sewage and water systems, victims of the investment collapse of the 1980s, played an important role in allowing cholera to return to the continent in 1991 after a gap of over sixty years.

While Latin America is not as poor as Africa or parts of Asia, it leads the world in inequality and after 1982, inequality worsened. According to CEPAL, the decade to the mid-1990s saw 'an increase in the inequality of income distribution in most countries'.[35] The Economist put it more bluntly, commenting that 'stabilisation and structural adjustment have brought magnificent returns to the rich'.[36] Even during the worst years of recession, the poor became poorer, and the rich really did become richer, especially the very rich. According to Forbes magazine, the number of Latin American billionaires rose from 6 in

1987 to 42 in 1994, although the Mexican crash of 1995 subsequently reduced their numbers for a few years.[37] Latin American inequality is on such a scale that a comparatively minor move towards a fairer distribution of income could eradicate poverty overnight, according to the World Bank's 1990 *World Development Report*: 'Raising all the poor in the continent to just above the poverty line would cost only 0.7 per cent of regional GDP – the approximate equivalent of a 2 per cent income tax on the wealthiest fifth of the population'.[38]

There is a vigorous debate over the relationship between structural adjustment and rising poverty – is it the cure or the cause? The World Bank believes that 'without adjustment, the condition of the poor would undoubtedly have been worse'.[39] Other voices within the world of the international financial institutions are far less upbeat. Most notable is the Inter-American Development Bank (IDB), which in 1993 concluded:

> There is growing doubt as to whether macro-economic policy can move from adjustment to growth, whether reforming the trade regime can move from removing distortions to stimulating dynamic export growth, and whether private sector reforms will increase output and employment sufficiently to meet the wider social goals of social equity, political participation and environmental balance.[40]

Organisations such as the British development agencies Christian Aid and the Catholic Fund for Overseas Development (CAFOD), which work on a daily basis with Latin America's poor, are in no doubt about the connection. Christian Aid believes that 'throughout the third world ... Structural Adjustment Programmes spell hardship for people in every aspect of their lives – health, education, work, culture'.[41]

One way to try and reach some firmer ground beyond the war of words is to look at adjustment's impact on each of the main elements which determine the daily livelihoods of poor Latin Americans. There are many ways that economic changes can affect people's quality of life: incomes, taxes, working conditions, prices, state services and the impact on home life and the family. Adjustment and stabilisation measures have a profound influence on all of them.

A living wage
The rural poor sometimes have a plot of land on which to grow food, but the urban poor have few assets beyond their labour, so their well-being depends to a large extent on what they can earn. According to CEPAL, the main causes of increasing poverty and inequality were the 'massive decline in real wages, ... the rise in unemployment and ... the number of people employed in very low-productivity jobs'.[42] Government cutbacks led to numerous redundancies, but their main impact was a sharp fall in wages among remaining public employees, the sector worst hit by adjustment. Public-sector pay packets shrank by 24 per cent in Costa Rica (1981–88)[43] and 56 per cent in Venezuela (1981-90).[44] Many of those worst affected were middle class, thousands of whom ended up joining the ranks of the 'new poor' created by adjustment policies. At a regional

level, between 1980 and 1986, wages fell faster for those with more than nine years of schooling than for any other sector of the workforce,[45] and many professionals were forced to take second or even third jobs to make ends meet.

Adjustment policies sought to 'flexibilise' labour. In practice, this meant cracking down on trade unions and making it easier for managers to hire and fire employees, shift to part-time work and to cut costs by subcontracting work to smaller companies, often little more than sweatshops. The proportion of the workforce employed by large companies fell from 44 per cent to 32 per cent between 1980 and 1990,[46] the slack being taken up by a boom in small companies and the informal sector, where wages were generally lower. In Chile, the neoliberal tiger, a labour force once accustomed to secure, unionised jobs has been turned into a nation of anxious individualists. According to a World Health Organisation (WHO) survey over half of all visits in Chile's public health system involved psychological ailments, mainly depression.[47] In Argentina such changes meant that having a job was no longer enough to stave off hunger. By the early 1990s, 23 per cent of wage-earners in the manufacturing sector were living below the poverty line, whereas before the debt crisis a job in a factory virtually guaranteed a pay packet big enough to keep a family out of poverty.[48]

Stronger growth after 1990 boosted wages in Chile, but failed to improve incomes in the other major economies. By 1997, average real wages in Peru, a late entry to the neoliberal game, were down to just 41 per cent of their 1980 value, while they had still not recovered their 1980 value in Argentina, Brazil or Mexico.[49] Significantly, these were the very countries whose adjustments were being lauded by the international financial community as neoliberal triumphs. Furthermore, despite strong growth, Argentina's unemployment rose from 6 per cent in late 1991 to 15 per cent by 1997.[50] Like Britain, much of Latin America was experiencing the phenomenon of jobless growth – the recovery in the Latin American economy was in danger of bypassing its citizens. Incomes for non-wage-earners also took a battering at the hands of adjustment. Government cutbacks whittled away at Latin America's already paltry welfare system, as the elderly in particular saw state pensions dwindle in value.

Overall, CEPAL discerns a pattern in which economic shocks exacerbate poverty, but subsequent upturns fail to repair the damage. It concludes: 'The experience of several countries has shown that even after the economy picks up again, it takes longer to bring poverty levels down to where they were previously and much longer still before any new reduction can be achieved.'[51] A prime example is Mexico, where real wages slumped after the 1995 financial crisis, but then failed to recover, even though the Mexican economy achieved extremely high growth figures in subsequent years. By 1997, wages were still 30 per cent down on their 1994 levels.[52]

Taxes
The tax system is important in determining what portion of income actually reaches the home, as well as how much the government has to spend on social services. From the late 1980s, tax reform also gained increasing importance as a means of balancing government budgets and curbing inflation. However, some of the resulting changes in the tax regime further penalised the poor. On the positive side, as part of their adjustment programme, several countries improved their level of income tax collection either by closing loopholes (Mexico, Argentina), or in some instances (Chile 1990, Colombia 1992) by increasing taxation rates.[53] Most countries, however, switched away from income taxes (already among the lowest in the world, since the Latin American elite has always been violently averse to parting with its wealth) towards greater emphasis on sales taxes. Governments argued that this was easier to collect, especially where in some cases over half the workforce were in the informal sector and therefore were not registered to pay taxes.

Credit
The neoliberal understanding of the economy is essentially monetarist, believing that cutting the amount of money circulating in the economy is the best means of curbing inflation. Removing money from the economy means reducing credit, which was largely achieved by imposing high interest rates to make borrowing more expensive. The result was a collapse in demand for credit and a deep recession in many countries, as local industry suddenly found it impossibly expensive to take out loans for investment.

When many economies returned to growth in the late 1980s, they often relied for their success on continued inflows of foreign capital, which had to be lured in by offering appetisingly high interest rates. The squeeze on borrowers continued, as only the largest firms were able to borrow abroad at lower interest rates. From the late 1980s, privatisation also did away with numerous state banks, some of which targeted at least some of their credit to small and medium-sized farmers and small businesses in the towns. Experience shows that, left to their own instincts, Latin America's private banks prefer to lend to big business. Just as millions of people were joining the informal sector, they saw their attempt at self-help crippled by the scarcity of credit.

Prices
Inflation has been aptly described as 'a tax on the poor'. In a high-inflation economy, the better-off usually find ways to defend their incomes from its erosive effects by investing their money in index-linked bank accounts or turning it into dollars. The poor have no such options, and for them, the fall in inflation in the 1990s was neoliberalism's single greatest achievement. CEPAL estimates that the Real plan which curbed Brazil's hyperinflation in 1994 raised some 8 million Brazilians out of poverty in just two years.[54] However, they had to wait nearly a decade to reap the reward, for under adjustment Latin Amer-

ica first saw its inflation levels rise until the end of the 1980s (barring a short fall caused by the heterodox experiments of 1984–87), before they fell back again after 1990.

Adjustment also saw the end of government subsidies and price controls on many basic foods and fuel. This created both winners and losers, since peasant farmers could now charge higher prices for their food crops, but the urban poor were especially hard hit. The sudden removal of fuel subsidies and the subsequent increase in public transport fares were one of the commonest causes of anti-IMF rioting in the region. Most governments replaced general subsidies with attempts to 'target' subsidies at the poorest. Although the neoliberal argument (that general subsidies are a waste of money and often end up subsidising the wealthy, middle-class consumer) is at first sight convincing, talk of targeting was in practice often little more than a smokescreen for government cuts, while the logistical difficulties of identifying the poor and getting subsidies to them often meant that many slipped through the extremely tattered safety net. When Jamaica replaced a general subsidy with a targeted subsidy, it managed to reach only 49 per cent of those identified as the target group. Those it reached were much better off than under the general subsidy, but the remainder were faced with a jump in food prices and no help from the state.[55] Trade liberalisation was one positive development for the urban poor, bringing cheaper food imports. Removing protective tariffs on imports often meant lower prices and higher quality for the consumer.

State services
Despite the pressures on public spending in the wake of the debt crisis, over the region as a whole health indicators such as infant mortality continued to improve, though at a slower rate than in previous years. According to CEPAL, however, the overall improvement concealed numerous 'situations where the tragedy of poverty continues to be felt with extraordinary force'.[56] Such cases included the spread of malaria, cholera and tuberculosis in the 1990s. CEPAL put continued improvements down to the spread of low-cost, effective technology such as vaccinations. These helped counteract the fall in wages and rising poverty which took place under adjustment. Decent education and health care are two of the most effective ways of lifting people out of poverty, and from the late 1980s onwards, the World Bank and other institutions began to urge Latin American governments to increase spending on health and education, the areas of social spending which most affect the poor. Across the region, spending per child fell by 28 per cent during the 1980s, while lack of resources, family pressures and inadequate teaching gave Latin America the highest school repetition rates in the world.[57]

From 1990, the pressure from the World Bank, coupled with the growing realisation that cutting social spending was undermining the region's prospects for growth, began to lead to policy changes. After the cuts of the 1980s, all the intensively adjusting countries increased spending on health, and all but Brazil increased their education budgets.[58] Many governments encouraged the middle classes to 'opt out' of the crumbling state system and put their money into the burgeoning private education and health-care sectors. The World Bank concluded that 'by targeting the richest segments of Chilean society, the [new health insurance funds] impoverished the rest of the social insurance system …. They have "skimmed" the population for good risks, leaving the public sector to care for the sick and the elderly.'[59] Chile's move to a two-tier health-care system exacerbated General Pinochet's legacy of social inequality. A study for Chile's Ministry of Health in 1993 showed that infant mortality was 7 per 1,000 births for the richest fifth of the population, and 40 per 1,000 for the poorest 20 per cent, the Chilean underclass.[60]

Although the Bank pushed for increased government spending, it also pressed governments to improve 'cost recovery', its euphemism for introducing charges for what used to be free health and education services. In Nicaragua the adjustment programme introduced by Violeta Chamorro in 1990/91 hit the health budget so severely that individual health centres were only able to stay open by introducing charges, even though it had not yet become official government policy. The volume of drugs bought by the health service fell to just an eighth of its 1989 figure, forcing patients to buy their own medicines.[61] The inevitable effect was to make health care impossibly expensive for large numbers of poor Nicaraguans.

Home and family

At the eye of the social and economic storm unleashed by the silent revolution lay the family. The central figure in the Latin American family is the mother. Traditionally, her main role may have been childbearing, child-rearing and housework, but economic and social change added new tasks to her workload. Women formed an increasing percentage of the workforce, rising from 22 per cent in 1980 to 45 per cent by the mid-1990s. Among the 25–49 age range, there was little difference between the proportions of women and men in work.[62] Many of the new, low-waged or part-time jobs generated by adjustment went to women, while many men lost their role as family breadwinner as full-time waged jobs disappeared, or wages fell so far that a single income became insufficient to feed a family. On top of this 'double day' of work and running the home, the deterioration of social services, especially in urban areas, forced women into a third role, taking responsibility for running their communities, fighting or substituting for inadequate state services in schools, health, drainage, water supply, or roads.

Adjustment made all these tasks more vital to the family's survival and more exhausting: 'flexibilisation' often meant lower wages, longer hours and greater insecurity, just as cuts in state subsidies brought steep price rises in basics like food and public transport. A study by Caroline Moser offers a unique glimpse of how adjustment and the debt crisis affected the women of one poor community in Guayaquil, Ecuador's largest city.[63] From 1978 to 1988, Moser regularly visited and studied the community of Indio Guayas, an area of swamp-land shanty town which in 1978 had about 3,000 residents. She was therefore able to take a series of socio-economic snapshots of the community as the Ecuadorean government adopted eight different stabilisation/adjustment pack-ages between 1982 and 1988. Moser found that women reacted in three dif-ferent ways to the impact of adjustment on their lives. About 30 per cent of the women were coping, juggling the competing demands of their three roles in the workplace, home and community. They were more likely to be in stable rela-tionships with partners who had steady jobs. Another group, about 15 per cent of the women, were simply 'burnt out', no longer able to be superwomen 24 hours a day. They were most likely to be single mothers or the main breadwin-ners, and were often older women, physically and mentally exhausted after the effort of bringing up a family against such heavy odds. They tried to hand over all household responsibilities to their oldest daughter, while their younger chil-dren frequently dropped out of school and roamed the streets. The remaining group, about 55 per cent, Moser described as simply 'hanging on', sacrificing their families by sending sons out to work or keeping daughters home from school to help with the housework.

Working the streets

Over 80 per cent of new jobs in the 1990s were in the so-called 'informal sec-tor' of the self-employed, spanning everything from rubbish recyclers to street vendors, with a sprinkling of high-powered business consultants.[64] The infor-mal sector became the last and only resort for millions of Latin Americans entering the job market for the first time, as well as those sacked during reces-sion and 'rationalisation'. By 1998, *The Economist* reported that 57 per cent of Latin America's workforce was operating in the informal sector.[65] The thou-sands of new arrivals ended up in a self-defeating scramble for survival. Here, at least, the laws of supply and demand work all too well; as the streets of Latin America's cities became clogged with street vendors desperately seeking cus-tomers, income fell. By 1989 the income of the average Latin American work-ing in the informal sector had shrunk to just 58 per cent of its 1980 figure, so it was harder hit than even the public sector.[66]

Adjusting the countryside

Although structural adjustment's greatest impact was in the cities, it also exacted a high human price in the countryside. The half-hearted agrarian reform programmes of the 1960s and 1970s were swept aside by the cut and thrust of the 'export or die' mentality. Public spending cuts and the determina-tion to leave everything to the market meant the end for a range of institutions which at least gave some limited support to peasant farmers: state development banks, state marketing boards and guaranteed prices for their crops were all curtailed (although in some cases this allowed farmers to charge higher prices). Import liberalisation produced floods of cheap imports, undercutting peasant crops such as potatoes and maize. The NAFTA opened the door to cheap US maize for Mexico's urban masses, but spelled disaster for nearly two million peasant farmers whose livelihoods face ruin from the competition.[67]

As elsewhere, in rural areas the deregulated market increased inequality. Banks lent to big landowners and transnationals with collateral, and ignored small peasants with nothing to pledge. Peasants were squeezed off the land by bankruptcy or offers which they could not refuse, and ended up becoming paid workers on their former lands. In Chile, just six large firms controlled 52 per cent of fresh fruit exports,[68] and the richest 10 per cent of the rural population saw their income rise by 90 per cent between 1987 and 1990. The share of the poorest 25 per cent fell from 11 per cent to 7 per cent.[69] In Costa Rica, another pioneer of non-traditional exports, agricultural credit to small farmers halved between 1984 and 1988, while the value of government bonds to exporters (effectively a state subsidy) rose by 1,900 per cent, with 80–90 per cent of the benefits from the bonds going to five transnational corporations.[70]

A painful wait

By 1998, after 16 years of debt crisis, adjustment and undoubted pain, most Latin Americans were still waiting for the long-promised benefits of structural adjustment to 'trickle down' to their neighbourhoods. Although the rich had had a vintage decade, most of the region's people were poorer and more insecure; their homes, communities, schools and hospitals were collapsing around them. Latin America was left trying to find its way in a cut-throat global economy, saddled with a population weakened by poverty and ignorance. Neoliberals had moderated their tone and now talked more about social cost and public spending, but their basic recipe remained unchanged as they insisted that the pay-off lay just around the corner. Small wonder that so many doubted their good faith and that disillusion with politicians of all hues was growing daily.

Table 1.1   *Latin America: key economic indicators*

Year	GDP Growth[a]	Exports[b]	Imports[c]	Net resource transfer[d]	Debt[e]
1981	0.7	96	98	11.3	288
1982	−1.2	88	78	−18.7	331
1983	−2.6	88	56	−31.6	353
1984	3.7	98	58	−26.8	367
1985	3.4	92	58	−32.2	377
1986	3.7	78	60	−22.5	393
1987	3.2	88	67	−16.2	428
1988	0.8	101	77	−28.8	420
1989	1.0	111	82	−28.0	423
1990	0.3	122	95	−15.4	442
1991	3.5	121	112	4.2	453
1992	3.0	127	138	26.4	469
1993	3.9	134	149	31.3	524
1994	5.4	153	171	7.65	57
1995	0.2	264[f]	279	16.7	608
1996	3.5	294	302	20.3	629
1997[g]	5.3	326	354	26.3	645

Notes
a   % change in regional GDP
b   value of regional exports of goods free on board (fob) (US$ billion)
c   value of regional imports of goods fob (US$ billion)
d   overall flow of resources into/out of the region. A positive figure indicates a net inflow, a negative figure a net outflow (US$ billion)
e   total external debt (US$ billion)
f   export and import figures from 1995 onwards include services as well as goods.
g   preliminary estimate.
Source: CEPAL.

Notes

1 UN Economic Commission for Latin America and the Caribbean (CEPAL) *Balance preliminar de la economía de América Latina y el Caribe*, 1987 and 1993 and 1993 (Santiago).
2 CEPAL, *Balance preliminar*, 1993, p. 47.
3 CEPAL, *Balance preliminar de la economía de América Latina y el Caribe*, 1997 (Santiago, CEPAL) p. 59.
4 *Ibid.*, p. 60.
5 Inter-American Development Bank (IDB), *Economic and Social Progress in Latin America*, 1990 Report (Washington, DC), p. 297.
6 *Ibid.*, p. 267.
7 IDB, *Economic and Social Progress in Latin America*, 1988 Report, (Washington, DC, IDB, p. 29.
8 CEPAL, *Balance preliminar*, 1997, p. 51.
9 *Ibid.*, p. 49.
10 A short-term finance package, as opposed to the Extended Fund Facility.
11 CEPAL: *Balance preliminar* 1997, p. 59.

12 *Ibid.*, p. 60.
13 *Ibid.*, p. 58.
14 CEPAL, *Estudio económico de América Latina y el Caribe*, 1996–97 (Santiago, CEPAL 1997), p. 134.
15 *Ibid.*, p. 87.
16 *Ibid.*, p. 129.
17 CEPAL, *Balance preliminar*, p. 60.
18 West Merchant Bank, *Investment Review* (London, August 1994).
19 R. Devlin, 'Privatisations and Social Welfare', CEPAL Review, 49 (1993), p. 159.
20 CEPAL, *Estudio económico*, p. 50.
21 CEPAL, *Balance preliminar*, 1993, p. 35.
22 CEPAL, *Panorama económico de América Latina*, 1994 (Santiago, CEPAL, 1994), p. 18.
23 *Latin America Monitor* (Mexico, August 1995), p. 3.
24 CEPAL, *Estudio económico*, p. 57.
25 CEPAL, *Balance preliminar*, 1997, p. 2.
26 Oxford Analytica, *Latin America in Perspective* (Boston, MA, Oxford Analytica, 1991), p. 236.
27 *CEPAL Review*, 50 (August 1993), p. 44.
28 CEPAL, *Panorama económico*, p. 8.
29 R. Ffrench-Davis and M. Agosín, 'Liberalización comercial y desarrollo en América Latina', *Nueva Sociedad* (September/October 1994).
30 CEPAL, *Estudio económico*, p. 59.
31 *Ibid.*, p. 122.
32 *Ibid.*, p. 60.
33 CEPAL, *Social Panorama of Latin America 1996* (Santiago, March 1997), p. 19.
34 Latin American Newsletters Special Report, *Poverty: An Issue Making a Comeback* (London, October 1992), p. 3.
35 CEPAL, *Social Panorama*, p. 41.
36 *The Economist*, 'A Survey of Latin America' (London, 13 November 1993).
37 *Latin America Weekly Report*, 14 July 1994.
38 *Financial Times*, 26 March 1993.
39 G. Psacharopoulos *et al.*, *Poverty and Income Distribution in Latin America: The Story of the 1980s* (Washington, D C., World Bank, December 1992).
40 IDB, *Socio-economic Reform in Latin America: The Social Agenda Study* (Washington, DC, 28 April 1993).
41 J. Madeley, D. Sullivan and J. Woodroffe, *Who Runs the World?* (London, Christian Aid, 1994), p. 26.
42 CEPAL, *The Social Summit: A View from Latin America and the Caribbean* (Santiago, CEPAL, 1994), p. 16.
43 CEPAL, *Social Equity and Changing Production Patterns: An Integrated Approach* (Santiago, CEPAL, 1992), p. 37.
44 CEPAL, *Panorama social de América Latina*, 1993, (Santiago, CEPAL, 1993) p. 16.
45 CEPAL, *Social Equity*, p. 38.
46 R. van der Hoeven and F. Stewart, *Social Development during Periods of Structural Adjustment in Latin America* (Geneva International Labour Organization, 1994), p. 5.
47 *El Mercurio*, 30 September 1993.
48 CEPAL, *Panorama social*, 1993, p. 8.
49 CEPAL, *Balance preliminar*, 1997, p. 52.
50 West Merchant Bank, *Investment Review*
51 CEPAL, *Social Panorama*, 1996, p. 25.
52 CEPAL, *Balance preliminar*, 1997, p. 52.
53 E. Cardoso and A. Helwege, *Latin America's Economy: Diversity, Trends and Conflicts* (Cambridge, MA, MIT Press, 1996), p. 178.
54 CEPAL, *Social Panorama*, p. 29.

55 Van der Hoeven and Stewart, *Social Development*, p. 24.
56 CEPAL, *Social Equity*, p. 42.
57 *Financial Times*, 30 June 1994.
58 World Bank, *World Development Report* (New York, World Bank, various years).
59 World Bank, *World Development Report* (New York, World Bank, 1993), p. 162.
60 Oxfam, 'Structural Adjustment and Inequality in Latin America: How IMF and World Bank Policies have Failed the Poor' (mimeo, Oxford, 1994), p. 16.
61 Talk by Trevor Evans, CRIES, at the Catholic Institute of International Relations, London, 12 July 1994.
62 CEPAL, *Social Panorama*, p. 64.
63 C. Moser, 'Adjustment from Below: Low-income Women, Time and the Triple Role in Guayaquil, Ecuador', in S. Radcliffe and S. Westwood (eds.), *'Viva': Women and Popular Protest in Latin America* (London, Routledge, 1993).
64 *Latinamerica Press* (Lima), 24 November 1994, p. 7.
65 *The Economist*, 21 March 1998.
66 Van der Hoeven and Stewart, *Social Development*, p. 14c.
67 H. Browne, *For Richer for Poorer: Shaping US–Mexican Integration* (Albuquerque and London, Resource Center Press/Latin America Bureau, 1994), p. 24.
68 E. Díaz, *Impact of the Export Model on Workers and the Environment: Analysis of the Fruit and Fishing Sectors* (Santiago, June 1994).
69 CEPAL, *Panorama social*, p. 22.
70 K. Hansen-Kuhn, *Structural Adjustment in Central America: The Case of Costa Rica* (Washington, DC, The Development Gap, June 1993), p. 12.

2

Institutions and democratic consolidiation in Latin America

GEORGE PHILIP

It may be a truism that every Latin American country has its own particular history and social structure, and that no two are exactly alike. However, there are general issues of governance that arise across the region, at any rate in countries with democratic political systems. This chapter deals with political institutions in democratic Latin America, and it argues that the progress made by most countries of the region in respect of democratisation and economic recovery has not so far generally been matched by the development of effective state institutions. To the extent that there has indeed been effective institution-building, this has been achieved much more in the narrow field of macroeconomic management than anywhere else. Without the professionalisation of the state as a whole, it will be difficult for elected governments to maintain public confidence in existing political arrangements, to satisfy the reasonable expectations of democratic electorates or even (in some cases at least) to maintain public order. If elected governments consistently fail in these respects, the gains made in terms of democratisation and economic reform will be put at risk.

This focus on state institutions, though loosely based on the work of Douglass North,[1] is not intended to suggest any kind of historical inevitability. Human beings, when convinced of the need, in principle can create and develop effective institutions. The point is simply that Latin American elites have so far been more successful at democratising than at creating state institutions which work well. This situation holds out the permanent threat of state failure. This chapter departs from the argument that the problem of the poor performance of existing state institutions can be seen as a consequence of three interacting variables: the increased empowerment of capitalist forces (including illegal and disreputable ones) arising from globalisation; political resentments on the part of those who have lost out as a result of economic change; and the traditionally weak and patrimonially structured Latin American state.

It is evident that internal politics in Latin America are to some extent subject to international forces, which are institutional as well as purely economic. International financial institutions are influential policy-makers and we also live in a world of increasingly influential NGOs. Under some circumstances global-isation may actually help the development of domestic institutions. The glob-alisation of economic activity and related dimensions of IMF conditionality may actually increase some kinds of state autonomy.[2] However, globalisation is not just a matter of cops, but also of robbers. The international trade in illegal drugs is globalised, and the practice of corruption on a global scale is most cer-tainly damaging to institutions.

Turning from international to domestic conditions, it is worth noting that power in the region was many times in the past exercised informally rather than though legal institutions. Landowner power was very real, as was the power of the Church. During the nineteenth century, state institutions were in many countries too weak to protect political authorities from violent overthrow. It was not until the turn of the century that South American military establish-ments could genuinely be said to monopolise force, and it was not until the 1930s that the same could be said of the military in Mexico. From that time, the military itself developed an increasingly formalised organisational struc-ture. However, it was not generally able or willing to reform the state in its own image. It looked for civilian allies with which to maintain power and therefore tended to fall in with traditional patterns of negotiated or patrimonial politics. Moreover, the military itself was quite willing to act illegally when faced with threats to its political authority, or simply when faced with attractive financial opportunity. Military governments in Latin America were not generally 'mod-ernising authoritarians' on the East Asian pattern. They were, for the most part, more politically exclusionary than seriously developmentalist.

The argument that it is both possible and necessary to develop professional state institutions if democracy is to work well in Latin America has not been one to which social scientists, on the whole, have given sufficient attention. During the 1970s both social scientists and political actors took it as virtually axiomatic that social and class conflict were the leitmotifs of Latin American politics, and that the distribution of power and wealth within the region was determined by the outcome of political engagement rather than policy studies or competent administration. The Left called upon the people to revolt against capitalism and offered social transformation. The Right, for its part, was not really convinced by the virtues of democracy at all. Fascism was not applied as thoroughly in Latin America as it was in Europe during the 1930s, but neither was it as convincingly defeated in 1945. Conservative authoritarians, secular and clerical alike, tended to respond to political challenge by calling upon the military. There is no doubt that social and political repression played important roles in preserving the social order during the region's long periods of author-itarian or semi-authoritarian rule. Elites did not need to organise state institu-tions capable of meeting the aspirations of ordinary voters because they were far from convinced that there was any point in meeting them.

When democracy arrived once more in Latin America, there quickly developed a significant scholarly literature based upon the question of its survivability. However, the conventional wisdom tended to discuss political institutions in isolation from state institutions. At the risk of some simplification, pacts and consensus were seen as good. Polarisation and mobilisation were seen as bad. This notion may well have been highly applicable to democratisation in Southern Europe, where previous authoritarian governments had already built moderately effective states, and where membership of the European Union (EU) would significantly transform state institutions. A combination of moderate politics and sound administration may, in such cases, have been a recipe for success. However, in Venezuela, and to some extent other Latin American countries where 'pacted democracy' was taken seriously, political compromise largely made state-building impossible.[3] Instead, state institutions were subordinated to bargaining over spoils by the established parties and then parcelled out on a patrimonial basis to meet whatever outcome had been negotiated. Such arrangements did not prevent democratic transition (although they may initially have made it easier), but they later posed real problems for democratic performance and democratic stability.[4]

Another factor informing much academic literature on Latin America was the fact that, starting in 1982, the region underwent a deep economic crisis, which produced an enormous amount of angst but no clear-cut solutions. In the end, the 1980s came to be seen as a 'lost decade' due to falls in GDP across the entire region. Democratically elected governments in countries such as Brazil, Argentina, Peru and Bolivia could not wholly be blamed for their failure to cope with the crisis, since this largely reflected the adverse consequences of decades of over-indebtedness and flawed macroeconomic management. Nevertheless, authors such as Przeworski[5] expressed concern that democratically elected governments might be unable to solve the most basic economic problems affecting the region. This, too, was an argument which generated considerable literature but ultimately failed empirically.

By the early 1990s, it was becoming clear that an increasing number of Latin American governments were committing themselves to market-oriented economic reforms. Success varied enormously, from the genuine achievements of Menem in Argentina to the much more doubtful performance of Pérez in Venezuela and Collor in Brazil.[6] It remains the case that some Latin American economies are very much more successful than others: this has been quite a normal state of affairs during the past century or more. What is noteworthy, however, is that neither the economic crises of the 1980s nor the radical kinds of economic reform carried out during the 1990s led to full-scale democratic breakdown. There were some fairly close calls, including Fujimori's closure of Congress in 1992 and two coup attempts in Venezuela during the same year (see Chapter 5), but the democratic system of government survived.

Democracy in Latin America has survived for a reasonable period and democratic leaders at times have proved capable and decisive economic managers.

These facts now seem clearly established. It therefore seems appropriate to raise a different question. How much can reasonably be expected from democratisation in the longer term? Human rights are certainly better respected than they were under military rule, although human rights abuses still occur under democratic government (see Chapter 8). Unfortunately, casual crime, organised crime and political violence continue to exist on a worrying scale in some countries. Violent disorder, including misconduct by security forces, can be as much a threat to individual rights as political authoritarianism. In Colombia, which has remained a democracy for longer than most countries in the region, it was estimated early in 1998 that there were some 20,000 military members of (several different) insurgent groups, and that much of rural Colombia was suffering from conditions of civil war. Neither the military nor the state as a whole is currently able to cope with the turmoil. Many thousands of people have died in political violence, including hundreds of people assassinated while seeking to exercise their democratic rights (see Chapter 6). There has been untold damage to property and to Colombia's economic prospects. These problems are intermixed with Colombia's position as a major supplier of cocaine to the United States and Europe. President Samper was accused by his critics of accepting money from drugs traffickers and Colombia was decertified by the US government as cooperative on drugs issues in 1995 and 1996.[7] Certification was grudgingly restored in 1997 because the US national interest demanded it (see Chapter 5). Readers who believe that democracy on its own is a sufficient condition for the existence of a successful political society should study Colombia and think again.

Human rights apart, another area in which democratisation should have provided some hope is social inequality. It is generally accepted that global capitalism has widened income differentials within countries, and most First World electorates have looked to government to counteract this tendency to some degree. Latin America already suffered from comparatively high levels of social inequality prior to the adoption of market-oriented reforms. Since then there is at best limited evidence that economic growth, where this has resumed to any significant degree, has tangibly benefited the poor. A positive case can be made in the cases of Chile and Argentina, and perhaps (allowing for the fact that growth recovered from a very low base) Peru. However, it is reasonable to conclude that, at the minimum, free market economics has not been accompanied by any extensive programmes of effective social reform.

Another more controversial judgement is that the absence of effective social reform does not seem to be explained satisfactorily by the characteristics of market-oriented economic reform itself. It is true that radical market-oriented reform in Britain and the United States was first advocated by politicians such as Margaret Thatcher and Ronald Reagan, who were seen as anti-labour and instinctively opposed to the use of the state to redistribute income, but it is much harder to make the same point about Latin American leaders such as Menem, Cardoso or Fujimori. Furthermore, the debate about the role of the state in First World countries is largely irrelevant to the reality of Latin America. In Britain, after 17 years of 'free market' economics, the government still takes and spends around 40 per cent of GDP. In Peru in 1990 the government's tax take was around 5.5 per cent of GDP. This low tax take characterised the end of a period of so-called populist, not market-oriented, economics. Despite Fujimori's privatisation policies, the share of Peruvian GDP taken by taxes has significantly increased since 1990. In Mexico, non-oil taxation currently amounts to around 9 per cent of GDP. Until 1988 virtually nobody in Mexico was pursued for tax fraud except for transparent political reasons. There was simply no institutionalised taxation system worth the name. The point is that, in order to reach the situation which currently exists in the most market-oriented First World economies, Latin American states would have to achieve an enormous *increase* in both the role and effectiveness of government. This would also be clear, only more so, if we contrasted the role of government in Latin America with its role in the 'Asian tiger' economies which, despite recent difficulties, have achieved an impressive record of success in the longer term. While it may be true that the IMF, the World Bank and other international financial institutions are not enthusiastic proponents of any expanded role for central government, there is nothing in the political economy of globalisation to prevent Latin American governments from taxing more effectively than they currently do. Without an effective system of taxation, governments have to choose between doing nothing to help the poor and embarking on risky macroeconomic experiments (fiscal populism) which have quickly led to high rates of inflation and capital flight.

The third area in which democracy might be expected to make a difference relates more specifically to economic issues. Here the picture is rather surprising. When democratically elected governments brought down high rates of inflation, they were rewarded at the polls. Today in the late 1990s average rates of inflation across the region are significantly lower than they were during periods of authoritarian rule (Venezuela being the only significant exception). Market-oriented reform, too, has happened on a significant scale. Free market economics is not peculiar to democratic forms of government any more than state planning is peculiar to authoritarianism. However, it is clear that most democratically elected governments which replaced military rulers across the region did not become more economically nationalist but less so. Two conclusions follow from this. One is that the one area in which ordinary Latin Americans are incontrovertibly better off than they were in the 1970s is reduced inflation. The other is that a combination of privatisation and the abandonment of many forms of government regulation has itself done something to change the role of the state. Many of the region's previous institutions for generating patrimonialism and corruption (such as industrial protectionism, price and exchange controls, and poorly controlled state-owned enterprises) have been dismantled. However, as was the case in Gilded Age USA, free market economies can certainly coexist with clientelistic public administration and a high degree of corruption. Withdrawing the state from areas characterised by corrupt mismanagement has certainly made a change, but one which is far from sufficient on its own.

The ability of some governments in the region to associate free market economics with falling rates of inflation has nevertheless allowed a period of radical reform which would have surprised most observers during the 1980s. There is also some optimism that, where radical economic restructuring has been allowed to take place, popular living standards should gradually rise. However, the possibility that free market economics may eventually help poorer Latin Americans is a far weaker and more tenuous ground for optimism than might have been provided by a successful programme of social reform. While it may be an exaggeration to view free market economics as 'savage neoliberalism', it is certainly the case that the global capitalist system has savage aspects. It would be reasonable to expect that a democratic state might do something to mitigate these, even if the constraints of global capitalism do put some significant limits on what might be achieved.

We return, then, to the observation that institutions in Latin America ought to work better than they generally do. While there are exceptions to this rule, these show up the general problem even more. If Venezuela can run an efficient state oil company, then why are there so many difficulties with its education system? If Petróleos de Venezuela (PdVSA) is generally honest, then why is the judicial system in the country so generally corrupt? There can be no doubt that most Latin American voters do actually want honestly run and effectively functioning state institutions. The rest of this discussion relates to the problems of developing such institutions.

Political institutions and presidentialism

Latin American executives are generally presidential. This fact has been seen by some observers, famously by Juan Linz, as an obstacle to democratic stability.[8] Linz characterises presidentialism as a system of dual legitimation, with President and Congress separately elected and autonomous in their respective spheres. The President selects the cabinet and generally exercises day-to-day control over policy. There is no prime-ministerial role as such and the President does not have any direct power (such as via dissolution) over the legislative body. Presidentialism is therefore to be distinguished not only from parliamentary systems of government, but from semi-presidential systems (such as France), in which the Executive does have a clear relationship with the legislature. In pure presidential systems (as defined by Linz), congressional power is inherently separate from presidential power, and this is alleged to present an ever-present danger of deadlock. In practice, though, total separation rarely exists, which is a weakness in Linz's argument. For example, the danger of deadlock may be reduced where the Constitution allows a president to bypass Congress and rule by decree under certain circumstances. By the same token,

Congress generally has a right to impeach or otherwise remove a president from office. There has been a very considerable literature on the whole issue of whether presidentialism is good for democracy. The literature is now rightly sceptical of the notion that there is a direct link between presidentialism *per se* and democratic breakdown.[9]

However we now need to move beyond discussing the direct threat of democratic breakdown to considering the general quality of democratic government in the region. In this context two preliminary points can be made. One is that the power of Congress in Latin America is commonly underestimated in the literature. In practice, presidents do need support in Congress if they are to succeed in policy terms or even to survive. South American congressional institutions have impeached two presidents for corruption since 1990 (Collor de Mello in Brazil in 1992 and Carlos Andrés Pérez in Venezuela in 1993), and removed a third (Assad Bucaram in Ecuador in 1997) for alleged 'mental instability'. A fourth president, Siles Suazo in Bolivia in 1985, chose to resign following a congressional vote of no-confidence and a fifth, Raul Alfonsín, voluntarily agreed to leave office three months early in order to give his successor an opportunity to confront Argentina's 1988–89 economic crisis. Furthermore, even though presidential impeachment remains comparatively rare, congressional censure of cabinet ministers is relatively common. There is therefore no real evidence that democratic Latin America has created any kind of super-presidentialism, above all kinds of political accountability. The only presidential institution which has until recently been all-powerful is that of Mexico, where democracy has not been fully established.[10]

The second general point is that Latin American executives have rarely been subjected to autonomous law enforcement. There is here an important point of contrast with the President of the United States. The architects of the US Constitution realised that it was necessary to have a system of political authority, but they were more exercised by the fear that the Executive might have too much power rather than too little. The Constitution itself famously specified that every man had the right to 'life, liberty and the pursuit of happiness'. This essentially meant economic and religious freedom – more exotic interpretations of 'the pursuit of happiness' came later – and was deliberately designed to reduce the field over which political action could be taken. The US Constitution (including the First Amendment) gives very definite powers to individuals. Adults have not only the power to bear arms but also to issue writs. An enormous amount of policy is made in the United States through court decisions given on cases brought by individuals (*Roe v. Wade* on abortion, *Brown v. Topeka Board of Education* on desegregation). The US Supreme Court has always been willing to interpret the Constitution to the disadvantage of the President of the day if it so decided.

In Latin America, by contrast, issues of rights, courts and judicial power have historically been taken much less seriously. There is generally no power of judicial review as such. Supreme Courts do not interpret the Constitution to the disadvantage of the executive power. Nor has the political culture placed the same degree of stress on individual rights. This was even more obviously the case when countries of the region were subjected to authoritarian rule. It is therefore a reasonable generalisation (allowing for some local variations and differences of emphasis) that executive power has been exercised more freely and with less regard to individual rights in Latin America than in the United States. Clearly the over-privileging of executive power is a threat to good government wherever it occurs, but this is not an issue of presidential government as such.

This situation may, however, be seen as something which can change. Both elite and popular political culture in Latin America were once more influenced by collectivist ideas (derived from fascism in some cases, and from socialism in others) than was the case in the United States. Latin America has also lived with social institutions which are far more authoritarian than their US counterparts. These have included an entrenched landed elite, which, as Rueschemeyer, Stephens and Stephens point out[11], is negative for democratic institutions. The Catholic Church was also a significant authoritarian influence for many years. A key issue for the future is how much and in what way this political culture is itself changing.

A further point is that the presidency is seen in most Latin American countries as a focal point for political action because of inadequacies in other political institutions. Whether or not one sees populism as dangerous, the nature of Latin American presidentialism does allow radical outsiders to run for office and win. The strength of party systems varies significantly between countries (this is addressed further below), but these are weak and perhaps weakening further in several countries. This, too, is relevant to the issue of presidentialism. The discrediting of political parties clearly explains why a Fujimori or a Collor could win the presidency without previous party affiliation or government experience. What should be noted, though, is that such figures do not always prosper.

For all of these reasons, presidentialism as such does not seem to be significantly at fault for the continuing weakness of state institutions. Where there are weaknesses, they need different kinds of explanation. Moreover, presidentialism has positive aspects as well. Presidents can be held accountable when things go wrong. They do need to pursue their objectives 'politically', via some degree of compromise and bargaining, if they are to succeed. Where electorates have rejected the party system as a whole, there are good reasons for this. Some degree of centralised presidentialism may, in any event, be necessary if a country is to avoid being fully at the mercy of global capital markets and powerful domestic social forces. There seems to be a greater danger of too little government in Latin America than of too much.

State institutions, party systems and the issue of clientelism

When looking for institutional weakness in the region, a good place to start is with the state bureaucracy. Nineteenth-century Europe essentially invented the 'Weberian' bureaucracy, and the professionally managed corporation was developed in the United States around the same time. The two types of organisations have similar characteristics. Latin America has not until recently had much experience with professionally-managed organisations, except for the military, which did indeed develop authentic bureaucratic characteristics during the course of the present century.

In essence, the Weberian bureaucrat or company manager is recruited on the basis of qualifications, experience and appropriate personal characteristics. His or her job is generally full time, with outside commitments secondary at best. The job is defined by a series of formal rules, clear procedures and targets. Performance is evaluated by superiors (either subjectively or through some form of procedure) and there is normally a system of promotion on merit. Although resignation or dismissal are certainly possible, there is an expectation that a manager/bureaucrat will stay in position for a significant period of time in order to permit some gathering of experience in the course of doing a particular job.

A clientelist appointee will be recruited mainly on the basis of personal or political loyalty, though some evidence of capacity may be taken into account as well. Performance in the job is likely to be weakly evaluated and relatively unimportant in any event. The most important consideration in future career development is likely to be the success or otherwise of the political cause with which the individual is associated. To the extent that performance evaluation matters, this is likely to have a significant political component. Financial controls over a bureaucratic position are likely to be limited, and it is accepted that a clientelist appointee will use his or her position to benefit family and friends. 'To one's friends one does justice', go the words of an old Brazilian proverb, 'but to one's enemies one upholds the law.'

It would be too much to say that all European state bureaucracies are purely Weberian while all Latin American ones are clientelist, but there is an important difference in emphasis. It has been shown by Douglass North and others[12] that the Spanish Crown, during the period when it ruled in the Americas, was in a financially precarious state. It therefore sought to 'sell' public office for ready cash to office-holders who would seek to make a profit from the right to collect taxes. Clientelism and corruption went hand in hand, and both were manifestations of state weakness. A similar pattern could be seen in much of Latin America during the nineteenth century, where evidence of state weakness was also very clear.

The first major institution to bureaucratise in South America (more precisely than Latin America) was the military. Under the influence of European military advisers, army reforms in the early part of the century created an effective system of youth entry into the service, officer training and promotion on merit within the officer corps. Promotion from the ranks of non-commissioned officer (NCO) was restricted or abolished altogether. It was precisely the tension between the clientelistic practices of civilian politicians and the belief of senior military officers in meritocracy (defined according to military criteria) which contributed to the 'young officers' movements of the 1920s and 1930s which played an important political role in Brazil, Chile and (to a lesser extent) Argentina.

In more recent years, military government in the region was strongly associated with economic planning and an expansion of the role of the state. O'Donnell even famously referred to the military governments of the 1960s as 'bureaucratic authoritarian'.[13] Some military officers specifically saw state enterprise as a means of translating the norms of Weberian bureaucracy and/or professional management into a culture where recruitment and promotion to private sector companies was still largely based on traditional or familial criteria. However, with limited exceptions, military government did not succeed in professionalising the state apparatus of those countries subject to military rule. For the most part, the military simply governed via traditional methods, which included clientelism and corruption. Control was given a greater weight than efficiency and state bureaucracies were 'militarised' rather than professionalised.

Today the quality of Latin American state institutions varies considerably. Some are clearly more effective than others. The Chilean public sector, for example, clearly operates more effectively than that of Venezuela. Even in Venezuela, the state oil company (PdVSA) is a genuine meritocracy. However, across the region, many state institutions have a clientelist element, and some are quite simply run for the benefit of those who work in them. The rule of law and financial accountability are weakly applied, though perhaps a little bit less weakly than a generation ago. The system of clientelism, unsatisfactory though it may be in many ways, is internally coherent and capable of surviving largely unchanged for quite long periods of time. There is an obvious point of contrast between the 'activist' aspirations of many Latin American presidents and the manifest incapacity of the bureaucracy to make policy impartially or even efficiently. This caused a lot of frustration to reforming governments in the region that found it hard, in practice, to get anything done. This failure, in turn, tended to induce left-leaning presidents to manipulate the macroeconomy in order to achieve outcomes that might, under other circumstances, have been better sought by a more targeted approach.

The existence of clientelist patterns of recruitment to public office clearly influences the composition and behaviour of political parties. Where party activists are motivated by the hope of government jobs or favours in public policy terms, they are much less likely to reflect any kind of serious political consciousness. For this reason, political parties may end up defined more by their attitude to the state than by any particular ideology or form of organisation. Duverger described such organisations as 'cadre parties',[14] although some Latin

American parties have been heterodox combinations of (authoritarian-run) affiliate organisations and direct membership parties. In any event, there does seem to be a close relationship between Latin American countries where state institutions work comparatively well, and strong party systems. Most observers would identify Chile and Uruguay as places where institutions work best. They also have the most effective party systems. Interestingly, they also have legally very different forms of presidentialism, which suggests that presidentialism itself is not the most important variable. The Chilean Constitution of 1980, though somewhat amended, is still the basis of presidentialism in that country. As might be expected from any document drawn up under General Pinochet, it provides for an extremely strong executive power. The Uruguayan Constitution, by contrast, offers much less power to the President and much more to the Congress, to the point where some critics of presidentialism have described Uruguay as semi-parliamentary.

While it might seem logical to believe that powerful and well-organised political parties make for good government, the actual direction of causality may be the reverse. Party systems are likely to work well when government is seen as reasonably successful. When government fails seriously, as happened in Peru in the 1980s, then the party system may attract most of the blame.[15] Government failure can be a powerful solvent of political parties. A good place to look at the decay of political parties is Venezuela. The Punto Fijo pact, according to which the leaders of Venezuela's main political parties agreed to work together, was seen by a whole generation of political analysts as a paradigm way of bringing democracy to the region. Party elites subsequently governed by bringing business elites and, to some extent, the main trade union confederation into a consensual mode of decision-making. Unfortunately they also adopted clientelist recruitment patterns which brought the judiciary and the state administration under the control of the political parties. When these became corrupted, partly due to their links with business and their need to run hugely expensive election campaigns, corruption spread into the state apparatus and judiciary as well. Economic mismanagement and fluctuating oil prices finally made the situation intolerable, and the dominant parties went into a decline from which they show no sign of recovering.[16]

While the radical decay of party systems in countries such as Peru and Venezuela must be attributed in part to the severe economic problems suffered by both countries, a purely economic explanation is insufficient. In the eyes of the majority of Peruvians and Venezuelans, the major parties had become fatally discredited through their association with corruption. This perception does not seem grossly out of keeping with the known facts.

Economic structures and institution-building

Societal authoritarianism and inertia are clearly not sufficient explanations for weak institutions. We also need to know why transformative influences have, to date, not succeeded in changing patterns of state organisation. Latin American societies have changed significantly over time. Some areas of Latin America began industrialising a century ago, and the first experiences of representative government also date from the previous century. Despite the occasional severe setback, there has been significant per capita growth and extensive social change during the twentieth century. It was during the 1960s that Latin America changed from being a predominantly rural to an essentially urban society: today it is around 70 per cent urban. Moreover, democracy is now largely accepted as a form of government and competition for elective office is routine. The media are free and quite ready to denounce corruption. Most Latin Americans are literate, and a growing number have university degrees. Nor is evidence of policy stagnation manifest in other areas. As we have seen, there have been major economic policy innovations in the region over the past decade. So why has it been so difficult to change public policy in other respects?

If economic growth and social change have had less of a transformative effect than might have been expected, one possible clue may be found in the actual pattern of economic change. This was a familiar theme in the 1960s writings of social scientists on Latin America, but it is important not to caricature Latin American economic development in a way that was done a generation ago. Latin America has changed significantly since 1965. Brazil and Mexico have become large-scale exporters of industrial products. While it is true that some of the smaller Latin American countries are still mainly exporters of primary products, they are no longer generally dependent on a single commodity. Nor are commodity-exporting countries generally less successful economically than countries whose main exports are manufactured products. Since the mid-1980s, the Chilean economy has been one of the most successful in the world. Even where single-commodity export dependency remains (as in Venezuela), the pattern of enclave foreign ownership has changed. PdVSA is one of the most efficient state-owned enterprises anywhere in the Americas.

Moreover, while there is significant foreign ownership of industry in Latin America (as there is in Europe), it is no longer tenable to draw a contrast between efficient transnational capital and uncompetitive ('oligarchic') local interests. Every major Latin American economy has produced powerful and efficient local capitalists with international links.[17] Such companies have nothing in common with the corrupt 'comprador bourgeoisie' criticised by sociologists a generation ago or with the family-run businesses which were locally dominant in parts of the region in the 1950s and 1960s. Indeed, it is precisely the less competitive kinds of enterprise which have lost heavily from economic liberalisation. It is therefore difficult to see much merit today in the traditional left-wing argument that Latin America's dominant classes are less serious economic modernisers than was the European bourgeoisie of a century ago.

Nevertheless, there may be an argument to the effect that there were strategic weaknesses in the pattern of import-substituting industrialisation (ISI) pursued across the region between 1945 and 1982. It became too easy for Latin American governments to borrow from abroad, and foreign indebtedness became an attractive substitute for effective public policies. The contrast between the experience of the Latin American and Asian economies makes this point clear. There is also no doubt that a combination of commodity wealth and largely unregulated borrowing from abroad reinforced a culture of corruption. Enormous amounts of money flooded into Mexico and Venezuela during the oil-boom years, but the developmental effect of this inflow was certainly not beneficial, and probably quite negative. The belief that an inflow of capital from abroad was an effective substitute for a professionally-run state proved to be wrong.

An optimist would argue that the ending of ISI and the inability of Latin American governments to acquire significantly more debt should therefore force an improvement in the quality of policy-making. There can be little doubt that economic policy in Latin America as a whole is less sloppy, more considered and generally more sophisticated than was the case a generation ago. In most countries economic policy is in the hands of properly qualified technocrats who are able to discuss issues with the IMF or the World Bank on the basis of intellectual equality. At the upper level of most Latin American states there is far less authoritarianism of attitude, far less social irresponsibility and far more understanding of the technical requirements of good policy-making than was the case a generation ago. The problem, though, is that the general public has still not seen the benefit of these changes. While few academic commentators have a good word to say about the governments of López Portillo (1976–82) in Mexico or Pérez (1974–79) in Venezuela, these were periods of booming employment and real wages which were higher than they are today. Governments which relied on high commodity prices and foreign borrowing may have triggered an unsustainable boom, but they also engendered social memories of better times which made it harder for populations to accept the hardships inherent in any determined programme of market-oriented reform. Only where the ghost of 'fiscal populism' was exorcised by hyperinflation did popular opposition to economic restructuring largely disappear.

Where modernising elites, in alliance with international institutions, have enjoyed sufficient political autonomy to carry through major market-oriented economic reform with visible success, the political agenda does seem to have moved to post-reform mode. There seems little likelihood of major policy reversal in Chile or Argentina, and perhaps not in Peru or Bolivia either. In all of these cases, issues of institutional reform have either been addressed to some extent or at least put securely on the political agenda. However, where free market reforms have either not been seriously attempted or not really worked, then resentment on the part of poorer Latin Americans has been evident. With repression no longer an option, popular resentment is likely to take the form of support for those individuals who most convincingly reject the existing order. The result is something of a lottery. Some individuals elected as outsider candidates have been spectacularly successful, while others have failed totally and deepened the institutional crises in their respective countries. In such cases, a lack of economic success may undermine the social consensus necessary for democratic institution-building.

The consequences of economic failure may be particularly dangerous today because income distribution seems to be worsening in parallel with (and perhaps as a result of) the process of globalisation. The resulting danger is that economic failure may become self-reinforcing. If the economy does not grow fast enough to allow the per capita income of the majority of the population to rise, angry voters, rioters and strikers may react in ways which may make economic problems more difficult to resolve. Wealth-holders are attuned (perhaps overattuned) to political and exchange rate risk in Latin America and may respond simply by exit. There was an enormous outflow of private capital from the region during 1981–82, just before the debt crisis struck. This outflow enormously deepened the recession suffered by the region after 1982. Similarly, the Tequila crisis of 1994 was triggered principally by the outflow of Mexican-owned capital.

All of this means that successful economic policy-making may be a necessary, though not a sufficient, condition for the professionalisation of the state. The risks inherent in economic globalisation can subsequently be reduced to some extent by effective state institutions, provided that these can somehow be brought into existence. Pension reforms can raise the savings rate. The inflow of short-term capital can be discouraged by taxation. Long-term capital inflows (which may be a stabilising factor) can be attracted by deregulation and reforms which end restrictions on foreign ownership of banking or other strategic sectors. There are also, undoubtedly, technical issues to be addressed. However, none of these policy measures can detract from the problem that, under conditions of global capital movement, economic growth is dependent upon a degree of domestic political stability, professional government and social consensus, which globalisation is itself not only unable to provide but potentially undermining.

Thus, although Latin America may well have a more effective modernising elite than was the case a generation ago, there may still be a political bill to be paid for the economic setbacks of the 1980s. Public opinion may refuse to follow where the elites wish to lead. Democratic politics provides abundant opportunity for the expression of rebellion through the ballot box. The development of effective state institutions therefore remains dependent upon the vagaries of day-to-day politics.

In conclusion, it would seem that the main obstacles to effective institution-building stem from a combination of rampant global capitalism, popular resentment at the poor performance of democratic political authority, and the traditional weakness of the Latin American state. If one wants to see how these forces can interact to devastating effect, a good place to start is the trade in illegal drugs. There is no country in which illegal drugs are the principal economic activity, though they are significant to both Bolivia and Colombia. However, the billions of dollars which go into organised crime are more than enough to complicate the political process in all countries in which the illegal drugs trade is significant. The relationship between drug money and insurgent violence – a relationship which is principally opportunistic from both viewpoints – adds enormously to the destabilising potential of the trade. So, too, does the perception that the United States is engaged on a self-righteous but ineffective policy of blaming individual governments within Latin America for their inevitable failure to deal with the drugs trade.

Most Latin Americans live in countries which have the great good fortune not to be heavily involved in the illegal drugs trade. Here, at least, there is no real doubt about the ability of the state to meet the standard Weberian criterion: the ability to monopolise force. However, even where this primary condition is met, it is far from clear that state institutions can provide the 'secondary' conditions which are taken for granted in most of the developed world. These relate to state honesty and respect for procedures, impartial rule enforcement and some respect for individual rights.

Will social modernisation be enough?

The final question asked here is whether social modernisation, in all of its aspects, makes what might be called institutional modernisation more likely to occur. A weakening of traditional societal authoritarianism throughout Latin America is evident and surely significant politically. The educated classes in Latin America are, for the most part, fully involved in the contemporary enlightenment with its fairer treatment of sexual minorities, women and people from diverse ethnic backgrounds. Latin American electorates have repeatedly shown themselves more willing to vote for women, homosexuals and people of non-Hispanic origin than their US counterparts. Traditional military views on patriarchy and manhood now sound hopelessly anachronistic to most Latin Americans, and for this reason alone it is hard to see military officers again being taken seriously as national rulers. The influence of the Catholic Church is also far less than it was. Birth rates are falling across the continent. Very few people take Catholic teachings on marriage and divorce too literally. And Latin American social mores have changed significantly.

Unfortunately, however, ancestral voices may still have something to say about institution-building. Can a libertarian society coexist with an effective state? It may be asked whether there is not an inherent contradiction between the necessarily top-down process of institution-building and the contemporary stress on individual rights and dislike of coercion in all of its forms. As the case of Colombia shows clearly, personal freedom, compromise and tolerance, while desirable in themselves, are insufficient qualities to sustain public order. Now that democracy has become more or less established in the region, the need for consensual but effective public institutions to keep order and, where necessary, impose discipline are greater than ever. It is not yet clear whether and to what extent this need is likely to be met.

Notes

1 *Institutional Change and Economic Performance* (Cambridge, Cambridge University Press, 1990).

2 N. Phillips, 'Globalisation, State Power and Democracy in Latin America', paper presented at the Annual Conference of the Society for Latin American Studies, Liverpool, 17–19 April 1998.

3 See J. Buxton, 'Venezuela', in J. Buxton and N. Phillips (eds), *Case Studies in Latin American Political Economy* (Manchester, Manchester University Press, 1999).

4 See, for example, T. L. Karl, 'Petroleum and Political Pacts: The Transition to Democracy in Venezuela', *Latin American Research Review*, 22 (1987) and D. Levine, 'Venezuela Since 1958: The Consolidation of Democratic Politics', in J. Linz and A. Stepan (eds.), *The Breakdown of Democratic Regimes: Latin America* (Baltimore, Johns Hopkins University Press, 1978).

5 A. Przeworski, *Democracy and the Market: Political and Economic Reforms in Eastern Europe and Latin America* (Cambridge, Cambridge University Press, 1991).

6 See C. M. Lewis, 'Argentina', J. Buxton, 'Venezuela', and F. Panizza, 'Brazil', in Buxton and Phillips (eds), *Case Studies*.

7 See B. McBeth, 'Colombia', in *ibid.*

8 J. Linz, 'Presidential or Parliamentary Democracy: Does It Make a Difference?', in J. Linz and A. Valenzuela (eds.), *The Failure of Presidential Democracy: The Case of Latin America* (Baltimore, Johns Hopkins, 1994).

9 S. Mainwaring and M. Soberg Shugart, *Presidentialism and Democracy in Latin America* (Cambridge, Cambridge University Press, 1997).

10 See S. Peschard, 'Mexico', in Buxton and Phillips (eds), *Case Studies*.

11 D. Rueschemeyer, E. Stevens and J. Stevens, *Capitalist Development and Democracy* (London, Polity, 1992).

12 *Institutional Change.*

13 G. O'Donnell, *Modernization and Bureaucratic–Authoritarianism: Studies in South American Politics* (Berkeley, University of California Press, 1973).

14 M. Duverger, *Political Parties, their Organisation and Activity in a Modern State* (London, Methuen, 1964).

15 See J. Crabtree, 'Peru', in Buxton and Phillips (eds), *Case Studies*.

16 See J. Buxton, 'Venezuela', in *ibid.*

17 A. Salas Porras, 'The Mexican Business Class and the Processes of Globalization: Trends and Countertrends' (unpublished Ph.D. thesis, University of London, 1997).

3

Electoral and party politics

DANIEL HELLINGER

As the millennium approached, academics and politicians spoke of a situation, historically unprecedented, where every nation in Latin America with the exception of Cuba was ruled by civilian, elected governments and has set out to implement, to one degree or another, neoliberal economic reforms. This came to be called the 'Washington Consensus' in support of 'free markets and democracy'. As Joseph Tulchin commented, 'The Washington Consensus seemed global in its reach. It was the economists' version of Fukuyama's end of history.'[1] That is, consistent with Francis Fukuyama's thesis, the movement towards Western-style electoral democracy seemed historically inevitable in the aftermath of the collapse of the Soviet Union and linked to opening Latin American economies up to market reforms and international trade.[2]

There were ample grounds for pessimism as well. Theorists from antiquity to the present have contended that a strong middle class and economic equality are crucial to democratic stability. The economic structural adjustment packages implemented throughout the region have clearly accentuated the endemic inequality in Latin America. Middle-class residents can look out of the windows of their high-rise apartments and see the burgeoning slums. Teachers, bureaucrats, university professors, doctors and nurses, engineers and other employees wonder how their meagre salaries of several hundred dollars per month can cover their rents or mortgages, along with all of their other expenses. From the perspective of the poor in these makeshift communities, the prospect of education for their children is farther off than ever before. In much of Latin America the state (municipal services, including the police, education, sanitation, the courts, etc.) has retreated from these communities, leaving them with dangerously climbing crime rates and vigilante justice in place of the rule of law. Can a less educated population with declining health and educational standards, facing great personal insecurity, possibly be a healthy environment for the institutionalisation of elections?

One might assume the only reason why elections are held in Latin America is to satisfy the United States, but it would be a mistake to regard the practice of elections as merely a product of decisions made in Washington. In favour of a consolidation of electoral democracy, one must consider the following five trends, some aided from abroad, others not. First, the collapse of Eastern communism and crisis confronting the Cuban Revolution have influenced most of the Latin American Left (with notable exceptions) to take elections seriously as a necessary, if not sufficient, condition for democracy. Second, the international movement for human rights has sunk deep roots in Latin America, particularly among religious and women's organisations, which often took the lead in fighting the dictatorships from within (see Chapter 8). While some of these movements have faded without the unifying factor of opposition to dictatorship, they have left an imprint on the culture, providing experience in organising and monitoring elections to reduce the danger of fraud, and serving to train new political leaders. Third, the flowering of new social movements has contributed to a culture of resistance to co-optation by political parties, and commensurably a determination to hold these parties accountable in government. Fourth, significant new political parties linked to, but not in control of, these movements have emerged. Although none has triumphed in elections (a possible exception being in Nicaragua in 1984), they have significantly influenced the party and electoral systems. Fifth, business organisations seem to have made a more concerted effort to represent their interests through parties and influencing elections, making them less reliant upon state coercion.

International influences on electoral politics

Just like US Treasury officials, the IMF and the IDB limited the economic policy options available to the new democracies, the United States has not left the matter of elections in Latin American hands alone. William Robinson, in his studies of US intervention in elections, illuminates the influence of the quasi-governmental National Endowment for Democracy (NED).[3] The NED provides US taxpayer dollars to a variety of NGOs based in the United States, including the two major political parties, unions, officially sanctioned human rights organisations, women's groups, and other civic bodies. These groups receive NED money ostensibly to aid their counterparts abroad in a variety of efforts to build democratic institutions, including help in organising, monitoring and conducting elections. Robinson contends that the NED, along with other US aid programmes and covert operations on the part of the Central Intelligence Agency (CIA) are designed to ensure that democracy in Latin America remains weak: what US political scientists approvingly call 'polyarchy' as opposed to 'popular democracy', which connotes a more participatory system which would challenge the property structure and economic rules of the game associated with neoliberalism, if not with capitalism itself. While US expenditures to influence elections abroad are only a tiny percentage of the huge US budget, they can significantly influence political and social forces toward North American notions of democracy.

The United States has been much more zealous in promoting immediate elections in the aftermath of revolution than it has been in promoting them after the military seized power in Brazil in 1964, Uruguay and Chile in 1973, Argentina in 1966 and 1976, and so on. US intervention against elected governments attempting significant structural changes in their economies includes Guatemala in 1954, the Dominican Republic in 1965, Brazil in 1964 and Chile in 1973. On some occasions, pressure from the United States has not produced a coup but electoral defeat. In Jamaica, Michael Manley faced a US orchestrated campaign of destabilisation which contributed to his loss in 1980. In both Nicaragua in 1979 and Cuba in 1959, revolutionary regimes came to power as a result of mass insurrections against highly corrupt and brutal dictatorships. In both countries, there existed a mistrust of electoral democracy precisely because political elites had often sold out on promises of reform and democracy in the past, often inviting US military intervention as a preferred alternative to real change. In both countries, martyrs of past revolutionary struggles (José Martí in Cuba and Augusto César Sandino in Nicaragua) left a legacy promoting national unity based on unifying the peasants and poor in a single revolutionary party. This legacy is offered as a rationale by the Cuban government, which has thus far escaped the same fate and managed to develop a highly participatory and egalitarian system which compares well with the region's liberal democracies. However, it has done so at a price, which includes political prisoners and limitations on the range of permissible debate in civil society and elections.

Latin America's political parties are well aware the world has changed since the fall of the Berlin Wall in 1989. The absence of a superpower capable of countervailing the power of the United States, the struggles of Cuba to survive, the electoral defeat of the Sandinistas and the inability to imagine an alternative to neoliberalism have induced many socialist and populist politicians to reinvent themselves as 'responsible' democratic leaders who now embrace rather than criticise market-oriented economic policies. Many speak of moderating the resulting inequalities, but with the (very debatable) exception of Chile, none has succeeded. Even in Cuba the ruling Communist Party has found it impossible to introduce wider space for markets and private foreign investment without generating wider social and economic inequality, which in turn threatens the legitimacy of the government. But this only makes Cuba more like, not different from, its counterparts with multi-party systems.

General trends

As the gap between rich and poor has widened, the political party systems of Latin America have become not more but less ideologically polarised. One explanation for this paradox is the weight of the recent experiences with harsh military governments which smothered all party politics, not just those of the Left. Furthermore, the restoration of democracy has usually been in the form of a pact among party leaders, providing a common commitment to work together to preserve the electoral system.[4] This tendency can be seen at work in Colombia and Venezuela, where political and other elites negotiated pacts in the 1950s. As Venezuelan political scientist Juan Carlos Rey explains, in negotiations among civilian sectors to unite in opposition to the military, and later in negotiations during the transition itself, political parties agreed to moderate demands, limit the participation and influence of revolutionary parties, and share responsibility for government in the post-military era. The agreements sent the military back to the barracks but decades later, even as the new generation has almost entirely replaced the original founders of these 'pacted democracies', politicians have tended to moderate their differences short of breaking the underlying consensus.[5] Populist and leftist criticism of neoliberalism is tempered by knowledge that economic crisis and political polarisation were forerunners of democratic collapse, and without a clear alternative to the Washington Consensus few politicians care to risk the destabilising consequences of rejecting structural adjustment.

This is a weak basis for institutionalisation of elections, and in many countries the integrity of the electoral processes is seriously in question. In Venezuela, a stalwart of democracy throughout the era of military rule, the transparency of the voting process is suddenly in doubt. Thousands of ballots favourable to the Causa R (Radical Cause) party were found in rubbish dumps shortly after the 1993 elections. In Mexico, President Carlos de Salinas de Gortari, the architect of the NAFTA, was probably elected by fraud in 1988. News media and academics in developed countries praise reports by international observers of relatively clean presidential elections, but fraud and stealing of congressional elections and local elections remain common. Only established parties, particularly when they control the government, have the resources to place observers at every polling station. These partisan poll workers tend to take as their function guaranteeing the victory of their candidates, not guarding the integrity of the process.

During El Salvador's civil war of the 1980s the inability to show a stained thumb could have life-threatening consequences, as the country's military and death-squads made it clear that failure to vote was tantamount to treason, and treason meant one was marked for death. In the Paraguayan legislative contest of 1993 the incumbent Colorado Party was criticised for setting itself up as 'both judge and jury of the entire electoral process' when it agreed to review less than one-third of independent observers' challenges of fraud at 433 voting tables, and, in most cases, took little action.[6] In Peru, the victory of President Alberto Fujimori's Cambio 90 party in congressional elections 'was marred by scandals and confusion that delayed the vote count, disenfranchised thousands of voters, and left a trail of unanswered questions' about the country's electoral commission.[7] Often the process leading up to election day is far from transparent, with violence and intimidation frequent charges. Elections in Central America, Colombia and Jamaica have been notorious for these problems (although significant progress was achieved in the isthmus in the 1990s).

The process of obtaining a party's nomination is rife with uncertainty in many cases. Voters in Paraguay could be forgiven for being confused after President Juan Carlos Wasmosy, of the ruling Colorado Party, ordered the arrest of a retired general, Lino Oveido, who had won the Colorado nomination through a primary, resulting in the general's conviction and a ten-year prison sentence. The general had led the revolt which ended the 35-year dictatorship of General Alfredo Stroessner in 1989. In 1996, Wasmosy discharged Oveido for insubordination, but in 1998 Oveido won the Colorado primary by campaigning hard against Wasmosy's neoliberal economic policies, a point made through tireless grassroots campaigning and use of vast funds of uncertain origins for large construction projects in poor towns. Speaking the language of the masses, Oveido would eat in the homes of peasants and *barrio-* (slum-) dwellers, promising 'When I'm President, there'll be more meat in that pot.'[8]

To verify the integrity of an election is a complicated matter, requiring one to look beyond election day itself in evaluating a contest. While the European and North American media may be filled with optimistic reports the day after an election, there are often good reasons for voters in Latin America to believe electoral processes were not democratic. This mistrust, in fact, sometimes strengthens the hand of some elected presidents who have successfully used popular revulsion with parties and politicians to enhance their own power. President Alberto Fujimori used the military to disband Peru's elected Congress in 1992, attracting considerable criticism but no real consequences from abroad. President Jorge Serrano of Guatemala nearly accomplished the same in 1991, and Venezuela's Rafael Caldera used the threat of *fujimorización* to force highly questionable concessions from Venezuela's Congress between 1993 and 1998. In Argentina and Brazil, presidents were all manoeuvring in 1998 to change constitutional limits on their terms.

On the other hand, elected presidents have at times found their electoral mandate removed by Congress. Four elected presidents (Serrano in Guatemala, Fernando Collor de Mello in Brazil, Asaad Bucaram in Ecuador and Carlos Andrés Pérez in Venezuela) were removed by office in the 1990s. The causes for their removal, both in the legal and political sense, varied, and to some degree the victories of Congress can be viewed as a reaffirmation of commitment to representative democracy. On the other hand, these proceedings had little impact on economic policy. In all of these cases the unpopularity of structural adjustment plans at least contributed to the fall of the President, yet the fundamental direction of economic policy remained consistent with neoliberalism in the long run (see Chapter 2). Some studies promoted by the US and European institutes and universities contend that strong presidential government has not been harmful to democracy, but most Latin American political scientists disagree.[9] Guillermo O'Donnell warned that the new electoral democracy amounted to little more than 'delegative democracy', one where electoral processes are focused on the presidency, and contended that such democracies might endure, but are not consolidated. He agreed there was little immediate threat of a new wave of authoritarianism. However, he argued there was little sign of progress towards fuller representative democracy. In contrast, elected presidents tend to portray themselves above parties and contending interests.[10]

One must wonder how meaningful elections are to voters who see little correspondence between the electoral process and their social and economic well-being. I remember a conversation with a group of mothers in a *barrio* soup kitchen in Santiago in 1991, only one year after Chile's first presidential election, two years since these women had rejoiced after winning the plebiscite which forced dictator and General Augusto Pinochet to abandon the presidency. Were they still hopeful about democracy? 'We are proud of having forced Pinochet from office,' one told me, 'but nothing has really changed. I'm not sure what elections have earned us.' The sentiments of these women are representative of the ambiguous attitude towards elections in Latin America's civil society. On the one hand, the growth of new grassroots organisations generates a citizenry more capable of using the vote and resisting manipulation by parties (see Chapters 7 and 8). On the other hand, many new social movements promote a democratisation of the economy and society which is incompatible with a government committed to leaving poorer sectors to the mercy of the global market economy. Unions, for example, protest and resist privatisation of state companies. Peasant associations and new organisations of debtors (like Mexico's El Barzón) are making it difficult for the state to end subsidies which would result in loss of land and bankruptcies. Consumer groups demand government action to cap prices on basic goods. All of these measures are inconsistent with the neoliberal agenda.

Abstention rates are an indicator that, despite the general disrepute in which they hold military government, Latin Americans have their doubts about the value of the vote. It is worth noting that many Latin American systems go beyond granting suffrage to actually requiring citizens to vote. In Venezuela, where voting is compulsory, before 1978 abstention never exceeded 10 per cent of the electorate; in 1993, the rate rose to 40 per cent. In Honduras, another compulsory system, the rate was 41 per cent in 1997. Although the regulations are rarely enforced effectively, failure to provide proof of voting can result in loss of the right to have a passport or collect social security. (For this reason, observers often take the percentage of 'null and void' votes as an indicator of mass discontent.) This is an indication that an increasing percentage of Latin Americans, marginalised from the market economy and often living in deplorable conditions lacking in both minimum living standards and personal security, find little incentive to participate in elections. However, party organisation can make a difference.

The Mexican Partido Revolucionario Institucional (PRI, Institutional Revolutionary Party) is notorious for combining legal and skilful manipulation of electoral procedures with repression and fraud to control state and municipal elections in areas of opposition strength: for example, in Chiapas and southern Oaxaca.[11] Dan La Botz describes the desperation of a Mexican peasant woman who was directed to a special polling centre in 1994 when local officials in her village could not find her name on their registration list. After a half-day's travel to town, she found the special station had run out of ballot papers. In tears, she asked authorities to stamp her voting card or stain her thumb with indelible ink (a common practice, to prevent multiple voting). 'I was told that if I did not vote for the PRI that my child could no longer go to school, and I would lose the milk program. So I have to prove that I voted', said the woman.[12]

Most Latin Americans rejoiced at the return to the barracks of the military; even in countries (such as Colombia, Venezuela, Mexico and Costa Rica) where the military did not rule, the lessons of harsh human rights abuses and economic woes elsewhere in the hemisphere made the option of democratic reform more appealing than anything the generals had to offer politically. Political parties and their leaders enjoyed generally high prestige in the countries where these transitions took place. The 1990s saw most of this prestige squandered by a number of interrelated factors. Economic restructuring (especially fiscal austerity and privatisation) reduced the state's capacity to finance the goods and services available to politicians to build party support though patronage (jobs, contracts, construction, neighbourhood services, subsidies, welfare, etc.). In the pre-military era of populism, administration of such programmes was rife with corruption, but at least some redistribution 'trickled down' to the masses. Now the corruption remained, but the gap between rich and poor generally worsened, and the parties had few answers to propose.[13]

The functions of political parties are often defined as contesting elections and acting as transmission belts between the citizenry and the government, but in a region like Latin America, plagued by foreign intervention and military coups, parties may also collectively have the goal of maintaining and legitimising a system which, after all, rewards politicians with careers and avoids the costs of military rule. In Latin America, as in much of the Third World, a political party may also be the unarmed, political expression of a former guerrilla movement. Such was the genesis of the Frente Sandinista de Liberación Nacional (FSLN, Sandinista Front for National Liberation) in Nicaragua, the Frente Farabundo Martí de Liberación Nacional (FMLN, Farabundo Martí Front for National Liberation) in El Salvador and the M-19 in Colombia (see Chapter 6). Some parties, such as the Mexican PRI and the Partido Comunista de Cuba (PCC, Communist Party of Cuba), have, for a period of several decades after coming to power through revolution, consolidated and monopolised control of government in the name of promoting national unity and fundamental socio-economic change.

Our focus will be on how the neoliberal wave has affected the role of parties with regard to linking citizens and the state in the voting process. We will concentrate on the status and future of three different kinds of contemporary parties: (1) populist parties (of all ideological stripes) which have survived, at least in name, the military era; (2) parties with some kind of organic connection to new left organisations or revolutionary movements; (3) other kinds of electoral movements grouped around charismatic personalities which have emerged in the last decade (not a new phenomenon), or which are linked to new rightist and conservative organisations. For not only is there a 'new Left' in Latin America, but also a new Right. The growing importance of media in the neoliberal era has enhanced the influence of this new Right, which merits some discussion.

The dinosaurs: adaptation and extinction of populist parties

In this section we consider the fate of those political parties which dominated the Latin American landscape in the period between the Great Depression of the 1930s and what is widely regarded as the 'crisis of populism'. This crisis first fully manifested itself with the coup inaugurating 25 years of military rule in Brazil in 1964, included the collapse of Chile's impressive electoral democracy in 1973, and ultimately saw every country except Mexico, Colombia, Venezuela and Costa Rica fall under the jackboot. A hallmark of this period was the attempt by the military to depoliticise societies, which often included an outright ban on party activities. The Brazilian military took this process one step further, actually attempting to create an officially sanctioned pro-government party and an official opposition party.

Many of Latin America's most important parties can trace their founding moments to the nineteenth century, when groups of notables organised themselves into clubs, and formed the legislatures in the aftermath of independence. In most countries of Spanish-speaking America, a faction calling themselves 'Conservatives' tended to support the interests of landowners against more internationally oriented mercantile and financial interests, to whom they were often in debt. Conservatives also tended to support privileges for the Catholic Church, itself a major landowner. Liberals advocated a more secular approach and tended to support federalism, more liberal constitutional principles, individual property rights and the break-up of communal property owned by municipalities, the Church and the Indians. Liberals generally supported economic policies encouraging exports.

In fact, neither Liberals and Conservatives struck very deep roots among the people, except when *caudillo*[14] figures mobilised peasant armies to fight civil wars against one another. Over time, their differences were submerged as both parties appeared as little more than different factions of landed oligarchies. One or both of these parties eventually expired in most countries. However, some survived deep into the twentieth century (as in Chile, Colombia, Nicaragua, Honduras and Argentina) by adapting to the emergence of a middle and working class. The latter encouraged the emergence of parties, like the Radicals, who survive in Argentina and (dimly) in Chile, the Blancos in Uruguay, and Colorados in Paraguay. The early twentieth century saw socialist and communist parties emerge in countries with significant working-class sectors.

The process of party formation was uneven. In Central America the relative retardation of economic development produced systems which until the 1980s, with the exception of Costa Rica, remained little more than parties of notables, just like their continental counterparts in the nineteenth century. One result of the revolutionary upheavals of the 1980s was the emergence of the first truly mass-based parties reaching deep into the population, especially in El Salvador (FMLN) and Nicaragua (FSLN). In Brazil, not until the monarchy was overthrown in 1889 did parties of any consequence emerge. The vast size of Brazil, combined with a strong federal constitutional structure, made the creation of mass national parties difficult.[15] This remained the case until after the Second World War when José Vargas, a populist dictator, similar in many ways to Juan Perón, built two parties (simultaneously) to generate mass support from above. It was one of these parties, the Partido dos Trabalhadores Brasileiros (PTB, Brazilian Workers' Party), which President João Goulart later attempted to radicalise, contributing to the 1964 coup. Like the Peronists, the PTB relied upon entrenched patronage structures and control of unions and other organisations to win elections. While workers received some tangible benefits, the Peronists and the PTB smothered all efforts to make unions more independent, democratic, and directly responsive to workers. The military coups between 1964 and 1976 swept away these structures and links, with different consequences when the soldiers returned to the barracks. In Argentina, the Peronists reasserted their grip on labour, but under the leadership of President Carlos Menem in the 1990s veered sharply away from Perón's statism and radical nationalism. Political battles over neoliberalism are played out within Peronist ranks. In Brazil, by contrast, a new Workers' Party, the Partido dos Trabalhadores (PT), was formed in the struggle against the dictatorship, and has consistently resisted neoliberalism.[16]

Nationalist–populist parties

Examples of nationalist–populist parties would include the Alianza Popular Revolucionaria Americana (APRA, American Popular Revolutionary Alliance) in Peru, Acción Democrática (AD, Democratic Action) in Venezuela, the Movimiento Nacional Revolucionario (MNR, National Revolutionary Movement) in Bolivia, and the PRI in Mexico. These parties all sought to unite the middle class, working class, peasantry, and capitalists tied to domestic industries in a coalition which defined itself in terms of its enemies – the domestic landed elites, foreign capitalists, communism and dictators. Allowing for its greater degree of personalism, flirtations with fascist ideology, and its neglect of the peasantry, the Peronists probably came closest to fitting this category, if they fit any at all. Nationalist–populist parties all find themselves in crisis today. The MNR and APRA are in danger of extinction; AD and the PRI are in danger of losing their hegemonic status. All are riven by factionalism. The Peronists have been successful, but defeat in provincial and municipal elections in 1998 has touched off internal debate over support for Menem's neoliberal agenda and a call from Peronists in Congress to return to *justicialismo*, the vague mixture of fascism and worker-oriented populism which the party's late founder invented between 1946 and 1955. Control of the presidency may hold the party together behind Menem, but it is difficult to see what leader or philosophy can hold it together beyond his tenure.

Christian Democratic parties

Most Christian Democratic parties trace their roots to tendencies in the Catholic Church in the 1930s to define a social philosophy distinct from liberalism and Marxism. These parties remain strongest in Chile and Venezuela, although in the latter case the Comité de Organización Política Electoral Independiente (Independent Electoral Committee of the People, COPEI) has long shrugged off its image as a clerical party. Outside Chile, these parties are struggling, but their ties to European Christian Democracy and the Catholic Church provide them with an organisational base which may permit them to survive. However, neoliberalism rests uneasily with many rank-and-file Christian Democrats, who take seriously the social justice doctrines of the Church and are suspicious of business interests who support the party's modernising leadership.[17]

Communist parties

Largely marginalised with the collapse of the Soviet Union in 1991, communist parties were already in decline before the landmark event. While the Communist Party continues to rule Cuba, it draws as much upon the intellectual legacy of the nineteenth-century Cuban patriot José Martí, as it does on Lenin. In Chile and Costa Rica, communist parties retain some influence beyond their low electoral profile because of their influence in the labour movement.

Nineteenth-century catch-all parties

Catch-all parties include Argentina's Unión Cívica Radical (UCR, Radical Party), the Colorados in Uruguay and Paraguay, the Blanco Party of Uruguay, the Conservatives in Argentina and Colombia, and the region's various Liberal parties. In Honduras and Colombia the Liberals remain the single largest party, but election rules make for very weak party discipline and very heterogeneous ideological tendencies among candidates. The largest faction of the Liberals, the Partido Liberal Independiente (PLI, Independent Liberal Party), controls the presidency of Nicaragua and is the most important party after the Sandinistas. Liberals always have always been the main opposition to the Blancos in Paraguay, but were severely weakened by the 35-year dictatorship of a Blanco general, Alfredo Stroessner.

Socialist parties

All of the socialist parties have been influenced by Marxism but remained independent of Moscow. Some, like Chile's Partido Socialista (PS, Socialist Party) and Venezuela's Movimiento al Socialismo (MAS, Movement towards Socialism), have come more and more to resemble ideologically the social democratic and labour parties of Europe. In Chile and Venezuela, socialist leaders have joined centrist governments and been politically instrumental in selling neoliberal economic policies. Some on the left view this as a betrayal, others contend it demonstrates the maturation and responsible nature of the Latin American Left today.[18]

The military's attempts to re-engineer the party structures nowhere produced the desired outcome, but they did leave their mark. Upon their return to legality, party leaders showed little inclination to return to the policies of import substitution or to turn populism into a more radical or revolutionary direction, as leaders like Brazil's Goulart or Chile's Salvador Allende did. Even where outright military rule was averted, leaders of parties which had thrived during the era of import substitution tended to embrace the Washington Consensus. Often these leaders, most notably Carlos Menem of Argentina's Peronist Party and Carlos Andrés Pérez of Venezuela's AD, campaigned successfully as populists who would restore past good times and reclaim a measure of their country's influence internationally, but upon taking office they embraced neoliberalism fervently. Menem did so successfully, winning re-election in 1994, while Pérez was eventually removed from office by Congress in 1993 after mass rioting in 1989 and two coup attempts in 1992, stimulated by popular anger and his refusal to back away from his despised *paquete* ('package') of structural adjustment policies.[19]

The Peronists and AD historically relied upon patronage generated by the state to grease their political machines, yet both stuck with their presidential leaders (AD's congressional delegation voted to retain Pérez, but lacked a majority) in crucial votes. Why? Analysts cite the fear of even greater electoral losses from appearing divided and sanctions facing defectors from party discipline.[20] While patronage may be important to re-election, it is distributed through a party and a bureaucracy controlled by the president. If a *barrio* gets a new drainage system, a rural area a new paved road, a middle-class area a new set of squad cars for the police, or a working class district an extension on a steel mill earmarked for closing or downsizing, it is not because a local mayor, governor or legislator has convinced the bureaucracy to spend increasingly scarce resources, but because the party or a bureaucrat owing his job to the President has decided the investment should be made. And a local politician gets credit only if he or she is on the ballot to receive the grateful votes of beneficiaries.[21] In most Latin American nations (exceptions being Costa Rica, Colombia and, to some extent, Uruguay), party leaders, and often the President himself, directly control who appears on the ballot in legislative races. A recalcitrant party member faces the prospect of finding his or her political career ended, with little prospect of finding employment in a bureaucracy controlled by either the jilted party or the opposition.

Opponents of neoliberalism have yet to present a clear, programmatic alternative, and many politicians retain bitter memories of polarisation and the military rule which followed. Hence, even the most strident opponents of neoliberalism usually disavow any notion of returning to policies associated with import substitution. As a result, we find mid-level party leaders and officeholders often playing a delicate game. They criticise the government's policies in a piecemeal fashion, but they rarely assert their political power to reverse policies or oppose the president on crucial votes in Congress. Their parties have multiple personalities: populist in oratory and campaign style, especially during an election year, but neoliberal in control of the presidency and key cabinet posts.

Left parties and new social movements

Seeking more transparent government and resisting co-optation, many social movements in Latin America find some common ground with business-oriented neoliberals who see the state as too strong. On the other hand, these movements envisage a more participatory civil society, and they support an active role for the state, in stark contrast to the laissez-faire philosophy of neoliberalism. A number of important 'new left' parties in Latin America have either arisen as political expressions of these movements or at least present themselves as their allies. Among these are Causa R and the Patria para Todos (PPT, Homeland for All) in Venezuela, the PT in Brazil, the Partido Democrático Revolucionario (PRD, Democratic Revolutionary Party) in Mexico and Partido para la Democracia (PPD, Party for Democracy) in Chile. In some cases, these parties are little more than very loosely formed coalitions (the Frente Amplio in Uruguay, and Frente Grande in Argentina) with very open, sometimes loosely formed structures. To some extent, all of them have the appearance of an 'electoral movement' rather than parties with well-developed platforms and disciplined internal structure. By their nature they eschew the populist image of machines contesting elections. Although leftist, they generally reject the old (vanguard) model for parties inherited from Lenin and the experience of the Russian, Chinese, Vietnamese and Cuban revolutions.

In some ways the PRD of Mexico is prototypical of this type of party. Originating in a coalition of small leftist parties and dissenters from the Mexican PRI, the Left united behind Cuauhtémoc Cárdenas, who had broken from the PRI to run for the presidency in 1988. Subsequently, the parties and *priistas* (members of the PRI) who followed Cárdenas have struggled to build a party which can embrace moderate, progressive, former members of the PRI, small Marxist parties with regional strength, and leaders of social movements. Since 1994, the PRD also has had to manage an uneasy relationship with the Zapatistas in Chiapas, sharing their political aims without endorsing armed struggle. Cárdenas's crushing loss to the PRI's Ernesto Zedillo in 1994 might have shaken the fledgling party, but the enduring social crisis and strength of social movements in the capital contributed to his winning the mayoral race in Mexico City in 1997. This election also witnessed the conservative Partido Acción Nacional (PAN, National Action Party) and the PRD take enough seats together to control the lower House of Congress from the PRI, ushering in a new era in Mexican politics.

Movement parties have yet to control a presidency, but they are leaving a mark. The PT is Brazil's first national mass-based party. While its leader, José Ignacio da Silva, more widely known as 'Lula', has lost two runs for the presidency, the party has allowed for unprecedented participation and representation in Congress of blacks, indigenous peoples, and women. In Chile, the PPD, which split from the PS in order to project itself as a more movement-oriented socialist alternative has remained part of the Concertación coalition (of democratic parties) controlling the presidency of Chile since 1989. It is a vehicle for educational reforms and promotion of environmental policies.

On the other hand, the Venezuelan case puts in clearest relief the problems these parties have in developing governance structures which permit a degree of discipline but allow democratic control from below. The Causa R was founded in the 1970s not as a party, but as a movement aiming to empower Venezuelan slum dwellers and factory workers. Its founders were former guerrillas who decided that taking over the state through elections was less fruitful than deploying a patient strategy of organising new democratic unions and neighbourhood organisations. In a country where oil revenues have induced all parties to focus on control of government rather than grassroots organising, this was a major departure from the norm where the system of government was nicknamed 'partyarchy'.[22] By the 1980s, the Causa R's labour movement had won control over the most important unions in the huge steel and aluminium industries in eastern Venezuela (Guyana). In 1989, the party stunned AD by winning state and local elections in this bastion of AD control. The victorious gubernatorial candidate, Andrés Velásquez, was, like Lula in Brazil, a factory worker. Velásquez and his party then burst upon the national scene by making a strong showing in congressional and presidential elections in 1993. (Some Venezuelans believe Velásquez was deprived of victory through fraud.)

Causa R had appeal because it did not try to force its members and officials to toe an official line and because it was open to membership of anyone who agreed to put the interests of popular movements above party loyalty. However, with a share of power Causa R began to encounter problems rooted in what gave it appeal – its anti-party politics. The long years of organising had been led by a group of activists whose personal and philosophic disagreements could no longer be handled 'within the family' through an informal process. Openness could not be sustained without cost. In parts of the country where the party did not have deep roots in labour and community organising, opportunists with little commitment to the party's original project won office running on the party's slate but then governed in the old discredited ways.[23] These tendencies culminated in a split in 1997. One faction, led by Velásquez, retained the party name and opted to support a beauty queen-turned-technocrat, Irene Saez, who ran an independent campaign for the presidency in 1998. The other faction, the PPT, backed the leader of the failed coup attempt in 1992, Colonel Hugo Chávez, who also ran independently of the established parties and subsequently won the presidency.

Another type of new left party might include El Salvador's FMLN and Nicaragua's FSLN and other guerrilla movements (M-16 in Colombia and perhaps eventually the Zapatistas in southern Mexico) which organised themselves into political parties as part of a negotiated process ending armed hostilities. In all of these cases, the survival, if not triumph, of the guerrilla movement required active support from the masses. Upon taking power or ending armed struggle such groupings face the challenge of reorganising themselves to govern and/or contest for power through elections. They face the challenge of maintaining their revolutionary credentials in such a context, but they must also discard the habits inherited from clandestine and dangerous armed struggle. The FMLN's leader Rubén Zamora says, 'A history of exile and clandestine operations had transformed the party into a sect. To correct this, we made a conscious decision to deprofessionalize the party.'[24] Secrecy and discipline might be accepted in wartime, but they hold little appeal to popular social movements.

Winning a revolutionary struggle poses particular challenges of its own. The FSLN held power for 10 years before losing the 1990 elections. It is difficult to assess the extent to which US pressure influenced the voters. Many analysts believe Nicaraguan voters were punishing the Sandinistas for their own record when they voted in the majority for Violeta Chamorro, but the brutal economic and military war waged by the United States against them certainly affected the outcome to some extent.[25] The Sandinistas remain a potent force in Nicaragua, but continue in the 1990s to show the debilitating defects of excessive hierarchy as well as nepotism and personalism within their ranks.

Although the FMLN never had the opportunity to implement revolutionary reforms from a position of state power, internally it may have benefited by entering the electoral era in opposition. While the FSLN has struggled to recapture momentum since 1990, the FMLN has steadily increased its electoral share in a series of elections since the negotiated end of the Salvadorean struggle in 1991. What both former guerrilla movements have in common is that they have moderated their revolutionary zeal, a testimony to the way in which elections may act as a brake, not an accelerator, of radical change. On the other hand, both can take credit for having significantly democratised their political systems.

One might argue that Cuba's PCC belongs in this category, despite the party label and association with Lenin's vanguard theories. The contemporary party was formed well after the Fidelistas overthrew the Batista dictatorship in 1959. It was formed out of a fusion of the old Communists, who had backed the dictator and joined the Revolution late in the game, and other groups and parties in 1965. At the heart of Cuba's revolution have always been mass organisations, not the party. While these organisations cannot exist independently of the party's umbrella, the party relies upon the leaders and members of these organisations to vigorously debate and transmit, through party structures, opinions about important policy issues, such as education, taxation, space for the market versus rationing, social problems such as prostitution, etc. These popular, mass organisations are not going to disappear with Fidel Castro's exit, whatever path Cuba may pursue in the future. Whether a multi-party or single-party system emerges, the PCC will face challenges similar in many ways to those facing the other leftist parties.

The Right and the new caudillismo

Few genuine, business-oriented parties, like the Republicans in the United States or Conservatives in Britain, can be found in Latin America. One of the few long-standing parties of this type in Latin America is the PAN. It has long attracted the support of Mexico's powerful Monterrey industrialists and small landholders in the North. It also attracts support from religious voters resentful of the PRI's long-standing anti-clericalism. Since 1982 it served as a vehicle for those protesting corruption in the dominant party. Despite its business roots, the PAN has not spearheaded neoliberal economic policies in Mexico. Some PAN leaders fear the NAFTA privileges US businesses over potential partners in Europe and Asia. Probably, only the PRI could have implemented neoliberalism and the NAFTA in the context of Mexico's nationalist, revolutionary history, and this has not been without cost to its popular support.

In most of Central America until recent times parties have represented little more than factional differences among the oligarchy. In Guatemala, Panama and El Salvador the stronger parties had close ties to retired and active military officers. But the civil and revolutionary wars forced right-wing sectors to organise themselves to fight electoral contests more effectively. Some parties, notably the Alianza Republicana Nacional (ARENA, National Republican Alliance) in El Salvador, organised not only to violently persecute popular movements but to resist even the modest economic, land and political reforms implemented as part of the US-planned counter-insurgency war by the Christian Democrats. Much to the consternation of the United States, this nationalist appeal was effective. Among the parties in Nicaragua's divided right wing, the PLI has been most successful, its candidate (Miguel Alemán) winning the presidency in 1996 with a fiercely anti-Sandinista campaign. In control of the presidency, it should be noted, both the ARENA and the PLI have found it necessary to deal with the Left, not without angering more intransigent sectors in both the party and the United States. In both El Salvador and Nicaragua, the prospect of leftist parties winning presidential elections in the future is strong, and a major test for the new 'democratic' right is whether it can function as a responsible opposition.

The key point here is that a number of conservative political parties with substantial appeal to the masses have emerged in some Latin American countries, a relatively new development. In this respect they have been successful in the era of neoliberalism in achieving what one analyst denotes as a 'vertical appeal'.[26] That is, leftist parties generally have attempted to mobilise voters 'horizontally', by developing a populist appeal based upon class and exploitation. Conservative parties, whose firmest base tends to be among less numerous wealthy classes in society, have tended to mobilise support by appealing to social differences that cut 'vertically' through the classes, appealing to the poor, workers, peasants and the middle class with national patriotism (the ARENA's tactic against the centrist Christian Democrats and the FMLN), religion, ethnicity, and non-class economic interests (for example, consumers versus agricultural workers). Although studies of the new Right fail to consider gender among the potent issues which can be used to divide social classes, certainly one sees this factor present in campaigns which stress machismo or marianismo (the cult of the Virgin Mary) as predominant themes.

The Right, of course, has always been a factor in politics. However, business interests have usually found it as effective to work through centrist parties as to found their own. What is distinct about the present era in Latin America is the extent to which business interests favourable to the neoliberal model have developed capacities to do this using the media, and have institutionalised their presence in society by ties to think-tanks, both domestic and international, committed to promoting neoliberal ideas.[27] Two examples of this phenomenon can be seen in Chile and Peru.

In Chile, the Partido Nacionalista (PN, Nationalist Party), the product of a merger between the old Liberal and Conservative Parties, applauded the coup against Socialist Salvador Allende in 1973, but found itself banned during the Pinochet dictatorship. The Nationalists had relied upon the old Conservative agrarian base and the old Liberal base among industrialists and mining interests. While the Nationalists despised socialism and supported the 1973 coup, all its key support sectors had benefited from state subsidies and protection. These were uprooted by the policies of General Pinochet, who never took power simply to hand it back to the politicians.

When electoral democracy was finally restored in 1989, the right had to reorganise. In Chile, neoliberal intellectuals, dubbed the 'Chicago Boys', inspired by economists Frederick Hayek and Milton Friedman, colonised the economics schools of various universities, notably the Catholic University. Senator Jaime Guzmán, a Pinochet ideologue, established a centre and journal (*Estudios Políticos*) to promote neoliberal ideas. Guzmán not only promoted laissez-faire economic ideas but defended the brutal policies by which Pinochet crushed the Left and closed down all party activity during the dictatorship. As pressure grew to force Pinochet from the presidency and the need loomed for a party capable of promoting neoliberalism in elections, followers of Guzmán (assassinated in 1991) created the Unión Democrática Independiente (UDI, Independent Democratic Union). Politicians associated with the old Nationalists and Conservatives uneasy with endorsing Pinochet's regime founded the Renovación Nacionalista (RN, Nationalist Renovation). While these parties have not been able, even in coalition, to capture the presidency, they have used conservative religious appeals, middle-class fears of a return to leftist government, and sophisticated media campaigns to remain a force in Chilean politics. Their influence is enhanced by constitutional provisions making it difficult for the Centre and Left to translate electoral victories into congressional majorities.

In Peru, the novelist Mario Vargas Llosa drew upon deep popular anger directed towards the corruption and ineffectiveness of Peru's traditional parties, and against President Alan García Pérez. García was initially popular in 1985 for resisting paying the debt, but his disastrous mismanagement of the economy and rampant corruption profoundly alienated Peruvians. His nationalisation of the banking system alarmed elites and foreign investors, who looked favourably upon new think-tanks, notably Hernán de Soto's Liberty and Democracy Institute, to promote ideas seized upon by Vargas Llosa. A huge mass-media campaign by business interests gave Vargas Llosa a platform to exploit the discontent, spread the neoliberal gospel and become the heir-apparent to the disgraced García. Some of the parties excoriated by Vargas Llosa decided to join rather than fight him in the 1990 elections.

Peruvian voters stunned Vargas Llosa and the world in 1990 by electing instead a Peruvian of Japanese descent, Alberto Fujimori, who put together a coalition of parties, including the APRA and the Left, opposed to the novelist's neoliberal economic ideas. Fujimori also effectively appealed to race in predominantly Indian Peru, a nation with significant Afro and Asian populations as well. Fujimori characterised Vargas Llosa's supporters as white oligarchs out of touch with indigenous and mestizo (mixed race) masses, and he effectively appealed to the growing Protestant population, wary of the Catholic hierarchy's endorsement of his opponent.

In power, Fujimori turned on his supporters, closing Congress, aligning with the military and turning it loose to fight the Sendero Luminoso (SL, Shining Path) guerrillas (see Chapter 6) without human rights constraints and implementing the very economic policies promoted by Vargas Llosa. The vigorous electoral campaign on the part of Vargas Llosa, which associated neoliberal economic reforms with a discredited political class with no clear alternative, paved the way for anti-popular economic policies to be implemented by a president who had campaigned against them. Peru has no organised right-wing party to carry the neoliberal banner forward in future elections. However, as in many other Latin American countries, business interests can promote their agenda by penetrating party structures in other ways.[28]

Media and intellectual trends in the parties

Antonio Gramsci emphasised the educational and intellectual function of the party as its most important attribute, whether or not its leadership is recruited directly from a particular social class. 'In the political party the elements of an economic social group get beyond that moment of their historical development and become agents of more general activities of a national and international character.'[29] This is precisely the role being played by the new rightist parties and conservative elements linked to parties in Latin America, and their success has been considerably enhanced by the increased role of the media in electoral politics.

Throughout Latin America parties and candidates run populist campaigns promising relief from neoliberal economic policies, but once in power they leave economic policy-making to policy intellectuals trained in the United States or in local think-tanks heavily influenced by the United States. Jorge Domínguez calls these intellectual–politicians 'technopols'.[30] Unlike technocrats, who remain aloof from politics, technopols see their mission not only to design economic policy but to build political movements and interest groups dedicated to promoting neoliberal ideas. Some, like Brazil's President Fernando Henrique Cardoso, have built political parties to promote their ideas. More typical is Argentina's Finance Minister, Domingo Cavallo, who founded a think-tank (the Fundación Mediterránea, or Mediterranean Foundation) to promote market-oriented policies but moved into the Peronist Party at the invitation of Menem. Some, like Cardoso and Chile's Finance Minister Alejandro Foxley, had reputations as academic leftists but now promote little more than a humanised market system.

The importance of technopols is their ability, whether through their own business-oriented parties or by working within the framework of populist parties like the PRI in Mexico (Pedro Aspe) or the Christian Democrats in Chile (Foxley), to promote their policy prescriptions as the only possible ones in a globalised economy. Their connections with international business groups, US universities, and foundations provide them with links that other political and economic actors lack, links enforced by interaction with one another in conferences supported by these institutions. Their think-tanks train hundreds of like-minded technopols who can be imported into key ministries, displacing the politicians from state institutions which have been critical to party cohesion in the past.

The technopols use their intellectual credentials, experience with the media, and modern public relations techniques to propagate their market-oriented policies to the masses. Domínguez claims technopols have a 'passion' for a set of ideas and a shared responsibility to seek to implement them. He describes them as effectively merging their scholarly experience with political engagement, so they and their teams become 'partisans' in pursuit of their ideas. For Domínguez and his associates, this means they 'behave as "teachers to the nation," that is bearers of a more impersonal loyalty to a democratic regime, committed to educate the public about facts that may be inconvenient for their party opinions'.[31]

The rising importance of the media in political campaigning gives these technopols an important advantage in the political game. As the Argentinian analyst Oscar Landi puts it, 'When I am in a situation of hyperinflation, I am going to turn on the television to guide me in my daily action. I'm not going to visit the local headquarters of a party.'[32] Production of television commercials, focus groups, polls and advertising all cost significant amounts of money. A typical poll in Latin America costs $12,000 to $15,000.[33] These resources can be crucial in blunting challenges from leftist movements. In Brazil the PT seemed poised to win the presidency behind Lula in 1989, but international and national business sectors rallied behind Collor de Mello, a relatively inexperienced politician. Collor owned a television station in a peripheral state and was supported by the country's most important national television network. With money, media savvy, and the backing of Brazil's worried business community, Collor put together an effective campaign despite the lack of an established, organised party. Popular leaders like Lula and Cuauhtémoc Cardénas may have an organisational advantage, but often they have proved less skilful in debate formats. News organisations in both Brazil and Mexico, closely linked to monopoly business interests and heavily dependent on a friendly state, magnified poor performances by replaying heavily biased clips of debates and slanted news coverage.

Even where a well-orchestrated media campaign fails to win an election for the business community's preferred candidate, the message may influence the subsequent government, as clearly happened in Peru when Vargas Llosa lost to Fujimori. And, it is worth noting, among the most ready sources of money to finance the staggering costs of media-centred campaigns are the lords of the region's most dynamic export commodity, narcotics. Colombia's porous party system, made looser by rules permitting several slates of candidates for the same party to run in each state and district, is particularly vulnerable to such influence.

The agenda of political reforms in most countries is replacing the highly centralised, indirect methods of candidate selection with primaries, an import from the US electoral system. Some reform groups would like to replace the proportional system by which voters choose from closed lists of candidates with single-member district voting. Primaries permit candidates to bypass, for better or worse, the traditional politicians, but they also place a greater premium on advertising. Like Collor, Carlos Menem, though he was not an outsider but a veteran politician, was able to project through the media an image of *machismo*. Assuming an anti-politics-as-usual image, he was able to capture the Peronist Party nomination in that party's first open presidential primary.

The old personalism formed around *caudillos* and *caciques* ('bosses'). This still occurs, but as the prestige of the parties falls personalist leaders are as likely to come from the ranks of technocrats, beauty queens, failed coup-plotters, media personalities, sharp politicians who have turned against their own parties, former scholars, guerrilla chiefs and businessmen. Even in Venezuela, a system where parties seemed deeply entrenched and institutionalised, the four leading candidates for the presidency in 1998 were all running as anti-party candidates. One, former Miss Universe Irene Saez, has been a successful mayor of a wealthy Caracas suburb. Another led an unsuccessful coup in 1992. The inability of these parties to effectively utilise oil earnings, even during the 10-year boom between 1974 and 1983, paved the way for business groups to promote anti-statist ideas through the media and think-tanks for the first time since the 1930s. As oil prices collapsed and the foreign debt rose, the parties failed to respond effectively to popular revulsion against corruption. Although no presidential campaign has been won by an avowedly neoliberal candidate, recent presidents in Venezuela have advanced the neoliberal agenda, even Rafael Caldera (1993–98), who initially pursued a more heterodox economic policy.

Personalism is nothing new in Latin America, but new bottles do not contain merely the old wine of reactionary oligarchs, demagogic populists and regional discontent, but also the siren song of the market. As Landi has put it,

> The loss of state functions, the higher profile that the market is assuming in social relations, the internal intervention of external actors from other countries are external influences. Also there are the vices which properly belong to the parties themselves: old forms of clientelism, corruption, internal struggles for power, betrayals and sensibilities inherited from factional struggles. All of this appears on the accounts of the parties, and not the media.[34]

Conclusion

It is commonplace to note the weakness of 'democratic consolidation' in Latin America, and in many respects this chapter is hardly encouraging. Yet, for the foreseeable future, elections rather than coups are likely to be the most common way Latin American governments change hands. Barring a world economic calamity like that experienced in the 1930s, which cannot at all be entirely discounted, what can we say about the future of electoral politics in the wake of a still unfolding process of neoliberal economic and political change?

First, the crisis of the populist parties, regardless of their ideology, is definitive. Those which survive will do so because they have some institutional base of support, such as the Church in the case of the Christian Democrats, or because they have become catch-all parties with little function other than to recruit and serve as testing grounds for aspiring politicians. The middle class, labour and peasant organisations organically linked to these parties in the import substitution era have been severely weakened, depriving these parties of an important organisational base. Increasingly, they rely upon foreign-trained experts to run 'professional' media-oriented campaigns. Some will retain the ability to win elections; few have retained the ability to effectively represent popular needs. Market-oriented think-tanks and large domestic business interests tied to the world market (including narcotics traders) mean that business-oriented electoral politics is more firmly rooted than ever before in Latin America.

Second, highly centralised parties formed around dominant personalities will become more, not less, prominent. Anti-party sentiment, weaker established party organisations, the increased role of the media all mean that the 'new personalism' will continue. In particular, whenever some popular electoral force inimical to neoliberalism arises, it can be expected that the United States will actively support electoral opposition. Through the NED the hegemonic power has overt as well as covert means to respond to popular democratic movements.

Third, it is unlikely that vanguardist parties in the future will hold a monopoly of power, even in Cuba. The 'electoral movement parties' of the Left will succeed to the point that they develop organisational capacities to permit social movements and organisations to remain vital and independent, but supportive of their electoral aspirations. These parties lack a fully developed alternative programme to advance as an alternative to neoliberalism, and this is a weakness, but their most important task at present is to give Latin American citizens space to experiment with participatory and community-based economic and political alternatives to market policies.

Elections in Latin America have tended more often to act as a brake than an accelerator on social and economic change. When they have been used to advance revolutionary change, US intervention and military coups have been the response. The result has been costly, in both economic and human terms. This experience has created incentives for political parties and their leaders to elevate preservation of the system over mobilisation of popular discontent, which in turn limits the utility of elections and parties to voters disenchanted with neoliberalism.

Like everywhere, elections in Latin America have never resolved fundamental differences about the social and economic order. They tend to take place in the context of a predefined consensus. Latin America differs from most of Europe and North America in regard to the greater fragility of the consensus, due to the legacy of military and foreign intervention and the greater social and economic inequalities. On the other hand, the tendencies we see in Latin America – popular alienation from parties, declining participation, the increased role of the media and money in campaigning, crisis in the Left – are all phenomena we can well understand in Europe and North America. In this respect, the crisis of party politics in Latin America can be located within a more generalised, global crisis in party politics. Why would one expect effective parties to prosper in Latin America when they have been weakened almost everywhere else?

Notes

1 In J. D. Martz (ed.), *United States Policy in Latin America: A Decade of Crisis and Challenge* (Lincoln, University of Nebraska Press, 1997), p. 340.

2 F. Fukuyama, 'The End of History?', *The National Interest*, 16 (Summer 1989).

3 W. Robinson, *Promoting Polyarchy: Globalization, U.S. Intervention, and Hegemony* (Cambridge, Cambridge University Press, 1996).

4 A. Przeworski, 'Some Problems in the Study of the Transition to Democracy', in G. O'Donnell, P. C. Schmitter and L. Whitehead (eds.), *Transitions from Authoritarian Rule: Comparative Perspectives* (Baltimore, Johns Hopkins University Press, 1986).

5 J. C. Rey, *El futuro de democracia en Venezuela* (Caracas, Serie Estudios – Colección IDEA, 1982).

6 C. M. Conaghan, 'Troubling Questions: Looking Back at Peru's Election', *Latin American Studies Association (LASA) Forum*, 26 (Summer 1995).

7 M. A. Riquelme, 'Negotiating Democratic Corridors in Paraguay', *LASA Forum*, 24 (Winter 1994).

8 D. J. Schemo, 'Effort to Bar A Candidate Fuels Crisis in Paraguay', *The New York Times*, 22 March 1998, p. A9.

9 The former position is that of the editors and most authors in S. Mainwaring and M. Soberg Shugart (eds.), *Presidentialism and Democracy in Latin America* (Cambridge, Cambridge University Press, 1997). In contrast, see most of the authors in *Partidos y clase política en América Latina* (San José, Costa Rica, Instituto Interamericano de Derechos Humanos, 1995).

10 G. O'Donnell, 'Delegative Democracy', *Journal of Democracy*, 5:1 (1994).

11 J. W. Rubin, 'Elections, Repression, and Limited Reform: Update on Southern Mexico', *LASA Forum*, 18 (Summer 1967), p. 1.

12 D. La Botz, *Democracy in Mexico: Peasant Rebellion and Political Reform* (Boston, MA South End Press, 1995), pp. 213–14.

13 See the essays in *Partidos y clase política*, especially E. Torres Rivas, 'La gobernabilidad democrática y los partidos políticos en América Latina'.

14 A 'strong-man' of politics, whose power is based on personal charisma.

15 S. Mainwaring, 'Brazil: Weak Parties, Feckless Democracy', in S. Mainwaring and T. Scully (eds.), *Building Democratic Institutions: Party Systems in Latin America* (Stanford, Stanford University Press, 1995).

16 M. Keck, *The Workers' Party and Democratisation in Brazil* (New Haven, Yale University Press, 1992).

17 E. A. Lynch, *Latin America's Christian Democratic Parties: A Political Economy* (Westport, Praeger, 1993).

18 For the former, see C. Vilas, 'What Future for Socialism?', *NACLA Report on the Americas*, 25 (May 1992). See also the essays by Chilcote, Petras and Munck in R. Chilcote (ed.), 'Post-Marxism, the Left, and Democracy', edition of *Latin American Perspectives*, 17 (Spring 1990). For the latter view see J. Castañeda, *Utopia Disarmed: The Latin American Left after the Cold War* (New York, Knopf, 1993).

19 See chapter 5, this volume, and J. Buxton, 'Venezuela', in J. Buxton and N. Phillips (eds.), *Case Studies in Latin American Political Economy* (Manchester, Manchester University Press, 1999).

20 This discipline factor is cited by M. P. Jones, 'Evaluating Argentina's Presidential Democracy' and J. M. Carey, 'Strong Candidates for a Limited Office: Presidentialism and Political Parties in Costa Rica', both in Mainwaring and Shugart (eds.), *Presidentialism and Democracy*. See also J. Corrales, 'Why Argentines Followed Cavallo: A Technopol Between Democracy and Economic Reform', in J. Domínguez (ed.), *Technopols: Freeing Politics and Markets in Latin America in the 1990s* (University Park, Pennsylvania State University Press, 1997).

21 An excellent case study is J. Martz, *The Politics of Clientelism: Democracy and the State in Colombia* (New Brunswick, Transaction, 1997).

22 On the decay of the main parties, see M. Coppedge, *Strong Parties and Lame Ducks: Presidential Partyarchy and Factionalism in Venezuela* (Stanford, Stanford University Press, 1994).

23 D. Hellinger, 'The *Causa R* and the *Nuevo Sindicalismo* in Venezuela', *Latin American Perspectives*, 23 (Summer 1996).

24 'Democratic Transition or Modernization? The Case of El Salvador Since 1979', in

J. Domínguez and M. Lindenberg (eds.), *Democratic Transitions in Central America* (Gainesville, University of Florida Press, 1997), p. 176.

25 R. Harris, 'The Nicaraguan Revolution: A Postmortem', *Latin America Research Review*, 28:3 (1993).

26 E. L. Gibson, *Class and Conservative Parties: Argentina in Comparative Perspective* (Baltimore, Johns Hopkins University Press, 1996), pp. 17–18.

27 See the essays in D. A. Chalmers, M. do Carmo Campello de Souza and A. A. Borón (eds.), *The Right and Democracy in Latin America* (New York, Praeger, 1992).

28 J. Cotler, 'Crisis política, outsiders y democraduras, el "fujimorismo"', in *Partidos y clase política*.

29 A. Gramsci, *Selections from the Prison Notebooks* (New York, International Publishers, 1971), p. 16.

30 Domínguez, *Technopols*.

31 *Ibid.*, p. 11.

32 O. Landi, 'Outsiders, nuevos caudillos y media politics', *Partidos y clase política*, p. 210.

33 J. Rial, 'Percepciones sobre las instituciones democráticas y los medios de comunicación', in *Partidos y clase política*, p. 503.

34 Landi, 'Outsiders,' p. 210.

4

Global and regional linkages

NICOLA PHILLIPS

The orientation of Latin American foreign and foreign economic policies has changed significantly since the mid-1980s. From being a region characterised by inward-looking development models based on the import substitution idea, Latin American economies have been increasingly integrated with the globalising world economy, and countries have constructed a network of regional trade blocs to complement the 'internationalised' nature of economic policies. Increased openness to external trade and financial flows, consistent with the policy prescriptions embodied in the Washington Consensus (see Chapter 1), has led to the participation of the bulk of Latin American countries in the international processes of globalisation and regionalisation.[1]

The foreign policies of Latin American countries have followed the same pattern, and in many ways have been tailored to complement the new orientation of economic strategies. From the mid-1980s the consensus held that in order to address the problem of the external debt which troubled the region from the Mexican default in 1982, governments were not going to benefit from maintaining hostile positions vis-à-vis foreign creditors, particularly the United States. With the election of a 'new generation' of presidents such as Menem in Argentina, Fujimori in Peru and De la Madrid/Salinas in Mexico, foreign policy became oriented to the task of mending fences with the international community, in the interests of securing enhanced market access, favourable debt terms, international investment flows and bargaining power in international institutions. In this way, it seems clear that foreign policy became the instrument of foreign economic policy in Latin America, consistent perhaps with the growing dominance of economic (rather than military or security) affairs in the post-Cold War world.

This chapter is concerned with the external linkages of Latin American countries, and specifically with the 'internationalisation' of economic strategies. It examines the nature of countries' participation in the globalised world economy and the development of regional trade and investment patterns which are seen largely as 'stepping stones' to meaningful participation in the multilateral environment.[2] Foreign policy shifts will be analysed in the context of the development of foreign economic policy. The central contention is that Latin American political economy now operates on three interconnected and interactive levels: the global, the regional and the national.[3] The changes in countries' approaches to the first two of these levels, however, were initially designed to reflect priorities at the third: that is, they were part and parcel of the redefinition of the relationship between states and markets and hence bound up with the processes of neoliberal economic reform and political change at the domestic level. Most importantly, the 'internationalisation' of economic policy acted to 'lock in' the changes occurring at the domestic level, and thus facilitate the consolidation of economic (and political) reform.

Latin American foreign relations: towards economic integration

Since the late 1980s/early 1990s, the climate of relations between Latin American countries and the rest of the world, particularly the United States, has changed beyond recognition. This change is visible in both the economic and the political arenas. Apart from the sorts of economic cooperation that will be analysed below, Latin American countries now support and vote with the United States in such fora as the UN, participating in the Gulf War, Somalia, and other multilateral military and humanitarian exercises. As an example, the Argentine government decided to send two frigates to the Gulf War in September 1990 (decree 1971/90), and in 1991 there was an Argentine presence also in the UN missions UNIKOM (Iraq–Kuwait), MINURSO (the Western Sahara) and UNTAC (Cambodia), as well as in the former Yugoslavia from May 1992, as part of UNPROFOR.[4] These all aimed to demonstrate the commitment of the Argentine government to the Western alliance, and particularly the United States, as well as the reformed character of the Argentine armed forces.

As such, since the late 1980s, Latin American countries have turned away from positions of nationalist hostility to the United States and the rest of the industrialised world, and abandoned a 'third-worldist' foreign policy in favour of integration into the mainstream of international activity. This is particularly evident in countries such as Argentina and Mexico which, incidentally, were those most involved with the Third World movement and the New International Economic Order (NEIO) movement in the 1970s.[5] In addition, institutional forms of cooperation, notably the Organization of American States (OAS), were significantly revitalised in the early 1990s.[6]

These shifts can be attributed to changes in American foreign policy, which has become far less confrontational and unilateral since the end of the Cold War (and also to this international transformation itself), but also, more importantly, to the multidimensional process of change which has swept Latin America in recent years. On the one hand, the process of democratisation facilitated both the redefinition of the role of militaries in Latin America (see Chapter 5) and the insertion of Latin America into a democratic, post-Cold War global order. As US foreign policy shifted towards an increased emphasis (at least in rhetorical terms) on democratic governance and human rights, the process of political liberalisation in Latin America allowed for cooperation on precisely these issues. The OAS was reconstituted on the basis of a collective concern for the defence of democracy.[7]

On the other hand, the process of economic reform necessitated the construction of more positive international relations for Latin American countries, in the interests of attracting foreign capital and market access. The experiences of the 1980s, characterised by reticence following the Falklands War and the debt crisis, were moved aside in favour of a set of economic and political choices which facilitated this more positive engagement with the rest of the economic and political world. It seems clear that the new pattern of international relations is far more easily explained with reference to growing levels of *de facto* economic integration, recently formalised into a set of regional treaties, than with reference to the democratisation process. When Mexico signed the NAFTA, for example, political liberalisation was only just in its early stages. There is no doubt that both international and regional integration have positive implications for the maintenance of democracy, however, which constitutes an important incentive for membership.

The growing engagement with the international community and the 'West', therefore, was largely a function of the need to repair political relations in the interests of securing support for the process of economic reform. Foreign economic policy was the priority of Latin American governments concerned with establishing an outward-looking economic strategy based on neoliberal restructuring. As a result of these changes, diplomacy was reformulated to emphasise a multilateral foreign policy, oriented particularly towards relations with the United States and Europe. Many of the instruments and mechanisms by which this was achieved, in addition, were economic, such as the summitry 'of the Americas', the restoration of economic links between Argentina and Great Britain, the signing of the NAFTA and the bilateral free trade agreements with countries around the world. These developments in Latin American countries' foreign relations allowed for a more meaningful participation in the world economy, as well as more productive bilateral relationships and links with international financial agents.

Engagement in the globalisation process

The process of globalisation in the world economy has generated a shift in the structures of 'rewards and punishments'. At the same time as the rewards for conformity with the dominant policy consensus encapsulated in such constructs as the Washington Consensus have become more significant, the costs of non-conformity have visibly increased. On the one hand, competitiveness has become central to successful and continued economic development, and the way to achieve it is premised in large part on the attraction of foreign investment flows. This in turn depends on the establishment and maintenance of the 'right' policy framework, and of economic and political stability. Given the importance of country risk assessment and credit ratings in the current climate, Latin American governments have been eager to achieve both the competitiveness and the credibility on which access to finance depends. Even institutions such as the UN Economic Commission for Latin America and the Caribbean (ECLAC), which has spent much of the post-war period championing the cause of import substitution, is now producing titles such as *Policies to Improve Linkages with the Global Economy*.[8]

Such developments and constraints have reinforced the idea that there is currently no realistic alternative to the neoliberal policy orientation. Very few countries seriously question it. Venezuela has been the most tenacious in attempting to steer an alternative course, but in the event proved unable to sustain its position. This is not to suggest, however, that countries have simply 'fallen into line' with the international financial institutions and other global financial agents. In Venezuela, for example, the IMF agreement signed in 1994 was abandoned, and in Argentina there has been a series of renegotiations of the terms of such agreements. The debate in the second part of the 1990s on labour flexibilisation has resulted in a package of reforms which is not to the liking of the IMF. In part, these trends can be attributed to the greater flexibility in the negotiating style of the international financial institutions themselves. In addition, however, they highlight the fact that to assume too great a degree of convergence and uniformity is mistaken. One interpretation suggests that countries are acting to maximise their insertion into the global processes of economic activity, by producing a policy environment which is sustainable as a result of its compatibility with the realities of domestic politics. Another scenario might hold that resistance to globalisation is on the increase, and Latin American countries are likely to seek to forge their own path increasingly as the process advances. In many ways it is still too early to tell which alternative is the most likely in the long term, but at the moment, for the majority of countries, the first still seems to hold sway.

The inflows of foreign capital to Latin America as a result of the economic reform programme are evidence of the rewards available to countries which 'toe the line'. Argentina, for example, had become the third largest recipient of foreign direct investment world-wide by 1994. On the other hand, perhaps even more visibly, the process of globalisation has created a situation in which the punishments are much more harshly felt. On a general level, the Asian crises of 1997 and 1998 can be seen as the first of the 'crises of globalisation'. The withdrawal of funds from emerging markets following these and the Mexican crisis of 1994/95 indicate a fundamental truth about the contemporary world economy: that capital flows out quite as easily as it flows in. At the time of writing, the full impact of the market panic following the devaluation of the Brazilian Real in January 1999 has still to make itself visible. In the case of Mexico,

Asia and Brazil, apart from any more general observations about the crisis-generating nature of global capitalism, the policy 'lessons' were clear. The maintenance of fiscal deficits and overvalued currencies, for example, tend to be punished by the markets and by international investors, which are more reticent now than earlier in the 1990s about emerging markets generally. Equally, when Argentine Economy Minister Cavallo was talking in late 1991 and early 1992 about modifying the exchange rate system under Convertibility, his proposals were effectively vetoed by the hostile reaction of the markets.[9]

In this sense, it is clear that economic reform at the domestic level in Latin America was both intended to generate this type of insertion into the global economy, but also that its consolidation was furthered by precisely the same policy convergence. Neoliberal reforms were, to an extent, 'locked in' by the exigencies of attracting investment capital and maintaining trade opportunities. In a more direct way, reforms were necessitated and reinforced by agreements with the international financial institutions. These are the most concrete manifestation of commitments at the global level into which Latin American governments have entered. Such loan agreements are no longer entirely instances of external imposition of US preferences, as was the perception during much of the 1980s, but rather a situation in which the agreement of packages with the IMF and other institutions offers national governments additional bases for the consolidation of neoliberalism. As such, the establishment of working relations with the international financial institutions is seen to add credibility to the processes of domestic reform, and therefore to serve the more general development goals of Latin American countries.

This, again, is not to argue that neoliberalism has become entrenched without significant questioning. As argued in the Introduction, and illustrated in Chapters 1 and 2 especially, the neoliberal model is currently undergoing something of a re-evaluation. It may well be the case that Latin American countries have accepted that there are few realistic policy alternatives in the current globalised trade and financial systems. Even opposition parties and groups (including the Frente para el País Solidario (FREPASO, Front for the Solidarity of the Country) in Argentina and the PAN and PRD in Mexico) do not propose to abandon the overall economic orientation, but rather to place more emphasis on redressing its shortcomings, in areas such as social policy and employment. (The only exception would be presidential candidate 'Lula', Luiz Ignacio da Silva, in Brazil.[10])

The particular blend of policies varies from country to country, and the range demonstrates the ways in which it is mistaken to assume too great a degree of homogeneity and convergence. Chile, for example, retains controls on short-term capital flows, and other countries are following suit. After the Mexican crisis, a variety of countries were concerned to put in place safeguards in the banking and financial sectors, in order to guard against the deleterious effects of capital flight in the event of further economic difficulties in Latin America or in other parts of the world. Argentina, for example, increased reserve requirements in the banking sector and established a reserve fund to act as a cushion against future capital movements. By contrast, the Mexican government's response to the peso crisis was to deepen and expand the neoliberal agenda, raising VAT and promising more vigorous privatisation and further deregulation of the banking sector.

The increased caution in the region generally coincided with the start of a genuine debate on the globalisation dynamic and Latin America's place in it. The general orientation of this debate appeared to be a consideration of how best to mitigate what were perceived to be the negative effects of globalisation. These essentially related to the uncertainty and volatility of capital flows, as well as problems associated with issues of specialisation, trade flows and industrial production. Although the process of regional integration was proceeding apace at this time, it received an added impetus precisely as a result of this debate. Regionalism in Latin America has always been seen as a 'stepping stone' to greater integration at the global level, but also as a way of overcoming some of the immediate problems of integrating a national economy into the global economy. In a variety of ways, therefore, regionalism has emerged as an important alternative to global economic activity which represents a certain buffer against the vagaries of international capital, without yet becoming particularly closed or protectionist. At the moment, regionalism as contingency plan, regionalism as intermediary between the global and the national, and regionalism as market strategy appear to coexist in Latin America.

Regionalism in Latin America

Regionalism in Latin America has always been conceived as an example of 'open regionalism', in which there is no incompatibility between the pursuit of preferential trading arrangements with neighbouring countries and the pursuit of a multilateral trade strategy which involves links with the rest of the world. The adoption of 'open regionalism' is a direct reflection of the preponderance of global imperatives, which emphasise global economic and financial liberalisation. These combine with the processes of economic restructuring and unilateral liberalisation pursued to varying degrees in the member countries. The construction of regional integration is an attempt on the part of the member countries to improve their competitive positions in the globalised international economy both individually and as a bloc. The nature of regional integration, furthermore, has been characteristically 'outward looking' to date, contributing to the maximisation of trade policy through the enhancement of competitiveness, participation in the process of hemispheric integration (see below), and meaningful insertion into the global economy.[11]

The second important characteristic of Latin American regionalism is that it was conceived, and remains, oriented towards economic objectives. Political coordination between Latin American governments has not, contrary to many expectations, emerged.[12] The agreements refer to such issues as tariff reductions and trade liberalisation, and are intended to generate economic integration far more than any sort of political union *à la* European model. Although there are political elements to the integration process, therefore, such as agreements on nuclear non-proliferation and the condition of democratic government for membership, integration in Latin America remains without significant supranational institutional constructs. Those institutional arrangements which do exist, for example, in the Mercosur, are entirely intergovernmental rather than being discrete entities with decision-making capacities (like the European Commission). Resistance to institutionalisation remains firm, particularly in Brazil. Although there is a traditional/historical scepticism regarding the effectiveness of regional institutions,[13] the more pertinent explanations for the reluctance would focus on the reduced room to manoeuvre that institutionalisation would imply for the larger countries, and possibly also the difficulties that would be encountered in the maintenance of 'open regionalism'.

One of the most important effects of globalisation has been to create a situation in which 'successful implementation of domestic policy adjustment increasingly required inter-state negotiated bargains'.[14] This policy adjustment in turn was occasioned by the changing structures of rewards and punishments in the international economy as a result of the same process of globalisation. The political advantages, therefore, of locating domestic adjustment processes in the external environment are most easily achieved at the regional level, and the incentives to regionalisation are thus enhanced. It may well be that globalisation (rather than regionalisation) was the highest priority for Latin American countries, and regionalisation therefore a means to an end. There is certainly a suggestion that Argentine Economy Minister Cavallo himself was never particularly interested in regional integration for its own sake, despite a recognition of the importance of the Brazilian market, but rather far more concerned with the challenges of international opening.

In this way, it appears to be the case that regionalisation acted to reinforce the processes of economic reform which were already underway at the national level. In many ways, trade policy from the late 1980s was kept on an 'even keel' by such regional commitments. Liberalisation is much easier to achieve at the regional level than at the multilateral level, where the number and diversity of interests to be accommodated is much greater. Liberalisation is also more likely to be reciprocal, and hence to avoid the difficulties with issues like market access and uneven preference structures that currently dominate in multilateral trade negotiations. In addition, if liberalisation schedules and policy measures are agreed at the regional level, it is far less easy for national governments to reverse decisions or deviate from the agreed commitments. On a broader theoretical level, policy coordination has the major function of facilitating the 'accommodation of economic interdependence through reciprocal market liberalisation'.[15] This coincides with explanations of regionalisation as a mechanism for responding to globalisation and increasing levels of national and regional competitiveness in the globalised international economy.

Currently in Latin America (excluding the NAFTA from consideration), there are four customs unions (that is, regional blocs that have adopted a common external tariff): the Mercosur, the Andean Group, the Central American Common Market (CACM) and the Caribbean Community (Caricom).[16] These examples of 'spoke–spoke' initiatives (as opposed to a possible hub-and-spoke type arrangement with the inclusion of the United States) are accompanied by a proliferation of bilateral agreements, which creates the impression of a 'patchwork quilt of trade arrangements' in the Western Hemisphere.[17] Given the present shortcomings of the multilateral trading system, furthermore, the most realistic scenario for South America can be seen as the continuation of a 'bottom-up' process of integration, by which possibilities are opened up for more comprehensive regional and global integration.[18] At the same time, the policy conditions necessary for such participation in such integration processes are 'locked in' through the commitments agreed at the regional level, and thus accorded a degree of irreversibility. The most significant of the regional initiatives and, consequently, the principal mechanism by which these dynamics are generated, is clearly the Mercosur.

The Mercosur
The Mercosur is currently the most dynamic and successful example of regional integration between developing countries. The four core or 'full' members – Argentina, Brazil, Uruguay and Paraguay – are joined by Chile and Bolivia on the basis of 'associate membership'. On this basis, the associate members are not obliged to accept the common external tariff (CET), but are not automatically entitled to seats in the decision-making fora. Peru and Venezuela are currently the next in line for accession to the expanded Mercosur.

Article 5 of the Treaty of Asunción, which formally established the Mercosur in March 1991, aimed to achieve 'progressive, linear and automatic tariff reductions accompanied across the board by the elimination of non-tariff restrictions or equivalent measures ... with a view to arriving at a zero tariff and no non-tariff restrictions for the entire tariff area by 31 December 1994'.[19] The initial schedule for tariff reductions is shown in Table 4.1 below.[20] In addition to the programme of tariff reduction, the Treaty provided for the establishment of a CET in the interests of external competitiveness, and the introduction of equal tax treatment for products from all member countries with respect to local products.[21]

Table 4.1   *Mercosur: timetable for tariff reductions %*

30 June 1991	31 Dec. 1991	30 June 1992	31 Dec. 1992	30 June 1993	31 Dec. 1993	30 June 1994	31 Dec. 1994
47	54	61	68	75	82	89	100

Source: GATT: *Argentina 1992: Trade Policy Review* (May 1992), Vol. 1.

The tariff reduction programme was implemented as planned, despite fears throughout 1993 that the timetable would have to be revised, and despite minor changes to Argentine trade policy in the aftermath of the 1994/95 Mexican crisis. The CET was agreed at a summit in Montevideo in December 1992. Under the agreement, most products were subject to a maximum tariff of 20 per cent, with the exception of a relatively short list of goods that operated with a maximum of 35 per cent, to be gradually reduced between the years 1995 and 2001.[22] The customs union that took effect on 1 January 1995 with the Treaty of Ouro Preto was seen as 'almost' full[23]: it was agreed that between 5 and 10 per cent of total trade between the four countries would remain protected by national tariffs until 1999 in order to lessen the initial impact on uncompetitive industries. In addition, a further 10 per cent of total trade composed of 'sensitive' or 'strategic' products would not adopt the CET until 2001 (or 2006 for telecommunications and information technology products).[24]

As Tables 4.2 and 4.3 demonstrate, to date tariff liberalisation has spurred a significant growth in Mercosur trade, both within the region and with extra-regional partners. Although the relative significance of the former shows the most dynamic increase (Table 4.3), the overall expansion in trade flows is seen across the board. This is important evidence also of the 'open' nature of South American regionalism. So far, problems associated with the supposedly inherent protectionist nature of a regional bloc do not appear to have affected trade patterns in any particularly negative way. However, this growth is concentrated in the two largest economies – Argentina and Brazil. Paraguay and Uruguay remain more oriented towards regional trade than their larger partners,[25] although on the other hand, Argentina's interest in the regional market is far more pronounced than Brazil's. The problems associated with these asymmetries are discussed in more detail below.

Table 4.2   *Mercosur trade (US$ million)*

	1990	1991	1992	1993	1994	1995	1996	1990–96
Intra-Mercosur Exports	4.12	5.10	7.21	10.02	12.04	14.38	16.90	–
Growth rate (%)	–	23.60	41.40	39.00	20.20	19.40	17.50	309.50
Total exports from Mercosur countries	46.43	46.21	50.48	54.04	62.12	70.40	75.85	–
Growth rate (%)	–	-0.50	9.03	7.10	15.00	13.30	7.70	63.40
Intra-Mercosur exports / total exports (%)	8.90	11.00	14.30	18.60	19.40	20.40	22.30	–

Source: Argentine Embassy in Brazil (from the Comisión Parlamentaria Conjunta del Mercosur (CPC), Buenos Aires).

Table 4.3   *Evolution of the Structure of Mercosur Exports to the World*
(in percentages)

	1990	1991	1992	1993	1994	1995	1996
Intra-Mercosur	8.9	11.0	14.3	18.6	19.4	20.4	22.3
European Union	31.1	32.0	30.3	26.8	27.0	25.6	24.3
United States	20.7	16.9	17.1	17.6	17.5	15.3	14.6
Rest of LAIA[a]	7.1	9.0	18.6	10.3	9.9	9.7	9.5
Rest of the world	32.2	31.1	19.4	26.8	26.2	29.0	29.3
Total	100.0	100.0	100.0	100.0	100.0	100.0	100.0

Note: a Latin American Integration Association
Source: Argentine Embassy in Brazil (from Comisión Parlamentaria Conjunta del Mercosur (CPC), Buenos Aires).

The other principal effect of the Mercosur has been on investment flows, again both inside and outside the region. Foreign direct investment generally had more to do with the processes of privatisation which advanced throughout this time, particularly in Argentina, but the regional integration has produced a marked increase in the establishment of local operations by giant transnationals, particularly in the automobile, food and drink, petrochemical and textiles sectors.[26]

An analysis of the effects of integration on trade liberalisation and investment flows demonstrates the ways in which domestic reform efforts were 'locked in' at the regional level. In Argentina, as an example, the average tariff rate in mid-1994 before the implementation of the CET was 18.98 per cent (including the statistical surcharge). The average CET by the end of the first Menem administration a year later was 12.1 per cent.[27] Similarly, regional integration had important effects relating to the attraction of investment from both inside and outside the Mercosur network. Intra-regional investment flows were augmented by such mechanisms as agreements on representation, distribution and productive complementarity, joint ventures, participation in the capital structures of existing firms, the creation of affiliated companies and the formation of 'strategic alliances'.[28]

On a political level, therefore, the simultaneous and mutually reinforcing nature of the processes of unilateral and regional liberalisation gave rise to a valuable mechanism by which governments could strengthen support coalitions for their policy agenda and thus facilitate the consolidation of reform. Sectoral resistance to the adjustment occasioned by such policy shifts was offset by the perceived benefits to be derived from increased access to regional markets, and therefore from integration more generally.[29] In this sense, then, the Mercosur may be seen as having attenuated the post-implementation difficulties of opening the domestic economy. This reduction in the adjustment costs of structural reform (as opposed to initial stabilisation) was supplemented from around 1993 by the extra cushion provided by abundant inflows of foreign capital.

Hence it may well be the case that most developing countries that seek integration do so for reasons of domestic discipline, particularly when there is the need, as in most Latin American countries at the time, to consolidate a sea change in economic policy and the development paradigm that informs it. Integration, therefore, is about the enhancement of national competitiveness in the globalised international economy and about the maximisation of the effectiveness of domestic economic strategies, in addition to its association with a particular set of neoliberal policies. However, the arguments about the 'locking-in' of a certain set of policies refer only to a specific set of international and domestic circumstances around the start of the 1990s, rather than to any general link between integration and neoliberalism.

Towards a Free Trade Area of the Americas (FTAA)?

With growing global integration and this new pattern of relations, diplomatic activity has increased significantly. The first Summit of the Americas at Miami in December 1994 appeared to usher in a new period in inter-American relations. This built on Bush's 1990 Enterprise for the Americas initiative,[30] and subsequently the start of negotiations for a hemispheric free trade area at the second Summit of the Americas in April 1998 in Santiago, Chile. This new diplomacy was complicated, however, by the Mexican peso crisis at the end of 1994[31] and the reaction in the United States to the $20 billion rescue package that it was obliged to assemble.[32] If previously Congress had been reticent about the possible expansion of the NAFTA, after the Mexican crisis this was simply moved off the agenda. The FTAA negotiations in some way compensate, but are for the same reasons likely to be politically complicated.

The FTAA was projected to take effect from 2005. Despite the intention for a hemispheric bloc (excluding Cuba), however, the most likely scenario at the present time appears to be that integration will take the form of an alliance between blocs: the NAFTA in the north and the Mercosur in the south (possibly expanded into a South American Free Trade Area, or SAFTA). It seems increasingly likely that the other older blocs in the region – such as the Andean Pact and the Central American and Caribbean units (CAC and Caricom) – will be subsumed into these two dominant arrangements. The expansion of the Mercosur has gained significant extra impetus in the light of these hemispheric negotiations. One motive is the perceived need to counteract the negotiating strength of the United States which, for obvious reasons, prefers to negotiate on a country-by-country basis, while the Mercosur prefers to negotiate as a bloc. The other motivation may be that a SAFTA could function as a contingency plan in the event that the FTAA collapses or never comes to fruition.

Mexico and Brazil appear at present to be the most reticent about the

FTAA.[33] Mexico's reservations are also based on a defence of its preferential access to the North American market, which would be compromised by the negotiation of hemispheric integration along the proposed lines. While most other Latin American countries continue to conduct trade relations with the rest of the world as well as North and South American partners, Mexico's trade structure is almost exclusively dominated by trade in the NAFTA.[34] Therefore, Mexican objectives in both regional and hemispheric trade negotiations diverge significantly from the rest.

Although it has avoided being cast as the villain of the piece, Brazil is the principal counterweight to the United States[35], and has voiced differences of opinion regarding tariff reduction schedules as well as doubts concerning the scope of the negotiations. From a Brazilian perspective the United States is seen to be promoting provisions which go beyond those agreed during the Uruguay Round, while Brazil's preference in the short term is to consolidate the measures agreed in the World Trade Organization (WTO). Similarly, Brazil and most other South American countries are concerned principally with trade issues, while the United States' objectives are more focused on 'newer' issues such as services, intellectual property rights, competition policy and government procurement.[36] Brazil was also at the forefront of the calls for a SAFTA from early 1994.

This throws up another set of issues concerning the disparities between the objectives of the United States and Latin American countries. Sceptics of hemispheric integration argue that optimism is based on a one-sided analysis of hemispheric relations. The United States, it is argued, holds different views on such issues as democratisation, the environment and security, and these are all presented as potential stumbling blocks. In addition, it is not perceived to be in the interests of the United States to lock itself too tightly into a regional relationship in view of the strongly multilateral nature of its trade policy, and also its attention is likely to remain most focused on Mexico and the Caribbean rather than South America.[37] To this we can add the comments made above concerning Brazilian multilateral concerns, and an overall desire on the part of Latin American countries to build links with other parts of the world, notably Europe and the Asia Pacific. Furthermore, it is unlikely either than Mexico will readily sacrifice its preferential access to the US market, or that the preferential market arrangements in South America will be willingly opened up to competition from the north of the hemisphere. In this respect, it is perhaps mistaken to see subregional arrangements as the building-blocks of a potential FTAA.[38]

On another level, South American countries are far less pressed to negotiate with the United States than Mexico. Although they all trade with the United States, Mexico remains by far the most dependent, and far more affected by tariff and other barriers to the United States market. For South American countries, on the other hand, most tariffs are already quite low (particularly for agricultural products), and in any case most benefit from preferential treatment under the terms of the Generalized System of Preferences.[39]

Problems of Latin American integration

These observations also shed some light on the main difficulties associated with the consolidation of regionalism in South America. It should be noted, in advance, that integration in South America began with a set of highly ambitious goals in a complicated macroeconomic situation. Given the initial environment, the achievements and survival of the Mercosur is noteworthy. The principal problems of contemporary regionalism in Latin America relate to the 'deepening' of integration and the management of the 'expanded market'. Although the 'formal' elements of integration have proceeded well, the phase of 'easy' integration is currently giving way to the question of deepening, which is usually seen to involve macroeconomic policy harmonisation and institutionalisation.[40] The main obstacle to this remains associated with macroeconomic differences between countries, generating issues of policy convergence or harmonisation. Brazil, the largest economy, remains hostile to the idea of macroeconomic policy coordination, whereas Argentina and the smaller countries are generally in favour. Argentina focuses in particular on present imbalances in the exchange rate regime: since the adoption of the Convertibility Plan in 1991,[41] Argentina's currency is pegged at a 1:1 parity with the dollar, while Brazil remains free to devalue at will.

The second main issue of the agenda – institutionalisation – does not find much favour in the region generally. There is some question of whether integration can proceed with the development of supranational decision-making structures, but for the time being none of the countries is particularly anxious to press the issue. The smaller countries are the least opposed to institutionalisation, and argue for some kind of central dispute resolution mechanism at the very least. Given the general difficulties for smaller countries in any regional arrangement in pressing their interests vis-à-vis the more powerful members, a degree of institutional development would probably serve Uruguayan and Paraguayan interests well. Similarly, the administrative implications of the expansion of the Mercosur may well necessitate some advances in this area. The principal drawback, of course, is the implied movement away from economic exchange towards the politicisation of regional integration. Although any process of integration is inherently and necessarily political, especially in a highly intergovernmental variant such as the Mercosur, there is a resistance to any developments which push the arrangements towards an overtly political agenda which compromises the intergovernmental (and perhaps 'open') nature of South American regionalism. Brazilian resistance, furthermore, is strongest for the same reasons as mentioned above in the context of the FTAA: given that its interests are not especially closely focused on the region, it is anxious to guard its multilateral credentials.

The other significant area of divergence lies in economic orientation. While Argentina and the smaller countries have pursued liberalisation with some vigour, Brazilian economic policy remains oriented towards a relatively high level of state intervention, an active industrial policy and a somewhat ambivalent attitude to economic reform. Brazil has demonstrated a marked propensity to prioritise domestic industrialisation objectives over liberalisation. These imbalances in economic orientation are reflected in indicators of the economic relationship between the countries, as well as differences in economic circumstances. Argentina has been hard pressed to shake off a persistent trade deficit with Brazil, while Brazil has long been struggling with high levels of fiscal deficit and an overvalued currency. Both of these circumstances make the threat of Brazilian economic difficulties worrying. The feared devaluation of the Brazilian currency in January 1999 will undoubtedly have serious implications for the rest of the region. On a very basic level, although the feared 'agricultural specialisation' of Argentina (as a result of Brazil's manufacturing superiority) did not happen[42], around 30 per cent of Argentina's total exports are directed to Brazil. The full regional implications of the Brazilian crisis have yet to become apparent.

A last thought : the internationalisation of politics?

The emphasis on global and regional economic relations does not obscure the implications for the conduct of politics at all three of the levels mentioned at the start of this chapter. We have already seen the ways in which foreign policy and diplomatic relations were transformed along with (and for the purposes of) international economic relations. Similarly, and perhaps more importantly, the regional integration process was facilitated by democratisation, creating the conditions for increased interaction as a result of diminished political and military rivalries.[43] At the same time, the task of democratic consolidation was propelled further by precisely this process.

This last observation, however, is more complex than it appears at first glance. Apart from a regional or international defence of democracy (as in the case of the attempted coup in Paraguay), the process of engagement with external actors and structures has created a situation in which the political economy of Latin American countries has become genuinely internationalised. Economic reforms have become locked in through a set of global and regional commitments and obligations. Similarly, however, the sorts of political reform that accompanied neoliberalism have been reinforced by Latin American countries' insertion into international processes of change. These political changes (and reforms) have involved the reorganisation of political power at the domestic level.

The first manifestation of this is the privileging of business and the private sector over labour. In effect, both domestic governments and the nature of the process of globalisation have constructed a new 'support coalition' for this type of economic change which centres on business actors. At the domestic level, this has usually involved the incorporation of business sectors into the mainstream of the policy-making process, along with the dominance of technocrats in office. In essence, Latin American governments have constructed an alliance between the holders of political power (the state) and the holders of economic power, both at the domestic and at the international levels. This state–business nexus can be seen as essential to the survival of the sort of 'neoliberal democracy' that has taken root in Latin America.[44] It is essential for the successful consolidation of the neoliberal economic orientation, which depends on the vitalisation (and vitality) of the private sector, which in turn is essential for the maintenance of political legitimacy at the domestic level.

The second manifestation is the consolidation of the state as the pivot or hinge of the new economic and political models. The state has always been dominant in Latin American countries, and even with its reformulation as a result of economic reform, it remains at the centre of the political process. First, the international economic negotiations and commitments of Latin American countries are conducted largely by governments with, until recently, minimal input from societal actors. The Mercosur, for example, is exclusively intergovernmental in its structure (as mentioned above), and interests at the societal level have generally channelled their participation and lobbying efforts through their national governments. Even business interests were largely articulated through the structures of the state, and 'secondary' actors such as political parties, trade unions and social movements have constructed some linkages with counterparts in the region, but have not participated in the integration process in any particularly visible or effective independent way.[45]

Both of these developments contributed in the early part of the 1990s to the establishment of the sorts of centralised and insulated styles of government of which Menem and Fujimori are prime examples.[46] Although, as the chapters in the second part of this volume show, the demobilisation of civil society is starting to give way to new demands for and forms of political participation, the 'internationalisation' of the state, perhaps as a result of the internationalisation of economic activity, acted to remove the policy-making process even further from the influence of domestic societal actors. As such, the sorts of political reforms implemented in a variety of countries, intended to strengthen business over labour and reconstitute the state after a damaging period of political and economic crisis, were 'locked in' by the growth of economic and political linkages at the global and regional levels.

This has often been seen to lead to the derogation of accountability, as both economic and political power become located in the hands of external, unaccountable actors or else a government that is not responsive to societal interests. This was clearly inimical to the development of participatory democracy in the early part of the 1990s, although with the round of elections in the region at the end of the 1990s there are some grounds for optimism that politics will become more democratic in this respect. In other ways, however, this 'internationalisation of politics' may offer advantages for political development, in that increasing global integration (economic and political) has increased the pressure that is brought to bear on subversive or belligerent elements of civil society. Globalisation is not a force for world peace, has not produced homogenisation or stability, and has generated increasing tendencies towards subnational fragmentation. Nevertheless, there is a certain argument to be made that global integration has acted to reduce the feasibility of political extremes in the world, and at the national level. In Latin America, it appears that there are far more demands for inclusion, even from the Zapatistas in Mexico, than examples of 'opt-out' opposition. The question concerns the nature of the political system, and the economic model, into which previously marginalised groups will be incorporated.

Conclusion

The above discussion has shown that the development of the global and regional linkages of Latin American countries has acted to sustain and consolidate the neoliberal economic orientation at the domestic level, and also to open up a new set of possibilities for economic development and foreign policy objectives. The integration of Latin American countries into the international political economy is therefore a means to an end in many respects: the consolidation of economic reform (and associated sorts of political reform) at the domestic level was strengthened in the first instance by commitments and obligations outside the boundaries of the national state.

In many ways, however, the real debates are only just beginning. The economic model, globalisation, the nature and future of regional integration, relations with the international financial institutions and the reconciliation of global, regional and domestic priorities are all increasingly open to question. Issues of political development, particularly the need for the democratisation of politics in the region, are linked to all of these issues: the questions revolve around the sorts of political processes that can be (and need to be) constructed at the domestic level in the context of the globalisation of political and economic activity.

Notes

1 For the purposes of this chapter, the term 'international' will be taken as an umbrella term covering the global and the regional. 'International' and 'global' are not used interchangeably. In the same way, 'internationalisation' refers to the location of activities at both the regional and the global levels.

2 For an analysis of the motives for regional integration, see A. Hurrell, 'Explaining the Resurgence of Regionalism in World Politics', *Review of International Studies*, 21:4 (1995).

3 See N. Phillips, 'The Future Political Economy of Latin America', in R. Stubbs and G. R. D. Underhill, *Political Economy and the Changing Global Order*, second edition (Oxford University Press, 1999).

4 A. Fontana, 'Argentina and the Politics of International Security' (mimeo, Buenos Aires, 1997), p. 1. Since the early 1990s, Argentine forces have also been active in various capacities in Honduras, Angola, El Salvador, Israel, Nicaragua, Mozambique, Cyprus and Haiti. See D. L. Norden, 'Keeping the Peace, Outside and In: Argentina's United Nations Missions', *International Peacekeeping*, 2:3 (Autumn 1995).

5 See G. P. Atkins, *Latin America in the International Political System*, third edition (Boulder, Westview, 1995), pp. 250–1.

6 For a discussion, see H. Muñoz, 'A New OAS for the New Times', in A. F. Lowenthal and G. F. Treverton (eds.), *Latin America in a New World* (Boulder, Westview, 1994).

7 A. Hurrell, 'Regionalism in the Americas', in L. Fawcett and A. Hurrell (eds.), *Regionalism in World Politics: Regional Organization and World Order* (Oxford, Oxford University Press, 1995), pp. 265–6; J. Grugel, 'Latin America and the Remaking of the Americas', in A. Gamble and A. Payne (eds.), *Regionalism and World Order* (Basingstoke, Macmillan, 1996), p. 158.

8 (Santiago, 1995).

9 P. Gerchunoff and J. L. Machinea, 'Un ensayo sobre la política económica después de la estabilización', in P. Bustos (ed.), *Más allá de la estabilización: Argentina en la época de la globalización y regionalización* (Buenos Aires, Fundación Friedrich Ebert, 1995), p. 45.

10 See Chapter 3 and F. Panizza, 'Brazil', in J. Buxton and N. Phillips (eds), *Case Studies in Latin American Political Economy* (Manchester, Manchester University Press, 1999).

11 J. Fuentes, 'Reconciling Subregional and Hemispheric Integration', *CEPAL Review*, 45 (December 1991), p. 99.

12 M. Hirst, 'The Obstacles to Regional Governance in the Western Hemisphere: Old Regionalism in a New World Order', Serie de Documentos e Informes de Investigación, 180 (Buenos Aires, FLACSO, May 1995), p. 21.

13 J. Fuentes, 'El regionalismo abierto y la integración económica', *CEPAL Review*, 53 (August 1994), p. 83.

14 R. Higgott, 'Economic Co-operation in the Asia Pacific: A Theoretical Comparison with the European Union', *Journal of European Public Policy*, 2:3 (September 1995), p. 363.

15 A. Moravcsik, 'Preferences and Power in the European Community: A Liberal Intergovernmentalist Approach', *Journal of Common Market Studies*, 31 (1993), pp. 486–7.

16 The Mercosur: Argentina, Brazil, Uruguay, Paraguay (plus Chile and Bolivia as associate members); the Andean Group: Bolivia, Colombia, Ecuador, Venezuela, Peru; the CAC: Costa Rica, El Salvador, Guatemala, Honduras, Nicaragua, Panama; the Caricom: Antigua and Barbuda, the Bahamas, Barbados, Belize, Dominica, Grenada, Guyana, Jamaica, St Kitts–Nevis, St Lucia, St Vincent and the Grenadines, Trinidad and Tobago.

17 J. Whalley, 'CUSTA and NAFTA: Can a WHFTA be Far Behind?', *Journal of Common Market Studies*, 30 (1992), p. 126.

18 D. Tussie, 'In the Whirlwind of Globalization and Multilateralism: The Case of Emerging Regionalism in Latin America', in W. D. Coleman and G. R. D. Underhill (eds.), *Regionalism and Global Economic Integration: Europe, Asia and the Americas* (London and New York, Routledge, 1998), p. 92.

19 General Agreement on Tariffs and Trade (GATT) *Argentina 1992: Trade Policy Review* (May 1992), Vol. 1, p. 62.

20 *Ibid.*, p. 66. Significantly, the agreement allowed for a significant number of products to be exempt from the liberalisation scheme: 324, 394, 439 and 960 for Brazil, Argentina, Paraguay and Uruguay, respectively. These exemptions were subject to a separate timetable of tariff reductions, which reflected the differential treatment accorded to smaller member countries: Argentina and Brazil were required to implement annual reductions of 20 per cent from 31 December 1990, Uruguay and Paraguay 10 per cent reductions in 1990 and 1991, and 20 per cent thereafter (*ibid.*, pp. 67–8).

21 Report of the Argentine Government to the GATT Trade Policy Review of Argentina, 4–5 March 1992. Printed in GATT, *Argentina 1992*, Vol. 2, p. 33.

22 *Latin American Regional Reports – Southern Cone*, 4 February 1993.

23 *Ibid.*, 29 December 1994.

24 For an account of the controversies and difficulties surrounding the establishment of the customs union in 1995, see *El Economista* (Buenos Aires), 16 December 1994.

25 Inter-American Development Bank and Institute for the Integration of Latin America and the Caribbean (IDB/INTAL), *Informe Mercosur*, no. 1 (July–December 1996), p. 8.

26 *Ibid.*, p. 13. See also *The Economist*, 'Remapping South America: A Survey of Mercosur', 21 October 1996, pp. 10–12.

27 R. Bouzas, 'Mercosur and Preferential Trade Liberalisation in South America: Record, Issues and Prospects', Serie de Documentos e Informes de Investigación no. 176 (FLACSO, Buenos Aires, February 1995), p. 17.

28 *Informe Mercosur*, p. 12.

29 R. Bouzas, 'La agenda económica del Mercosur: Desafíos de política a corto y mediano plazo', *Integración & Comercio* (IDB/INTAL, January–April 1996), p. 68.

30 For an analysis, see R. Porter, 'The Enterprise for the Americas Initiative: A New Approach to Economic Growth', *Journal of Interamerican Studies and World Affairs*, 32:4 (Winter 1990); A. Payne, 'The United States and its Enterprise for the Americas', in Gamble and Payne (eds.), *Regionalism and World Order*; R. Bouzas and N. Lustig, 'Apertura económica, integración subregional y la iniciativa para las Américas', Serie de Documentos e Informes de Investigación no. 132 (Buenos Aires, FLACSO, July 1992); R. A. Pastor, 'The Bush Administration and Latin America: The Pragmatic Style and the Regionalist Option', *Journal of Interamerican Studies and World Affairs*, 33:3 (Fall 1991); S. Weintraub, 'The New US Economic Initiative Toward Latin America', *Journal of Interamerican Studies and World Affairs*, 33:1 (Spring 1991); F. Rojas Aravena, *América Latina y la iniciativa para las Américas* (Buenos Aires, FLACSO, 1993); R. Gitli, 'Latin American Integration and the Enterprise for the Americas Initiative', *Journal of World Trade*, 20:4 (August 1992); UN Economic Commission for Latin America and the Carribbean (ECLAC), *América Latina Frente a la iniciativa Bush* (Santiago, 1990).

31 See S. Peschard, 'Mexico' in Buxton and Phillips (eds), *Case Studies*.

32 For analysis of the Mexican crisis, see H. J. Wiarda, 'After Miami: The Summit, the Peso Crisis, and the Future of US–Latin American Relations', *Journal of Interamerican Studies and World Affairs*, 37:1 (Spring 1995); G. L. Springer and J. L. Molina, 'The Mexican Financial Crisis: Genesis, Impact and Implications', *Journal of Interamerican Studies and World Affairs*, 37:2 (Summer 1995).

33 P. S. Wrobel, 'A Free Trade Area of the Americas in 2005?', *International Affairs*, 74:3 (July 1998), p. 557.

34 D. Tussie, 'Multilateralism Revisited in a Globalizing World Economy', *Mershon International Studies Review*, 42 (May 1998), p. 192.

35 For an analysis of power relations and hierarchical structures in the Americas, see G. Mace, L. Bélanger and J. P. Thérien, 'Regionalism in the Americas and the Hierarchy of Power', *Journal of Interamerican Studies and World Affairs*, 35:2 (Summer 1993).

36 P. Da Motta Veiga, 'Brazil's Strategy for Trade Liberalisation and Economic Integration in the Western Hemisphere' (Inter-American Dialogue, June 1996), pp. 6–7.

37 A. Hurrell, 'Latin America in the New World Order: A Regional Bloc of the Americas?', *International Affairs*, 68:1 (1992).

38 M. Naím, 'Toward Free Trade in the Americas: Building Blocks, Stumbling Blocks, and Entry Fees', in S. Weintraub (ed.), *Integrating the Americas: Shaping Future Trade Policy* (New Brunswick, Transaction, 1994), p. 49.

39 S. Haggard, 'The Political Economy of Regionalism in Asia and the Americas', in E. D. Mansfield and H. V. Milner (eds.), *The Political Economy of Regionalism* (New York, Columbia University Press, 1997), p. 41.

40 J. Lucángeli, 'La integración de la Argentina en el Mercosur: Revisión de antecedentes y evaluación del desarrollo y perspectivas del acuerdo regional', Centro de Estudios para el Cambio Estructural (CECE), Serie de Estudios no. 26 (Buenos Aires, April 1998), p. 50. See also R. Lavagna, 'Coordinación macroeconómica, la profundización de la interdependencia y derivaciones para el Mercosur: Notas sobre la oferta y demanda de coordinación', *Desarrollo Económico*, 36:142 (July–September 1996).

41 See C. M. Lewis, 'Argentina', in Buxton and Phillips (eds), *Case Studies*.

42 *Latin American Special Reports*, 'Latin American Trading Blocs: The State of Play' (April 1995).

43 M. Hirst, 'Mercosur and the new circumstances for its integration', *CEPAL Review*, 46 (April

1992), p. 139.

44 J. Grugel, 'State and Business in Neo-Liberal Democracies in Latin America', *Global Society*, 12:2 (1998).

45 M. Hirst, 'La dimensión política del Mercosur: actores, politización e ideología', Serie de Documentos e Informes de Investigación no. 198 (Buenos Aires, FLACSO, November 1995).

46 See N. Phillips, 'Globalisation, State Power and Democracy in Latin America', paper presented at the Annual Conference of the Society for Latin American Studies, Liverpool, 17–19 April 1998.

Part II

TRADITIONAL AND EMERGING ACTORS

The military in Latin America:
defining the road ahead

CRAIG L. ARCENEAUX

On 4 February 1992, Venezuela awoke to coordinated military uprisings at garrisons located in four of the largest urban centres in the country: Caracas, Maracay, Maracaibo and Valencia. Sporadic fighting along city streets between the rebellious troops and loyalist units left some 300 casualties, with 78 dead and 1,100 soldiers under arrest. President Carlos Andrés Pérez barely escaped with his life. By late afternoon the uprising was quelled, but the victors had little to celebrate. In many areas the rebels were greeted by civilians who waved flags in marches, honked car horns and banged on pots and pans as signs of support. When Lieutenant Colonel Hugo Chávez, a rebel leader, was made to announce his surrender on national television, he declared that the attempt would be terminated '*por ahora*' (for now), a phrase soon echoed by Venezuelan groups with various economic or political grievances against the government. An environment of coup rumours plagued the country for months, until 27 November, when a second unsuccessful military coup occurred as a reaction to the personnel discharges and promotional oversights caused by the first coup attempt.

Why did factions within the Venezuelan armed forces rebel? Was it a populist reaction to the economic deprivation of the lower classes? Was it a crusade to purge the political class of corruption and imprison the culprits? Was it a move by soldiers upset by the soft position taken by Pérez on border disputes with Colombia, Brazil and Guyana? Or was it a response to growing guilt in the ranks over their role in the repression of the 1989 socio-economic unrest that left hundreds of civilians dead – a role which was forced upon them by the government? The Venezuelan case highlights the variety of economic, political and professional elements that define the military role in Latin American politics. Moreover, these coup attempts occurred in a country where civilian rule was viewed as stable and during a time when democratic civilian rule was advancing in the region. What happened in Venezuela in 1992 thus demonstrates the fact that the military will continue to play a role in the region. What that role is and how it is likely to develop is the subject of this chapter.

The military in Latin America and the Latin American militaries

Latin America does not stand out as a particularly 'militarised' area of the world. Since the democratisation processes of the mid–1980s, defence expenditures have declined and have remained well below world averages. In 1985, Latin American countries spent on average 3 per cent of their GDP on the armed forces. In 1995 this figure was 1.9 per cent and by 1996 it was 1.8 per cent.[1] The 1996 figure stands far below expenditures found in Europe outside NATO (North Atlantic Treaty Organization) (3.8 per cent), the Middle East and Africa (6.8 per cent), Central and South Asia (5.3 per cent), East Asia and Australasia (4.6 per cent) and Sub-Saharan Africa (3 per cent). NATO countries come closest at 2.3 per cent.[2]

Recent trends in military spending show a sharp divergence between Central and South America. Both regions were hit hard by the debt crisis and experienced a decline in military spending during the 1980s. But over 1991–95, average South American military expenditures increased 5.2 per cent, while those of Central America decreased 11.9 per cent.[3] The contrast largely reflects the Central American peace processes, which call for significant levels of demilitarisation. Table 5.1 shows military expenditures for 20 Latin American countries. Unsurprisingly, it demonstrates that larger countries with larger economies tend to spend more on the armed forces. More interesting are the measurements of burden placed upon the economy and government spending. Cuba, Chile, Ecuador, Colombia and Uruguay rank highest when military spending is measured as a percentage of GDP. Nonetheless, only Cuba exceeds the global average of about 4 per cent. When military expenditures as a percentage of central government expenditures are examined, Argentina, Ecuador, Chile, Colombia and Guatemala come out on top, although most countries fall below the world average of about 10 per cent and developing world average of 13 per cent.[4] The Chilean and Ecuadorean figures partly reflect the legal assurances given to military expenditures in these countries. In Chile, the military is assured revenue equal to a portion of sales from the copper industry, and there is also a constitutional floor placed on the military budget, and in Ecuador the military has a legal right to proceeds from petroleum exports. Colombia's appearance in both measures reveals the intensity of the guerrilla war.

The general decline in military budgets has had a significant impact on the armed forces of the region. Strapped for finances, most remain poorly trained and inadequately equipped. Latin American military budgets are distinguished by excessive personnel costs (they often represent up to three-quarters of military expenditures). This leaves little for operations, maintenance, procurement or research and development.[5] Nonetheless, these personnel costs do not provide adequate salaries for NCOs and most officers. Pension outlays are still pay-

Table 5.1 *Military expenditures of selected Latin American countries* (constant 1995 $)

	$m			$ per capita			% of GDP			ME/CGE[a]	
	1985	1996		1985	1996		1985	1996		1995	
Argentina	4,945	3,732	(2)	162	108	(2)	3.8	1.5	(9-11)	27.0[b]	(1)
Bolivia	173	152	(12)	27	18	(14)	2.0	2.1	(6/7)	9.5	(6)
Brazil	3,209	10,341	(1)	24	63	(4)	0.8	2.1	(6/7)	3.9	(17)
Chile	1,696	1,990	(4)	140	138	(1)	7.8	3.5	(2)	17.5	(3)
Colombia	579	1,846	(5)	20	52	(6)	1.6	2.6	(4)	16.2	(4)
Costa Rica	40	50	(18)	15	14	(15/16)	0.7	0.6	(19/20)	2.7	(18)
Cuba	2,181	686	(8)	216	62	(5)	9.6	5.4	(1)	n/a	
Dominican Republic	70	101	(16)	11	13	(17)	1.1	1.1	(17)	9.1	(8)
Ecuador	388	528	(9)	41	44	(7/8)	1.8	3.4	(3)	18.3	(2)
El Salvador	344	122	(13)	72	21	(13)	4.4	1.5	(9-11)	7.4	(10)
Guatemala	160	154	(11)	20	14	(15/16)	1.8	1.4	(12/13)	14.2	(5)
Honduras	98	57	(17)	22	9	(19)	2.1	1.3	(14/15)	8.7	(9)
Jamaica	27	28	(20)	12	11	(18)	0.9	0.6	(19/20)	1.4	(19)
Mexico	1,695	2,582	(3)	22	28	(11)	0.7	0.8	(18)	5.1	(16)
Nicaragua	301	36	(19)	92	8	(20)	17.4	1.5	(9-11)	5.3	(14/15)
Panama	123	109	(15)	56	40	(9/10)	2.0	1.4	(12/13)	5.3[b]	(14/15)
Paraguay	82	110	(14)	22	22	(12)	1.3	1.3	(14/15)	7.3	(11/12)
Peru	875	1,061	(6)	47	44	(7/8)	4.5	1.9	(8)	9.3	(7)
Uruguay	326	270	(10)	108	85	(3)	3.5	2.3	(5)	7.3	(11/12)
Venezuela	1,125	903	(7)	65	40	(9/10)	2.1	1.2	(16)	6.3	(13)

Note

a Military expenditures as a percentage of central government expenditures.

b Denotes 1994 figure.

Source: International Institute for Strategic Studies, *The Military Balance 1997/98* (London, Oxford University Press, 1998), pp. 295–6; ME/CGE from US Arms Control and Disarmament Agency (USALDA), *World Military Expenditures and Arms Transfers* (Washington, DC, 1988), pp. 58–98.

ing for the larger militaries of the past, and only the highest-ranking officers draw decent salaries.

Finally, the region fails to make a significant mark on the extent of armed conflict found throughout the world. Only 3 of the world's 24 major armed conflicts were found in Latin America in 1996 and 2 of these are waning. In Guatemala, the implementation of the final peace accord in December 1996 ceased conflict between the armed forces and the Unidad Revolucionaria Nacinal de Guatemala (URNG, Guatemalan National Revolutionary Unity) guerrilla front, and in Peru, military success has substantially reduced the strength of the Sendero Luminoso and the Movimiento Revolucionario Túpac Amaru (MRTA, Túpac Amaru Revolutionary Movement). Only in Colombia, where the military continues to battle the resurgent Fuerzas Armadas Revolucionarias de Colombia (FARC, Revolutionary Armed Forces of Colombia) and Ejército de Liberación Nacional (ELN, National Liberation Army) guerrilla forces, do we find a particularly grave armed conflict, one that represents a real challenge to the existing political system.[6] The regional level of combat stands in stark contrast to the Latin America of the 1960s and 1970s, when active guerrilla groups were found in nearly every country (see Chapter 6).

The threat of interstate conflict remains very low in the region. Only four significant interstate conflicts have occurred in the twentieth century, and only one of these, the 1932–35 Chaco War in which Paraguay wrested control of territory claimed by Bolivia, was particularly destructive and affected broad sectors of society. The 1995 January border dispute between Ecuador and Peru stands as the second most violent conflict of the century, with about 300 casualties, but it should be emphasised that the battle remained localised and left major population centres unscathed.[7] The other two disputes, a 1941 skirmish between Peru and Ecuador and the 1969 'soccer war' between El Salvador and Honduras, lasted just 7–10 days and were neither particularly violent nor destructive.

Low military expenditures and a dearth of interstate wars do not mean that the armed forces have been inactive in the region. Unfortunately, Latin American militaries historically have tended to turn their operations inward and have concerned themselves more with internal security rather than national defence. This pattern became institutionalised during the Cold War, when the United States accepted responsibility for external defence and expected the armed forces of each country to provide for internal security. This division of labour to combat the perceived threat of communist expansion was made clear through US training missions, provision of material, and, in the case of perceived failure, direct military intervention. The Inter-American Treaty of Reciprocal Assistance (the Rio Pact), signed by 21 Latin American states and the United States in September 1947 at Rio de Janeiro, has provided the formal–legal justification for direct military action by the United States. The treaty deems any armed attack (including internal uprisings) against any country in the region an attack against all, and calls for a military response after a 2/3-majority vote. US political and economic pressure has assured responses in its favour and the United States has taken advantage of the vague language to take unilateral action. The United States has been, and continues to be, a 'hovering giant' in the region.[8]

The emphasis on internal security means that although force size and defence expenditures may not be particularly high, militaries continue to have a significant impact on society (simply put, internal security is less costly than external defence). Human rights abuses were rampant under the military regimes of the 1960s and 1970s, and the search for resolutions to these abuses continues to plague the region. Amnesties passed in Argentina, Brazil, Chile, El Salvador, Guatemala, Honduras, Peru and Uruguay place prohibitions on the prosecution of officers suspected of human rights abuses. These amnesties are viewed as unjust by many human rights organisations (see Chapter 8), but motions to abrogate them usually meet with military threats of reintervention.[9]

Human rights abuses by soldiers or the military police have fallen dramatically, but countries of special concern include Brazil, Colombia, Guatemala, Mexico and Peru.[10]

Although the discussion thus far has recognised basic similarities among the armed forces of the region, it is incorrect to speak of a 'Latin American' military. Just as a variety of socio-economic settings, cultural traits, and levels of political stability characterise the region as a whole, so the Latin American militaries demonstrate a range of diversity which overwhelms simple classification schemes. High levels of professionalism distinguish the South American militaries, but distinctions remain. The Colombian and Venezuelan militaries are identified by their regard for civilian supremacy, Peru and Ecuador have traditionally had progressive/populist oriented militaries in contrast to the acceptance of neoliberal policies found in the Brazilian, Chilean, Argentine and Uruguayan militaries, and the Paraguayan military, in its supportive role under the *caudillo* Stroessner, harked back to an earlier period in Latin American history. The apparent unity of the Central American militaries is equally deceptive. The attempts to instil revolutionary doctrine and party domination placed the Nicaraguan military closer to its Caribbean neighbour Cuba, and one cannot overlook the elimination of military institutions in Costa Rica and Panama. The Mexican military stands alone with its combination of professionalism, acceptance of civilian supremacy, and revolutionary mythology. Finally, for most Caribbean countries the norm has been national police forces, or paramilitary organisations such as the 'Tonton Macoute', which ruled under Haiti's Duvalier.

In light of these cautionary comments, a general distinction can be drawn between the Central American and South American militaries. Millet notes five attributes typical of the Central American militaries.[11] First, aside from the Honduran air force, navy and air force units are placed within the army command hierarchy. Second, there is a tendency to include national police or paramilitary forces within the army institution (although recent reforms are changing this). These attributes have contributed to the political power of the army and lead it, on an ordinary basis, towards involvement in internal security matters. Strikes, protests and other forms of public disorder are often immediately addressed by military units. Internal security brings a number of responsibilities under the armed forces, including immigration, customs at borders, ports and airports, and tax collection. Officers too often fall to the corrupt opportunities provided by these duties. All told, this sort of involvement in internal security contributes to the divide between soldiers and citizens, and the poor impression of the armed forces in society.

The last three attributes are associated with the low level of socio-economic development in Central America. First, NCOs are marked by an inordinate deficiency in training, and their social standing relative to commissioned officers represents a divide that inhibits military careers and contributes to the isolation of the elite officer corps. Second, a low level of development means that

Central American countries lack strong, organised labour unions, political parties, public interest groups, business groups or professional bureaucrats to challenge national military power. Varas corroborates the budgetary impact of underdevelopment on military power, noting that in 1987 the military budget was greater than outlays for health and education (considered individually) in Bolivia, Cuba, El Salvador, Guyana, Honduras, Nicaragua, and Peru.[12] On the other side of the development continuum, Hunter has noted how pork-barrel pressures in Brazil, Argentina, and Chile have led politicians to reduce military prerogatives as budget priorities are shifted to other groups.[13] A final attribute of Central American militaries is their greater dependence on the United States for training and equipment, a dependence cultivated by the intense security concerns held by the United States in the region. Historically, the United States has displayed a greater propensity to overlook human rights abuses in Central American countries than in South American countries in order to maintain military ties. Stringent arms embargoes due to human rights considerations were placed on Argentina, Brazil and Chile in the 1970s, and these actions in fact spurred the independent development of defence industries.[14]

Table 5.2 disaggregates the 'Latin American military' concept by illustrating the distribution of military power throughout the region. Brazil stands alone as the undisputed power. But after Brazil, the rankings are more muddled than they appear. Colombia, Peru and Mexico are ranked above Chile, but the former three armed forces have stronger internal orientations. Less occupied by internal threats and security concerns, the Chilean military is better prepared to project its military power outward (note that the disparities in army size are not found in navy and air force size). Overall, the table demonstrates the contrast between the larger South American militaries and those in Central America and the Caribbean. Two exceptions are Cuba and Uruguay, although Cuba, once a significant military power, has fallen to eighth place due to the cut in Soviet Cold War funding. The country should descend lower as equipment repairs decline and opportunities for training exercises fade, although one should not expect it to fall too far insofar as it is arguably the only country in the hemisphere that faces a significant military threat from its neighbours. Uruguay, the smallest South American country represented in the table, is below Cuba, Guatemala, El Salvador and the Dominican Republic. Nonetheless, Uruguay's number one ranking under military personnel per 100,000 population and relative navy and air force sizes indicate an ambitious response to the South American model.

Although the predominance of the army within the armed forces is clearly established by Table 5.2 for all countries, the stark division between the more professional armies of South America and those of Central America should be noted. Even the landlocked countries of Bolivia and Paraguay have larger navies than those found in Central America.[15] A final comparison of interest illustrated by the table is the amount of military personnel per 100,000 population. Uruguay, Chile, Peru, Bolivia and El Salvador have the largest armies as

Table 5.2 *The 20 largest Latin American militaries and force distribution (1996 active personnel, 1,000s)*[a]

		Army	Navy	Air force	Para-military	Total	Per 100,000 pop. (rank)
1	Brazil	200.0	64.7	50.0	385.60	700.30	423 (13)
2	Colombia	121.0	18.0	7.3	87.00	233.30	647 (7/8)
3	Peru	85.0	25.0	15.0	68.60	193.60	788 (3)
4	Mexico	130.0	37.0	8.0	15.00	190.00	203 (18)
5	Chile	51.0	29.8	13.5	31.20	125.50	861 (2)
6	Argentina	41.0	20.0	12.0	31.24	104.24	299 (17)
7	Venezuela	34.0	15.0	7.0	23.00	79.00	346 (16)
8	Cuba	38.0	5.0	10.0	19.00	72.00	647 (7/8)
9	Bolivia	25.0	4.5	4.0	30.60	64.10	755 (4)
10	Ecuador	50.0	4.1	3.0	0.27	57.37	471 (10/11)
11	Guatemala	38.5	1.5	0.7	12.30	53.00	471 (10/11)
12	El Salvador	25.7	1.1	1.6	12.00	40.40	688 (5)
13	Domincan Republic	15.0	4.0	5.5	15.00	39.50	498 (9)
14	Paraguay	14.9	3.6	1.7	14.80	35.00	670 (6)
15	Uruguay	17.6	5.0	3.0	2.50	28.00	875 (1)
16	Honduras	16.0	1.0	1.8	5.50	24.30	387 (14)
17	Nicaragua	15.0	0.8	1.2		17.00	382 (15)
18	Panama	–	–	–	11.80	11.80	429 (12)
19	Costa Rica	–	–	–	7.00	7.00	198 (19)
20	Jamaica	3.0	0.15	0.17	0.20	3.52	142 (20)

Note: a The figures do not include rural defence militias and other semi-autonomous paramilitary groups. Peru, Mexico, Colombia, Cuba and Guatemala all have significant numbers in these groups. Nor do the figures include the state militias in Brazil, which total 385,600 and are considered to be army reservists. Panama's army was abolished in August 1994, and Costa Rica's in December 1948. *Source:* International Institute for Strategic Studies, *The Military Balance 1997/98* (pp. 205–29).

a proportion of their population, while Jamaica, Costa Rica, Mexico, Argentina, Venezuela and Nicaragua stand on the other side of the continuum.

The continuing search for theory in Latin American civil–military relations

There is no doubt that the armed forces have played a significant role in Latin American politics. Only Cuba, Colombia, Costa Rica, Mexico and Venezuela remained unscathed by military intervention in the 1960s and 1970s. The question that divides scholars is why the military has intervened in politics. The question is important, because only with such understanding can we guard against future unwarranted military incursions into civilian affairs. That the military ought not to trespass outside its professional duties has not always been a consensus among researchers. Early modernisation theorists such as Shils and

Pye argued that, as the most modern institution in a traditional society, the military could transfer its expertise in bureaucratic organisation and rationality to other institutions in society and government.[16] Johnson applied the argument specifically to Latin America.[17] Although the perspective was popular for a time, the rise of repressive military regimes made scholars sceptical of the putative developmental role of the military. A strict analytical separation between military matters and civilian affairs began to develop, largely based upon Samuel Huntington's detailed work on the professional duties of the armed forces.[18] Any movement away from these professional duties and toward the social, political, or economic concerns of the country would initiate an endless spiral of involvement in civilian affairs. Hence, Welch asserted, 'having received or requested responsibility for presiding over extensive social change, the military inherently develops vested interests in political action'.[19]

Theoretical approaches to the Latin American military blossomed in the 1960s. Most of these submerged the armed forces within the greater concerns of political development. Set within weighty forces such as mobilisation, institutionalisation or cultural change, the military held little chance to be regarded an autonomous agent. Thus, according to Huntington, mass praetorianism causes military coups.[20] A society falls to mass praetorianism when it lacks strong political institutions (especially political parties) to channel social demands properly through government. In this situation of praetorianism, students protest, the poor riot, workers strike, politicians and bureaucrats fall to corruption, and the military stages coups.

Finer took a slightly more complex approach.[21] A modernising force within the military itself, professionalisation, produces frustration as the armed forces compare their own capabilities to the purportedly inept politicians within an underdeveloped political culture. Ironically, this modernising force then leads the armed forces to disrupt the political development of the country. José Nun also looked to developmental forces, although from an economic perspective.[22] According to Nun, because most officers have middle-class origins, the military intervenes to protect this class in times of crisis. In his theory of bureaucratic authoritarianism, O'Donnell identified three developmental processes leading to military intervention.[23] The first is an economic crisis produced by the exhaustion of import-substitution industrialisation policies. The second is a socio-political process in which the populist coalition affiliated with import-substitution breaks down and gives way to mass praetorianism. The third is the general professionalisation of the military, which increases both its unity and perception of threat. These three processes engender a coup coalition consisting of business and technocrats who want to replace the exhausted import substitution model with a free market model, and the military who are reacting to the corporate threat they perceive in mass praetorianism.

Despite the prevalence of developmental approaches, some researchers began to study the military as an actor in its own right. Janowitz and Abrahamsson detailed how processes of recruitment, military socialisation, and professionalisation detach soldiers from society and allow the armed forces to formulate independent corporate interests.[24] Nordlinger noted how corporate interests such as the military budget, non-political criteria for promotions and assignments, and educational training free from outside political manipulation determine the propensity for militaries to intervene in politics.[25] The message was simple: grant the armed forces due respect and do not draw them into civilian squabbles, and civilian control will be advanced. Fitch returned the armed forces to their socio-economic setting, but maintained the attribution of autonomy that had been developed.[26] Survey data on the Ecuadorean armed forces unveiled distinct attitudinal predispositions within military factions. The rise of factions with interventionist propensities determined the motive to intervene, while developmental conditions (economic crisis or socio-political conflict) determined the opportunity to intervene.

The attention given to psychological dispositions led researchers to study the impact of military doctrine. Military doctrine explains the *raison d'être* of the armed forces and establishes military mission, broadly defined. Many researchers pointed to the growth of a 'national security doctrine' (NSD), in which the military redefined security to encompass development, and thereby justified the seizure of government during economic and social crises. NSD promoted a concept of 'total war' in which all the resources of society were to be mobilised and coordinated for development, all in the name of national security. A Manichaean perspective led to the view that any criticism of the developmental plans of the government was subversive activity and should be repressed.[27]

Researchers turned their queries from 'why do militaries intervene?' to 'why do militaries withdraw from power?' as military regimes began to fall throughout Latin America in the 1980s. Although some analysts emphasised economic development or societal opposition,[28] the growing appreciation of the military as an independent actor remained. Remmer constructed an institutional model to explain differences in regime durability.[29] Variances in the concentration of power and the integration of military personnel into government offices determine the capacity of a military regime to endure economic crises and stifle politicisation in the ranks. Thus, economic downturn or social unrest need not end a military regime if the armed forces could effectively respond to the crisis. Farcau also centralised the military with his concentration on the role of factions during democratic transition. He argued that 'competition between the factions was one of the guiding forces in the transition process, and the external factors of political and economic events were often simply tools that the factional leaders were able to use to enhance their positions' whether their intention was to continue military rule or to force a withdrawal.[30]

The retreat of military regimes in Latin America has not diminished the importance of civil–military studies. Horowitz notes that 'military power is sometimes consonant, other times contradictory, with democratic forms of rule', and hence 'the simple correlation of militarism and dictatorship, or conversely, civilianism and democracy, cannot be sustained by the available evidence'.[31] The question of civilian control is now central to civil–military studies. At first thought, the answer appears clear: civilians must extend direct control of all military affairs in order to guard against incursions into civilian affairs. Hence, according to Varas, military autonomy is the antithesis of civilian control.[32]

The portrait of a zero-sum game between military autonomy and civilian control is at first glance intuitively appealing and convincing in its simplicity. But as argued by Pion-Berlin, the proponents of this framework 'want to have it both ways. On the one hand, they lament the past, when civilian meddling in military affairs resulted in more fragmented and politicised armed forces .... On the other hand, these same scholars now criticise military insularity, arguing that it can only isolate the military', and allow the development of misunderstandings and anti-democratic orientations. Indeed, recent empirical studies highlight the costs of relentless civilian management in military affairs. In Venezuela, divide-and-rule tactics and fragmentations of the ranks have been used to promote civilian control since democratisation in 1959.[33] The strategy worked so long as socio-economic unrest was at a minimum, but the debt crisis and IMF-imposed austerity measures of the late 1980s reversed the Venezuelan economy. Disgruntled middle-ranking officers found an opportunity to mobilise factions within the fragmented command lines, and expressed themselves in the 1992 coups.[34] The Argentine military uprisings in 1987 and 1988 provide a second example. Norden documents how the rebellious officers were motivated less by political interests than by institutional concerns.[35] These revolts were not attempts to replace the standing Alfonsín government, rather, they were military responses to uncertainty in the human rights trials, budgetary cuts, the lack of training and provisions, media attacks on the prestige of the military institution, and inept military commanders. In the eyes of the military, they were defensive in nature and were a reaction to civilian derision of the professional interests of the military.

Hence, the simple zero-sum relationship between military autonomy and civilian control is illusive. Pion-Berlin notes that autonomy simply refers to independent behaviour and, as such, is not necessarily pernicious. The military, like all professions, must develop some autonomy if it is to attain the corporate identity which is so central to professionalisation.[36] Without this autonomy, the military is vulnerable to divisive political influences from civilians, more easily drawn into civilian disputes, and consequently more prone to intervention. This institutional autonomy is distinct from military political autonomy, which is inherently offensive in nature. Political autonomy refers to the desire of a military to usurp civilian authority and extend its decision-making outside core professional interests. With this distinction, we can see that military autonomy in areas such as junior-level personnel decisions, military education, training procedures and research institutions is not necessarily as detrimental as military autonomy in intelligence-gathering, internal security concerns or senior-level personnel decisions. Civilian recognition of institutional autonomy can promote civilian control as the armed forces reciprocate with respect for civilian authority in political affairs. Pion-Berlin has provided an important framework that distinguishes between institutional and political autonomy. Continued work in Latin American civil–military studies will examine how civilian authorities can best work to reduce political autonomy and gratify institutional autonomy, especially in a period of declining budgetary expenditures.[37]

The Latin American militaries and the road ahead

Distinct levels of professionalism, varying success in civilian control and an assortment of socio-economic settings mean that Latin American militaries will embark upon different roads in the future. Some will reintervene in politics, some will accept civilian supremacy, and others will remain defiant in the face of civilian rule. Nonetheless, there are some general processes at hand that present common challenges and opportunities for all countries in the region. These general processes are the end of the Cold War, continued economic globalisation, and democratisation.

For Latin America, the Cold War was not some distant confrontation between superpowers. Cold War concerns led the United States to intervene in the area at numerous levels and the armed forces of the region viewed communism as their primary threat. Guerrilla groups were consistently portrayed as agents of international communism. The anxiety over communist subversion was most brazenly manifest in the intervention-inducing NSDs. It is thus no surprise that the end of the Cold War has significant consequences for Latin American militaries, both in terms of US–Latin American relations and domestic civil–military relations.

During the Cold War, the containment of communism was the predominant security interest of the United States throughout Latin America. Whether policies called for development, counter-insurgency training, or military cooperation, they all shared this same goal. There existed only a difference in degree of influence between Central and South America. In the post-Cold War era, the United States has concentrated on a series of new security interests, and the region as a whole has been 'disaggregated'.[38] That is, as we move from one issue to the next, different countries rise and fall in importance to the United States. For example, drug interdiction is now a predominant concern for the United States, but the concern dominates relations with Bolivia, Colombia, Peru and Mexico.[39] These countries endure intense scrutiny annually, when the United States certifies drug interdiction efforts. 'Decertification' means a loss of bilateral aid. Latin American countries see two 'double standards' at work. First, the certification process places the onus of the drug trade on supply factors and completely ignores the demand for narcotics in the United States which drives drug production.[40] Second, many Latin American countries (especially Colombia and Mexico) tie difficulties in reducing drug production and trafficking to the flow of small arms from the United States. Hence, while the United States emphasises the supply-side efforts in the drug war, it does little to stem the supply of arms from within its own borders. Unfortunately, neither of these double standards is likely to disappear in the near future because they are driven by domestic concerns. The high visibility of the certification process allows US politicians to demonstrate to constituents a concern over the international drug trade, and any effort to restrict access to small arms meets the resistance of powerful interest groups such as the National Rifle Association.

According to the United States, drug production can best be curtailed with a 'militarisation' of the anti-narcotic effort, that is, the direct involvement of military units in such activities as crop eradication, destruction of drug-processing laboratories, and arrests of involved individuals.[41] As early as the November 1987 Meeting of American Armies, Latin American military leaders were united (except Chile, which was still under military rule) in their opposition. They argued that militarisation would encourage corruption and disrupt discipline in the ranks, and that it could lead to more 'dirty wars' against their own people, especially in such complex countries as Bolivia, where coca use is ingrained in the culture of the indigenous population.[42] In the 1990s, many countries have trained specialised or paramilitary military units for drug interdiction to shelter the military command structure from corruption (with varying degrees of success), but human rights abuses remain. Moreover, such efforts are nearly impossible in Colombia and Peru, where drug production and the guerrilla war are thoroughly intertwined.[43]

The United States also views many Caribbean countries as important to the anti-narcotics effort. The concern here is not drug production, but related activities of money-laundering, contraband and drug-transit operations. Specified countries of concern include Aruba, the Netherlands Antilles, the Bahamas, the Dominican Republic, Haiti and Jamaica. The United States has put pressure on Caribbean countries to sign on to the US Maritime and Overflight (shipriders) Agreement, which allows patrols and searches by the US Navy and Coast Guard, seizures and arrests by US law enforcement agencies, and overflights and forced landings of planes, all within the national boundaries signatories.[44] The 'agreement' represents a clear move by the United States to assume military and police functions within these states.

The end of the Cold War has also produced a change in the democratisation and human rights policy of the United States. Previously, the perceived threat of communist subversion led the United States to downplay criticisms of repressive activities. This was especially the case with Mexico and Central America, given their proximity. But in the 1990s, the United States has played a more active role, as demonstrated by its emphasis on human rights at the April 1998 Summit of the Americas[45] and willingness to scrutinise the demilitarisation and democratisation processes in Central America.[46] But once again, disaggregation is the key. Whether or not security concerns will be given greater priority than human rights is now determined on a case-by-case basis. Neighbouring Mexico seems to retain immunity from significant human rights abuse criticism, and the strengthening guerrilla movement in Colombia has recently led the United States to resume military aid, despite continuing human rights violations by the armed forces.[47]

One more security-related issue of importance to the United States that affects the region unevenly is that of the arms trade. The July 1997 decision by the United States to lift its ban on advanced conventional weapons systems will be most important to the larger, more professional armies of the Southern Cone and Brazil.[48] United States policy-makers argue that the new policy will allow civilian leaders to indulge better the professional interests of the armed forces and thus dampen their political concerns. If the case of Brazil is an indicator, there is little reason for such optimism. This country consciously pursued the 'indulge' strategy in the latter 1980s, but military influence over the defence sector proved to be 'a springboard for enhanced political influence on a broad range of issues'.[49]

The end of the Cold War has also produced significant changes within the Latin American militaries themselves.[50] Although the existence of border disputes and other regional contentions should not be overlooked, the end of the Cold War withdrew from the militaries their single most important and visible external threat – that of international communist expansion. An 'existential crisis' has developed for many Latin American militaries.[51] New missions, new roles, and new enemies are being sought as the militaries seek to justify their existence. New roles range from the growing Argentine involvement in UN peacekeeping missions[52] to the Honduran Green Battalions, which are charged with reforestation. Even the region's strongest military power seems to be eschewing traditional external roles. In the November 1996 publication of its new National Defence Plan, Brazil recognised as its main national security threats drug trafficking and international organised crime.[53] Although Latin American militaries have historically acted outside traditional defence roles, they are increasingly involved in infrastructure development, the construction of schools and hospitals, anti-smuggling operations, disaster relief, the provision of food and health services, environmental protection, drug interdiction and public order tasks.[54]

The rise of new military missions raises two concerns. The first emphasises the impact of expanded military operations on civilian organisations. In its zeal to assume new duties, the military may 'crowd out' civilians from activities they have traditionally fulfilled, or should fulfil. In Brazil, the military continues to play an important role in the technology sector, and the already expansive activities of the Ecuadorean army now include tourism and agro-industry.[55] In Chile, the military is strongly urging their 'Interior Borders' operation, which would involve it in infrastructure development and civic action projects to spur economic and population growth in the far north and south, and its eastern border with Argentina.[56] The military may often be the only organisation capable of fulfilling some demands on short notice, but governments must remain wary of the impact such involvement will have on the future development of the country if civilian organisations lose their chance to develop.

The second concern is mission creep, a phenomenon discussed above. One can refer to the case of Ecuador, where civic action in the hinterlands has allowed the military to impede the political activity of progressive church groups and indigenous movements, and to support the efforts of right-wing evangelical groups.[57] While 'crowding-out' and mission creep are relevant concerns, they ought not lead one to associate automatically internal missions with all things bad and external missions with all things good. In underdeveloped countries, and especially in the hinterlands, the military often represents the only capable organisation for the task at hand. And there is no intrinsic reason why a military should be more subservient to civilians just because it is involved in an external mission. The key is to ensure that in any operation undertaken, civilians remain in decisional control. Indeed, a recent study on military operations in South America shows that civilians have been about equally successful at controlling internally and externally based missions.[58]

Second, the future of Latin American militaries will also be affected by economic globalisation. The greater mobility of business means that states must compete for investment as never before. States have little choice but to reduce business taxes and inflationary government expenditures to lure investors. Hence, states too must 'downsize'.[59] Military budget reductions in a period of changing security relations demand serious thought about military reform, but civilians lack such expertise and militaries guard the status quo as best they can, fearing that reforms would open even greater cuts. In many countries the result is not that the military is learning to effectively cope with less, but that it is simply trying to do the same with less.[60] The resulting frustration could lead to reassertions of military power if the armed forces view their institutional interests as threatened.[61]

A second consequence of globalisation emerges from the related growth of regional economic integration schemes (see Chapter 4). In this context, there is a concern that economic integration may foment neo-nationalism within the armed forces.[62] It is the duty of a military to defend national territory, and there remain suspicions as well as existing border disputes among many Latin American militaries. Indeed, in Bolivia, when political leaders began to study the prospects of greater economic cooperation with Chile, military leaders moved to the verge of insubordination, with public announcements that territorial disagreements would have to be resolved before economic negotiations could take place.[63] Uruguayan military leaders reacted contentiously to the Argentine recommendation that military integration be incorporated into the regional economic organisation, the Mercosur, realising that they would be overwhelmed by the Argentine and Brazilian militaries. In what could be interpreted as a veiled threat, Uruguayan commanders publicised a document which stated that such a move would effectively remove territorial defence as its mission, and leave only vigilance against the threat of subversion.[64]

Third, democratisation will significantly affect Latin American militaries in the future. Democracy is now the norm in Latin America, and international efforts are being devised to restrain deviations. At the June 1993 meeting of the Organization of American States, a 'defence-of-democracy' resolution (no. 1080) called for the Permanent Council of the OAS to meet and coordinate a response to any interruptions in democratic procedures. Invocations of the resolution and official condemnations helped reverse the presidential attempt to dissolve Congress in Guatemala in May 1993. Similar international actions stimulated the democratic reopening of the Peruvian Congress after this body had been dissolved by President Fujimori in April 1992. In October 1991 the resolution led to economic sanctions after a military coup in Haiti.[65] Paraguay experienced the most recent threat to democracy in April 1996. Weary of the constant policy pressure from General Lino César Oviedo, President Juan Carlos Wasmosy requested that he resign. Oviedo's refusal was met by an outpouring of foreign pressure and social protest, enough to tip the balance against Oviedo.[66] The case illustrates how democracy itself provides certain defences against military intervention. Wary of the pendulum-like swings that characterise the region's democratic history, countries have no desire to stand idle when neighbouring democracies are threatened. The memory of authoritarianism was enough to push Paraguayans into the streets.

Research supports the view that democracy itself can reduce military prerogatives. The democratic game calls for all actors, be they societal or bureaucratic, to negotiate with politicians. As noted by Hunter, 'the more directly the armed forces impinge on the ability of legislators to enhance their electoral interests, the more likely members of Congress will be to enact such reforms to reduce military prerogatives'.[67] In her study of Brazil, Hunter found that politicians contested military supervision of labour policy to cater to the interests of labour unions, and reduced the military budget to shift resources toward politically lucrative pork-barrel projects. On the other hand, the military retained much of its autonomy to design security policy in the Amazon. Politicians not only lack an incentive to challenge the military in this area, but they also lack expertise. This highlights the fact that although democracy does provide inherent mechanisms to reduce military prerogatives, they are not enough. Greater communication between civilians and officers, civilian-based security research centres and more widespread exchange programmes between civilian and military schools are required if civilians are to develop the expertise necessary to challenge military prerogatives effectively and legitimately.[68] Lacking such knowledge, it is little surprise that in both Argentina and Uruguay, politicians have had greater success in reducing the military budget than in managing military reform.[69]

Conclusion

Latin American civil–military relations have reached a critical juncture. In a region in which military intervention and political influence had been the rule, civilian control and democracy have emerged as the new norm. But the combined impact of the end of the Cold War, economic globalisation, and democratisation does not provide clear signals for the future. Rather, it provides both challenges and opportunities. The end of the Cold War may bring an end to anxiety-ridden US policy, but it may also give rise to troubling new military missions. Economic globalisation legitimates reductions in military budgets, but it may also incite a military backlash. And although democracy provides important mechanisms to deepen civilian control, past democratic failures in the region confirm that democracy *per se* is not a sufficient barrier to military intervention in politics.

The key is to realise that political leaders stand apart from these conditions. Latin American leaders are found in a diverse range of socio economic settings, face various levels of military professionalisation and security challenges, and look back upon different histories of democratic experience and civilian control. The 'initial conditions' in one country may prove more conducive to democracy than those in another.[70] Political leaders must work within their own particular situation to magnify the positive aspects of the post-Cold War era, economic globalisation, and democratic procedures, and to counter or at least endure the negative aspects. The future of the Latin American militaries will proceed on a case-by-case basis, with political leaders centre stage.

Notes

1 The region stood well below world averages even during the military dictatorships of the 1970s. For 1978, military expenditures as a percentage of GNP (gross national product) average 1.7, and military expenditures as a percentage of central government expenditures average 7.4. The same figures for the developing world as a whole are 6.4 per cent and 21.6 per cent. The disparity holds throughout the 1970s. See US Arms and Disarmanent Agency (USACDA), *World Military Expenditures and Arms Transfers* (Washington, DC, USACDA, 1988), pp. 43–5.

2 International Institute for Strategic Studies, *The Military Balance 1997/98* (London, Oxford University Press, 1998), p. 298.

3 *World Military Expenditures.*

4 Cuba is undoubtedly ranked high here as well, but figures are unavailable. Argentina's ranking is largely an anomaly, produced by a severe economic crisis on top of a resolute policy of privatisation and government downsizing which was especially harsh in 1994.

5 *The Military Balance 1997/98*, p. 200.

6 In Guatemala, armed conflict has caused over 46,000 deaths since 1967, with 25 in 1996. In Peru, armed conflict has caused 28,000 deaths since 1980, with an estimated 50–200 in 1996. And in Colombia, over 30,000 have been killed since 1970,, with an estimated 400–1,000 killed in 1996 (*SIPRI Yearbook* 1997, p. 20). Significant guerrilla activity is currently found in Chile and Mexico as well, but nowhere near the level found in the three aforementioned countries.

7 For a good analysis and historical overview of the Peru–Ecuador dispute, see D. S. Palmer, 'Peru–Ecuador Border Conflict: Missed Opportunities, Misplaced Nationalism, and Multilateral Peacekeeping', *Journal of Interamerican Studies and World Affairs*, 39:3 (February 1997).

8 C. Blaiser, *The Hovering Giant: U.S. Responses to Revolutionary Change in Latin America, 1910–1985* (Pittsburgh, University of Pittsburgh Press, 1985).

9 For important analyses of human rights policies, see A. Barahona de Brito, *Human Rights and Democratization in Latin America, Uruguay and Chile* (New York and Oxford, Oxford University Press, 1997); J. Pasqualucci, 'The Whole Truth and Nothing but the Truth: Truth Commissions, Impunity and the Inter-American System', *Boston University International Law Journal*, 12:2 (1994); and L. Weschler, *A Miracle, a Universe: Settling Accounts with Past Torturers* (New York, Pantheon, 1990).

10 US Department of State (Bureau of Democracy, Human Rights, and Labor), *Reports on Human Rights Practices for 1997 – Latin America and the Caribbean* (Washington, DC, US Department of State, 30 January 1998).

11 R. Millet, 'The Central American Militaries', in A. F. Lowenthal and J. S. Fitch (eds.), *Armies and Politics in Latin America* (New York, Holmes and Meier, 1986).

12 A. Varas, 'Introducción', in *Cambios globales y América Latina: Algunos temas de la transición estratégica* (Santiago, CLADDE-FLACSO, 1993).

13 W. Hunter, 'Civil–Military Relations in Argentina, Chile, and Peru', *Political Science Quarterly*, 112: 3 (1997).

14 J. O. Maldifassi and P. A. Abetti, *Defense Industries in Latin American Countries* (Westport, Praeger, 1994).

15 Navies in Bolivia and Paraguay play an important and legitimate security role. Rivers often provide the primary means of transport in many areas owing to the thick jungle terrain and/or undeveloped infrastructure. Naval river patrol thus plays an important role in controlling migration, containing smuggling operations, and drug interdiction. River patrol, cartographic river exercises and involvement in the fishing industry are important operations for most South American navies.

16 E. Shils, 'The Military in the Political Development of the New States' and L. Pye, 'Armies in the Process of Political Modernization', both in J. Johnson (ed.), *The Role of the Military in Underdeveloped Countries* (Princeton, Princeton University Press, 1962).

17 J. Johnson, *The Military and Society in Latin America* (Palo Alto, Stanford University Press, 1964).

18 S. P. Huntington, *The Soldier and the State: The Theory and Politics of Civil–Military Relations* (Cambridge, MA, Belknap Press of Harvard University Press, 1957).

19 C. E. Welch, Jr, *Civilian Control of the Military: Theory and Cases from Developing Countries* (Albany, State University of New York Press, 1976), p. 31; also see A. Stepan, 'The New Professionalism of Internal Warfare and Military Role Expansion', in Lowenthal and Fitch (eds), *Armies and Politics*.

20 S. Huntington, *Political Order in Changing Societies* (New Haven, Yale University Press, 1968).

21 S. E. Finer, *The Man on Horseback: The Role Of the Military in Politics* (New York, Praeger, 1962; 1988).

22 J. Nun, 'The Middle-Class Military Coup', in C. Veliz (ed.) *The Politics of Conformity in Latin America* (London, Oxford University Press, 1967).

23 G. O'Donnell, *Modernization and Bureaucratic Authoritarianism: Studies in South American Politics* (Berkeley, University of California Press, 1973).

24 M. Janowitz, *The Professional Soldier: A Social and Political Portrait* (Glencoe, Free Press, 1960) and B. Abrahamsson, *Military Professionalization and Political Power* (Beverly Hills, Sage, 1972).

25 E. A. Nordlinger, *Soldiers in Politics: Military Coups and Governments* (Englewood Cliffs, Prentice-Hall, 1977).

26 J. S. Fitch, *The Military Coup d'Etat as a Political Process: Ecuador, 1948–1966* (Baltimore, Johns Hopkins University Press, 1977).

27 J. Comblin, *The Church and the National Security State* (New York, Orbin Books, 1979); G. Herrera Arriagada, *El pensamiento político de los militares* (Santiago, Centro de Investigaciones Socioeconómicas, 1981); D. Pion-Berlin, 'Latin American National Security Doctrines: Hard- and Softline Themes', *Armed Forces and Society*, 15:3 (Spring 1989).

28 J. M. Malloy and M. A. Seligson (eds), *Authoritarians and Democrats: Regime Transition in*

Latin America (Pittsburgh, University of Pittsburgh Press, 1987); E. Baloyra, *Comparing New Democracies: Transition and Consolidation in Mediterranean Europe and the Southern Cone* (Boulder, Westview, 1987).

29 K. Remmer, *Military Rule in Latin America* (Boston, Unwin Hyman, 1989).

30 B. W. Farcau, *The Transition to Democracy in Latin America: The Role of the Military* (Westport, Praeger, 1996), p. 83.

31 I. L. Horowitz, 'Militarism and Civil–Military Relationships in Latin America: Implications for the Third World', *Research in Political Sociology*, 1 (1985), pp. 79–80.

32 A. Varas, 'Military Autonomy and Democracy in Latin America', in A. Varas (ed.), *Democracy Under Siege: New Military Power in Latin America* (New York, Greenwood, 1989).

33 For example, the services lack an effective institution to coordinate negotiations with the government, military policy and budgetary requests are not unified within a single institution, and retirement regulations create rapid turnovers in the higher ranks.

34 C. L. Arceneaux, 'Democratic Consolidation or Deconsolidation?: Military Doctrine and the 1992 Military Unrest in Venezuela', *Journal of Political and Military Sociology*, 24:1 (1996).

35 D. Norden, 'Democratic Consolidation and Military Professionalisation', *Journal of Interamerican Studies and World Affairs*, 32:3 (October 1990).

36 D. Pion-Berlin, 'Military Autonomy and Emerging Democracies in South America', *Comparative Politics*, 25 (1992); also see Huntington, *The Soldier*.

37 David Pion-Berlin develops a compelling institutional framework to explain how civilian decisional authority varies by policy area (*Through Corridors of Power: Institutions and Civil–Military Relations in Argentina*, University Park, Pennsylvania State University Press, 1997) and Samuel Fitch has emphasised the importance of developing new democratically based military doctrines 'Military Professionalism, National Security and Democracy: Lessons from the Latin American Experience', *Pacific Focus*, 4:2, 1989.

38 D. Mares, 'Nuevas tendencias en la seguridad hemisférica: El aporte norteamericano', in *Cambios globales y América Latina: Algunos temas de la transición estratégica* (Santiago, CLADDE-FLASCO, 1993).

39 Studies on US international drug policy and the effect of drugs-trafficking on Latin American politics include B. M. Bagley and W. O. Walker III (eds.), *Drug Trafficking in the Americas* (Coral Gables and New Brunswick, University of Miami, North-South Center and Transaction, 1994) and E. Joyce and C. Malamud, *Latin America and the International Drug Trade* (New York, St Martin's Press, 1998).

40 K. E. Sharpe, 'The Military, the Drug War and Democracy in Latin America: What Would Clausewitz Tell Us'?', in G. Marcella (ed.), *Warriors in Peacetime: The Military and Democracy in Latin America* (Portland, Frank Cass, 1994).

41 P. Zirnite, 'The Militarization of the Drug War in Latin America', *Current History*, 97:618 (April 1998).

42 J. Malamud Goti, 'Los militares y la guerra contra las drogas', Nueva Sociedad, 130 (March–April 1994), p. 172.

43 N. Richani, 'The Political Economy of Violence: The War System in Colombia', *Journal of Interamerican Studies and World Affairs*, 39:2 (1997); J. Simpson, *In the Forests of the Night: Encounters in Peru with Terrorism, Drug-Running and Military Oppression* (New York, Random House, 1994).

44 A. T. Bryan, 'The New Clinton Administration and the Caribbean: Trade, Security, and Regional Politics', *Journal of Interamerican Studies and World Affairs*, 39:1 (1997), p. 107.

45 *Los Angeles Times*.

46 T. M. Leonard, *Central America and the United States: The Search for Stability* (Athens, University of Georgia Press, 1991). Sceptics of the new emphasis on human rights point to recent revelations of torture instruction in US training missions (*Washington Post*; 21 September 1996; *Washington Post*, 28 January 1997), and the reluctance of the United States to turn over government documents that implicate human rights abusers in Haiti, Guatemala and El Salvador because they may also implicate US intelligence agencies (D. McFayden, 'Consorting with

Tyrants', *NACLA Report on the Americas*, 30:1, July–August 1996; *Los Angeles Times*, 23 July 1992).

47 *Washington Post*, 27 December 1997.

48 *Los Angeles Times*, 8 October 1997.

49 K. Conca, 'Technology, the Military, and Democracy in Brazil', *Journal of Interamerican Studies and World Affairs*, 34:1 (Spring 1992), p. 142.

50 For a Latin American perspective, see C. Buchruker and O. A. Mendoza (eds.), *El nuevo orden mundial y nosotros* (San Juan, Argentina, CEILA-FLACSO, 1993).

51 C. Perelli, 'El nuevo ethos militar en América Latina: Las crisis existenciales de las fuerzas armadas de la region en los 90s', PIETHO Working Paper no. 80 (Montevideo, PIETHO, 1991).

52 While Latin American militaries have served in peacekeeping forces in the past, they are currently serving in greater numbers, and some countries are even modifying their defence doctrines to reflect international peacekeeping. Argentina leads in involvement, but the role is also important in Brazil, Chile, Uruguay and Venezuela. See A. L. Pala, 'The Increased Role of Latin American Armed Forces in UN Peacekeeping: Opportunities and Challenges', *Air Power Journal* (1995 Special Edition).

53 *The Military Balance 1997/98*, p. 199.

54 G. Aguilera, 'Fuerzas armadas, redefinición de seguridad y democracia en América Latina', *Estudios Internacionales*, 9:1–6 (1994).

55 M. Hens and J. A. Sanahuja, 'Seguridad, conflictos y reconversión militar en América Latina', *Nueva Sociedad*, 138 (1995), pp. 53–4.

56 W. Hunter, *State and Soldier in Latin America: Redefining the Military's Role in Argentina, Brazil, and Chile* (Washington, DC, United States Institute of Peace, 1996), pp. 32–3.

57 J. S. Fitch, 'Military Role Beliefs in Latin American Democracies: Context, Ideology, and Doctrine in Ecuador and Argentina', paper presented at the XIX International Congress of the Latin American Studies Association, Washington, DC, 28–30 September 1995, p. 77.

58 D. Pion-Berlin and C. L. Arceneaux, 'Of Missions and Decisions: Military Roles and Civilian Controls in South America', paper presented at the Annual Meetings of the Western Political Science Association, Los Angeles, 19–21 March, 1998.

59 R. Rosecrance, 'The Rise of the Virtual State', *Foreign Affairs*, 75:4 (1996).

60 F. Rojas Aravena, 'Procesos de decisiones en el gasto militar latinoamericano', *Fuerzas Armadas y Sociedad*, 9:3 (July–September 1994).

61 P. Franko, 'De Facto Demilitarization: Budget-Driven Downsizing in Latin America', *Journal of Interamerican Studies and World Affairs*, 36:1 (1994).

62 Hens and Sanahuja, 'Seguridad, conflictos', p. 57; A. Romero, *América Latina: militares, integración, y democracia* (Caracas, Instituto de Altos Estudios de América Latina, Universidad Simón Bolívar, 1989), pp. 27–33.

63 *Foreign Broadcast Information Services (FBIS)* 2/10/93, 6/28/93.

64 *FBIS* 12/11/91.

65 P. Hakim, 'The OAS: Putting Principles into Practice', *Journal of Democracy*, 4 (July 1993).

66 A. Valenzuela, 'Paraguay: The Coup that Didn't Happen', *Journal of Democracy*, 8:1 (1997).

67 W. Hunter, *Eroding Military Influence in Brazil: Politicians Against Soldiers* (Chapel Hill, University of North Carolina Press, 1997), p. 70.

68 A. Stepan, *Rethinking Military Politics: Brazil and the Southern Cone* (Princeton, Princeton University Press, 1988), pp. 128–33.

69 Pion-Berlin, *Through Corridors of Power*.

70 F. Agüero, *Soldiers, Civilians, and Democracy: Post-Franco Spain in Comparative Perspective* (Baltimore, Johns Hopkins University Press, 1995).

6

Guerrilla movements

PETER CALVERT

Guerrilla movements appeared from time to time in Latin America before 1917 and they continue to exist today after the fall of communism. This demonstrates conclusively (if proof were needed) that those who, like Ronald Reagan, believed that they were caused by an international communist conspiracy were wrong. It was Reagan's belief that 'the Soviet Union underlies all the unrest that is going on' and that 'If they weren't engaged in this game of dominoes there wouldn't be any hot spots in the world.'[1] The alternative explanation, favoured in the past by US liberals, was that the main cause of insurgency was social and economic deprivation, or, to put it more crudely, poverty.[2] The purpose of this chapter is to look at the origins, aims and strategies of recent Latin American guerrilla movements, to re-evaluate their causes and to look beyond the present context of democratisation and neoliberal economic reform programmes to examine how the trends and actors will evolve in the long term.

Guerrilla warfare originated in a war against foreign intervention and even in the 1980s, many of the best-known examples regarded themselves as national liberation movements. In the Western Hemisphere, this took the form of rallying opposition to the economic and political hegemony of the United States. However, locating guerrilla movements within a wider economic and social context is not easy. Economic conditions do not specifically require people to join guerrilla movements; though they may seem to leave insurgents little choice, in fact it is rare for individuals not to have the alternatives of accommodation (accepting things as they are and trying to make the best of it) or emigration. Joining an armed movement against one's own government involves such a high level of risk compared with the expected gains that at any time only a few have been prepared to try it. Hence, paradoxically, the leaders of a successful guerrilla movement usually come from the same political class as the government they are trying to overthrow rather than that of their followers.

Moreover, waging war, even on a limited level over a long period of time, requires an economic base. Guerrilla forces require not only leadership, personnel and goals to fight for, but also material facilities,[3] and a successful campaign requires a large amount of funds. Guerrillas fight outside the rules of war, often without uniform, and use surprise as a central strategy. As a result they are treated by governments and their security forces as terrorists or bandits. The main thing that protects them from prompt reprisals is their superior knowledge of the territory in which they operate. For both these reasons, they require the support of the local population, which is more likely to be forthcoming if they seem in some way to be representative either of them or of their desires.

A guerrilla movement will not survive for long, therefore, unless it is embeds itself in the social structure of the region in which it operates. Moreover, since its strategy is a strategy of weakness, not of strength, it must utilise to the full the political impact of its military actions. Almost invariably, such movements operate at two levels, the 'legal' and the 'illegal', or, to put it another way, movements which do not usually fail to survive the first stages of conflict. Parallel with the armed organisation, there is a much larger network of political supporters and sympathisers. It is through this network that funds are raised and arms and supplies purchased. Details of military counter-measures are also fed back, and the information which the armed command wish to reach the outside world disseminated for maximum effect. Insurgent movements may even conduct a form of diplomacy and receive a degree of recognition and support from overseas.

The complex relationship between these two levels and between leadership, personnel, goals and facilities can be illustrated well with reference to the principal guerrilla movements that have been active since 1945. The two that have been 'successful' are the 26 July Movement in Cuba and the Frente Sandinista de Liberación Nacional (FSLN, Sandinista National Liberation Front) in Nicaragua. In the 1990s, the main theatres of guerrilla conflict in Latin America have been Colombia, Peru and Mexico.

Cuba

Cuba, like Spain, had a past history of guerrilla warfare in its search for independence. The idea that guerrillas can successfully overthrow their own government derives more from the native Cuban tradition of insurgency than from any foreign model. Again, the leadership came from the educated middleclass, marginalised by the lack of opportunities under a dictatorial regime. Fidel Castro Ruz, the son of a well-to-do immigrant Galician planter, was an active student politician who took his inspiration from José Martí, the precursor of Cuban independence.[4] Following General Fulgencio Batista's open seizure of power in the previous year, Castro and some friends tried to raise a revolt by seizing the military barracks in Cuba's second city, Santiago, on 26 July 1953. While his fellow-conspirators were rounded up and shot, he was able to use his knowledge of the mountains in which he had often gone hiking[5] to evade pursuit for a few days before falling into the hands of a military patrol which happened to be led by a former school friend. Saved from immediate execution by this stroke of fortune, he was tried and sentenced to a short term of imprisonment, from which he was released in a general amnesty in 1955.

Castro took refuge in Mexico, and it was from there that he set sail for Cuba towards the end of 1956. On landing, he and his companions were ambushed by Cuban government forces. The 15 survivors took refuge in the mountains of the Sierra Maestra, where, largely by trial and error, they formed the nucleus of a guerrilla force. The ultimate success of the Cuban Revolution created a myth of the intrepid guerrilla, which Castro himself certainly did nothing to check. Few at the time noted that the ultimate success of the 26 July Movement was due as much to a mass urban insurrection by workers in Havana as to the guerrilla campaign in the countryside, nor that the rural recruits to the movement were plantation workers rather than the peasants of left-wing legend. As in other cases, the rural insurrection could not have survived but for the support of its civilian wing, the *llano*, dominated by urban groups until the failure of the general strike of 9 April 1957.

Other Latin American guerrilla movements of the 1960s, including one in Guatemala which was to last for more than thirty-five years.[6] were inspired both by Cuban example and by the account of them given in the writings of Castro's second-in-command, Che Guevara (1928–67). Shortly after victory he wrote his account of the campaign[7] and a short handbook for the guerrilla fighter.[8] The latter also enunciated three principles which were to be of much greater theoretical appeal. They were: (a) that popular forces can win a war against the army; (b) that it is not necessary to wait until all conditions for making revolution exist, but rather the insurrection can create them; and (c) that in underdeveloped America the countryside is the basic area for armed fighting.[9]

The theory of the *foco* (focus), a small group as the vehicle of social revolution, was elevated to a doctrine by a French-born Professor of the University of Havana, Régis Debray.[10] *Foquismo* had a profound influence on insurgents in Latin America and a lesser impact on the rest of the Third World well into the 1970s. But Guevara himself died in Bolivia in 1967, partly owing to the many organisational failures of his expedition,[11] but also because the theory's emphasis on action ignored political realities.[12] The land reform of the 1950s had been partial and incomplete, but at least it had given Bolivian peasants something. The bearded Cubans, regarded with deep suspicion by the local inhabitants, had nothing to offer them.[13]

Nicaragua

The death of Guevara and the destruction of his *foco* did not immediately end guerrilla warfare in Latin America, but by the beginning of the 1970s government responses had reduced the surviving groups to insignificant levels, even in

Guatemala, where they were already divided. The one major exception, the Sandinista movement in Nicaragua, attained power in 1979 as a result of quite exceptional circumstances: the fact that Anastasio Somoza Debayle had concentrated so much power and wealth in his own hands that he had totally alienated all major support groups except his National Guard.[14]

The Sandinistas were divided initially into three factions. One, the insurrectionist faction, favoured the traditional Marxist–Leninist strategy, based on organised labour. The second, the Guerra Popular Prolongada (GPP, Prolonged Popular War), followed a Maoist line, relying on a guerrilla campaign in the countryside. The third faction, the *Terceristas*, led by Daniel Ortega Saavedra, called for a cross-class alliance and it was they who won out, forming a broader alliance with non-Marxist opponents of the regime, to whom they were often related. Helped by the precipitating factor, anger that the money that had been subscribed for the victims of the Managua earthquake of 1974 had not reached its intended destination, they were able to put together a coalition with allies as unlikely as the Church[15] and the Conservative Party, and to fight their way into what was left of Managua in a two-pronged military campaign which enjoyed support from socialist Cuba, military–populist Panama and democratic Costa Rica.

The coalition victory was rapidly followed by the outbreak of civil war in neighbouring El Salvador. There the combined effects of immigration, economic recession and the total resistance of the authoritarian regime had stoked up pressures for change. But the oligarchy was not divided, and by immediately resorting to force it was able to resist the insurgents until massive quantities of US aid and support began to arrive. Meanwhile, Ronald Reagan had come to power in Washington and the Sandinista government of Nicaragua was reclassified as a 'renegade state,'[16] bent on regional domination by the support of the Salvadorean insurgency.

The US response was clandestine. The Fuerza Democrática Nicaraguense (FDN, Nicaraguan Democratic Force), usually known by their Sandinista nickname of 'contras' (for counter-revolutionaries), was set up by the CIA under a National Security Decision Directive, NSDD 17, signed by Reagan in November 1981, and led by Colonel Enrique Adolfo Bermúdez, who had entered the elder Somoza's National Guard in 1952. Its two separate, interrelated civil and military wings coincided with a major fault-line between the former national guardsmen and the civilians, disaffected members of the Nicaraguan elite. The seven members of the FDN directorate were paid US$84,000 a year, tax free, by the US government, an astonishing figure by Central American standards.[17]

The FDN, however, lacked local support except in the Miskito region on the Caribbean coast, whose English-speaking people resented what they saw as their forcible incorporation in the dominant Hispanic culture of revolutionary Nicaragua.[18] Though primarily a guerrilla force, most of its activity was directed towards 'soft' or 'economic' targets such as coffee mills and warehouses, with the aim of driving the country into bankruptcy. It is also believed to have been implicated in the assassination of municipal leaders and the attempted assassination of Edén Pastora ('Commander Zero'). It was not successful. Though its activities were wound down after the Iran–Contra scandal broke in 1986, the US Congress continued to provide funds for the contras and blocked all successive attempts at a negotiated peace. As Shuman and Harvey write: 'US support for the Contras set back democratisation and development of Nicaragua for at least a decade.'[19]

US pressure on Nicaragua only ended in 1990 when its people voted the Sandinistas out of office. In the aftermath of defeat, there was a keen debate about what had gone wrong.[20] However, the main cause seems to have been war-weariness and the hope among the electorate that, by voting for Violeta Barrios de Chamorro and Unión Nacional Opositora (UNO, National Opposition Union) which counted among its fourteen components the traditional Communist Party, the United States might be prepared to relax its grip and peace might come. But peace did not come. By 1993, as a result of the contra war and the new government's austerity programme, more than 70 per cent of the economically active population had no work.[21] The contras did not demobilise, some of the Sandinista groups took up arms in self-defence and it was not until 1996 that the last of the dissident groups roaming the countryside was formally disbanded. Meanwhile, peace agreements were worked out with the help and support of the UN in El Salvador in 1992 and Guatemala in 1997.

Colombia

Colombia has a strong and well-diversified economy with a significant manufacturing component. It was the only country in Latin America to weather the 1980s without having to reschedule its debts, and its Human Development Index (HDI) ranking considerably exceeds its ranking on GDP per capita.[22] At first sight it would seem an unlikely theatre for guerrilla warfare. In fact, however, its economy has been seriously distorted by the impact both of the drug culture and of the US-sponsored coca-eradication programme, and these are important elements in explaining the persistence of violence there.

Colombia is also a divided society, fragmented both by region and by the competing political allegiances which flared into La Violencia in 1948.[23] It has a history of well-established guerrilla movements dating back to the 1940s.[24] Three were formed or reorganised in the 1960s as part of the global effect of disagreement among the revolutionary Left. These were the armed wing of the Colombian Communist Party, known as the Fuerzas Armadas Revolucionarias de Colombia (FARC, Revolutionary Armed Forces of Colombia), founded in 1964 by a group of 46 men under the leadership of Manuel Marulanda Vélez, known as 'Tirofijo'; the Maoist Ejército Popular de Liberación (EPL, People's Liberation Army), founded in 1968, after the split between Moscow and Beijing; and the pro-Cuban Ejército de Liberación Nacional (ELN, National Liberation Army). A fourth originated as the armed wing of the Alianza Nacional

Popular (ANAPO, Popular National Alliance) of the former dictator, Gustavo Rojas Pinilla. With the collapse in 1970 of ANAPO's hopes of gaining power by election, in 1973 many of its members reformed as a guerrilla movement under the leadership of Alvaro Fayad. It was called the Movimiento de 19 Abril (M-19, 19 April Movement) after the date of the 1970 election which they claimed had been rigged against them.

The Colombian Communist Party's attitude towards the armed struggle, however, remained ambiguous and a move in 1967 for the FARC to link up with the pro-Cuban ELN came to nothing. It was not until 1983 that an alliance with both the ELN and M-19 was concluded. Given the way in which the so-called 'independent republics' of Marquetalia and El Chocó had succumbed to the Colombian army in the early 1960s, the FARC deliberately avoided the creation of regional centres and sought to hit at the government wherever it could. The ELN, founded in 1964 by a group of students under the leadership of Fabio Vázquez Castaño, achieved widespread publicity soon after its foundation by recruiting the dissident priest, Camilo Torres Restrepo (1929–66). Torres had left the priesthood in 1965 in order to work for the poor of Colombia and had subsequently decided that this could only be done through armed struggle. He was killed in his first skirmish and the political organisation he had founded, the People's United Front, broke up.

It was the M-19, however, that dominated the scene in the 1970s, and in 1976 a state of siege was reimposed, while successive Liberal governments struggled to contain the situation. By 1982, the Liberals had, however, become divided between the Centrists, who dominated the party organisation and the nominations, and the so-called 'New Liberals', who saw that greater commitment to change was necessary if the guerrillas were to be outflanked. Denied the Liberal nomination, which went to ex-president López Michelsen, the New Liberals ran their own candidate, Dr Luís Carlos Galán Sarmiento. The Conservative, Dr Belisario Betancur Cuartas, was the surprise winner.

Betancur, taking up the populist call for reform, had promised to negotiate with the guerrillas to bring them within the democratic system and gain peace. By the middle of 1985 he had been successful to a surprising extent and had gained the agreement in principle of three of the four major guerrilla groups, the FARC, M-19 and the EPL, to renounce violence and enter democratic politics. Though the FARC persisted in transforming themselves into a legal political party under the title of the Unión Patriótico (UP, Patriotic Union), the ranks of their activists were systematically decimated by assassination squads as they tried to prepare for the 1986 elections. The EPL withdrew from talks with the government in August 1985, and the ELN refused to enter into any agreement. In June 1987, despite the fact that the truce still formally held, the FARC resumed operations, with an attack on a military patrol.

It was, however, the M-19 who had ended any possibility of peace when in December 1985 they seized the Supreme Court Building on the Plaza Bolívar, only a block from the presidential palace, the Palacio de San Carlos. Eleven members of the Supreme Court were killed and the court building itself gutted by fire after the army had shelled it. In the aftermath the army established effective control of the political process from behind the scenes, and four years passed before the strategy of negotiation was resumed.

Since 1985 the ELN has emerged as one of Colombia's most active guerrilla groups. Under the leadership of another former priest, Manuel Pérez, over the next three years it carried out over a hundred attacks on the country's main oil pipeline, netting in the process a large sum in ransom money. A parallel campaign for the nationalisation of the oil industry, as in Venezuela in the 1970s, was also popular. However, it has been the rise in the later 1980s of Colombia as the world's major centre for the illegal trade in cocaine that has fuelled both the resumption of guerrilla activity and right-wing retaliation on the attempts of the Left to use this source of funds.

As a result, in January 1989 the government of President Virgilio Barco (1986-90) agreed to direct talks with the M-19, and a formal basis was established for a cessation of hostilities, leading to quadripartite talks between the government and the three main guerrilla groups. In congressional and municipal elections in March 1989 the Liberals won 72 seats in the Senate as against the Conservatives' 41 and the UP's 1. The sole UP Senator, Bernardo Jaramillo Ossa, was killed at El Dorado airport, Bogotá, by a 16-year old hired assassin soon afterwards. By April 1989 a spectacular increase in drug-related violence had already begun, some (but not all) of which had significant political overtones. The assassination of the governor of Antioquia, Antoni Roldan Betancurt, a strong advocate of human rights and opponent of the drug barons (4 July), was followed on 18 August by the killing at a political rally of the immensely popular Senator Galán, who had been expected to be the Liberal standard-bearer in the 1990 presidential elections. It was Senator Galán's death that demonstrated the critical pass into which the government had drifted and finally provoked the previously hesitant President to proclaim the drug cartels the government's major target. Within days, on 5 September, the US President, George Bush, reinforced this new-found decisiveness by announcing a massive programme of aid to Colombia to counter drug production and trafficking. The drug cartels responded by declaring open war on the government, giving immediate evidence of their formidable capacity to strike at will.

Despite this, the M-19 signed a new peace treaty with the government on 9 March 1990, formally completing the peace process begun in January 1989, and participated for the first time in the presidential elections of 1990. History repeated itself, as their candidates were gunned down. The 39-year-old M-19 leader and presidential candidate of the new left-wing alliance, Convergencia Democrática (CD, Democratic Convergence), Carlos Pizarro León Gómez, was shot dead by a contract killer while on a commercial flight from the capital to Barranquilla on 26 April, and in the two weeks before the election on 27 May 37 died and 324 were wounded in incidents of violence. The Liberals won decisively. However, a proposition to establish a Constituent Assembly to reform the Constitution of 1886 achieved overwhelming support later in the year, and at elections for the Assembly held in a calm atmosphere on 9 December, M-19 members or sympathisers emerged as the largest grouping, though well short of a majority over the 'dinosaurs' of the two traditional parties. Meanwhile, both the FARC and the ELN had regrouped and remained active.

The presidency of César Gaviria Trujillo (1990–94) coincided with the collapse of communism and again the time looked favourable for dialogue with the revolutionary Left. At first Trujillo had some success. Under a decree of 22 January 1991, the Partido Revolucionario de Trabajadores (PRT, Revolutionary Workers' Party) laid down its arms, and on 1 March the EPL was reborn as the Esperanza, Paz y Libertad (EPL, Hope, Peace and Liberty) party. In return it received two nominated seats in the Constituent Assembly, which met for the first time on 5 February with 73 members, of whom 70 were directly elected. To coincide with the opening of the Assembly the FARC and the ELN, now linked by a joint directorate, the Simón Bolívar Guerrilla Coordinating Board (CNGSB), launched a new nation-wide offensive. In the first elections under the new Constitution, the Alianza Democrática (AD, Democratic Alliance)/M-19 obtained 9 seats in the Senate and 15 in the House, though its support, at 10 per cent, was well down on its 1990 figure. It joined the government but withdrew after the government broke off peace talks in March 1992.

In June 1994, Ernesto Samper Pizano (PL), a 43-year-old economist who had previously served as Development Minister, was elected President with just 50.37 per cent of the vote. His political opponents were believed to be behind strongly denied reports that his campaign had been financed by the Cali cartel.[25] In September and October indications came from both the FARC and the ELN that they were prepared to enter into dialogue, and on 17 November, the President stated that his government was prepared to enter into peace talks without preconditions. Since then the FARC and the ELN have been able to wage a campaign on two fronts, varying their tactics by sabotage and kidnapping key figures. Dialogue has continued, but three factors have prevented it reaching a peaceful conclusion.

First, President Samper, weakened by his constant association with the Cali cartel, has lacked the authority to deal either with the guerrillas or with the army. Other members of his Cabinet have also been the subject of suspicion: Guillermo González Mosquera, appointed in February 1997 to the key post of Defence Minister, was forced to resign a month later when evidence was circulated that in 1989 he had accepted a campaign contribution from a leading drug trafficker.[26]

Second, the guerrillas have not been defeated, so the army still believes in the possibility of a 'military solution'. It has been most reluctant to accept the need for a dialogue, though this is hardly surprising, given the history of failed initiatives to incorporate the guerrillas in regular politics. Meanwhile, the army continues to suffer casualties; in January 1998 three senior officers were retired after a successful FARC attack killed 10 soldiers.[27]

Third, neither the FARC nor the ELN have any difficulty recruiting supporters. The main reason is the US-sponsored coca-eradication programme, which is deeply unpopular among the Colombian peasantry and which has generated all-out resistance, discreetly aided by the coca barons. In 1995 popular protests spread across the southern departments of Guaviare, Putumayo, Caquetá, Meta and Cauca, leading to the deaths of at least 18 people in clashes with police and troops. Though agreement was reached with the Putumayo growers, the President insisted that violence in Caquetá was fuelled by 'hidden interests' and talks were suspended on 23 August, while both protests and guerrilla violence continued at a high level.

Peru

The military–populist regime of General Juan Velasco Alvarado carried out significant social reforms in Peru between 1968 and 1975. These were, however, reversed to some extent by his successor, and the civilian governments of the 1980s had to contend both with the legacy of debt and the effects of the El Niño weather system. After four decades, in 1980 the Alianza Popular Revolucionaria Americana (APRA, Popular American Revolutionary Alliance) finally elected a President, who promised land reform and refused to accept the dictates of the international financial community. Within months his government was bankrupt and the challenge to it stronger than before.

Two revolutionary movements have featured in Peru in the past decade, and both have used guerrilla tactics as part of their repertoire. The Communist Party of Peru – Shining Path (PCP–SL, Partido Comunista del Perú–Sendero Luminoso), better known simply as Sendero Luminoso (SL), is, as its name suggests, a splinter group of the Partido Comunista Peruano (PCP, Peruvian Communist Party). After a split in 1964, Abimael Guzmán first joined the Maoist PCP-Bandera Roja (Red Flag) and then in 1970 led a faction dedicated to armed struggle out of its youth movement, recruiting a considerable number of his students at San Cristóbal de Huamanga University in Ayacucho as 'weekend guerrillas'. Guzmán, alias 'Presidente Gonzalo', was 'a middle-class, Spanish-speaking, Kantian philosopher from Arequipa'.[28] The name he chose for his faction, 'the shining path', is taken from a phrase of the Peruvian Marxist writer, José Carlos Mariátegui (1895–1930). Philosophically the movement (which went underground in 1977) has taken a very hard line and rejected all forms of collaboration, either with government or non-Marxist opposition. Strategically it has pursued the Maoist path of the GPP, laying great emphasis both on secrecy and on building a secure base in the department of Ayacucho and surrounding areas. Though the Peruvian peasantry had already been mobilised in the 1960s,[29] the SL was an urban-based movement dedicated to the total restructuring of Peruvian society.[30]

The SL opened its campaign on 17 May 1980, the day Peru returned to civilian government after 12 years of military rule, with a carefully planned campaign designed to emphasise its ability to strike both in its rural heartland of the department of Ayacucho but also in the cities. In what became a trademark operation, electricity pylons were blown up, plunging Lima into darkness. Initially care was taken to avoid open confrontation with the armed forces, concentrating instead on building up a 'people's revolutionary army', estimated to number up to 3,000 activists, by sabotage, kidnapping and the assassination of local officials.[31]

Every effort was made to disrupt the presidential elections in April. However, these went ahead, and the second phase of the SL's campaign began when the new APRA President, Alan García, offered them an amnesty. The offer was not accepted: indeed, a striking feature of the movement at this early stage is the rarity and brevity of public statements issued in its name. Sporadic violence continued, until on 18 June rebels inspired mutinies in three prisons, Lurigancho in the suburbs of Lima, and El Frontón and Santa Bárbara at Callao. To recapture the prisons, troops using tanks, heavy weapons and explosives killed over 250 inmates, 'at least' 100 of them, according to the President, massacred at Lurigancho after they had surrendered. He promised to arrest those responsible, but, despite a Lima court detaining General Jorge Rabanal, commander of the armoured division at Lurigancho, the President conspicuously laid the blame for the massacres on the police, although they were part of the military command structure and acted throughout under military orders.

Though the loss of key elements in the SL's command structure and the fear of a new military government seemed at first to have resulted in a substantial reduction in the scale, if not the number, of its attacks, a reprisal attack on a tourist train at Cuzco, which killed 7 and wounded at least 28, was a reminder of the movement's continued strength in the provinces. In October 1986, 39 insurgents were killed, including the reputed number three in the SL hierarchy. But the assassination of Admiral Gerónimo Cafferata on 14 October confirmed its continuing power, and the state of emergency in Lima was renewed. Meanwhile, impatience at the slow fulfilment of APRA's promised land reform led to a wave of spontaneous land occupations in the southern highlands.[32]

In 1987, having established control of the Upper Huallaga Valley,[33] the SL began to benefit from the huge profits of Peru's illegal narcotics trade. Despite the creation by the government of a unified military command structure in April, the movement's strategy continued to be directed at either dividing the armed forces or provoking a military coup, but this did not happen. Instead police captured Guzmán's deputy and military commander, Osman Morote, in early June 1988, although, as Taylor points out, this was only the second leading member of the organisation to be captured since it began operations, and in both cases it seemed to be more by accident than by design.[34]

Certainly the evidence is that the security forces, confronted by a well-funded, well-armed enemy, who knew more about them than they did about it, were thoroughly demoralised. The discovery of 5 bodies in an unmarked grave during the previous month confirmed the massacre by soldiers of 28 peasants in Cayará. However, President García, who had initially been critical of such excesses, indirectly defended the armed forces, who had been increasingly insistent that he should do so. The government, which had extended the state of emergency to cover Ayacucho, five neighbouring provinces and Lima itself, was also thought to be behind the emergence of a right-wing counter-terrorist group, the so-called Commando Rodrigo Franco. Amnesty International confirmed that there had been a sharp increase in reported cases of torture and unlawful killing in the Andean emergency zone since 1987, and even government sources admitted in 1988 that between 11,500 and 15,000 were known to have died since 1980, and since 1982 at least 3,200 people were said locally to have 'disappeared'. The government lacked an effective intelligence organisation and did nothing for the highland peasantry. Instead, they saturated the highlands with troops who, by operating a 'shoot to kill' policy, were more effective recruiters for the SL than they were themselves. Indeed, given the SL's use of the 'armed strike' (that is, coercing peasants into support by threatening to shoot them), they were lucky that the García administration was so incompetent.

On 26 July 1988 a Lima daily newspaper published an interview with Abimael Guzmán, which was accepted to be the first public statement of the 53-year-old revolutionary leader's views in 10 years. Following precisely the line laid down by Mao Zedong,[35] Guzmán called for a new, third stage in the struggle. 'Our process of the people's war has led us towards the apex', he claimed. 'We have to prepare for insurrection, which will be the taking of the cities.' By November, when the power lines between Lima and the Mantaro hydroelectric plant in the central Sierra were severed and a state of emergency was declared in Junín, seven more departments were under martial law and the insurgents seemed well on their way to their objective. They were by then active not only in their heartland of Ayacucho and in the cities, but in Cuzco, Puno, the Upper Huallaga Valley, Junín and surrounding departments, and even in Ancash in the north.[36]

On 10 May 1989 the SL declared an 'armed strike' in the Central Andean departments of Junín, Pasco and Huancano, and both the violence and the criticism of President García spread rapidly. Later in the year SL tactics focused on the disruption of the municipal elections on 12 November. A daring demonstration in the heart of Lima on 1 November became a hour-long gun battle in which several passers-by were casualties, and led President García to place the capital itself under martial law. In the countryside, where more than fifty mayors had been killed and many candidates had in consequence withdrawn, it proved impossible to hold elections in some sparsely populated areas.

Despite all efforts to prevent them, however, presidential elections were held in 1990, resulting in the unexpected election of a political unknown, Alberto Fujimori, a businessman of Japanese descent, running on a populist platform of pure change (Cambio 90). Lacking as he did a majority in either house of Congress, he formed a government of national unity of non-aligned and independent members, with military figures in the key positions of Defence and Interior, under a Prime Minister, from the conservative Acción Popular (AP, Popular Action Party), and requested emergency legislative powers for 180 days to tackle the crisis of hyperinflation compounded by an escalating guerrilla war. Aiming to break the alliance of drug trafficking and insurgency, his government soon reversed its initial refusal to accept US money for crop substitution, and by the end of the year the privatisation of the banking system initiated a programme of free market reforms, which soon brought the approval of the international financial community. In 1995 the President was able to announce that, under the Brady Plan, agreement had been reached with Peru's 250 creditor banks. The agreement, for $10,000 million of commercial debt, would enable a new agreement to be made with the Paris Club and the IMF.

Meanwhile, in the first weeks of the new government constitutional guarantees were suspended over some two-thirds of the country. The Servicio de Inteligencia del Ejército (SIE, Army Intelligence Service) was reorganised and, under the leadership of a close confidant of the President, Vladimir Montesinos, began to bring results.[37] Not long afterwards, Amnesty International claimed that under the Fujimori government 120 people had already 'disappeared', making a total of some 3,700 since 1980. Soon the government's austerity programme began to meet widespread resistance and on 5 April 1992, with the aid of a well-executed military coup, President Fujimori suspended the Constitution and dissolved Congress and the judiciary.[38]

However, the results were not at all in accordance with the SL's strategy of 'the intensification of contradictions'. In September, after 12 years of conflict which cost some 23,000 lives, Guzmán himself was arrested. Though the President immediately claimed this justified his dictatorial measures, Guzmán was not captured by the army but found by efficient police work in a 'safe house' in Lima, where he was seized, together with his alleged 'number Two', Elena Reboredo Iparaguirre, and 19 other members of the Central Committee. The decisive clue, it was reported, had been the discovery in a dustbin of used bottles of the unusual medicine Guzmán used for psoriasis. After he had been exhibited like an animal in a steel cage to the press on 24 September, he was tried secretly at La Punta naval base at Callao and sentenced to life imprisonment.[39]

In the ensuing months many of Guzmán's key followers were also captured, though violence continued in the rural areas and much of the country continued to be under martial law. On 1 October the President claimed before the UN that Guzmán, from the naval prison at Callao, had made a formal offer of peace. Subsequently a major split was reported in the movement between its imprisoned leader and armed militants led by Oscar Ramírez Durand ('Feliciano'). Casualties had fallen to some 300 in 1993 and 6,000 former guerrillas surrendered under the government's 'Law of Repentance' before it expired on 31 October 1994. On 28 July 1994 the President had claimed that terrorism had been defeated.

In Peru, economic crisis had played into the hands of the guerrillas in the 1980s. But with their defeat, Fujimori, with his classless background, proved adept at wooing the peasant vote and in April 1995, in an election marked by an exceptionally high turnout, he became the first Peruvian president to be re-elected for a consecutive term. In an election marked by a high turnout, he obtained between 60 and 70 per cent of the vote in the shanty towns of Lima and in the poverty-stricken central and southern highlands.[40]

In fact, terrorism had not been defeated, even if by 1996 the SL no longer represented a serious challenge to the government. A rival group, the Movimiento Revolucionario Túpac Amaru (MRTA, Túpac Amaru Revolutionary Movement), founded by Luis Varese Scoto, had begun an armed campaign in 1984 with the seizure of a radio station. As its name suggests, it was a pro-Cuban movement which sought to capitalise on Peru's indigenous tradition of nationalism and resistance to foreign domination, rather than to present itself as a new version of Marxism. It was, in effect, the armed wing of Varese's Partido Socialista Revolucionario (PSR, Revolutionary Socialist Party). The truce which it had declared unilaterally at the accession of Alan García in 1985 was soon lifted, but the movement remained relatively small, clashing on occasions with the SL, against which the main military effort was directed. On 28 April 1989 the army successfully ambushed a MRTA cell near the village of Molinos in the Department of Junín, killing 62. Soon afterwards, its leader, Víctor Polay Campos ('Comandante Rolando'), was arrested but escaped from custody in July 1990; he was rearrested in San Borja in June 1992. Following the collapse of the SL, several MRTA leaders were arrested in 1995, including Cistero García Torres ('Comandante Ricardo'). Two bombs which exploded near a police station on 26 July 1996 were also attributed to the MRTA. By the end of the year a total of 400 suspects were held on a variety of charges many in sub-human conditions, in tiny, damp and overcrowded cells.

The well-planned action of 17 MRTA guerrillas in seizing the Japanese Embassy with 490 hostages, including the President's own brother, on the night of the Emperor's birthday, 17 December 1996, was a bold attempt to reverse this situation. It came as a complete surprise to President Fujimori. Refusing either to negotiate or to admit any degree of responsibility for the welfare of the hostages, the President watched as, over the next two weeks, several batches were released. At year-end only 81 of those most closely connected with the government, the security forces and the President himself remained in the heavily armed compound. The guerrilla leader, Néstor Cerpa Cartolini ('Comandante Huerta'), held a press conference inside the compound to reiterate his refusal to yield his central demand, the release of all 400 MRTA prisoners. Five rounds of talks were held between him and a government negotiator between 11 and 24 February. The talks were broken off on 7 March when the guerrillas, detected tunnelling activity and, despite successful efforts by the Japanese government to find a country willing to accept the guerrillas both they and the government refused to agree to a deal. On 19 March both the Interior Minister and the national police chief resigned. Their replacements, General César Saucedo Sánchez and General Fernando Diaderas, took the decision to launch the carefully planned attack on 22 April 1997. Lulled into overconfidence, four of the guerrillas, including Cerpa himself, were killed outright when a mine was exploded under the basement where they were playing football. Commandos then burst into the building from all sides. Two soldiers died and one of the 72 hostages, Supreme Court Judge Carlos Giusti, died shortly afterwards of a heart attack, but all the guerrillas were summarily shot, including both those who tried to surrender and those who had been wounded. President Fujimori was again triumphant, and it seemed unlikely that the MRTA would be able to carry out its threat of reprisal.

Mexico

On New Year's Day 1994, the previously unknown Ejército Zapatista de Liberación Nacional (EZLN, Zapatista National Liberation Front) seized control of three towns in the southern Mexican state of Chiapas: Ocosingo, Altamirano and Las Margaritas. They also attacked a fourth, the historic tourist site San Cristóbal de las Casas, where they ransacked the Palace of Justice and set fire to it before retreating into the mountains. The former State Governor, retired general Absalón Castellanos Domínguez, was seized at his cattle ranch, bundled into a truck with two of his cows, and taken with them as a hostage. In their manifesto, 'Today we say enough!', the EZLN made the reason clear. The regional bosses (of whom Domínguez was the most hated) had, they said, stolen their lands from them. 'We possess nothing, absolutely nothing,' it said, 'no home, no land, no work, no education.'[41]

The operation had been deliberately timed to coincide with Mexico's entry into the NAFTA, which the insurgents believed would further increase their misery. Within a week, the guerrillas had extended their control to the towns of San Miguel and Guadalupe Tepeyac, the country was on nation-wide alert, a fifth of Mexico's army had been deployed to the region and more over 145 people had been killed, some by summary execution and other atrocities. On 10 January President Carlos Salinas de Gortari reshuffled his cabinet, dismissing his Secretary of the Interior (*Gobernación*), José Patrocinio González Garrido, a former governor of Chiapas. Two days later he accepted the urgent advice of the Bishop of San Cristóbal, Monseñor Samuel Ruiz, called a truce, and appointed as negotiator Manuel Camacho Solís, the Secretary of External Relations, who had been passed over for the presidential nomination in 1993. Over the next few weeks, while the truce held, the negotiations continued.

The choice of the name 'Zapatista' for the new movement was significant. Though the celebrated Mexican agrarian leader had no connection with the state, his name had long been used by the ruling Partido Revolucionario Institucional (PRI, Revolutionary Institutional Party) to legitimise its near-monopoly of political power. Chiapas was the poorest State in Mexico and the insurgents wanted investment, land reform, and the opportunity to choose their own political leaders.[42] Chiapas not only suffered from the general economic crisis of Mexico in the 1980s; bypassed by the land reform of the 1930s, the indigenous population suffered particularly acutely from the impact of state-directed modernisation.[43] A third of households had no electricity and 40 per cent had no running water. The state ranked last on major indicators of literacy (which is, as ever, measured by literacy in Spanish). It was also the state from which there have long come the most persistent accusations of violations of human rights, especially the use by landowners of *pistoleros* (gunmen) to drive the Indians off their traditional lands, in conjunction with the army and the police.

Though the movement demanded traditional rights for the native Indian population, however, its charismatic leader, ski-masked 'Subcomandante Marcos', made use of portable computers and the Internet to circumvent government blocks on communications. Asked about the reasons for opening the armed struggle in Chiapas in an interview in March 1994, 'Marcos', who was actually Rafael Sebastián Guillén Vicente, a university teacher and son of a well-to-do Tampico furniture dealer, was quite frank:

> The project of preparing a war, an armed struggle, means that you have to think everything through. You have to put together an army in conditions of secrecy. You're not going to form an army just by acting like other guerrillas; rather, you have to prepare before acting. You need geographic conditions of isolation, security, depopulated zones, places where you won't be detected.
>
> In addition to this, you need areas that are propitious for political work. The panorama narrows at that point, but there continue to be various options in states such as Oaxaca and Guerrero. Then the other element of our army appears, the other initiators: the indigenous campesinos from here who got to know some of the compañeros that began this. They said to us: 'why don't you come here?; here there are mountains where you can go; if we are fucked up, it's precisely because nobody comes here.' So it was these campesinos who proposed Chiapas, and so this is how we ended up here.[44]

During the summer, while the government was preoccupied with the presidential election campaign, there was an effective stand-off between insurgents and the army, and parts of Chiapas deteriorated into near-anarchy. On the eve of his inauguration on 8 December, governor-elect Robledo offered to resign if the FZLN laid down its arms. However, he did not do so and on 19 December the guerrillas, who by this time controlled about one-fifth of the state, demonstrated their ability peacefully to slip through the army cordon by erecting roadblocks, proclaiming 'liberated zones' and occupying the town of Simojovel and, it was claimed, 37 other municipalities.

The government had advance warning of this move. On 21 December it tried to take advantage of it to devalue the new peso while placing the blame on the guerrillas. However, within 24 hours, while fresh troops and tanks moved into place around the guerrilla bases, the devaluation had revealed the fundamental weakness of the Mexican economy, its dependence on short-term loans. As capital flooded out of the country, the government lost control of the financial situation. The peso fell to unprecedented depths, precipitating a major crisis of confidence among investors. By contrast, the rebels appeared to gain legitimacy. In these circumstances the new president, Ernesto Zedillo Ponce de León, prudently decided to resume negotiations on the rebel demands.[45]

Dialogue continued in the early weeks of 1995, though sporadic attacks on the insurgents continued in parallel and it was not always clear how much the army was in fact following government orders or acting on its own initiative. The Zapatistas attracted great international attention with a well-publicised Continental Meeting for Humanity and against Neoliberalism held in La Realidad on 4–8 April 1996. A further 'international encounter' held between 27 July and 3 August was attended by some 3,000 sympathisers from 43 countries.[46] On 29 August talks were again broken off, the EZLN alleging government failure to honour previous accords, but one of their leaders was given safe conduct to attend a conference of indigenous peoples in the capital in October. Meanwhile, a series of disclosures suggested that the Salinas administration had been much more closely involved with major drug interests than had ever been suspected at the time.

Talks between the government and the EZLN insurgents were resumed following conciliatory statements by the latter in January 1997. Seven alleged guerrillas had been released on 3 January after a judge overturned their convictions for terrorism. In August troops were withdrawn from three areas of Chiapas, and on 12 September unarmed Zapatista guerrillas participated without incident in a public rally in the capital. Meanwhile, however, the killing of Indians by paramilitary groups in Chiapas continued, leading to fears that the government was in fact masking its real intentions to seek a 'military solution'. When 45 Tzotzil were massacred in a single attack by right-wing paramilitaries on 22 December at Acteal, near San Cristóbal de las Casas, the government denied responsibility, but both the Interior Minister and the state Governor were forced to resign.[47] The EZLN high command was quick to voice its suspicions that a covert military occupation of the entire state was under way and the official report published on 23 January 1998 confirmed that the police had abetted the killings.[48]

On 28 June 1996, meanwhile, a new and potentially much more threatening guerrilla group, the Ejército Popular Revolucionario (EPR, People's Revolutionary Army), had announced its presence in the State of Guerrero with an armed demonstration in the village of Atoyac de Alvarez. Guerrero had a history of insurgency dating back to the years of independence and it was in this village that an earlier guerrilla leader, Lucio Cabañas, had been killed by the army in 1974. The army responded with the deployment of some 10,000 heavily armed troops with intelligence support, it was said, from France, Israel, Peru and the USA. On 30 August thousands more troops were deployed in southern states after the EPR, on the two previous days, had staged coordinated attacks on seven widely spaced sites in Oaxaca, Guerrero and the State of Mexico, and there were reports of numerous skirmishes and some arrests.[49] A statement published in the *Excelsior* newspaper called for the armed overthrow of President Zedillo's government, but the EPR, having admitted that it lacked the resources to defeat the army, called a temporary ceasefire on 25 September to allow local elections to take place in the state.[50]

Following a six-month lull, in May 1997 fresh clashes between EPR guerrillas and security forces were reported from Guerrero, and on 27 May 3 soldiers died and 10 were wounded in two attacks at Atoyac de Alvarez; the guerrillas, however, again announced a unilateral truce for the period of the elections. In the meantime the position of the Zapatistas has been gradually eroded, as much by the continuing economic penetration of the state as by creeping conquest by the armed forces. Massive forest fires have devastated the Lacandón jungle, depriving the guerrillas of their traditional refuge.

Conclusion

Guerrilla activity, therefore, continues in Latin America, and despite the many formidable advantages of governments it is too early to say that their day is over. Throughout Colombia, Peru and Mexico, economic crisis and structural adjustment have disarticulated both urban and rural society, offering insurgent movements a ready-made mass of disaffected supporters. However, the movements themselves are very different, and in the case of the SL in particular, the actions of individuals on both sides have clearly altered the outcome.

Their impact on the political process has also varied with local conditions. In Colombia a weak government has been unable either to defeat the guerrillas or to negotiate a settlement. In Peru, President Fujimori has built a successful political career on a combination of market-led reform and hardline opposition to terrorism. In Peru, after initial blunders, the government of President Zedillo has acted with great caution, but the threatened link-up between the movements in Chiapas and Guerrero has not happened, and with continuing movement towards democratisation, a national insurrection is not on the cards.

Increasing demands on guerrilla resources have emphasised the need to raise substantial funds, and in all recent cases in Latin America drug interests have been involved on one side or the other (or indeed, as in Colombia, both). And the increasing pressure on Latin America's very scarce land has exacerbated the situation, institutionalising conflict between government and rural workers. However, the modern movements are poised uneasily between the need for rural support and the growth of Latin American populations, where the real power is and where they are most vulnerable. It is hardly necessary formally to authorise the use of paramilitaries and 'death squads' since (it seems clear) there are plenty of volunteers. Given that none of the movements discussed above has entirely disappeared, it can safely be expected that guerrilla movements will continue to influence Latin American politics for some years to come. However, as Che Guevara himself believed, they are unlikely to be successful as long as the possibility of change by peaceful means remains open.[51]

Notes

1 R. Dallek, *Ronald Reagan: The Politics of Symbolism* (Cambridge, MA, Harvard University Press, 1984), p. 141, quoting from *The Wall Street Journal*.

2 L. Schoultz, *National Security and United States Policy towards Latin America* (Princeton, Princeton University Press, 1987).

3 P. Calvert, *A Study of Revolution* (Oxford, Clarendon Press, 1970), p. 4.

4 S. Balfour, *Castro* (London, Longman, 1992), pp. 9, 42.

5 *Ibid.*, p. 23.

6 M. González, 'The Culture of the Heroic Guerrilla: The Impact of Cuba in the Sixties', *Bulletin of Latin American Research*, 3:2 (1984), is critical.

7 E. Che Guevara, *Reminiscences of the Cuban Revolutionary War* (London, Allen and Unwin and Monthly Review Press, 1968).

8 E. Che Guevara, *Guerrilla Warfare* (New York, Monthly Review Press, 1967).

9 *Ibid.*, p. 2.

10 R. Debray, *Revolution in the Revolution?* (Harmondsworth, Penguin, 1969); see also R. Debray, *Strategy for Revolution*, ed. R. Blackburn, (London, Jonathan Cape, 1970).

11 P. Calvert, *Revolution and International Politics*, second edition (London, Pinter, 1996), pp. 105–7.

12 L. Mercier Vega, *Guerrillas in Latin America: The Techniques of the Counter-State* (London, Pall Mall, 1969), p. 76.

13 E. Che Guevara, *The Complete Bolivian Diaries of Che Guevara and Other Captured Documents*, ed. D. James (New York, Stein and Day, 1968); R. L. Harris, *Death of a Revolutionary: Che Guevara's Last Mission* (New York, Norton, 1970).

14 E. Crawley, *Dictators Never Die: A Portrait of Nicaragua and the Somozas* (London, Hurst, 1979).

15 T. S. Montgomery, 'Cross and Rifle: Revolution and the Church in El Salvador and Nicaragua', *Journal of International Affairs*, 36 (1982), pp. 209–21.

16 H. Smith, 'The Conservative Approach: Sandinista Nicaragua's Foreign Policy', in S. Chan and A. J. Williams (eds.), *Renegade States: The Evolution of Revolutionary Foreign Policy* (Manchester, Manchester University Press, 1994).

17 E. Bradford Burns, *At War in Nicaragua: The Reagan Doctrine and the Politics of Nostalgia* (New York, Harper and Row, 1987), pp. 63–5.

18 See also C. R. Hales, *Resistance and Contradiction: Miskitu Indians and the Nicaraguan State, 1894–1987* (Stanford, Stanford University Press, 1994).

19 M. H. Shuman and H. Harvey, *Security Without War: A Post-Cold War Foreign Policy* (Boulder, Westview, 1993), p. 45.

20 A. Kapcia, 'What Went Wrong? The Sandinista Revolution', *Bulletin of Latin American Research*, 13:3 (1994); M. González, *Nicaragua – What Went Wrong?* (London, Bookmarks, 1990).

21 J. Nef, 'The Politics of Insecurity', in J. Knippers Black (ed.), *Latin America, Its Problems and Its Promise: A Multidisciplinary Introduction*, third edition (Boulder, , Westview, 1998), p. 243.

22 United Nations Development Program, *Human Development Report 1994* (New York, Oxford University Press, 1994), pp. 94–5.

23 O. Fals Borda, 'Violence and the Break-up of Tradition in Colombia', in C. Véliz (ed.), *Obstacles to Change in Latin America* (New York, Oxford University Press, 1965).

24 V. L. Fluharty, *Dance of the Millions: Military Rule and the Social Revolution in Colombia, 1930–1956* (Pittsburgh, University of Pittsburgh Press, 1957).

25 Keesing's 40225.

26 Keesing's 41533.

27 Keesing's 42004.

28 D. Poole and G. Réñique, 'The New Chroniclers of Peru: US Scholars and the "Shining Path" of Peasant Rebellion', *Bulletin of Latin American Research*, 10:2 (1991), p. 143.

29 H. Blanco, *Land or Death: The Peasant Struggle in Peru* (New York, Pathfinder, 1972); H. Béjar, *Peru, 1965: Notes on a Guerrilla Experience* (New York, Monthly Review, 1969); R. Gott, *Guerrilla Movements in Latin America* (London, Nelson, 1970).

30 Poole and Réñique, 'The New Chroniclers'.

31 D. S. Palmer (ed.), *The Shining Path of Peru* London, Hurst, 1992.

32 L. Taylor, 'Agrarian Unrest and Political Conflict in Puno, 1985–1987', *Bulletin of Latin American Research*, 6:2 (1987).

33 This is one of the principal coca-growing regions of Peru.

34 L. Taylor, 'Counter-Insurgency Strategy, the PCP–Sendero Luminoso and the Civil War in Peru, 1980–1996', *Bulletin of Latin American Research*, 17:1 (1998).

35 M. Tse-tung and E. Che Guevara, *Guerrilla Warfare* (London, Cassell, 1964).

36 Taylor, 'Counter-Insurgency Strategy', p. 45.

37 D. Poole and G. Réñique, *Peru: Time of Fear* (London, Latin American Bureau, 1992).

38 See J. Crabtree, 'Peru', in J. Buxton and N. Phillips (eds), *Case Studies in Latin American Political Economy* (Manchester, Manchester University Press, 1999).

39 Keesing's 39091–92; 39138.

40 Keesing's 40498.

41 General Command of the EZLN, EZLN Communiqué 1/1 1993, http://ezln.html

42 P. Howard and T. Homer-Dixon, *Environmental Scarcity and Violent Conflict: The Case of Chiapas, Mexico* (Toronto, University of Toronto Press, 1995).

43 F. Alvarez, 'Peasant Movements in Chiapas', *Bulletin of Latin American Research*, 7:2 (1988).

44 Interview with 'Marcos' in the Lacandón jungle by Irish journalist Michael McCaughan, March 1994, http:// www.igc.apc.org/nacla/mexico.html

45 Keesing's 40316.

46 K. Kampwirth, 'Creating Space in Chiapas: An Analysis of the Strategies of the Zapatista Army and the Rebel Government in Transition', *Bulletin of Latin American Research*, 15:2 (1996).

47 Keesing's 41952, 41953.

48 Keesing's 42003.

49 Keesing's 41136, 41223.

50 Keesing's 41223, 41264.

51 Guevara, *Guerrilla Warfare*, p. 2.

7

NGOs and the retreat of the state: the hidden dangers

LAURA TEDESCO

If the 1980s were the 'lost decade' for Latin American countries, the 1990s have been a decade of radical change. While Latin America suffered a deep crisis during the 1980s, it is currently considered primarily as an 'emerging market'. This more positive image masks an ongoing process of crisis and struggle.

This chapter considers the emergence of new actors and the gradual weakening of others in Latin America over the 1990s. The state has traditionally been seen as the agent of development. Today, the state shares this role with international or national non-governmental organisations (NGOs). In some areas it is now little more than a spectator of the development process. The chapter analyses the rise of NGOs and the decline of the state as two interrelated processes. It argues that the increasing reliance on NGOs for the carrying-out of developmental activity brings with it significant risks, as the state ceases to exercise responsibility for the provision of basic rights.

Conceptualising the state

An understanding of these risks follows from our conceptualisation of the state and civil society. NGOs are part of civil society. Civil society is often seen as an area of freedom beyond the state: the sphere of the market, in which every individual becomes a citizen. The benign definition of civil society sees it as a sphere where differences disappear and we are all citizens and equals. Civil society, that is, appears to be a place of autonomy. However, here civil society is understood more as an area of coercion. The market is seen as a coercive force, where individuals are not equals and class differences make citizenship a weak concept.

The state has been defined in many different ways. Here it is defined as a form of domination. More specifically, the capitalist state is a form of class domination. The state dominates through institutions, values, norms, and, mainly, social relations. The economic and political role of each class conditions the state's social relations. The latter are dynamic because there is a constant tension between classes to either maintain or improve their economic and political position. In response, the state is also dynamic and assumes different characteristics at different moments. The capitalist state can be defined as 'developmentalist', 'populist' or 'neoliberal'. These are simply different forms of class domination, different structures of power relations between classes. The 'developmentalist' state dominates through the image of 'development from above and for all'. The 'populist' state dominates through the image of 'the state as organiser of and provider for the working class'. The 'neoliberal' state dominates through the image of the state as guarantor of 'democracy, law and order, efficiency and provider of the legal framework for civil society and/or the individual to flourish and express itself'.

The continual dynamism of social relations is reflected in periodic crises of the state. Crisis is neither 'economic' nor 'political.' The concepts of 'economic' and 'political' are specific to capitalism since 'the relations between slave and master or serf and lord were indistinguishably economic-and-political relations'.[1] Thus, the concepts of 'economic' and 'political' are fetishised categories which reflect the superficial fragmentation of capitalist society. The notion of crisis, applied to social and historical developments, refers to 'hard times' as well as to turning points.[2] Although crisis presents itself as economic, it expresses the structural instability of capitalist social relations, 'the instability of the basic relation between capital and labour on which society is based'.[3]

As Holloway and Picciotto suggest, each development of the state must be seen as a particular manifestation of the crisis of the capital relation. Crisis of the capital relation inevitably involves a restructuring of social relations which take economic and political forms.[4] Crisis involves a process of struggle. The outcome of this struggle determines the nature of the new pattern of accumulation. Thus, crisis is a crisis of the capital relation; a crisis of an historically specific form of class domination; a crisis of accumulation which involves the totality of capitalist social relations. Crisis is composed of both breakdown and restructuring, and 'between crisis-as-rupture and crisis-as-restructuring there is a whole world-history of struggle'.[5]

Thus, historically, in Latin America the breakdown of the social relations which sustained the 'populist state' produced a process of struggle. Inward-oriented strategies became unsustainable. While the dominant class was fighting to repress the working class economically and politically by changing the social relations of populism, the latter was fighting to maintain its political and economic 'inclusion'. The 1980s witnessed the process of struggle between the collapse of inward-looking strategies and the emergence of outward-looking strategies. This was a struggle over income distribution, rather than for radical transformations. It was a struggle over the nature of the welfare state and the continuing validity of Keynesianism. The 1990s have seen the results of this struggle: the implementation of new social relations and a new type of domination. The main characteristics of this new form of domination are the introduction of democracy, the economic retreat of the state and the promotion of a strong civil society. These changes were brought about in order to perpetuate the structure of domination inherent in the structure of social relations upon which the state is based. Importantly, the prime purpose was neither to enhance the efficacy of development polices nor to transform income distribution, but to maintain the class structure of domination.

Latin American neoliberalism in the 1990s

In the 1990s, economic growth has become the main concern of Latin American governments. The focus has been on macroeconomic stability, liberalising and deregulating the economy and attaining greater economic growth. This has entailed the economic retreat of the state. The state is no longer directly an economic actor, only the regulator of market activity. The market has become the allocator of resources *sine qua non*. In this sense, social issues have in effect become economic issues, and citizens have become customers.

In the 1980s, Latin America saw the development of two contradictory processes. On the one hand, the military dictatorships began to fall. On the other hand, the external debt crisis emerged. The debt crisis provided the first real opportunity to implement a neoliberal programme.[6] As outlined by Duncan Green in Chapter 1, the so-called Washington Consensus was the set of policies that was suggested as a uniform solution for all Latin American countries, despite the considerable differences between them. The Washington Consensus has been defined as consisting of macroeconomic prudence, outward orientation and domestic liberalisation.[7] The main policy instruments were defined as fiscal discipline, the reduction of public expenditure, tax reform, market-determined interest rates, a competitive exchange rate, import liberalisation, the promotion of foreign direct investment, privatisation, deregulation and new laws on property rights.[8]

The main criticism of the Washington Consensus was that in the face of spiralling interest payments on the debt, public expenditure could not easily be cut. This forced the new democratic governments to look for reductions in social expenditure, cutting back their already minimal 'welfare states'.[9] The philosophy behind the Washington Consensus was that internal structural reforms were necessary to stabilise the economy and to enable the debtor countries to pay off the external debt. These structural adjustment programmes have become the principal method for promoting neoliberalism in Latin American countries and the foundation of economic policies throughout the region.

In 1992, 39 per cent of the total households of the metropolitan areas of Latin America lived below the poverty line.[10] Out of a total population of 470 million in Latin America, 150 million people still live in poverty. The neoliberalism of the 1990s has not changed the most notable aspect of the Latin American economy, namely, the profoundly unequal distribution of wealth. Trade liberalisation in Latin America has reduced real wages in the short term as a result of real exchange depreciation and has increased unemployment.[11] Fiscal austerity has required changes to social security programmes, 'leading to a reduction in the proportion of the labour force covered by public programmes'.[12] According to Bulmer-Thomas's analysis 'a strong case could easily be made that full implementation [of the NEM] will lead to an increase in both income inequality and poverty unless the New Economic Model (NEM) is associated with rapid economic growth'. He goes on to argue that the 'NEM in Latin America is not a sufficient condition for the reduction in poverty and an improvement in income distribution'.[13] The reason is that the NEM has not achieved the expected growth rates. On the contrary, 'the rate of growth in real GDP per head since the start of the NEM is below the rate before the debt crisis in most countries'.[14] The superiority of the NEM over the inward-looking strategy cannot easily be assumed.

NGO activity in Latin America

NGOs are defined as 'associations formed within civil society bringing together individuals who share some common purpose'.[15] There are international NGOs which are based in one country (generally an Organization for Economic Cooperation and Development, or OECD, country) and help to develop other countries, and national NGOs, which are based in a Third World country. These two types are also known as Northern NGOs (NNGOs) and Southern NGOs (SNGOs), respectively. There is also a distinction between those NGOs that seek to provide benefits only to their members and those that seek to provide public benefits. This distinction is important regarding accountability: while the former are accountable to their members, the latters' accountability is less clear. The former are also known as grassroots organisations (GROs), or community-based organisations.

NGO activity has increased significantly since the end of the Cold War. During the Cold War period there were 'three worlds': the First World (capitalist and developed), the Second World (Communist and developed), and the Third World (underdeveloped). The First World combined economic inclusion (in which economic life included the majority of people), individualism and political democracy. With the collapse of communism and the fall of most authoritarian regimes these three principles were adopted by the majority of the nation-states.[16]

The post-Cold War period has seen an increase in United Nations activity as a consequence of the end of the log-jam in the Security Council. This has transformed North–South relations as the humanitarian relief work undertaken by the UN has grown in importance. Thus, the main features of the post-Cold War period are an ongoing wave of democratisation and economic liberalisation, a new role for the UN, and restructured North–South relations. In this context, NGOs have become key players, acting as intermediaries between the North and the South.

In Latin America, political democratisation was followed by economic liberalisation. NGOs were seen as vehicles for democratisation and the strengthening of civil society. They act as a counterweight to the state 'opening up channels for communication and participation, providing a training ground for activists promoting pluralism and protecting human rights'.[17] Western donors saw NGOs as tools to improve not only the economies of developing countries, but also their polities. It is estimated that international NGOs, 'through their relationship with SNGOs, assist some 60 million people in Asia, 25 million in Latin America and 12 million in Africa'.[18] While in Asia and Africa, NGOs have displaced governments in the health sector, the Latin American case has been historically different.

During the military dictatorships, Latin American NGOs were opposed to government regimes and worked alongside a number of political parties for the return to democracy. NGOs were considered by donor nations as vehicles for democratisation and strengthening of civil society. Indeed, during the 1970s, NGO activity was deeply influenced by the political situation. Since all political activity was banned, NGOs were one of the few legitimate forms of organisation and participation. NGOs were *anti*-governmental rather than *non*-governmental organisations – 'they were perceived and, above all, perceived of themselves, as a form of oppositional political action under conditions of authoritarianism'.[19] Under these conditions, the political aspect of NGO activity was emphasised. One of the characteristics of NGOs was their marginality, their lack of involvement with the state. They established a close relationship with local organisations opposed to the authoritarian regimes, for example in El Salvador, although there were some exceptions, such as in Guatemala. In El Salvador there were continuous suspicions of strong links between NGOs and the FMLN, while in Guatemala NGOs tried to maintain political independence.[20]

During the 1970s, there were tensions between Latin American NGOs and Northern NGOs. The former disliked the control that foreign agencies exercised over their activities. They asked for the abandonment of paternalism, decentralisation of power and solidarity to challenge state power. Although Macdonald recognises small changes in the relationship between Northern and Latin American NGOs, she also points out that 'old habits die hard and the majority of Northern NGOs have failed to respond in a serious way to criticisms from the South'.[21] Another crucial feature of those years was the role played by the Catholic Church. The Church is the most powerful organisation in Latin American civil society, and in some countries (especially Brazil) it played a crucial role in confronting the military dictatorships. During the dictatorships, those NGOs protected by the Church were the only survivors of social movements.

Latin American NGOs have not been isolated from the region's 'changing era'. With the breakdown of authoritarian regimes, NGOs have gradually begun to accommodate themselves to the new reality of the 1990s, playing a role as development agencies rather than as political activists against state oppression. During this period, NGOs 'had not only survived but had grown in importance and numbers, increasingly identified as an agent of development rather than social transformation'.[22] Thus, the combative aspect of Latin American NGOs was modified after the re-emergence of democracy. The '*anti*-governmental' approach was replaced by 'collaboration' with national governments, foreign governments and international agencies, the aim being to gain access to funds. Although some NGOs are still reluctant to be involved with governments (especially in Brazil) most of them have given up their fight against the state and have begun to comply with the 'neoliberal' rules of the game. Consequently, NGOs have begun to assume the responsibility for implementing development programmes previously executed by the state.

Some authors have welcomed the transformation of NGOs, while others remain very critical. Lehmann argues that NGOs have helped to strengthen the demands for citizenship rights put forward at the grassroots level,[23] and Friedmann argues that NGOs have the ability to pressure the state to be 'more responsive to the claims of the disempowered'.[24] From a critical point of view, Rivera-Cusicanqui criticises NGOs working in highland Bolivia. According to her analysis, NGOs operate with Western values which are inappropriate in the Andean community.[25] The Bolivian case is a good example of the role of NGOs in the 1990s. The government contracted a church-based NGO (Fe y Alegría, or Faith and Joy) to manage a number of secondary schools. While teachers were paid the same as in public schools, the Fe y Alegría schools were preferred to public schools because there was an 'exceptional esprit de corps among students, parents and staff'.[26] In Bolivia, NGOs are involved in smallholder agriculture, primary health care and education, the last two being clearly basic rights hitherto provided by the state.[27]

In Recife, Brazil, children between the ages of 7 and 14 receive basic education through a network of community organisations serviced by the Luiz Freire Centre. This NGO provides basic education for children and illiterate adults, legal assistance, communications services and health care. In Brazil there are over 2,000 NGOs associated with the protection of the environment, education, land reform, community development, gender issues and human rights.[28] In Chile, research-oriented NGOs play a significant role in formulating and implementing health policy.[29] In Santiago there are almost a hundred NGOs working with the small business sector.[30] In Peru, NGOs are involved in the health sector and environmental programmes.[31]

In the 1980s the state's role in development was clearly defined: it was the main promoter and director of development. In the 1990s this role is more difficult to define. The state is still a promoter of development, but it is no longer the principal 'doer' of development. It is no longer directly involved in the process of development to the same extent. NGOs are also undergoing a metamorphosis. In the 1980s their role was 'to be allies to the poor, to increase their access to some of the fruits of growth, to contest much of the project of modernisation, to criticise the forms in which the state intervened and to be voices for a more democratic form of development'.[32] In the 1990s, NGOs have seen their functions change. They have become the only alternative to the state in the practical implementation of development. They have assumed responsibilities, such as secondary schooling in Bolivia, which were previously exclusive to the state. In this sense, they have accepted the rules of the neoliberal game.

There are exceptions. Some NGOs are trying to maintain a slightly more critical role. Brazilian NGOs have tried to keep their 1970s approach and avoid replacing the state. According to Durao,

> Brazilian NGOs have no significant links with the market, having relatively small investment in activities directly connected to production. Small-scale development experiences have already been exhaustively questioned, criticised and abandoned by most NGOs. There has been some going back, for example, to work centred on alternative technologies in agriculture. But even these are not conceived by NGOs as economic or productive projects divorced from politics and education; on the contrary, they are taken up as political and educational projects.[33]

Brazilian NGOs are part of the political world, they are involved in human rights defence and they are struggling for the construction of citizenship and the democratisation of the state. They have maintained their autonomy from the government and political parties. Their target population is that deprived of its basic rights. According to Bosch, the NGOs are moving 'from a basic needs to a basic rights focus in their work'.[34]

However, such examples are the exception. After an attempt by the Carlos Salinas government to regulate them, NGOs in Mexico have achieved a different treatment by Ernesto Zedillo's government, which in 1995 consulted NGOs on the so-called National Development Plan. The new Plan promotes the participation of NGOs in the formulation, execution and evaluation of public policies.[35] Mexican NGOS are engaged in activities shaping public policies, and there is a strong interaction between NGOs and the state. Mexican NGOs, therefore, have apparently accepted the rules of the game and have become implementers of public policy.

The interrelationship between neoliberalism and the rise of NGOs

We have outlined how NGOs have increased their role in the 'neoliberal era'. This raises the question of the relationship between the rise of NGOs and neoliberalism. Theoretically, neoliberalism promotes a strong civil society. It believes in the greater efficiency of the private sector. The poor performance of the public sector in Latin American countries encouraged a search for more efficient ways of providing services. As a result, aid donors advocated the participation of NGOs, and civil society in this sense became key to the provision of a range of services. According to the neoliberal dogma, the market and the private sector are more efficient than the state and the public sector in achieving economic growth and in providing services. NGOs are now 'seen as the pre-ferred channels for service-provision in deliberate substitution of the state'.[36] Neoliberalism sees NGOs as a vehicle for democratisation and as a means of helping to strengthen civil society. Neoliberalism sees civil society as non-coercive, a sphere of freedom for all.

The rise of NGOs is neither a 'natural phenomenon' nor a 'natural response' to local and/or voluntary action. The popularity of NGOs with governments and official aid agencies is not an isolated event. In the post-Cold War period, development and aid policies have been dominated by what Robinson calls the 'New Policy Agenda'.[37] This Agenda, although with differences between countries, 'is driven by beliefs organised around the twin poles of neoliberal economics and liberal democratic theory'.[38] The main paradox of our times is that processes of democratisation, which meant the political inclusion of all, were accompanied by economic liberalisation and structural adjustment, which meant the economic exclusion of the majority. This is why the concept of state and citizen has changed. While the state is no longer a provider but an 'implementer', the citizen is no longer entitled to expect services from the state. This implies that the responsibility of the state has also been modified. As Wood points out, 'the state as guarantor and regulator implies a different view of responsibility to the state as implementer'.[39]

Thus, implicitly, NGOs have made a contribution to the rolling-back of the state, since one of the reasons for the increasing importance of NGOs is the assumption of the state's inefficiency. NGOs have filled the gap left by the retreat of the state, acting as a smokescreen to hide the fact that public services, as such, are disappearing. NGOs appeared as alternatives to the state, masking the fact that the state has obligations towards its citizens: equal opportunities to education, health, safe water, and so forth. NGOs are no longer fighting an authoritarian state, they are replacing an indifferent state. Moreover, the rise of NGOs is understood as a sign of state failure: the role of NGOs is rising due to the state's incapacity to achieve its objectives. The point is that NGOs, despite their good intentions, have helped the retreat of the state to appear legitimate and to create the conditions in which the disappearance of the state does not seem dangerous. In reality, NGOs are a manifestation of the retreat of the state rather than its solution.

Assuming this new role has been difficult for NGOs. They are confronted with a state which is handing over many of its obligations to the private sector and is looking at civil society to resolve social crises. If NGOs take on the responsibility, they will be accomplices to the retreat of the state and its abandonment of social responsibility to its citizen. NGOs would be playing the neoliberal game, legitimising it. If they confront the state, they will lose financial resources and consequently importance, due to their increasing dependence on international aid agencies and OECD governments. They cannot confront the 'neoliberal dogma' without confronting their main source of funds. They are, in this context, facing a Catch-22 situation. They are caught 'between the macro-level political imperatives and their micro-level social/development roles'.[40]

The shortcomings of NGOs: the distinction between rights and needs

We have argued that NGOs help legitimise neoliberalism. But why should we be worried about this? There are a number of shortcomings in the role played by NGOs. First, the assumption that NGOs are more efficient providers of services than the state is questionable. According to Turner and Hulme,

> there is little evidence that NGOs are more cost-effective than government agencies, as is often believed, and the data available on performance are very limited. NGOs are often able to work with the poor, but their capacity to assist the poorest of the poor is limited. Aid agencies have been reluctant to observe the limitations of NGOs: small size, restricted impact, distance from policy decisions, professional and technical limitations, poor co-ordination, problems of representatives and accountability'.[41]

Indeed, NGOs in Latin America only reach 25 million people out of the 150 million living below the poverty line. Another consequence of the involvement of NGOs is that state inefficiency becomes a 'self-perpetuating reality'.[42] There is no incentive to change state inefficiency. The solution is either to privatise the sector or to open it up to NGOs. In this sense, the danger of filling the gap is that while NGOs are gaining legitimacy, the state is ignoring its obligations.

Second, despite their good intentions, NGOs are constrained by their dependence on international and national donors, one of which is the World Bank.[43] Increasing amounts of official aid are being channelled to and through NGOs. There are already warnings concerning the likely corruption of NGOs 'from closer relationships with, and financial dependence on, official aid'.[44] The traditional strength of NGOs was based on their flexibility, innovation and beneficiary participation; they were supposed to be accountable to the people and to be independent actors in civil society. All this is undermined if NGOs are financially dependent on official aid. NGOs are gradually becoming closer to international aid donors than to 'the people'. In becoming mere implementers of state-designed policies, NGOs are losing one of their most precious features: their flexibility.[45]

The World Bank had devoted an increasing proportion of its aid to structural adjustment loans and many other development agencies and bilateral donors have also made their aid conditional on the recipient government's acceptance of the neoliberal agenda. This ever-tightening network of 'cross-conditionalities' has given international aid donors unprecedented influence to shape both macroeconomic and social policy in developing countries. The IDB has required, *inter alia*, the privatisation of irrigation projects and of the irrigation system as preconditions for an assistance loan to the Peruvian agricultural sector.[46] NGOs are being caught in this network of 'cross-conditionalities', losing their flexibility and autonomy. NGOs cannot be against the neoliberal agenda when their main donors are the very promoters of it.

A third danger is that with the rise of NGOs, development[47] has become more of a technical issue, centred on technical expertise. Much of the development agenda is losing its social connections. There are, of course, technical aspects to development projects, but development has economic, social, political and cultural dimensions. If development becomes seen as a purely technical issue it is depoliticised and therefore becomes disconnected from themes such as income distribution. It has been argued that 'non-governmental groups managed by half a dozen professionals have shown that they can change the course of decision-making about a country they may never have seen'.[48]

There is also a danger that the presence of NGOs leads to development being seen as an individual project rather than a collective action. The economic, social, political and cultural dimensions of development need collective action. This is the obligation of the state *and* civil society working together. NGOs cannot take responsibility for primary health care or education, as is now the case.[49] These are issues which must be the focus of collective action. The increasing role of NGOs in the provision of basic public services (basic rights) signals the privatisation of these services. The state does not take full responsibility for the provision of these services, and citizens' rights are minimised in the neoliberal state. A crucial consequence of this is the depoliticisation of the social agenda. As Segarra points out, 'where once the social agenda, expressed through social services, was firmly in the public domain, management of these services is now relegated to the technical expertise of international actors, NGOs, and state planners. Social policy under conditions of restructuring the state becomes a technical problem and therefore outside politics.'[50]

If development is understood as a technical theme and social issues as economic ones, nobody takes responsibility for their provision. Thus, development in all its dimensions is being depoliticised. There is no collective action towards the achievement of sustainable development, only isolated projects financed by international donors. This has also established a new relationship between North and South, whereby the North has disengaged from the South's problems by placing between them the international agencies and NGOs. Bennett argues that 'the growth in humanitarian relief lies at the very centre of policies reflecting a profound change in North–South relations: relief, as a policy model, is a form of disengagement from the South'.[51]

Finally and most fundamentally, the changing role of the state implies that its citizens are losing their rights to services formerly provided by the state. Wood captures the idea extremely well:

> To what extent do citizens lose basic political rights if the delivery of universal services and entitlements is entrusted to non-state bodies which would at best only be accountable to the state rather than directly to those with service entitlements? Can the state devolve responsibility for implementation without losing control over policy (since practice is policy) and therefore losing responsibility for upholding the

rights of its citizens? If the answer to the first question is 'yes' and to the second is 'no', then we have states without citizens. The irony, of course, is that the international advocates of the process of democratisation are the same ones who wish to privatise the functions of the state, thus rendering the purpose of democracy toothless and meaningless.'

If the market becomes *the* allocator of 'public services', this means that one has only 'exchange entitlements but not rights'. Moreover, Wood assesses that 'the loss of rights in the state is not adequately compensated for by acquiring them in the market'.[52]

We have seen, for example, that the World Bank has praised the example of the provision of educational services by the Fe y Alegría in Bolivia. But the 'success' of this NGO surely raises a number of more fundamental concerns, such as whether is it right that the government should contract an NGO to run public education; whether the NGO is accountable to the state, the parents or the pupils; and whether the NGO has the power to organise or change the curricula. Is the international or national donor involved, directly or indirectly, in the educational system? Can an educational system be modified (especially in the long term) by an NGO or an international or national donor? Is it not a state's obligation to provide free and equal education to all its citizens?

It is now widely accepted that the state is changing, and, according to the World Bank *World Development Report 1997*, the international context has influenced this. There are four developments which have unleashed the changes: the collapse of the Soviet Union, the fiscal crisis of the welfare state, the role of the state in the development of East Asia, and the collapse of states and the explosion of humanitarian emergencies all around the world. According to the Bank, 'the determining factor behind these contrasting developments is the effectiveness of the state'. An effective state is considered to be essential not only for the provision of goods, services, rules and institutions but also to 'allow markets to flourish and people to lead healthier, happier lives'. Experience has taught that 'the state is central to economic and social development, not as a direct provider of growth but as a *partner, catalyst and facilitator*'.[53]

If the state is not *obliged* to provide, it is because somewhere, sometime, citizens have lost the right to demand. The crucial issue is the concept of effectiveness. To be effective is to be able to bring about the intended result; therefore it is essential to look at the objectives of the state. According to the World Bank's *Report* cited above, 'states with weak institutional capabilities should focus on providing the pure public goods and services that markets cannot provide (and that voluntary collective initiatives under-provide), as well as goods and services with large positive externalities, such as property rights, safe water, roads and basic education'. It also points out that the 'state, at all levels of institutional capability, should respect, nurture, and take advantage of private and voluntary initiatives and competitive markets'.[54] Therefore, the state must promote private initiative to help it to provide goods and services. The only services that the state must itself directly provide are those with positive externalities. But the concept of positive externality is extremely subjective. While one person could regard health, unemployment benefits and access to higher education as issues with the largest positive externalities, another person might argue for a more restrictive definition, suggesting that property rights bring more important externalities than, say, education. Is it the market, again, that decides the hierarchy between positive externalities?

The role of NGOs in the 1990s has been to try to repair effects rather than attack causes: 'if you see a baby drowning you jump in to save it; and if you see a second and a third, you do the same. Soon you are so busy saving drowning babies that you never look up to see that there is someone there throwing these babies in the river.'[55] NGOs have been trying to save babies; the real need is to stop babies being thrown in the river. The need is to radically change the state, to transform social relations and to achieve an egalitarian income distribution, which is the first step towards sustainable development. This change cannot be carried out through NGOs which are supported by the same governments and organisations which promote structural adjustment, nor can it be externally directed. It has to be done by redefining the state's objectives.

It is the distinction between basic needs and basic rights which is the key to appreciating the hidden dangers of the role of NGOs. NGOs have neglected to highlight the fact that there are basic rights, not merely basic needs. A focus on basic rights would imply that the state still has the responsibility to provide certain services. NGOs would then need to change their role, from replacing the state as agents of development, to fighting against the state's failures.

Conclusions

NGOs have played a valuable role in Latin America, for example, in raising the profile of certain topics. But there are dangers where NGOs come to replace the state. The rights that have been acquired through the Keynesian class collaboration need to be maintained. Neoliberalism has led to the economic exclusion of the majority of the population in Latin America. NGOs, as part of the private sector, are not able to correct this to any significant extent. NGOs should be aware of this and concentrate on promoting the struggle to maintain basic rights, rather than aiming to replace the state.

It is essential to redefine concepts such as democracy and citizenship to include economic and social rights. What is the meaning of citizenship when one is unemployed and unable to provide education for one's children? The rights gained, such as free education and health, cannot be transferred to either private institutions or NGOs. It is the obligation of the state to provide equal opportunities for all. The neoliberal state dominates through the idea of democracy, a strong civil society and private initiative. This gives the impression that an individual has the capacity to achieve his or her objectives. But defining the neoliberal state as a new form of class domination corrects the misperception that civil society is a neutral, non-coercive sphere. This reveals the limitations and dangers of relying too heavily on initiatives – including those of NGOs – in the private sphere. As Wood points out, 'civil society is now in danger of becoming an alibi for capitalism'.[56]

Latin American NGOs are assisting people who have been abandoned by the state. The danger is that, through this assistance, NGOs are legitimising the fact that the state, is ignoring basic rights. NGOs are there when nobody else is present to provide minimum levels of service provision. However, the fundamental danger is that NGOs in Latin America are, in some instances, beginning to replace the state not only in the provision of basic needs, but also in the provision of basic *rights*. Due to the presence of NGOs' the state is better able to ignore the fact that it is not assuming full responsibility for the fulfilment of its citizens' rights. The worry is not so much where NGOs are replacing the state in the promotion of development, but where they are active in the promotion of basic rights. Implicitly or explicitly, NGOs are out there filling the gap left by the retreat of the state, as an older brother tidies up his little brother's bedroom in order to avoid their mother's anger.

In this context, NGOs are promoting market-based strategies for development rather than society-based solutions. If, in the 1980s, NGOs were vehicles for democratisation, some of them have, in the 1990s, become vehicles for 'neoliberalisation'. NGOs should be raising the issue of basic rights rather than 'filling the gap'. At present, they are deflecting attention away from the root causes of the still growing inequalities in Latin American societies.

Notes

1 J. Holloway, 'Crisis, Fetishism, Class Composition', in W. Bonefeld *et al.*, *Open Marxism*, Vol. 2 (London, Pluto, 1992), p. 160; P. Anderson, *Lineages of the Absolutist State* (London, Verso, 1979).

2 Holloway, 'Crisis, Fetishism', p. 146.

3 *Ibid.*, p. 159.

4 J. Holloway and S. Picciotto, 'Capital, Crisis and the State', *Capital and Class*, 52 (Spring 1977), pp. 77, 92.

5 Holloway, 'Crisis, Fetishism', p. 164.

6 V. Bulmer-Thomas (ed.), *The New Economic Model in Latin America and its Impact on Income Distribution and Poverty* (London, Macmillan and Institute of Latin American Studies, 1996), p. 302.

7 J. Williamson (ed.), *Latin American Adjustment: How Much Has Happened?* (Washington, DC, Institute for International Economics, 1990), p. 1.

8 This is the set of policies also called the 'orthodox approach'. Orthodoxy is well defined by Stallings and Kaufman as 'market-oriented approaches ... that emphasise fiscal and monetary restraint, reductions in the size of the state sector, liberalisation of trade restrictions, and collaboration with creditors'. A heterodox approach is defined as a policy where the state plays a more active role in regulation and investment decisions and more emphasis is placed on distribution and employment (B. Stallings and R. Kaufman eds, *Debt and Democracy in Latin America*, Boulder, Westview, 1989, p. 2). For a detailed account of the differences see J. M. Nelson (ed.), *Economic Crisis and Policy Choice: The Politics of Adjustment in the Third World* (Princeton, Princeton University Press, 1990); J. M. Nelson *et al.*, *Fragile Coalitions: The Politics of Economic Adjustment* (New Brunswick, Transaction, 1990); M. Kahler, 'Orthodoxy and its

Alternatives: Explaining Approaches to Stabilization and Adjustment', in Nelson (ed.), *Economic Crisis and Policy Choice*; and S. Haggard and R. R. Kaufman, 'The Politics of Stabilization and Structural Adjustment', in J. Sachs (ed.), *Developing Country Debt and Economic Performance, Vol. I: The International Financial System* (Chicago, University of Chicago Press, 1989).

9 P. Meller, 'What Washington Means By Policy Reform', in Williamson (ed.), *Latin American Adjustment*, p. 33.

10 Bulmer-Thomas (ed.), *The New Economic Model*, p. 317.

11 *Ibid.*, p. 297.

12 *Ibid.*, p. 298.

13 *Ibid.*, pp. 301, 308.

14 *Ibid.*, p. 309.

15 M. Turner and D. Hulme, *Governance, Administration and Development* (London, Macmillan, 1997), p. 200.

16 R. Dahrendorf, *La cuadratura del círculo* (Mexico City, Fondo de Cultura Económica, 1996).

17 Turner and Hulme, *Governance*, p. 207.

18 *Ibid.*, p. 204.

19 Spoerer, cited by L. MacDonald, *Supporting Civil Society* (London, Macmillan, 1997), p. 13.

20 A. Burge, 'Central America: NGO Coordination in El Salvador and Guatemala, 1980-1994', in J. Bennett (ed.), *Meeting Needs: NGO Coordination in Practice* (London, Earthscan, 1995), p. 147.

21 Macdonald, *Supporting Civil Society*, p. 13.

22 J. Pearce, 'Between Co-option and Irrelevance? Latin American NGOs in the 1990s', in D. Hulme and M. Edwards (eds), *NGOs, States and Donors: Too Close for Comfort?* (London, Macmillan and Save the Children, 1997), p. 267.

23 D. Lehmann, *Democracy and Development in Latin America* (Cambridge, Polity, 1990).

24 J. Friedmann: *Empowerment: The Politics of Alternative Development* (Oxford, Basil Blackwell, 1992), p. 158.

25 S. Rivera-Cusincanqui, 'Liberal Democracy and Ayllu Democracy in Bolivia: The Case of Northern Potosí', in J. Fox, *The Challenge of Rural Democratisation: Perspectives from Latin America and the Philippines* (London, Frank Cass, 1990).

26 World Bank, *World Development Report 1997: The State in a Changing World* (Oxford, Oxford University Press, 1997), p. 89.

27 H. Veltmeyer, J. Petras and S. Vieux, *Neoliberalism and Class Conflict in Latin America: A Comparative Perspective on the Political Economy of Structural Adjustment* (London, Macmillan, 1997).

28 Inter-American Foundation, *A Guide to NGO Directories* (Arlington: Inter-American Foundation, 1995.

29 C. Reilly (ed.), *New Paths to Democratic Development in Latin America* (Boulder, Lynne Rienner, 1995).

30 Inter-American Foundation, *A Guide*.

31 E. Dawson, 'Mobilisation and Advocacy in the Health Sector in Peru', in M. Edwards and D. Hulme (eds), *Making a Difference* (London, Earthscan, 1993).

32 A. Bebbington and G. Thiele, *Non-Governmental Organizations and the State in Latin America* (London and New York, Routledge, 1993), p. 200.

33 Cited in M. Bosch, 'NGOs and Development in Brazil: Roles and Responsibilities in a "New World Order"', in Hulme and Edwards (eds), *NGOs, States and Donors*, p. 234.

34 *Ibid.*, p. 235.

35 K. Piester, 'Targeting the Poor: The Politics of Social Policy Reforms in Mexico', in D. A. Chalmers *et al.*, *The New Politics of Inequality in Latin America: Rethinking Participation and Representation* (Oxford, Oxford University Press, 1997), p. 486.

36 Hulme and Edwards, *NGOs, States and Donors*, p. 6.

37 M. Robinson, 'Governance, Democracy and Conditionality: NGOs and the New Policy

Agenda', in A. Clayton (ed.), *Governance, Democracy and Conditionality: What Role for NGOs?* (London, Intract, 1993).

38 Hulme and Edwards (eds), *NGOs, States and Donors*, p. 5.

39 G. Wood, 'States Without Citizens: The Problem of the Franchise State', *Ibid.*, p. 83.

40 Pearce, 'Between Co-option and Irrelevance?', p. 258.

41 Turner and Hulme, *Governance*, p. 206.

42 Edwards and Hulme (eds), *Making a Difference*, p. 851.

43 See P. J. Nelson, *The World Bank and Non-Governmental Organizations* (London, Macmillan, 1997).

44 Edwards and Hulme (eds), *Making a Difference*, p. 850.

45 Bebbington and Thiele, *Non-Governmental Organizations*, p. 54.

46 J. Randel and T. German, *The Reality of Aid 1996* (London, Earthscan, 1996), p. 67.

47 One of the most comprehensive definitions of development includes an economic, political, social and cultural dimension. It is conceptualised by Turner and Hulme *(Governance*, p. 11) as follows:

– an economic component dealing with the creation of wealth and improved conditions of material life, equitably distributed;
– a social ingredient measured as well-being in health, education, housing and employment;
– a political dimension including such values as human rights, political freedom, enfranchisement, and some form of democracy;
– a cultural dimension in recognition of the fact that cultures confer identity and self-worth to people;
– the full-life paradigm, which refers to meaning systems, symbols, and beliefs concerning the ultimate meaning of life and history; and
– a commitment to ecologically sound and sustainable development so that the present generation does not undermine the position of future generations.

These are the main dimensions of sustainable development. Thus development is neither a purely economic term nor a technical issue.

48 Jha, cited by Edwards and Hulme (eds), *Making a Difference*, p. 21.

49 Veltmeyer, Petras and Vieux, *Neoliberalism and Class Conflict.*, p. 172.

50 M. Segarra, 'Redefining the Public/Private Mix: NGOs and the Emergency Social Investment Fund in Ecuador', in Chalmers *et al.*, *The New Politics of Inequality*, p. 490.

51 Bennett, *Meeting Needs*, p. xiv.

52 G. Wood, 'States without Citizens', pp. 81, 83.

53 World Bank, *World Development Report 1997*, p. 1 (emphasis added).

54 *Ibid.*, p. 40.

55 Edwards and Hulme (eds), *Making a Difference*, p. 13.

56 E. Wood, 'The Uses and Abuses of "Civil Society"', *Socialist Register*, 1990, p. 60.

8

The human rights movement and democratisation

ALEXANDRA BARAHONA DE BRITO

Latin America has been associated with images of human rights violations, such as the forced disappearance of people under military rule, abuses against indigenous populations, the violence of insurrections or civil wars, and the murder of street children or peasant leaders involved in land struggles under democratic rule. If one is so readily able to conjure up these images, however, this is largely because Latin America has given rise to one of the largest and most influential human rights movements with the largest number of human rights non-governmental organisations (HROs) in the world.

Thus, the disappeared bring to mind the Mothers of the Plaza de Mayo and their white handkerchiefs, the violations against indigenous peoples, and Guatemalan human rights activist and Nobel Peace Prize winner, Rigoberta Menchú. These activists and the organisations they represent have made the rest of the world aware of Latin America as a place where human rights violations are a fact of life, and one where the human rights movement has become a force to be contended with, as it mobilises domestic and international public opinion and forces governments to take human rights demands into account. This chapter examines the evolution of the human rights movement in Latin America, from its inception under military authoritarian rule to the present. It focuses primarily on the role played by HROs since the transition to democracy and the impact that they are having on the process of democratisation in the region.

The evolution of the human rights movement

Growth and development

Latin America's modern human rights movement emerged with significant visibility in the 1970s with the onset of military–authoritarian rule in response to the wave of repression unleashed by military and police forces in their battle against 'subversion'. HROs did exist before this period, but they were not very active.[1] The first organisations to emerge under military rule were those group-ing together the relatives of the victims of repression, such as the disappeared or political prisoners. These were followed by HROs working on behalf of vic-tims that denounced, disseminated information on and sought legal redress for violations. The movement was not uniformly strong or influential or similarly composed throughout the region, and was initially strongest in the Southern Cone, particularly in Argentina and Chile, but also in Brazil and Uruguay.[2]

The 1980s saw the growth of the movement, with the consolidation of exist-ing groups, the emergence of new organisations and the adoption of new themes, tactics and targets, particularly in countries undergoing transitions to democracy. In addition, various national movements developed regional net-works such as the Latin American Federación Latinoamericana de Familiares de Detenidos Desaparecidos (FEDEFAM, Federation of the Families of Disap-peared Prisoners) and the Servicio de Paz y Justicia (SERPAJ, Peace and Justice Service). Others were established with a regional reach, such as the Lima-based Comisión Andina de Juristas (CAJ, Andean Commission of Jurists).

Towards the end of the 1980s and in the early part of the 1990s, the move-ment spread geographically to countries that had not experienced military authoritarian repression but which suffered from serious human rights prob-lems, such as Colombia, Mexico, Peru and Venezuela. HROs also began to gain clout in various Central American countries with the initiation of the peace process in the region, and the 1990s saw the emergence of human rights move-ment in Cuba, the only country of the region that is not nominally a democ-racy. It is estimated that by the mid-1990s there were some 3,000 human rights groups in Latin America, operating nationally, regionally or locally.

From the outset, Latin America's human rights movement has been shaped by the partnerships it established. The support of the Catholic or other churches was crucial for the development of the movement in Brazil, Chile, Central America, Mexico and Peru.[3] Members of the Catholic Church hierar-chy in Brazil associated with the Protestant World Council of Churches (WCC), the Chilean Vicaría de la Solidaridad (Vicariate of Solidarity) and Peru's Comisión Episcopal de Acción Social (CEAS, Episcopal Commission for Social Action) and Consejo Nacional Protestante (CONEP, National Protestant Coun-cil) were instrumental in founding and protecting human rights activism. The adherence and support of important figures in the intellectual community were also important. The Academía de Humanismo Cristiano (Academy of Christian Humanism) in Chile and the Mexican Academía Mexicana de Derechos Humanos (AMDH, Academy for Human Rights) based in the Autonomous University of Mexico (UNAM) are cases in point.[4]

Links with activists or leaders of political parties opposed to military rule or in favour of human rights causes were also a key element shaping the move-ment in many countries. In Chile, for example, socialist and Christian Democ-ratic lawyers were linked with the first human rights organisation set up after the coup and in Peru, participation of left-wing parties was also essential to the growth of the movement in the 1980s.[5] Latin American political exiles also played an important role in raising the visibility of human rights violations in their host countries, organising exile committees focusing on human rights issues.

International alliances

International alliances also were of critical importance to the development of the movement.[6] Increased international visibility for isolated or excluded groups or previously ignored issues has often been the only or most effective means to change domestic human rights situations. Latin American HROs found allies in European- or US-based human rights international NGOs (INGOs) that began to emerge in the 1970s, such as Amnesty International, the first human rights INGO, the US-based Lawyers' Committee for Human Rights, Human Rights Watch and the Washington Office on Latin America (WOLA), as well as the Swiss-based International Commission of Jurists (ICJ). HROs also linked up with European and US Church foundations such as the WCC and the US Catholic Conference (USCC), with private institutions such as the Ford Foundation, and with groups linked with the Socialist and Christian Democratic Internationals. Latin America's HROs also gained the support of governmental and intergovernmental institutions that attached increased importance to human rights issues from the 1970s onwards, and the solidarity of international film-makers and journalists whose films and documentaries helped to publicise human rights violations around the world. Examples are *Missing* (1982), *Kiss of the Spider Woman* (1985) and *La Historia Oficial* (1985).

These transnational alliances were not only of critical importance for human rights work in Latin America. Human rights INGOs and their Latin American allies played a central role in promoting the beginnings of a 'human rights revolution' in the international arena in the 1970s. They contributed to legitimising global concern with human rights, propagating a human rights 'language', the incorporation of human rights issues into the foreign policies of individual states and to the fortification and creation of human rights instruments within the UN and the OAS. They also became active participants in the international and regional policy-making process, serving as advisers as well as sources of reliable information on the human rights situation in the countries of the region, and are now influential actors in the elaboration of the international human rights agenda.

It is in large part as a result of their activism that the UN's human rights machinery became more active and interventionist from the 1970s onwards. Chile was one of the first countries to be subjected systematically to international scrutiny for human rights violations. Regionally, the American Convention on Human Rights came into force in 1979 and the Inter-American Commission on Human Rights became more active in monitoring the human rights situation of OAS member states. In the United States, the House Subcommittee on Human Rights and International Organisations began to hold hearings on human rights violations abroad in 1973 and in 1975, the US Congress passed a law linking foreign aid and the human rights practices of recipient countries, the first such legislation ever passed. Under the Carter Administration the US State Department Bureau of Human Rights and Humanitarian Affairs began to take a more active role in incorporating human rights issues into foreign policy debates. In Europe, various countries also began to adopt human rights commitments in their cooperation and foreign policies, and the EC also began to take an active interest in such matters.[7]

The 1980s saw the institutionalisation of international concern with human rights, the completion of various new human rights conventions, an increase in UN monitoring activities, and the incorporation of human rights concerns in the foreign policies of various states, particularly among the Nordic countries and Canada. By the 1990s, Latin American HROs and INGOs were active participants in the formulation of international human rights agenda, participating in the 1993 UN Conference on Human Rights and the 1995 UN Conference on Women, and receiving increased recognition by governmental actors in the elaboration of platforms or programmes for international human rights action.[8]

Relations with the state and transnationalisation

Changing relations with the state

All the HROs working under dictatorial rule were similar in one respect: they worked in opposition not only to a 'government', but also in opposition to a 'system of rule'. They worked against the state which, supposedly responsible for guaranteeing rights, was instead responsible for the mass violation of human rights. Military leaders were soon faced with a 'moral opposition' centred around the defence of basic rights that called for the restoration of civil and political rights and of democracy as the only means to ensure respect for those rights.[9] Although opposition was 'moral' it was also eminently political: focusing on human rights violations was revolutionary, as the defence of rights indicted the system of rule and not just a particular government.

Since the transition to democracy, the nature of relations between the state and HROs has changed substantially, shifting from confrontation to partial cooperation. The shift from total opposition to critical engagement with the transition to democracy has not been easy, sometimes because HROs have been unable to adapt their strategies as they do not sufficiently distinguish between a democratic state (however flawed) and an authoritarian one, sometimes because the democratising state in some countries is still quite hostile to certain forms of human rights activism.

Overall, however, a more cooperative relationship is being established between HROs and democratically elected governments. The state has tended to acknowledge the seriousness of human rights problems. It has adopted and made legitimate many of the demands of the movement. It has established institutions and formulated policies that attempt to create the conditions for increased respect for human rights. It is also accepting the legitimacy and usefulness of HROs as actors in the policy-making process. Governmental policies of positive engagement with human rights issues at home and abroad are a product of the process of democratisation, of the intense and cumulative pressure from INGOs and HROs in Latin America for countries to improve human rights records, of the international 'human rights revolution' mentioned above, as well as of economic liberalisation, as the governments and civil societies of the developed countries often demand respect for human rights as corollaries to the signature of cooperation of trade agreements. The US House Committee on Foreign Affairs heard denunciations of human rights in Mexico for the first time in 1990, for example, largely because of the signature of the NAFTA.[10]

Positive engagement is also the product of changing government attitudes towards the limits of sovereignty where the issues of democracy and human rights are concerned. Since the 1990s, the countries of the region have begun to 'share' responsibility with fellow Rio Group or OAS members for the preservation of democratic governance and respect for human rights. The Rio Group requires that its members be democratic and provides for their exclusion when this commitment is violated. Hence the suspension of Panama and Peru in February 1988 and April 1992, respectively. Within the OAS, the adoption of various instruments promoting 'democracy and human rights' between 1991 and 1993 permitted the state to respond to the coup in Haiti in September 1991 and to the Serrano and Fujimori 1992 *autogolpes* (palace coups) in Guatemala and Peru, respectively.[11]

Governments are beginning to accept that external actors with whom they have trading or political relations have a stake in human rights commitments. Unlike in the 1960s and 1970s, today international concern with violations is accepted and no government engages in total denial, with most at least partially acknowledging human rights violations. In Latin America, governments have tended to accompany partial acknowledgement with 'self-corrective' statements which indicate that authorities are aware of the problem and are doing their best to resolve it.[12] Furthermore, governments have begun to invite HROs to participate in the policy-making process and many countries have been moving slowly away from what has been called the 'politics of shame', or adopting isolated actions after human rights crimes with little consideration for policy continuity, towards the elaboration of proper human rights policies. On 13 May 1995, for example, Brazil adopted a National Human Rights Programme, the first such plan launched in Latin America and the third of its kind in the world, the drafting and preparation of which actively involved the country's HROs.[13]

The establishment of Ombudsmen in some countries shows how the state is substituting or complementing work previously undertaken only by HROs. National Ombudsmen have been established in all countries of the region except Brazil, Chile, Uruguay and Venezuela. HROs in these countries work in close collaboration with the Ombudsmen, providing them with information, helping victims of abuse to present their cases and pressing for greater, more effective action by these bodies.[14]

The internationalisation of the movement

It is impossible to examine the significance of HRO activity in the region without assessing it from a wider international angle. The force of cosmopolitanism as a world-view, as well as the twin processes of transnationalisation and globalisation, are having an important impact on the human rights movement and democratisation, as well as on the links between the two. Cosmopolitanism expresses a conception of international relations that views individuals as members of a global political community rather than as citizens of a state. It therefore tends to minimise the significance of sovereign-bound notions of entitlements and duties. Cosmopolitanism has contributed to the creation of and has been reinforced by the emergence of transnational advocacy networks. These involve local, national, regional and international state and non-state actors working on various normative issues that are linked by shared values and a common discourse. These actors engage in a dense exchange of information and services and can mobilise information to pressurise governments and international organisations.

Cosmopolitanism and emerging transnational networks have also been reinforced by globalisation. This process is not a uniform, linear, homogenising or integrating one, equally affecting all realms of political and economic activity. Nonetheless, the emergence of a global society based on the diffusion of common values and a shared language is an observable phenomenon, and globalisation has involved the creation of a normative framework within which value- and principle-based conflicts are articulated. Non-enforcement and cultural relativism notwithstanding, the 'language of liberal human rights has moved in to fill the vacuum left by the demise of grand political narratives in the aftermath of the Cold War'.[15]

All of the above makes it increasingly difficult to limit the boundaries of the Latin American human rights movement, in terms of actors, issues and territoriality. There is no longer such a clear division between domestic and external actors. National or regional labels and identities can matter less than consensus on key rights questions within cosmopolitan networks. Cosmopolitanism, transnationalism and globalisation tend to reinforce the de-territorialisation of rights and duties, to shift the political playing field beyond the confines of the nation-state into the wider global arena, to promote the emergence of a common language of rights and to cut across sovereign barriers, promoting a new vision of global citizenship.

Human rights advocacy is being de-territorialised by transnational networks and the fusion of 'international and sub-national forces',[16] by the rapid evolution and lowered costs of all forms of communication that make it a 'practical

possibility for a transgression in one place to be felt nearly everywhere immediately',[17] as well as by the existence of a new 'global public' attentive to normative issues.[18] As the language and values of human rights 'spread', new actors
are forced to take normative issues on board, blurring the lines between traditional activists and new actors on the fringes of the movement. *Ad hoc*, temporary or strategic alliances between one and the other occur with growing
frequency. Thus, multinational consulting firms engaging in 'social auditing' to
assess labour conditions in companies operating in Latin America have become
the unlikely allies of HROs, pressing for equal rights for women in factories
that are part of transnational production systems.

In tandem with this, the range of what can be classed as 'human rights activities' is transcending the more limited set of concerns that characterised the
movement two decades ago. Newly emerging consumer rights groups are
'rights defenders', although they address non-traditional issues such as transparency and ethics in trade and production, competitive pricing or the quality
of private and public services. Anti-corruption groups are not HROs, but they
work on issues highly relevant to human rights, such as equality before the law
as well as governmental accountability and transparency, access to information
and 'good governance'. Indigenous leaders are not classic human rights
activists. Some groups belong to peasant movements, political or party coalitions or cultural associations.[19] However, they usually contribute to ensure the
'rights' of indigenous peoples. Environmental groups are not immediately iden-
tifiable as HROs, but they also quickly cut across thematic boundaries, as the
problems they deal with touch upon a number of human rights issues. As the
'indivisibility' of rights and the linkages between human, political, social and
environmental rights implicit in the notion of 'sustainable development'
become increasingly acceptable, the 'human rights universe' expands, making
it more complex and hard to classify or circumscribe.

Transnationalisation and globalisation are also affecting thinking about the
process of democratisation, requiring a better understanding about the links
between international and domestic political forces in shaping the process of
democratisation in Latin America. The terms 'democratisation' or 'democratic
deepening' refer here to the always unfinished process whereby the principles
and practices that characterise a democracy are extended to include all members of society, or the duties and entitlements integral to the promise of democracy encompass the *demos* as a whole. Traditionally, the key actors involved in
that process have been national civil and political societies and states, but the
process of democratisation, much like human rights activism, is being deterri-
torialised to some extent, as a new 'encounter' takes place between the nation-
state and 'a panoply of emerging transnational forces'[20] that have a growing
influence over domestic political outcomes.

Thus, the process of democratic deepening in any country has become intricately linked with the power of sub-state forces as well as by exogenous events
and forces that operate outside the boundaries of the state. The practice and

theory of citizenship and rights are shifting as a result of changes in the political, juridical and economic boundaries of the nation-state and international institutions produced by the processes of transnationalisation and globalisation. Single nation-states now face challenges that transcend their policy-making and executive capacities. International law and the internationalisation of political decision-making also tend to weaken state sovereignty. Various citizenship rights have become universalised, raising the question of 'whether the rights embodied in citizenship rights can any longer be sustained simply within the framework [the nation state] that brought them into being'.[21]

In this way, the contribution that Latin American HROs make to the process of democratisation must take into account the 'global potential and limitations of a cosmopolitan community of individuals'.[22] Ensuring rights and access to justice and redress necessarily challenges traditional conceptions of political sovereignty; its makes the business of nations the business of the international community, civil societies across the globe. As Held notes, 'in an era in which the fates of peoples are deeply intertwined, democracy has to be recast and strengthened, both *within* pre-established borders and *across* them' (original emphasis).[23]

From combating denial to demanding implementation

The human rights movement has focused on four key strategies: disseminating information, creating readily recognisable symbols for international consumption, applying moral or other pressures on international institutions and governments, often through the formation of strategic alliances, and finally, holding governments accountable to rhetorical or juridical commitments by contrasting the latter with a failure to stem abuses.[24] Although this holds true for all periods of human rights activism, the issues for which HROs have applied these strategies have evolved since the period of authoritarian rule.

During the period of dictatorial government, HROs concentrated primarily on three key areas: combating official denial of human rights violations; bringing international attention to bear on the situation of individual countries by disseminating information and engaging in international campaigns; and pressurising governments, the UN and the OAS to take punitive action against repressors by publicly condemning violations, cutting off aid or conditioning trade relations to improvements in human rights records.[25] With the transition to democracy, the central campaigning issue for HROs was to pressurise the new democratically elected authorities in their countries to call to account those responsible for violations.[26] Although each country met with varying levels of success in this enterprise, HROs, in alliance with sympathetic political leaders or prominent members of society, INGOs and governmental institutions, as well as international and regional human rights organisations, were vital to all efforts to bring violators to trial as well as in helping to produce reports about the realities or repression under military rule. Argentina, Bolivia,

Brazil, Chile, Paraguay and Uruguay in the Southern Cone and Guatemala, El Salvador, Honduras and Nicaragua in Central America have been among the countries to have undertaken partial efforts at 'truth and justice'.[27]

The issue of accountability for violations committed by the military is one which still lingers on in a variety of ways. Many domestic and international HROs are still attempting to put the issue back on the political agenda, or trying to gain the backing of regional or international bodies to press governments to take punitive action against repressors according to international legal responsibilities. The arrest of General Pinochet in London in 1998 and the request for his extradition by the Spanish authorities are the most important developments in this area. There are organisations still dedicated to the rehabilitation of torture victims, such as the Rehabilitation and Research Centre for Torture Victims in Copenhagen and the Centre for Victims of Torture in Minneapolis in the United States and others continue with the task of finding the bodies of the disappeared, developing a 'human rights forensic science' as a result of their efforts. Nonetheless, the issue of 'backward-looking accountability' has taken a back seat, as other more pressing problems have become apparent during the process of democratisation in the region.

Combating contemporaneous impunity

The central issue that the movement has taken on board is that of 'contemporaneous impunity', challenging existing 'authoritarian enclaves', deepening democracy and accountability. After more than a decade since most of the transitions occurred, it has become apparent that the region's democracies can coexist with often very high levels of human rights violations. Impunity under democracy is associated with lack of accountability of armed forces combating subversion, as in Colombia and Peru, of police forces fighting crime in urban areas, as in Brazil and El Salvador, and of private groups, often linked with police or military officers, which engage in repressive activities designed to eliminate 'undesirables' ranging from drug traffickers, peasant activists or trade-union leaders, street children and criminal elements living on the fringes of society. Impunity results both from the inability of formal systems of justice to enforce the rule of law as well as from deliberate political decisions not to prosecute state agents responsible for violations.[28]

The region's HROs have thus concentrated on the rights of the most vulnerable groups in society, of the 'undesirables' excluded from the benefits of effective citizenship. One such group is the region's prison population. Latin America's prisons hold around half a million inmates. Not only have prison conditions remained very poor and even worsened, but inmates are also subject to torture as well as to prolonged imprisonment due to incomplete judicial proceedings. In 1996–97 there were massacres, riots and other forms of violent protest in Bolivia, Brazil, Colombia, Ecuador, Guyana, Honduras, Jamaica, Mexico, Panama, Peru and Venezuela. HROs have cooperated with governmental authorities to take action in this area, particularly in conjunction with national Ombudsmen. Various countries, notably Argentina, Chile, Costa Rica and Uruguay, have played a key role in pressing for the establishment of a UN mechanism to monitor the treatment of prisoners, consisting of the adoption of an Optional Protocol of the Convention Against Torture, permitting the creation of a UN Subcommittee which has the authority to visit the prisons of signatory states.[29]

Another sector of the population which has received increasing attention are children, particularly street children and those forced to engage in child labour. Although only 7 per cent of the estimated world total of 250 million working children between the ages of 5 and 7 are in Latin America, child labour is a problem in a number of the countries of the region.[30] Moreover, the issue of violence against street children is a serious problem in countries such as Brazil, Colombia, El Salvador and Guatemala, where child and adolescent criminality are problems and where death-squad activities against children are covered with a mantle of impunity. Similarly, conditions in children's institutions are often appalling and there is little control over the authorities running such establishments and abuses occurring within them.[31] The strongest human rights movement dedicated to the rights of children has emerged in Brazil. An estimated 200 organisations existed prior to the transition to democracy in 1985, most of them coordinated by the Movimento Nacional de Meninos e Meninas da Rua (MNMMR, National Street Children's Movement) established in that year. Since the transition to democracy, these groups have played a major role in making this issue a 'human rights' problem rather than one of law and order, in pressurising the government to introduce legislation on children's rights.[32]

Revisiting old campaigns: the rights of women and indigenous peoples

The issue of indigenous rights has also taken on renewed force in the 1990s. The last two decades saw a 'cultural renaissance and a political awakening' among the region's indigenous peoples, who have 'organised themselves into sophisticated political networks and are now struggling to improve their condition and expand their participation in governmental decisions affecting their development'.[33] As a result of their activism, 'indigenous rights has become a mainstream human rights issue within the international community'.[34]

This is a key issue for the process of democratisation in Latin America, as it raises particularly complex issues such as the nature of citizenship and sovereignty, the relationship between indigenous communities and the nation-state when demands for self-determination or forms of autonomous governance are called for, as well as the legitimacy and practicability of 'collective' rights in democracies based on the rights of the individual. In a region with an estimated 40 million indigenous people, exclusion from democratic institutions has not only 'perpetuated conflict between ethnic groups', but has 'postponed the creation of a broadly democratic society in Latin America, founded in law, embracing cultural diversity, and encouraging wide participation in decision-making and consensual governance'.[35] The demands raised by indigenous rights groups are particularly relevant in countries with large or geographically and culturally separate indigenous populations and communities, such as Bolivia, Brazil, Colombia, Ecuador, Guatemala, Mexico, Nicaragua, Paraguay and Peru.

Indigenous groups, be they regional, national, interregional or local, and associated HROs, church organisations and INGOs in these and other countries, have focused on four key issues: the wider political question of self-determination or autonomy the enforcement of territorial rights through land demarcation or the establishment of clear legal jurisdiction over land; access to natural resources and opposition to 'invasive' extractive activities in indigenous areas; and combating repression by military or police forces active in counter-insurgency or anti-narcotics operations.[36]

Demands for self-determination have been resisted by the Latin American governments, due to concerns over political and territorial issues. However, various countries such as Argentina, Bolivia, Brazil, Chile, Colombia, Mexico, Paraguay and Peru have adopted or are considering the adoption of constitutional reform measures, in order to make way for the increased political participation of indigenous groups in policy-making and to ensure the protection of their territorial or basic rights. Land rights and control over essential natural resources have also generated much tension between indigenous rights as well as environmental activists and governments in the region. The passage of laws permitting the sale of ancestral lands to non-indigenous groups or business interests has produced strong reactions among indigenous populations in Colombia, Mexico, the Brazilian and Peruvian Amazon region and Paraguay and has led to widespread rural violence. The pressure of the movement has contributed to the establishment of reserves in Bolivia, Brazil, Colombia, Ecuador, Nicaragua, Panama and Venezuela.[37]

Conflict over the use of natural resources such as water, minerals and metals, as well as oil and forest woods, is a feature of the struggle for indigenous rights in Brazil and Colombia, where the state contracts extractive or prospective rights to companies which 'invade' indigenous territory. Indigenous land or natural-resource claims often come into conflict with government economic development policies and, as such, raise complex questions regarding the legitimacy of development strategies based on trade liberalisation and individual property rights.

Finally, the violation of the basic rights of indigenous peoples by military, police or guerrilla forces in countries involved in anti-insurgency or wars against drugs is also a key issue. Isolated indigenous peasant communities living and working in drug-producing areas or in regions where insurgent forces are active are caught in the crossfire between security forces, drug traffickers and guerrilla groups. Such is the case of in various communities in Colombia in the Amazon, Sierra Nevada de Santa Marta and Cauca regions, where the FARC and M-19 insurgents and drug traffickers have become enmeshed in a complex web of complicity and conflict, in the Peruvian Amazon and highland areas where the MRTA, and drug traffickers are also connected and active,[38] and in Guatemala, where indigenous communities have long been the victims of counter-insurgency policies and forced relocation or recruitment into civil patrols (see Chapter 6).

The success of local, national and regional activism is intricately tied in with the internationalisation of the region's indigenous movement, the establishment of a dense network of relations between Latin American and North American indigenous groups and their increasing clout in the international arena. Indeed, it can be said that the Latin American indigenous rights movement was 'born transnational'.[39] Hemispheric indigenous groups were the driving force behind the 1977 UN International Non-Governmental Organisation Conference on Discrimination Against Indigenous Populations in the Americas in Geneva. This led to the establishment in 1982 of the UN Working Group on Indigenous Populations (WGIP), which has served as a forum for debate for NGOs, Indian organisations and governmental representatives, and laid the groundwork for the draft UN Declaration on the Rights of Indigenous Peoples - the adoption of which is a goal of the International Decade of the World's Indigenous Populations (1995–2004).[40]

The rights of women have also become an important campaigning issue in the 1990s, although NGOs working on women's rights or gender-specific issues had already emerged in the late 1970s and early 1980s (see Chapter 9). The increased visibility of women's rights issues in the 1990s is a reflection of the increased importance of women's rights as an issue in the international arena, and of the formation of an effective transnational network, as well as of the gradual recognition that gender issues should not necessarily be subsumed in the wider category of 'oppression'.

Among the most pressing issues on which women's rights groups have focused are conflict-related violence against women, including custodial violence and the use of rape as a form of political terror (in Colombia, Haiti and Peru, for example), adolescent prostitution, trafficking in women (in Brazil, for example), domestic violence and sexual assault – all widespread in most of the countries of the region. The Southern Cone Network Against Domestic and Sexual Violence set up in 1989, and the Latin American and Caribbean Network Against Domestic and Sexual Violence established in 1990, with coordinating offices in Argentina, Brazil, Costa Rica, Peru and Puerto Rico, have been active in this area.[41]

In addition, groups focus on increasing equal access to justice in countries where the judiciary, police and medical professions are permeated by discriminatory attitudes, combating state sponsored or tolerated discriminatory legislation and practices, as well as pressing for equal labour conditions, an issue which is becoming increasingly important as women participate in the process of labour globalisation and the formal and informal sectors. Various countries in the region still have legislation which discriminates or tolerates discrimination against women. In Guatemala, for example, the civil code allows husbands the right to prohibit wives from working outside the home and appoints husbands as representatives of all family concerns. In Mexico, the *maquiladora* sector is rife with discriminatory hiring and firing practices.

Governments have responded to NGO pressures by implementing various reforms. In Brazil, police stations staffed only by women have been created to permit easier reporting on domestic violence. Brazil, Chile, Colombia and Ecuador have adopted national programmes to prevent violence against women or have made constitutional changes to that effect, and Costa Rica has established programmes to train police and judiciaries to better understand gender-related issues. It is notable that 'most governments took these initiatives in the period 1988–92 after networks helped put the issue of violence against women on the international agenda', thus highlighting the important role played both by domestic Latin American NGOs and their international allies.[42]

Latin American HROs working on women's rights have not only made a significant contribution putting the rights of women on the Latin American political agenda; through participation in a transnational network focused on this question, they have also contributed significantly to making this an important issue in the UN. Pressures from this network have contributed to various important regional and international developments, such as the determination in 1992 by the UN Committee on the Elimination of Discrimination Against Women that violence against women is a form of discrimination that states must combat; the adoption by the UN General Assembly, in 1993, of the Declaration on the Elimination of Violence Against Women; and the appointment by the United Nations Human Rights Commission (UNHRC) in April 1994 of the first Special Rapporteur on Violence against Women. In February 1997, a draft text categorising gender violence as a crime against humanity was drawn up, a number of high-level officials, including UN Secretary-General Kofi Annan, US Secretary of State Madeleine Albright and World Bank President James D. Wolfenson, called for the inclusion of women's rights into national and international legislation and practices in 1997, and the Human Rights Committee of the International Covenant on Civil and Political Rights (ICCPR) began to pay increasing attention to violence against women. This 'surge of high-level pronouncements on women's human rights represented a watershed in the decade-long effort by women's rights activists from around the world to highlight human rights issues'.[43]

Mobilising around new issues: gay and lesbian rights
A relatively new issue mobilising human rights groups in some countries in Latin America is gay and lesbian rights. The movement is still in its early stages, uneven in regional coverage and still controversial for cultural reasons. It is important to note that the strongest gay and lesbian movement, in the United States, is itself only recent.[44] INGOs have taken these rights on board as a separate category only very recently. Amnesty International (AI) and Human Rights Watch (HRW), for example, only adopted specific action on these rights in 1991 and 1994, respectively. Furthermore, these rights have only lately

become an open part of the international human rights agenda. It was only in March 1993 that the International Lesbian and Gay Association was given consultative status on the Economic and Social Council (ECOSOC) and only in July 1993 that gay and lesbian groups were accredited to participate in the Vienna Conference on Human Rights.[45]

Gay and lesbian associations have been formed in Argentina, Mexico and Peru, which are linked with the US-based International Gay and Lesbian Association. Latin American activists have focused primarily on gaining basic recognition of gay and lesbian NGOs, defending gays and lesbians from violations against the right to life and various forms of inhuman and degrading treatment, as well as on repealing discriminatory legislation. Homosexuality is still a criminal offence in Chile, for example, in violation of the right to equal protection and the right to privacy of the ICCPR and of the UNHRC decision of 1995 condemning anti-sodomy legislation. In some countries governments have shown reluctance in recognising the legal status of NGOs working on gay and lesbian rights, and gays and lesbians, as well as activists working on these rights, have been subject to harassment and attack in various countries.

In 1992, the Argentine government refused to grant legal status to the NGO Argentine Homosexual Community. This decision was subsequently reversed after the case was presented to the Inter-American Court of Human Rights.[46] Two groups in Costa Rica and Honduras, Abraxás and the Association of Honduran Homosexuals Against AIDS, met with similar problems in 1995, the same year in which FUNDASIDA, the only non-governmental AIDS organisation in El Salvador, and Entre Amigos (Among Friends), were attacked and raided. Similarly, in 1996 the Costa Rican Triángulo Rosa (Pink Triangle) was forced to close down following repeated threats and acts of vandalism.[47] Both Argentina and Brazil have had cases of asylum presented to the UN High Commissioner for Refugees, which contemplates gays and lesbians as a group subject to discrimination. In Brazil, the express constitutional protection of homosexuals was discussed in 1993, and in Chile, activists initiated a campaign in 1995, seeking the repeal of the prohibition on homosexuality.[48]

Calling the private sector to account
The responsibility of business corporations for ensuring respect for human rights has become a key issue for human rights activists in Latin America, underscoring 'how far the debate has moved from earlier discussions of whether corporations even have a responsibility for human rights'.[49] Pressures exerted by local human rights groups in conjunction with INGOs has led governments, the International Labour Organization (ILO) and the European Parliament (EP), among other institutions, to take an interest in this issue. In May 1997, the ILO proposed the establishment of a 'global social label' to distinguish goods produced according to proper labour standards and the EP has also proposed that imported textile goods be labelled to the same end.

It is notable that local human rights NGOs work in conjunction with and alongside a multiplicity of new actors previously extraneous to any human rights-monitoring activities. In this area, given the relatively higher degree of globalisation evident in the chain of production established by various multi-national companies, the degree of cross-fertilisation of local, national, regional and international efforts is higher and has been quite effective in inducing change. The Apparel Industry Partnership (AIP) convoked by the US Government in 1996, for example, established a Workplace Code of Conduct on 18 April of that year to prevent child labour, harassment and discrimination, as well as to ensure freedom of association and collective bargaining. By 1997 various companies within the AIP had accepted that external monitoring for compliance could take place.

The Mandarín factory in the San Marco free trade zone in El Salvador is currently monitored by an Independent Monitoring Commission composed of Salvadorian NGOs. In 1997, labour and church groups as well as local NGOs in Guatemala created a committee for the monitoring of corporate codes of conduct. Also in Guatemala, an association between HRW and union organisers working in the Phillips–Van Heusen *maquiladora* factories, led to the acceptance of collective bargaining rights by the company and the first-ever instance of a collective bargaining agreement in the Guatemalan *maquiladora* sector in August 1997.[50] In Colombia, the contracting of military and police forces by oil companies working in the Casare and Arauca regions led to action both by HRW and British-based human rights groups, in conjunction with local populations and workers, in order to pressurise companies to change their security arrangements.[51]

As in other arenas, INGOs have played an important role in applying pressure on home companies and informing the public about the labour conditions under which certain garments are produced. Such is the case of the National Labour Committee and the Press for Change and Global Exchange, based in the United States, as well as the European coalition of NGOs led by the Dutch Clean Clothes Campaign, which includes Labour Behind the Label from the United Kingdom, Les Magasins du Monde in Belgium, the Artisans du Monde from France and FENECON, the Dutch industry organisation. Auditing companies such as Ernst and Young, as well as Coopers and Lybrand, have emerged as actors in this debate, offering to carry out 'social audits' of companies under scrutiny. Ernst and Young, for example, undertook a social audit of the Exporters Manufacturer's Association in Guatemala in 1997.[52]

Conclusions: the human rights movement, violations and democratisation

Latin America's HROs have contributed in various ways to improving the human rights situation in the region. They have played a very important role in 'embarrassing' reluctant governments into action and in working with more 'open' governments to design policies to reduce impunity in various countries throughout the region. In doing so, they are changing governmental attitudes to human rights, and strengthening democratic institutions. One of the most important contributions that the movement has made to the process of democratisation has been in the area of the dissemination of information and education about human rights, not only among those targeted for abuse but also within the institutions most closely associated with committing violations. HROs have contributed to solving individual cases, saving people from death or abuse; they have brought the language of human rights to the region, making it part of the political discourse of parties and governmental, non-governmental and regional institutions; they have widened the scope of the issues considered to be human rights issues, re-linking the issue of poverty and exclusion to the more classic issues of the right to life; and they have created a climate whereby impunity is no longer a protecting mantle which human rights violators can *automatically* count upon.

The relationship between human rights activism and the process of democratic deepening is characterised by a combination of tension and complementarity that mirrors the dynamics of relations between HROs and the state. HROs act as a necessary thorn in the side of the democratising state, cajoling hostile, resistant, indifferent or co-operative governments to widen the boundaries of political inclusion and citizenship, testing their democratic resilience and adaptability. In this sense, the activism of the movement is part and parcel of the democratisation process in the region. HROs are giving prominence to and mobilising around various new issue areas that challenge the democratic frontiers of the state, thus becoming key players in the process of regional democratisation. The region's HROs have realised that although they cannot act in 'opposition' to the democratic state, they must continue to press for the fulfilment of the conditions for widespread respect for human rights. In this sense, they act as the 'conscience' of their countries, calling attention to human rights violations and undertaking important work on the causes of continued crimes against the right to life.

The issues raised by the various sectors of the human rights movement in Latin America are those which pose the most 'uncomfortable' challenges to the various democratising states in the region. Indeed, the struggle for human rights and the relationship between NGOs and the state in that process reveal a paradox that is central to democratisation in the region. On the one hand, the violation of basic rights of the most underprivileged or marginal groups in society are those which raise the spectre of conflict and which place greatest pressure on government authorities with often scarce or fragile political, institutional and even financial resources, already beset by various conflicting demands related with economic development strategies and political reform. As such, the human rights movement and the demands it raises are seen as a source of trouble and instability. On the other hand, democratisation is exactly about extending and ensuring the rights of those presently excluded from the political process and decision-making mechanisms, and states which resist widening and even redefining the scope and nature of citizenship become obstacles to democratic deepening. In this sense, the struggle for human rights and the tensions which emerge from that struggle lie at the very heart of the question of democracy in Latin America. As such, HROs are protagonists in a dynamic process of confrontation, negotiation and cooperation with national, regional and international governmental, intergovernmental and institutional forces, which is defining the future of Latin America's democracies on a daily basis.

The outcome of that dynamic is uncertain. Every gain is made at the cost of losses in other areas. The course which democratic deepening takes depends on the ability and willingness of states to make choices which diminish tensions between different social groups and which gradually incorporate the 'excluded' into the political system. Put in another way, making rights work is part of a struggle for power among competing groups, and their realisation implies changes in forms of government and in relations between the governing and the governed.

Human rights have been abused massively in Latin America, as the state cannot assert its authority over society owing to the failure to reconcile contending political projects. Indeed, the political and economic history of Latin America has been characterised by successive postponements of a full incorporation of the large number of 'excluded' into the political system, and by an inability to create the socio-economic conditions for the effective exercise of citizenship. The most recent wave of transitions to democracy in Latin America occurred for the most part without social revolutions or radical alterations in the economic system towards greater redistribution. The incomplete nature of these transitions has led to the establishment of 'limited' democracies. Thus, Latin America's democracies are still without 'effective citizenship for large sections of the political community'.[53] Universal respect for human rights is the surest sign of a deep democracy where citizenship rights are effective. The fact that Latin America's democracies coexist with high levels of human rights violations reveals that these are still limited and incomplete.

Continued human rights violations testify to the durability of extremely hierarchical social and economic structures, non-democratic modes of power mediation in social and political life and social, political and cultural attitudes based less on a faith in a relationship between citizens and an impartial liberal democratic state and more on a continued reliance on relations of patronage and extra-legal forms of conflict mediation. They are also the product of persistent and acute socio-economic inequalities, as when inequality becomes embedded in the social fabric, it encroaches upon the principle of equality before the law upon which the observance of human rights is based. The human rights situation is a symptom of the duality of polities caught between authoritarian and democratic, 'traditional' and 'modern' forms of political, social and cultural relations. Governments may implement policies to reform and modernise the institutions of law and order which have the most direct impact on the human rights situation in the country, but they may also engage in the politics of patronage which directly contradict the logic of accountability and transparency and perpetuate relations of reciprocity with social groups implicated in or supportive of the violent suppression of social conflict.

The process of democratic deepening or consolidation in the country depends upon making citizens of the 'rightless', to create the conditions for their inclusion into the modern universe of institutions and values, which uphold democratic practices, and respect for the universal notion of human rights. Thus, resolving the human rights situation in Latin America lies at the heart of the process of democratic deepening, as it cuts across the various political, institutional, social and cultural and economic fault-lines which characterise the region's fragile democracies. Yet it is precisely because the human rights situation cuts across these various fault-lines that solutions to the problem are difficult to achieve; they eventually entail deep and widespread changes in the structural, political, sociocultural and institutional realities which give rise to the culture of violence underpinning the dynamic of human rights violations.[54]

In this context, the ability of HROs to change this dynamic is limited. Democratic deepening requires fundamental reforms, which transcend the scope of action which can be undertaken by the human rights movement. Despite its many achievements, adaptability and durability, the human rights movement in the region has not significantly managed to stem the tide of human rights violations which still characterise the politics of many of the countries of the region today. Indeed, in many countries, HROs and activists are still under attack from anti-democratic forces, which feel threatened by the action undertaken by these organisations.

The ability of HROs to definitively shape events is constrained by virtue of the fact that they are non-governmental and cannot take power and implement national policies. That role will always remain firmly in the hands of governments and state authorities. For HROs, the 'link to government is simultaneously the most powerful and the least dependable aspect of the work of the network, as it often depends on the individuals occupying key posts'.[55] In the absence of institutionalisation, only the commitment and good will of officeholders ensures positive attitudes to human rights, and if authorities change and there is no institutionalisation, the chances for respect for human rights to become embedded in national political life are slim.[56]

Yet some states are able to resist even the most intense pressures, such that the contribution of HROs depends upon the willingness of governments to take action, whether reluctantly or not. In turn, this will depend upon the capacity of local HROs to find powerful allies, be they non-governmental or governmental, and on the ability or willingness of the latter to impose 'sanctions' of one kind or another on an offending country. Even in these situations, success is sometimes elusive, as governments react not only to material but also to moral pressures, and if they are unconcerned about 'belonging to the democratic community of nations' they may be sanctioned and remain unmoved.[57]

It should also be noted that HROs are not a homogenous modernising and democratising force. The defence of 'noble causes' does not ensure that HROs are transparent, democratic, and accountable to those they claim to defend.[58] Nor does it guarantee that they do not contribute to existing dynamics of violence by generating tensions between competing client groups. Indeed, as part of the political and civic culture of the places where they operate, HROs often engage in the politics of personalism, patronage and clientelism, as do state agents or sectors of the political class. Indeed, as HROs have gained in power and influence, the issue of accountability becomes increasingly important. According to one estimate, Brazil's HROs, for example, administer approximately $700 million a year,[59] and critics claim that human rights have become an 'industry' in the country, giving jobs to various people in organisations competing fiercely for foreign funding.[60]

Whatever the development of the region's process of democratisation and the limitations of the region's powerful human rights movement, two things are certain: on the one hand, that Latin America's human rights movement cannot do without democracy and without the continued survival of a democratising state led by authorities willing to engage in reform, however inept and cumbersome; on the other hand, that Latin America's political and state authorities or institutions cannot do without the pressures for change and incorporation emanating from the movement as a whole, however uncomfortable the demands posed may be.

Notes

1 M. Keck and K. Sikkink, *Activists Beyond Borders: Advocacy Networks in International Politics* (Ithaca, Cornell University Press, 1998), p. 88; A. Brysk, 'From Above and From Below: Social Movement, the International System, and Human Rights in Argentina', *Comparative Political Studies* 26 (1993), p. 267; E. L. Cleary, *The Struggle for Human Rights in Latin America* (Westport, Praeger, 1997), p. 66.

2 For Argentina see I. Guest, *Behind the Disappearances: Argentina's Dirty War Against Human Rights and the United Nations* (Philadelphia, University of Pennsylvania Press, 1990); L. Martin and K. Sikkink, 'US Policy and Human Rights in Argentina and Guatemala, 1973–1980', in P. B. Evans, H. K. Jacobson and R. D. Putnam (eds), *Double-Edged Diplomacy: International Bargaining and Domestic Politics* (Berkeley, University of California Press, 1993). For Brazil and Uruguay see L. Weschler, *A Miracle a Universe Settling Accounts with Torturers* (New York, Penguin 1990). For Chile see P. Orellana and E. Quay Hutchinson (eds), *El movimiento de derechos humanos en Chile, 1973–1990* (Santiago, Centro de Estudios Políticos Latinoamericanos Simón Bolívar, 1991).

3 Cleary, *The Struggle*, p. 5. For Chile see also Human Rights Watch (HRW), *La Vicaría de la Solidaridad en Chile* (1987); P. Lowden, *Moral Opposition to Authoritarian Rule* (Oxford, Macmillan, 1996).

4 See J. M. Puryear, *Thinking Politics: Intellectuals and Democracy in Chile, 1973–1988* (Baltimore, Johns Hopkins University Press, 1994), pp. 44–6 and Cleary, *The Struggle*, pp. 31–2.

5 In countries where the human rights movement was connected to the political parties which won 'transitional' elections, as in Chile, the latter were stronger and better prepared to deal with the human rights problems inherited from military rule. See A. Barahona de Brito, *Human*

Rights and Democratisation in Latin America, Uruguay and Chile (Oxford, Oxford University Press, 1997).

6 K. Sikkink, 'The Emergence, Evolution, and Effectiveness of the Latin American Human Rights Network', in E. Jelin and E. Hirshberg (eds), *Constructing Democracy: Human Rights, Citizenship, and Society in Latin America* (Boulder, Westview, 1996), p. 59; J. Smith, 'Transnational Political Processes and the Human Rights Movement', in M. Dobkowski *et al.* (eds), *Research in Social Movements, Conflicts, and Change* (Greenwich, CT, JAI Press, 1995), pp. 185–219; Brysk, 'From Above', pp. 259–85.

7 For the United States see J. Donnelly, *International Human Rights: Dilemmas in World Politics* (Boulder, Westview, 1993); D. P. Forsythe, *Human Rights and US Foreign Policy: Congress Reconsidered* (Gainesville, University of Florida Press, 1988); L. Schoultz, *Human Rights and United States Policy Towards Latin America* (Princeton, Princeton University Press, 1981), esp. pp. 290–2. For the EC see A. Von Stechow, 'The Council of Ministers: The Constraint on Action', in G. Edwards and E. Regelsberger (eds), *Europe's Global Links: The European Community and Interregional Cooperation* (London, Pinter, 1990), pp. 161–3.

8 On the importance of NGOs in the UN system see D. Otto, 'Non-Governmental Organizations in the UN System: The Emerging Role of International Civil Society', *Human Rights Quarterly*, 18 (1996).

9 Lowden, *Moral Opposition*, pp. 1–7.

10 Cleary, *The Struggle*, pp. 34, 42.

11 For an analysis of the new inter-American democracy-promoting system see H. Muñoz, 'El derecho a la democracia en las Américas', *Estudios Internacionales*, 28 (1995); T. Farer, 'The Rise of the Inter-American Human Rights Regime: No Longer a Unicorn, Not Yet an Ox', *Human Rights Quarterly*, 19 (1997) and T. Farer (ed.) *Beyond Sovereignty: Collectively Defending Democracy in the Americas* (Baltimore, Johns Hopkins University Press, 1996); C. Cerna, 'Universal Democracy: An International Legal Right or the Pipe Dream of the West', *New York Journal of International Law and Politics*, 27 (1995).

12 These terms are used by Stanley Cohen in his analysis of government responses to human rights reports – 'Government Responses to Human Rights Reports: Claims, Denials and Counter-claims', *Human Rights Quarterly*, 18 (1996).

13 Ministério de Justiça, *Programa nacional de direitos humanos* (Brasília, Ministério de Justiça, 1996).

14 D. Gardner, 'Mexico', in P. Baehr, L. Sadiwa and J. Smith (eds), *Human Rights in Developing Countries Yearbook 1996* (Oslo, Nordic Human Rights Publications, 1996). Also see Instituto de Relaciones Europeas–Latino Americanas (IRELA), *Evaluación de la institución del Ombudsman en América Central, México y los países andinos* (Madrid, 1995).

15 R. Wilson (ed.), *Human Rights Culture and Context: Anthropological Perspectives* (London, Pluto, 1997), p. 1.

16 A. Brysk, 'Acting Globally Indian Rights and International Politics in Latin America', in D. Van Cott (ed.), *Indigenous Peoples and Democracy in Latin America* (Washington, DC, Inter-American Dialogue, 1994), pp. 29–30.

17 Wilson, *Human Rights Culture*, p. 11.

18 Keck and Sikkink, *Activists Beyond Borders*, pp. 14–15.

19 For Bolivia and Columbia, respectively, see X. Albó, 'From Kataristas to MNRistas? The Surprising Alliance between Aymaras and Neoliberals in Bolivia', and J. Avirama and R. Márquez, 'The Indigenous Movement in Colombia', both in van Cott (ed.), *Indigenous Peoples*.

20 Brysk, 'Acting Globally', pp. 29–30.

21 D. Held, *Democracy and the Global Order: From the Modern State to Cosmopolitan Governance* (Cambridge, Polity, 1995), p. 223.

22 Keck and Sikkink, *Activists Beyond Borders*, p. 215.

23 *Democracy and the Global Order*, p. 223.

24 Keck and Sikkink, *Activists Beyond Borders*, pp. 16–25.

25 See, for example H. Frühling, *Represión política y defensa de los derechos humanos* (Santiago,

Ediciones Chile América, 1986).

26 For the role of human rights movements in the transition to democracy see, for example, M. del Huerto Amarillo and A. Sabella Serrentino, *Movimiento de derechos humanos en el Uruguay* (Montevideo, IELSUR, 1986) for Uruguay; H. Fruhling, 'El movimiento de derechos humanos y la transición en Chile y Argentina', Cuadernos de Trabajo, 11 (Academía de Humanismo Cristiano, Santiago, 1991) for Argentina and Chile.

27 For Bolivia see HRW, 'Bolivia: Almost Nine Years and Still No Verdict in the "Trial of Disappearances"' (1992). For Argentina see HRW, *Truth and Partial Justice in Argentina* (1987) and *Truth and Partial Justice in Argentina, An Update* (1991); C. Acuña *et al.*(eds), *Juicio, castigos y memorias: Derechos humanos y justicia en la política argentina* (Buenos Aires, Ediciones Nueva Visión, 1995); A. Brysk, *The Politics of Human Rights in Argentina* (Stanford, Stanford University Press, 1995); D. Weissbrodt and M. Bartolomei, 'The Effectiveness of International Human Rights Pressures: The Case of Argentina', *Minnesota Law Review*, 75 (1991); Comisión Nacional Sobre la Desaparición de Personas, *Nunca más Argentina: Informe sobre la desaparición forzada de personas* (Buenos Aires, Eudeba, 1984). For Chile see, HRW, *Chile: The Struggle for Truth and Justice for Past Human Rights Violations* (1992) and 'Chile, Unsettled Business: Human Rights at the Start of the Frei Presidency' (1995); S. Brett, *Chile, A Time of Reckoning: Human Rights and the Judiciary* (Geneva, International Commission of Jurists, 1992); J. Correa, 'Dealing with Past Human Rights Violations: The Chilean Case After Dictatorship', *Notre Dame Law Review*, 67 (1992); M. A. Garretón, 'Human Rights in Democratisation Processes', in Jelin and Hirshberg (eds), *Constructing Democracy*; D. Weissbrodt and P. W. Fraser, 'National Commission on Truth and Reconciliation: Report of the Chilean Commission on Truth and Reconciliation', *Human Rights Quarterly*, 14 (1992); Comisión Nacional de Verdad y Reconciliación, *Informe de la Comisión Nacional de Verdad y Reconciliación* (Santiago, Talleres de la Nación, 1991). For Uruguay see Barahona de Brito, *Human Rights*; HRW, *Challenging Impunity: The Ley de Caducidad and the Referendum Campaign in Uruguay* (1989); L. Roniger and M. Sznajder, 'The Legacy of Human Rights Violations in the Southern Cone: Argentina, Chile and Uruguay' (Jerusalem, mimeo, 1997); Servicio de Paz y Justicia (SERPAJ), *Uruguay Nunca Más: Informe sobre la violación a los derechos humanos, 1972–1985* (Montevideo, SERPAJ, 1989).

28 For new sources of human rights violations under democracy see F. Panizza, 'Human Rights, Global Culture and Social Fragmentation', *Bulletin of Latin American Research*, 12 (1993) and 'Human Rights in the Process of Transition and Consolidation of Democracy in Latin America', *Political Studies*, XLIII (1995).

29 HRW, *World Report 1998*, pp. 414–15.

30 Report by the International Labour Organization (ILO), cited by HRW, *World Report 1998*, p. 380.

31 For death squads and the murder of street children in Brazil, see HRW, *Final Justice: Police and Death Squad Homicides of Adolescents in Brazil* (1994) and G. Dimenstein, *Brazil: War on Children* (London, Latin America Bureau, 1991). For Guatemala, HRW, 'Guatemala's Forgotten Children: Police Violence and Arbitrary Detention' (1997). For Colombia, L. Aptekar, *Street Children of Cali* (Durham, NC, Duke University Press, 1988).

32 Cleary, *The Struggle*, pp. 69–81.

33 Van Cott (ed.), *Indigenous Peoples*, p. 2.

34 For participation in UNCED see Y. Kakabadse and S. Burns, 'Movers and Shapers: NGOs in International Affairs', *World Resources Institute Working Paper* (Washington, DC, World Resources Institute, 1994).

35 See Brysk, 'Acting Globally', p. 31.

36 Van Cott (ed.), *Indigenous Peoples*, p. 12.

37 See, for example, T. McDonald, 'The Quichua of Eastern Ecuador', in S. Davis (ed.), *Indigenous Views on Land and the Environment* (Washington, DC, World Bank Development Report, 1992); Avirama and Márquez, 'The Indigenous Movement in Colombia'; and J. C. Tresierra, 'Mexico: Indigenous Peoples and the Nation-State' and E. Prieto, 'Indigenous Peoples in

Paraguay', both in van Cott (ed.), *Indigenous Peoples*.
38 I. Remy, 'The Indigenous Population and the Construction of Democracy in Peru', in van Cott (ed.), *Indigenous Peoples*.
39 Brysk, 'Acting Globally', p. 32.
40 For the negotiation process of the draft Declaration see R. L. Barsh, 'Indigenous Peoples and the UN Commission on Human Rights: A Case of the Immovable Object and the Irresistible Force', *Human Rights Quarterly*, 18 (1996).
41 Keck and Sikkink, *Activists Beyond Borders*, p. 180.
42 *Ibid.*, p. 194.
43 HRW, *World Report 1998*, p. 390.
44 J. D. Willetts, 'International Human Rights Law and Sexual Orientation', *18 Hastings International and Comparative Law Review*, 1 (1994).
45 D. Sanders, 'Getting Lesbian and Gay Issues on the International Human Rights Agenda', *Human Rights Quarterly*, 18 (1996), p. 91.
46 'Argentina: CHA Goes to the Inter-American Court of Human Rights', *International Lesbian and Gay Association Bulletin*, 15 (1992).
47 For an account of such attacks against gay and lesbian people and NGOs, see HRW, *World Report 1998*.
48 'Brazil's Constitution up for Review', *International Lesbian and Gay Bulletin*, 4 (1993) and 'Activists Launch Campaign to Repeal Chile's Sodomy Law', *International Gay and Lesbian Human Rights Commission, Emergency Response Network* (June 1995).
49 HRW, *World Report 1998*, p. 415.
50 *Ibid.* and HRW, 'Corporations and Human Rights: Freedom of Association in a Maquila in Guatemala' (1997).
51 HRW, *World Report 1998*, p. 420.
52 *Ibid.*, p. 417.
53 A. Przeworski, *Sustainable Democracy* (Cambridge, Cambridge University Press, 1995), pp. 34, 39.
54 See A. Barahona de Brito, 'Democracy and Social Justice: Some Preliminary Considerations', paper presented at the preparatory meeting of the V Euro-Latin American Forum, Social Development and Regional Integration, 16–17 October 1998; and F. Panizza and A. Barahona de Brito, 'The Politics of Human Rights in Democratic Brazil: A Lei não pega', *Democratisation*, December 1998.
55 Keck and Sikkink, *Activists Beyond Borders*, p. 103.
56 P. S. Pinheiro and P. de Mesquita Neto, 'O Programa Nacional de Direitos Humanos: avaliação do primeiro ano e perspectivas', *Estudos Avançados*, 11 (1997), p. 131.
57 A. Barahona de Brito, 'The Politics of Democracy and Human Rights Promotion: The European Union and the Mercosul', *Lumiar Papers* (Lisbon, Instituto de Estudos Estratégicos e Internacionais, 1998).
58 For problem of accountability see, for example, H. Béjar and P. Oakley, 'From Accountability to Shared Responsibility: NGO Evaluation in Latin America', in M. Edwards and D. Hulme (eds), *Beyond the Magic Bullet: NGO Performance and Accountability in the Post-Cold War World* (West Hartford, Kumarian Press, 1996), pp. 93–4, 98–9.
59 *Veja* (9 February 1994, no. 1326), p. 70.
60 Cleary, *The Struggle*, pp. 79–80.

9

Women and politics

FIONA MACAULAY

Since the mid-1980s profound social, economic and political changes have swept across Latin America, as authoritarian and military rule has crumbled and been replaced by liberal democracies, revolutionary wars have been fought, won and lost, and autocratic government has gradually given way to greater pluralism. The grand narratives of history are always told as if women were absent. However, not only have women been present during all these changes, but they have also been key collective and individual protagonists throughout all these shifts of regime. As countries emerge from conflict and authoritarian rule, and move to consolidate hard-won peace and democracy, how has the renegotiation of the rules of the political game affected women, and how, in turn, have women acted upon the political system in order to further their own interests, and to deepen democracy?

This chapter examines the complex interplay between changes in political regimes and the organised women's movement in Latin America, paying particular attention to the consolidation phase. In geographical terms, the chapter focuses, on the one hand, on countries which have emerged from authoritarian rule, such as those of the Southern Cone – Paraguay, Bolivia and Brazil. There are others, principally those of Central America, which have recently put an end to years of armed conflict. In others, such as Mexico or Peru, change is too partial and contradictory to be classified as a genuine transition to democracy. However, there is a striking degree of commonality between the agendas and strategies of national women's movements across the region. This is attributable not just to the well-developed regional networks of women that evolved during the 1980s and earlier, but also to the 'globalisation' of a set of normative values with respect to women's rights, born of the efforts of the UN and the women's movement internationally, and on which Latin American women's groups draw heavily. Like many aspects of women's organised political activity during the contemporary period, it is reminiscent of the early experiences and strategies of the 'first wave' of Latin American feminism at the turn of the century. This chapter outlines some of those common priorities and strategies in the mid-to late 1990s and argues that the consolidation phase of (re)democratisation has led women's movements throughout the region to engage in a new and contestational way with the institutional arena, seeking to act upon it and transform it into a better conduit for grassroots women's demands and a guarantor of women's hard-won rights.

Gender politics and regime change

Regime change and political crisis always entail a momentary breakdown in existing gender relations, which may subsequently undergo a shift as a result, or end up being shored up and reinforced. Transitions generally share a number of common features as far as women are concerned. They bring about a major change in the rules of the game, affecting electoral, constitutional and political relations. They are also characterised by a male elite-brokered settlement, in which certain pending social issues, such as gender equality, will be relegated to the consolidation phase once the democratic system is properly secured, or dismissed as divisive. Political parties move into dominance as a channel for interest representation and policy-making. Part of the negotiated settlement entails a demobilisation of civil society, which had played such a key role in protest against the incumbent regime and in creating the grassroots demand for a change of regime. As the parties move centre stage and the locus of politics shifts from the informal to the institutional, male politicians squeeze the women activists out of the soup kitchens, *barrio* committees and human rights groups.

Periods of regime breakdown and transition are contradictory moments for women. One the one hand, these critical junctures are driven by overriding dynamics to which all other considerations are secondary: the removal of the incumbent regime, or the end of a war and the installation of a new, democratic peace. It was therefore very difficult to get certain issues on to the agenda during the transition period. For example, the issue of new divorce legislation was considered taboo by the leaders of the Chilean centre-left coalition, the Concertación, during their first term in office, although women in the parties viewed it as a priority. The downplaying of 'private' issues sought not to antagonise the Church, to whose support the new leadership owed a great deal. On the other hand, opportunities open up for non-traditional political actors to come to the fore. The vacuum created by the absence, under military rule, of the traditional areas of politics in which men normally operate (parties, trade unions), is filled by women, protesting in the street and demanding political change. The Mothers of the Plaza de Mayo in Argentina, and other women's human rights groups in the region, are the most potent symbol of this gender-role transgression at times of crisis, even if many women justify their trespass into a male domain within the terms of maternalist discourse, arguing that they are in fact upholding, not subverting, established gender roles.[1] Male politicians are generally cognisant of the role of women in the popular movements and of their increased politicisation. Their desire to attract women's votes renders them more amenable to the demands from the women's movement to incorporate gender issues into their platforms. In Brazil, women managed to secure a number of commitments from the incoming centrist Partido do Movimento Democrático Brasileiro (PMDB, Brazilian Democratic Movement Party), notably the installation of women's police stations to combat violence against women, and of women's councils to advise on public policy at national and state levels.[2] In summary, regime breakdown opens the way for women to emerge as non-traditional actors in informal political settings. The transition offers them momentary leverage in the parties and political elite, even as politics is re-masculinised.[3]

In the late 1980s Central America began to emerge from a decade of civil war which affected virtually every country in the isthmus, directly or indirectly. The civil war in Nicaragua was ended in 1990 by the election of Latin America's third woman president, Violeta Chamorro. El Salvador signed peace accords in 1992 and Guatemala ended 36 years of violence with peace accords in 1996. The 'pacification' of Central America has brought mixed effects for women in a similar way. Like other kinds of transitions, opportunities opened up and priorities changed for those women who were already politically active, even though women were excluded from the post-war settlement and have had to battle for a voice. The wars in the area exacted a high price: some 120,000 women were widowed in the Guatemalan civil war, and have been represented by their own organisation, Coordinadora Nacional de Viudas de Guatemala (CONAVIGUA, National Coordination of Guatemalan Widows of Political Violence) since 1988.[4] Nicaraguan women were amongst those hardest hit by hyperinflation, rationing and the armed conflict, and voted decisively to end the war. For the 'mothers of the heroes and martyrs', and others, the cost to their families and households was too great. The 1990 elections were marked by the use of gendered imagery. White-haired, and conducting much of her campaign from a wheelchair, Chamorro projected a maternal and madonna-like image that stood in sharp contrast to the macho style of the incumbent President Daniel Ortega, who used a fighting cock as his campaign mascot. On the other hand, women feared the loss of many positive gains made during the revolution. The number of women elected to the National Assembly dropped from 18.5 per cent in 1990 to 10.7 per cent in 1996. Chamorro's government promised land and jobs to ex-combatants, who took precedence over women as they represented a more potentially destabilising force. Women bore the brunt of unemployment, and impoverished female-headed households became the norm. Issues of sexuality or reproductive rights, which the Sandinistas had downplayed in order not to antagonise the Catholic Church, were now rendered taboo in a government backed by the church hierarchy. Nonetheless, the departure from government of the FSLN left feminists and women in the party, and rural and urban unions far freer than before to campaign around such controversial agendas.

As in the transitions to democracy in South America, the ending of the conflict was brokered by male elites, in this case assisted by the international community, in the form of the UN mechanisms installed to monitor the peace accords. Women were largely excluded from this settlement and there ensued a struggle to ensure that civil society had a formal voice in the various bodies set up to oversee the transition. For example, violence against women was omitted from the 1994 Global Accord between the government and the armed opposition, and not considered by the UN Verification Mission (MINUGUA) to be within their mandate. Guatemala is perhaps exceptional in having a range of new civilian organisations in the discussion of the peace accords. After women were excluded from the Permanent Commissions women organised in 85 refugee camps in Mexico elected to negotiate their return. They pressed for women's needs to be considered and *Mama Maquín* (an organisation of indigenous women) was represented on return committees, with a network in the same refugee camps by 1994. Since 1992 women have been elected to both Permanent Commissions and have led groups returning to Guatemala. However, the National Women's Forum was not set up until May 1997, the last of the international community's commitments to create new civil society bodies under the peace accords. Revolution and civil conflict have both a devastating and galvanising effect on the civil population. These highly politicised conflicts encouraged women to organise, in defence of their families and communities, initiatives which were able to survive the period of crisis and maintain momentum through the transition, into what may be tentatively characterised as a consolidation phase in the region.

The consolidation phase of political democratisation has affected women's movements in a different way. Women's movements have begun to engage with the state and with the political parties in new ways, employing a language of citizenship, rights and entitlements that draws on the commitments made by national governments to international conventions, such as the UN Convention on the Elimination of All Forms of Discrimination against Women and the Platform of Action of the 1995 UN Conference on Women in Beijing. There is renewed strategic attention to the potential of formal, institutional arenas to deliver the policies and resources that women's grassroots movements have been demanding, such as labour legislation, health care and reproductive rights. Concerted efforts have been made by women's groups over the past few years in the reform of legal codes, constitutions, party and electoral systems, and representation, with the understanding that only structural change will actually see public policy for women debated with women's input, passed in Congress and implemented with adequate resources.

The formal political arena

Transitions to democracy in the region have changed women's relationship with the formal sphere of politics, with its representative institutions, decision-making bodies, and the key gatekeepers between civil society and political power – the political parties – as women's movements in the region begin to engage with the state with their own agenda and strategies, and on their own terms. Women activists in many countries were disappointed, and disbelieving, as they found themselves shouldered aside within the political parties as male politicians and leaders returned from exile. In most cases, the percentage of women elected to public office actually dropped in the first elections marking the transition to democracy – numbers were halved in Chile and dropped to zero in Uruguay. The low numbers elected reflected the scramble for power within the parties which seemed to worsen as the democratic system began to consolidate. For example, in Chile, women within the *Concertación* found that, in the second round of post-Pinochet elections in 1993, even women with a high profile in the party, or who already held seats, were finding difficulty being selected for winnable seats. Contrary to the 'common-sense' suppositions of modernisation and development theory, women's political participation in Latin America has not followed a smooth upward curve, but rather it has had some early peaks, and unexpected troughs following recent (re)democratisation. For example, in the six years following the granting of women's suffrage in Argentina in 1949, the number of women elected to the Chamber of Deputies rose to nearly 29 per cent. It then dropped very sharply to 2.2 per cent and below for the following 18 years, rising again to around 9 per cent in the 1973–75 period, President Juan Perón's third period of power. Following the transition to democracy after military rule, in 1983 Argentina elected a parliament with a mere 3.9 per cent women in the Chamber of Deputies and 6.5 per cent in the Senate. Table 9.1 details the percentage of women elected to national legislatures as of 1999, or the most recent available data, during which time some countries have introduced positive discrimination measures, to greater or lesser success.

Women have always been regarded as interlopers in the formal political sphere, even though in some countries, they have been enfranchised for over sixty years. The continent has seen only three women presidents,[5] and in some countries the number of women elected to the national legislature remains under 10 per cent. In part this is due to factors which afflict women everywhere, such as the culture within the parties, the relegation of women to the private domain under the liberal public/private rubric, and public resistance to accepting women as political actors. Authoritarian interludes frequently delayed the exercise of franchise. In Uruguay women were granted the vote in 1932 and first exercised it in 1942.[6] Elsewhere, suffrage, both male and female, was a sop to the international community by countries run by autocrats or family dynasties. Guatemala, Honduras, Paraguay and Nicaragua have no extended

Table 9.1   *Women in elected office in Latin America, 1999*

Country	Female suffrage secured	No. of women in Lower House (%)*	No. of women in Upper House (%)	Office last renewed
Argentia	1947	27.6	5.6	26 Oct. 1997
Bolivia	1952	n/a (7.7 1993)	3.7	1 June 1997
Brazil	1994	5.7	7.4	4 Oct.1998
Chile	1949	10.8	4.3	11 Dec. 1997
Colombia	1954	11.8	12.7	8 Mar. 1998
Costa Rica	1949	19.3	*	1 Feb.1998
Cuba	1934	27.6	*	11 Jan. 1998
Ecuador	1929	17.4	*	31 May 1998
El Salvador	1950	16.7	*	16 Mar.1997
Guatemala	1945	12.5	*	12 Nov. 1995
Honduras	1955	9.4	*	30 Nov. 1997
Mexico	1953	14.2	14.8	6 July 1997
Nicaragua	1955	9.7	*	20 Oct. 1996
Paraguay	1961	2.5	17.8	10 May 1998
Peru	1955	10.8	*	9 Apr. 1995
Uruguay	1932	7.1	6.5	27 Nov. 1994
Venezuela	1947	13.1	8.8	8 Nov. 1998

Notes
In countries where data from the most recent elections are unavailable, figures are given for the previous legislative period.
Lower House, or single house in the case of unicameral parliaments, are marked *.
Sources: Female suffrage: T. Valdés and E. Gómariz (eds) *Latin American Women: Compared Figures* (Santiago and Madrid, FLASCO and Instituto de la Mujer, 1995), p. 159. Numbers and percentage of women elected in the most recent elections: Inter-Parliamentary Union Web site.

democratic experience comparable, say, to Chile's. Women voters were regarded across the continent as inexperienced, apathetic and easily influenced by the Church, a prejudice which no longer holds water. On one measure, women are more active citizens than men: they now outstrip men as a percentage of registered voters and of voter turnout in many countries. The political upheavals of the 1970s and 1980s and subsequent transitions to democracy have politicised many women, in particular, who entered the political sphere as very non-traditional actors, as underground party activists, human rights campaigners and even guerrilla fighters. The formal political sphere has gained a new attraction: elections now do change political outcomes, and the parties have moved centre stage as mediators in struggles over power and resources as never before. The period of consolidation has coincided with a determined move by the women's movement to be represented at the highest governmental level, a response in part to some of the disappointments of the transition, in part to the sidelining of civil society and grassroots movements in the transition. The vote has more relevance than ever: women are more aware of their muscle, and make greater demands for candidates to promise change, at local as well as national levels.

In the transition to democracy in the region, political parties have come to dominate the political scene, squeezing out the social movements in which women are more likely to participate. As a result, politics itself has been 're-masculinised' and women excluded from a traditionally male ambit. As the gatekeepers of the political system, parties play a crucial role in setting the terms of which issues are represented in political life and by whom. Women's relationship with the political parties is now changing. During the periods of crisis and confrontation, whether the civil wars in Central America, or the movement to end military regimes in Brazil and the Southern Cone, party women (*las políticas*) remained deeply involved with party politics, even whilst exercising *doble militancia* (double militancy) as feminists. In Chile, as in its neighbouring countries, many women kept the organisational structures of the banned centre-left parties alive during the years of the Pinochet dictatorship, maintaining grassroots cells and activities whilst the (largely male) leadership was exiled abroad. The energies of women in the FSLN in Nicaragua, and the FMLN in El Salvador, were similarly absorbed by the drama of the civil wars in each country, and the struggle to defend the revolutionary party and its vision. Now women are setting the terms of participation in the party. They want to be in the party mainstream, not in a female ghetto, and they have pressed parties to take a 'gender agenda' on to their platforms.

Women were members and activists within political parties for decades before they gained the right to vote or run for office and in some, they actually constitute a majority of the membership. Many parties, such as the Chilean Radicals, Socialists and Christian Democrats, formed special 'women's departments' in the 1920s and 1930s to incorporate women. On assuming the presidency, Perón granted women suffrage in 1947 and established the Partido Peronista Femenino (PPF, Peronist Women's Party) to channel women's pro-Peronist energies and loyalties, a move which paid rich dividends electorally. In revolutionary Cuba and in Sandinista Nicaragua, the governments set up *oficialista* women's organisations that effectively functioned as the women's wing of the dominant revolutionary party: the Federation of Cuban Women and the Asociación de Mujeres Nicaragüenses Luisa Amanda Espinoza (AMNLAE, Luisa Amanda Espinoza Association of Nicaraguan Women).[7] These women's departments functioned parallel to the main party and did not, except in the case of the PPF, lead to substantial involvement of women in leadership roles or elected office, or provide a useful space within which women could build confidence within an otherwise male dominated structure. During the transition period, women in the parties have begun to replace women's departments with alternatives such as technical departments within parties to advise on gender issues (the Christian Democrats in Chile), the creation of the permanent post of 'women's' vice-president (the Socialist Party in Chile) and the installation of a women's 'secretariat' within the more collegial structure of the Brazilian PT.

The discovery of just how limited that transitional opening had been for women to set a new agenda, and press claims as new actors, has subsequently led many women in the parties to a new set of extra-party strategies. Clearly the internal party culture was more resistant than ever to women's presence in positions of power, despite the lip-service paid to women's grassroots work prior to the transition. Other barriers to women's political participation, such as the triple burden of home, work and political life, the gender division of labour and women's lack of resources, are all macro-level socio-economic issues that would not be solved overnight. The electoral system, political culture and resistance to selecting and promoting women could, however, be addressed via formal mechanisms that would enforce change. This attention to structural inequalities within the democratic political system itself has become a women's movement priority in the consolidation period.

Virtually all the countries of the region have either adopted, or are in the process of voting on, a number of measures, most commonly a quota system. Quotas first began to be debated in the region in the late 1980s, following the example of several European countries and centre-left parties who came into contact with Latin American women activists in exile. Finally, the UN Conferences on Women, firstly in Nairobi in 1985, and more emphatically in Beijing in 1995, stressed the importance of women's access to institutional power. Quotas are used principally in three ways in Latin America: to assure women of a certain percentage of seats on the governing body or executive of a political party; to guarantee women candidates a certain percentage of places, in a particular position, on a closed party list in a proportional representation electoral system; and to force the elected authorities to appoint a certain percentage of women to leading posts in the executive branch and administration. A fourth form of quota, that of guaranteeing to women *per se* as a sector, a certain number or percentage of seats in elected bodies, such as the national parliament, has not been employed in Latin America, as it has elsewhere in the world.

Argentina boasted the first party quota system, when the PPF was guaranteed 33.3 per cent of the party leadership positions and electoral places. The result was the highest percentage of women ever elected in the continent. In the current period, those parties which have adopted a quota for women in internal leadership positions are generally centre-left parties, or small and marginal parties. In Chile the PS and PPD have both had a 20 per cent quota since 1990, and the PT adopted a 30 per cent quota in 1991, copied soon afterwards by the Central Unica de Trabalhadores (CUT, Central Union Confederation), the largest trade union confederation in the country. The PT then sponsored a bill to secure 20 per cent of places for female candidates for city councillors in the 1996 municipal elections and it was extended to the election of deputies at state and federal levels for the 1998 elections (and raised to 25 per cent). Women have also had success with parties in Paraguay (all except the Partido Liberal Radical Auténtico (PLRA, Liberal Party)) and Mexico (PRI).

Argentina's 1991 Ley de Cupos (quota law) obliged all parties to select a female candidate in every third slot on their electoral lists. Ecuador's Ley de Amparo Laboral (labour protection law) of 1996, and Paraguay's 1996 electoral code set the floor at 20 per cent. Costa Rica and Bolivia have similar provisions, although they are not adequately fulfilled or enforced. However, a percentage on party lists may not result in an equal percentage being elected: this depends on the electoral system. Closed party lists are the best guarantee of an equivalent outcome, particularly if women candidates are inserted proportionally according to the quota from the top of the pre-selected list, rather than clustered among the lowest, unelectable positions. An open list is no guarantee, and in a majoritarian electoral system the first-past-the-post principle ensures a winner-takes-all mentality, and fierce competition within the parties for selection. For example, in the 1994 elections in Chile, which has a binominal system (two deputies elected per district) an impressive number of women, 49 (12.9 per cent of all candidates), ran for deputy, but at least half were run by small parties with no hope of election under the current system, and received under 5 per cent of the vote in that constituency. Only nine were elected. The women's movement in Chile is now proposing the introduction of a proportional representation system. The complex and highly competitive Uruguayan party system has also proven remarkably resistant to change: feminists have tried to persuade the parties to adopt a code of conduct since the 1980s, but both main parties (the Nationals and Colorados) have refused.[8]

One of the most noticeable results of over a decade of women's activism in the parties and demands for greater access to the political system is a change in the composition of elected representatives. Indigenous women have been elected for the first time to Guatemala's national assembly. In Brazil in 1994, the PT elected two women senators: Marina da Silva, the daughter of rubber tappers from the western Amazon, and Benedita da Silva, a black woman from a shanty town in Rio de Janeiro. Women elected to office have also shown greater willingness to work together in coalitions and networks, and across party lines. For example, Nicaraguan women succeeded in reforming the criminal code to have domestic violence recognised as a crime. The change, proposed by the Network of Women against Violence, was also backed by right-wing women legislators, who persuaded their male peers that the issue was not a 'leftist or Sandinista idea'. Similarly, in the run-up to the 1996 elections the cross-party National Coalition of Women, encompassing women party representatives from the FSLN to the ex-Contra supporters, presented a joint platform to their individual parties, stressing women's rights.

The Brazilian Constituent Assembly of 1986 saw an influx of feminists, who ran specifically so that they could influence the new Constitution, which they managed by mobilising women country-wide. Since 1994, Brazil has also seen its most cohesive *bancada femenina* (women's caucus), a cross-party grouping which has taken the Beijing Platform of Action and 14 priority areas of legislation as its collective agenda. This has, however, been less successful in Chile, where gender issues themselves have become politicised in the absence of other policy areas which might distinguish right from left, or one party from another. This makes cross-party collaboration almost impossible. The legislators themselves are also 'competing' with the women's ministry, SERNAM (Servicio Nacional de la Mujer).

It has taken a very long time for women to be appointed to public office in anything but token numbers, and the first portfolios occupied by women were in the area of social welfare: education, labour, social welfare and health.[9] This has begun to change in recent years, with a Brazilian woman minister of finance, an FSLN-appointed women head of police, an Argentinian woman minister of foreign affairs and a Chilean female minister of justice. The post of Human Rights Ombudsman in two countries (Bolivia and El Salvador) is now held by a woman. During the transition period Chilean women of the Concertación put forward a number of demands including the appointment of 30 per cent women to senior government posts. It was never adhered to or adopted as an official Concertación measure. In Colombia in 1993 deputy Yolima Espinoza presented a bill establishing a quota for women to be appointed to public posts, starting with 15 per cent in 1994 and rising to 50 per cent in 1999.

The demand for access to the formal arenas of power echoes the campaigns of the suffragists during the first decades of this century. Access is now sought, however, as a matter of *right*, no longer as a favour, in exchange for women's votes, or on the basis of the special 'maternal' qualities women might bring to humanise and moralise politics. Although women in social movements often employ such maternalist discourse and justify their public activism in terms of a private identity as mothers, it is debatable whether the *Supermadre* ('Supermother') is still a valid image of the politically active Latin American woman.[10] If women in the continent are now arguing for greater political representation as a matter of justice and right, then the issue of whether women in elected office represent 'women's issues' is less important than achieving a critical mass. Coalitions between women in different parties may be built temporarily on specific issues. Rather than counterposing practical gender issues (related to women's daily identity and needs in the family and community) against strategic 'feminist' goals, it is perhaps more useful to think of the women's movement adopting new strategic approaches to practical concerns. Long-term structural change in the state and political system is crucial to satisfying women's basic needs, as well as fundamental rights, over the long term as well as in the short term.

Grassroots politics

If the attention of the women's movement has turned to the formal, institutional sphere of politics, does this mean that women's social movement activity has disappeared following the crisis of regime change and transition to democracy? Have women been demobilised, or has female-dominated social movement activity adapted to the new reality? Rather than setting up misleading dichotomies, counterposing the formal with the informal spheres of politics, institutional action with 'autonomous' movements, grassroots women against middle-class and elite women in politics, or women's 'popular' organisations versus feminist groups, it is more useful to trace how they interact and interpenetrate. As noted earlier, marginalised groups of women such as rural workers, indigenous women and black women now have representation and voice, not just in national parliaments, but also in municipal and provincial government. Women's social movements have demanded an institutional input where none was offered, for example, CONAVIGUA in the refugee-return process in Guatemala. Women continue to gain ground within the trade-union and rural movements, and now play a leading role in the Paraguayan peasant movement, forming half of its national Executive. Rural women and domestic workers arrived in their hundreds in Brasília to lobby Congress and won full pension and labour rights for both groups of women. Women's groups have also adopted a new tactical and focused approach to the formal political sphere, building horizontal, regional and even international networks.

The three types of women's organisation which emerged under authoritarian rule and civil war – economic survival organisations, human rights groups and feminist groups – have not faded away following the transition. As international attention and funding have moved away from the region, this has led to an NGO-isation of social movements – women's and others – and they have had to turn their attention increasingly to lobbying the institutional realm, providing advocacy for their members and providing grassroots services, often in partnership with the state (see Chapter 8). Nor has the *raison d'être* for their existence disappeared. Hyperinflation continued to wrack Brazil until the mid-1990s. Following the 1990 elections in Nicaragua and the application of structural adjustment measures, unemployment rose to 70 per cent and 60 per cent of the population were said to be living in poverty. Soup kitchens and women's survival networks continue to sustain families and communities in Central America. The women-led human rights groups also remain active, their work incomplete, as abuses are still committed and investigated and the perpetrators arrested and tried, in spite of the amnesty laws introduced by the military before leaving office, which were left untouched in the name of national reconciliation. Women organised the plebiscite in Uruguay which came so close to overturning the amnesty law, and the Mothers in Argentina in 1998 saw General Videla, ex-president and junta leader, arrested for the abduction of the children of 'disappeared' parents.

In the war-torn countries of Central America, new women's groups formed during and after the transition, such as Las Dignas (Dignified Women) in El Salvador and Tierra Viva (Living Earth) and Puntos de Encuentro (Meeting Points) in Nicaragua. The FSLN's women's 'wing', AMNLAE, was already losing credibility as a representative voice for Nicaraguan women by the end of the 1980s, as dissent appeared among 'independent feminist' groups and the union-linked women's entities.[11] Nicaraguan feminism was given a boost in 1992, when it hosted the first Central American women's conference, and the region as a whole became more integrated into the Latin American feminist movement with the holding of the Sixth Feminist Meeting in El Salvador in 1994.[12] Inter-American networks of women have existed since the women's suffrage campaigns of the first decades of the century and the establishment of the Inter-American Commission of Women within the Organisation of American States in 1928,[13] leading to an increasingly vocal role for the region's women in international fora such as the UN Conferences on Women. In some countries, feminist organisations are more active than in others, but overall the picture is one of diversification and adaptation. Argentina has around 300 women's groups, and holds national conferences with attendances of 8,000. Brazil boasts hundreds of local groups, linked into networks that may be thematic (e.g. health or reproductive rights) or territorial (by state), involved in both institutional and informal politics. In Chile, however, independent women's organisations have become moribund, sidelined by the women's ministry, which has taken on a semi-representational function, or they have been co-opted into the state in partnership with SERNAM. This underlines the importance of maintaining women's grassroots activity in a dynamic relationship with initiatives directed at institutional political change, for it is at the grassroots that women's views and public policy ultimately are expressed. Women working in the formal sphere of politics rely on the mobilisation and credibility afforded them by the support of popular organisations in order to effect change.

Using political power

The transition to democratic rule in many countries in the region, combined with the impact of the UN Decade for Women and the two international conferences in Nairobi in 1985 and Beijing in 1995, have refocused the attention of women's movements in Latin America on the institutional arena. The Beijing conference, in particular, urged the rapid reform of archaic legal systems and the eradication of discriminatory legislation from two angles: that of improving civil rights, and of promoting development. The World Bank has also started to include violence against women in its agenda as a development issue.[14]

Taken regionally, the gender-specific public policy initiatives implemented, or demanded, fall into a number of categories: the drafting of a comprehensive government Plan of Action; the installation of an executive-level body to advise on, monitor, or carry out the implementation of this Plan; reforms of the Con-stitution, civil and penal codes, family and labour law; and a number of specific policy initiatives, for example, combating violence against women. These are not restricted to the national level: many interesting and important public poli-cies aimed at improving women's rights and quality of life have been imple-mented at provincial, or even municipal, levels. This is crucial: for it is at local level that public policy is actually delivered, that government is experienced at first hand by the population, and at the grassroots and community levels that women are most active in popular politics. Decentralisation and devolution of greater responsibility to local government are part of the package of consoli-dation-phase measures for deepening and extending democracy.[15] Whether decentralisation will be a 'good' or 'bad' thing for women very much depends on how it is conceived and implemented. At best it empowers non-traditional actors, particularly women, to influence government and policy. At worst, it may shore up the power of local elites and exclude women's voices still further.

All Latin American countries have signed the UN Convention on the Elimi-nation of all Forms of Discrimination Against Women (CEDAW), some with a number of reservations, and nearly all these countries have established some governmental organisation or national machinery for the advancement of women, in accordance with the recommendations of the CEDAW.[16] However, these mechanisms vary widely depending on their institutional status, budgetary and administrative autonomy, insertion into the executive governmental struc-ture, and technical capacity and authority. Only Mexico and Colombia lack a special agency, and some countries had mechanisms well before 1980. In several countries, 'women's issues' are elided with those of children or of the family: part of the SERNAM's founding mission in Chile is the welfare of the family. Others view women's rights as a subsection of human rights. The 'parent' min-istry often betrays much of the underlying conceptions of the mechanism, as they are placed variously beneath the aegis of ministries of justice, social wel-fare, education, culture and the office of the presidency. Some have full cabinet status, others have an advisory capacity. President Menem established a female 'shadow cabinet' in which women advise ministries on gender impact. Some have a separate budget allocation; others do not. Some are created by presi-dential decree, which is rapid, but depends on the political will of the incum-bent, and may be viewed as his or her personal project. Others are created by law, which is slower, but derives greater legitimacy and support from having passed through the legislature and all-party debate and consensus. Most of these mechanisms are vulnerable to some degree to changes in the executive branch and economic circumstances. Where agencies report only to the President, or to the state governor, or mayor in a federal system such as Brazil, and lack estab-lished legal regulations, they are vulnerable to changes in government. There is also a crucial difference between executive, technical bodies, as most of these are, and representative fora which are channels for input into civil society, such as the National Women's Forum established in Guatemala in 1997.

The agenda pursued by these government agencies is increasingly that of a comprehensive equal opportunities blueprint, modelled on that of Spain or, latterly, on the Beijing Platform of Action. Around half the countries of the region had formulated such a plan by the mid-1990s,[17] mostly countries which had undergone transitions to democracy. The Central American plans have followed later, subsequent to the peace accords. Despite decades of repressive rule under Stroessner, during which all dissent was quashed, the Paraguayan women's movement has emerged as one of the liveliest of the region, and during the transition period established a Secretaría de la Mujer (Secretariat for Women) attached to the President's office, and drew up an equal opportunities plan for 1997–2001. A demand for quotas in the parties was presented as early as 1990. In 1998, as in earlier elections, the Coordinación de Mujeres del Paraguay (Paraguayan Women's Coordination) presented a 13-point platform of feminist policy proposals to the new government. One of the differences that marks out the current period from previous attempts by isolated women politicians to enact social policy on behalf of women is the professionalisation of the design and implementation of those policies, the creation of a group of technical experts, or 'femocracy' to do so, and the emphasis on inter-sectoral approaches, which involve not only policy design, but also political·lobbying to secure adequate political support and resources to make blueprints for gender equality a reality.

Women across the continent have taken advantage of the opportunity offered by the constitutional revision that has frequently accompanied changes of regime, to do away with archaic and discriminatory clauses and to insert articles which explicitly outlaw sexual discrimination. The Brazilian Constitution of 1988 is one of the most liberal in this respect, the result of an intense process of public debate in which a diversity of social movements, including the women's movement played a key role. In 1986, the women's movement ran and elected a number of women candidates to the constituent assembly with the aim of influencing the debate. On the other hand, the Chilean Constitution of 1980 is a deeply conservative document drafted under an authoritarian regime. The women's movement and ministry (SERNAM) have so far failed to win all-party support to modify the phrasing of the clause specifying that 'All men are born free and equal in dignity and rights.'[18]

Throughout the region, legal codes are being subjected to scrutiny and reform by the women's movement. Most penal codes determine the honesty, honour and good name of the woman to characterise certain crimes, such as rape, adultery, abortion and infanticide, and determine their punishment. The penal codes of two countries justify the husband who kills his wife and her partner if they are caught *in flagrante*. Despite the fact that the 'honour defence' is inadmissible in a court of law, it continues to be used in Brazil. In several instances, rape is punished less severely if the victim is not deemed an 'honest' woman. No penal code classifies rape in marriage as a crime. Many countries penalise adultery more severely for women, and adultery was only decriminalised in Nicaragua in 1997. The honour of the woman is such a defining feature of these penal codes that several allow for legal procedings to be terminated or the charges dropped if offender marries the offended party.[19] The woman regains then what she has 'lost': her honour, viewed as a collective good. Reforms are under way in several countries that would make these crimes against the individual rights of the woman rather than against collective morality.

Most constitutions also establish equal pay for equal work, without distinction of sex. Most allow for maternity and even paternity leave, and frequently require workplaces with over a certain number of employees to provide a day-care centre. However, such ideal principles are rarely enforced. In Brazil employers frequently, and illegally, require would-be women employees to take a pregnancy test or provide a certificate to prove they have been sterilised. Both domestic and rural women workers are the worst protected in terms of unionisation and access to social security. Women workers are particularly prone to the effects of informal and service-sector activity, low unionisation, and flexibilisation of labour throughout the region. Labour law is frequently linked to welfare rights, which tend to discriminate against women whose insertion into the labour market does not correspond to the masculine norm. The feminisation of poverty at a time of globalisation and market opening will be more difficult to tackle, particularly in countries such as El Salvador, where women make up almost 65 per cent of the workforce in the informal economy, and 90 per cent of that in the Export Processing Zone. In the *maquilas* (assembly plants) of the Mexican/US border women comprised 78 per cent of the workforce in the section, although this had dropped to 59 per cent in 1993, with most in textiles and electronics.[20] Women's cheap and flexible labour is also a major factor in the success of Chile's booming agro-export sector. Casual women workers (*temporeras*) constitute 40–50 per cent of the workforce, and work on a seasonal basis, migrating with their children to the agro-export producing regions, mainly from the urban periphery.[21] Chile in particular has been very active in targeting low-income groups such as female heads of households in order to provide a buffer against poverty in the family. The government also provides an effective subsidy to the agro-export sector by assisting female seasonal workers with childcare and other provisions for the duration of the season. Although the consolidation period has been characterised by women's engagement with public policy, political representation and legal norms, the logic of economic globalisation is far harder to tackle through such means.

Violence against women is one of the most common areas of public policy in the region: it attracts foreign funding, it is relatively uncontroversial and there is a vast unmet need for some form of support to women who have been victims of sexual, domestic or other forms of violence. The model throughout the region has undoubtedly been Brazil's women's police stations, first set up in the mid-1980s. By 1997, Nicaragua had 'women's police stations' in nine cities, attached to local police stations, staffed by female officers and supported in part by foreign assistance, providing social and legal help to women. The 1996 Criminal Code reform law against aggression against women criminalised domestic violence for the first time, with a six-year jail term and restraining orders. The importance of taking an integrated, tactical approach to gender policy is illustrated by Ecuador, whose Minister of Government's promise in 1997 to create 31 women's police stations was thwarted by the Minister of Finance, who refused to approve the budget.

Conclusions

The contemporary women's movement in Latin America and its current concerns with respect to democratisation, civil rights, political representation, legal reform and public policy represent, not so much a break with the past as a strong historical continuity with the first wave of Latin American feminism in the early decades of this century. The demands for crèches in the workplace, equal pay for equal work, and outlawing of sexual harassment were all contained in the 1940s Consolidated Labour Code of Brazil's President Vargas, yet they now appear very modern items on a feminist agenda. This degree of continuity indicates more than anything else the slowness of women's access to the formal political sphere and, the continued existence of a number of structural barriers to gender equality. While this consolidation phase brings with it elements which are unique to the current conjuncture, the women's movement itself in Latin America draws on decades of experience. Battles which were begun at the turn of the century have yet to be won.

Women now engage in collective action in the formal sphere, not only in the informal sphere. It is the demand for full, unrestricted and uncontingent citizenship which characterises the consolidation period of political democratisation. Women are now demanding political power and resources as a matter of right, not as a favour, a trade-off or in recognition of women's 'special qualities'. Like their predecessors decades earlier, contemporary Latin American women have forged strong transnational networks and alliances, first in the struggle for democracy and human rights in the 1980s, then in thematic campaigns, for example around violence against women, or reproductive rights, and, more recently, in a concerted effort to make a reality out of the Platform of Action of the Beijing Conference. Similarly, the establishment of executive-level governmental bodies to advise on and implement public policy targeted at women is not altogether new: governments and political parties in some countries have been keen for some decades to mobilise women in support of a particular ideology or development paradigm. However, in the 1980s and 1990s such programmes have been the result in the main of women's grassroots organisation and lobbying, not a top-down edict. An agenda of civil and political rights will not in itself solve the problem of women's inequality in Latin America, but it does give women a greater voice within the political system to tackle much wider structural, and globalised, economic problems.

Notes

1 For a fuller account of the use of such 'maternalist' discourse see F. Miller, *Latin American Women and the Search for Social Justice* (Hanover, University Press of New England, 1991); J. Fisher, *Mothers of the Disappeared* (London, Zed, 1989) and *Out of the Shadows: Women, Resistance and Politics in South America* (London, Latin America Bureau, 1993); and S. A. Radcliffe and S. Westwood (eds), *'Viva': Women and Popular Protest in Latin America* (London, Routledge, 1993).

2 For a fascinating, detailed and nuanced account of this process, see S. E. Alvarez, *Engendering Democracy in Brazil: Women's Movements in Transition Politics* (Princeton, Princeton University Press, 1990).

3 Georgina Waylen outlines a number of general considerations about the impact of transitional politics on the organised women's movement, particularly in Chile: 'Women's Movements and Democratisation in Latin America', *Third World Quarterly*, 14:3 (1993), and 'Women's Movements, the State and Democratization in Chile', Institute of Development Studies (*IDS) Bulletin*, 26:3 (1995).

4 With a membership of 15,000 grassroots indigenous women, it campaigns for compensation, literacy and income generation.

5 Isabel Perón, who assumed the presidency after Juan Perón's death in Argentina in 1974, and Lydia Gueiler, interim president of Bolivia for six months in 1979–80. Neither was directly elected.

6 Female suffrage in Ecuador and Brazil was also followed by a coup.

7 In the other two countries which experienced social revolutions, women were marginalised, rather than incorporated and mobilised. In Mexico, it took nearly forty years for women's suffrage to be granted in 1953, in part because the party of the revolution (PRI) feared women's reputedly conservative voting preferences, a prejudice that by the 1950s had little substance. See A. Macias and C. Ramos Escandón, 'Women's Movements, Feminism and Mexican Politics', in J. Jaquette (ed.), *The Women's Movement in Latin America: Participation and Democracy* (Boulder, Westview, 1994). Mexican women were absorbed into the 'popular' sector within the corporatist structure of the party. The Bolivian MNR incorporated women into the party (the 'Barzolas') as a kind of intimidatory women's auxiliary. Women's suffrage was granted as part of universal suffrage when the party came to power in 1952. See G. Ardaya Salinas, 'The Barzolas and the Housewives Committee', in J. Nash and H. I. Safa (eds), *Women and Change in Latin America* (South Hadley, Bergin and Garvey, 1986).

8 The one to do so, with 30 per cent, is the Partido Socialista. The left-wing coalition, Frente Amplio, has also proved resistant. Ironically, Uruguay was one of the first countries to give women the vote in 1932.

9 For a list of the first women cabinet members in each Latin American country see T. Valdés and E. Gómariz (eds), *Latin American Women: Compared Figures* (Santiago and Madrid, FLACSO and Instituto de la Mujer, 1995), p. 161.

10 Elsa Chaney's influential work, the first substantial study of women in Latin American political life (in Peru and Chile), argued that women should use maternalist discourse as a strategy for gaining greater access: *Supermadre: Women in Politics in Latin America* (Austin, Institute of Latin American Studies, University of Texas at Austin, 1979).

11 See N. Stolz Chinchilla, 'Feminism, Revolution and Democratic Transitions in Nicaragua', in Jaquette (ed.), *The Women's Movement*, and M. T. Blandon, 'The Impact of the Sandinista Defeat on Nicaraguan Feminism', in G. Küppers (ed.), *Compañeras: Voices from the Latin American Women's Movements* (London, Latin America Bureau, 1994).

12 There have so far been seven regional feminist conferences, the first five analysed in N. S. Sternbach *et al.*, 'Feminisms in Latin America: From Bogotá to San Bernardo', *Signs*, 17:2 (1992), reprinted in A. Escobar and S. E. Alvarez (eds), *The Making of Social Movements in Latin America: Identity, Strategy and Democracy* (Boulder, Westview, 1992).

13 F. Miller, 'Latin American Feminism and the Transnational Arena', in E. L. Bergman (ed.),

Women, Culture and Politics in Latin America: Seminar on Feminism and Culture in Latin America (Berkeley, University of California Press, 1990).

14 L. L. Heise, A. Germaine and J. Pitanguy, *Violence Against Women: The Hidden Health Burden* (Washington, DC, World Bank, 1994).

15 Decentralisation – part of the World Bank formula for good governance – is clearly crucial to the larger federal nations such as Mexico, Argentina and Brazil, but has also been carried out in smaller countries such as El Salvador.

16 Valdés and Gómariz, *Latin American Women*, p. 185.

17 *Ibid.*, p. 188.

18 See *ibid.* for a full comparison of legal provisions and constitutions.

19 Guatemala still has this on the statute books; El Salvador repealed this in 1996.

20 A. Dwyer, *On the Line: Life on the US–Mexican Border* (London, Latin America Bureau, 1994), p. 18.

21 See S. Barrientos, 'Fruits of Burden: The Organisation of Women Temporary Workers in Chilean Agri-business', in H. Afshar (ed.), *Women and the Empowerment: Illustrations from the Third World* (Basingstoke, Macmillan, 1998).

10

The environmental agenda:
accountability for sustainability

JONATHAN R. BARTON

The environmental imperative

The trauma of recent Latin American history, including the long years of dictatorship, the complex political transition processes and the burden of debt, has given rise to significant socio-economic transformations. These transformations have included increased human rights mobilisation, extensive migration and urbanisation, new welfare and health demands, and changes in production and consumption patterns. While these are themes that have dominated social science literature from the 1960s, the environmental debates linked to all these changes only became well known during the 1980s.[1]

The political economy of the environment in Latin America has more often than not been hidden or excluded from negotiations and policies due to the seemingly overriding importance of other issues. It was the failure to recognise that environmental change was both a product of and a causal factor in the transformations that led to its absence from the 'relevant' discussions in Latin American affairs. During the 1980s, environmental connections were made in terms of political and economic change and health, but these were largely suppressed due to the prioritisation of transition processes and economic recovery by technocratic governments and multilateral institutions. Only during the 1990s have we witnessed more constructive approaches to integrating environmental change with a range of political and socio-economic developments.

While it is difficult to talk of turning points, the seed of environmental awareness within state apparatuses and civil society can be traced back to the 1970s. The 1972 Stockholm Conference on the Human Environment coincided with increased concerns regarding environmental degradation: industrial development had been promoted at all costs in the larger Latin American republics, leading to atmospheric, water and solid waste contamination; sanitation problems associated with urbanisation and poor municipal infrastructure were being highlighted; mining, forestry and agriculture were degrading regional environments; and infrastructure projects were also leading to severe social and environmental repercussions. In the 20 years from Stockholm to the 1992 Earth Summit in Rio de Janeiro, these issues have been increasingly prioritised within development strategies, in both the North and the South. While only two heads of state attended the Stockholm Conference, 120 attended the Rio Summit.[2]

It is this broad range of environmental issues that leads one to the conclusion that the environment is not a secondary feature of social, economic and political change. It is primary and imperative.[3] Environmental change results from policies in all areas of government and business activities, and it is also a consequence of decisions taken within civil society by communities and individuals. In this respect, there are local, regional, national and global components to Latin America's environmental debates. Some of these components are integrated across these geographical scales and others are more specific and localised, but a feature of all is that there are ramifications for livelihood and health. The environment is not an issue in itself, rather it is a set of conceptual and actual approaches to the human–nature relationship. Responses to environmental change, therefore, require multidisciplinary strategies and the inclusion of a range of actors.[4] The rubric within which many of these issues have been addressed has become known as 'political ecology'. This framework attempts to examine environmental change with respect to power relations (relating to political, economic and social actors and processes) within and across societies.[5]

The environmental agenda

The environment is a catch-all. In terms of impacts and policy options, it is best reduced to various agendas. In Latin America, it was the Amazon region – 'the lungs of the earth' – which was highlighted by international environmentalists during the 1980s. From the 1960s, national development policy in Brazil had been the 'march to the West', leading to resettlement policies, commercial activity promotion, and infrastructural projects. Major projects in particular, such as large-scale cattle ranching, the Grande Carajás iron-ore mine, the Tucurui hydroelectric project and the Transamazonian Highway, came under heavy international criticism. Ecosystem changes in Amazonia and global environmental issues were entwined and the 'Green Agenda' was established. This agenda is exemplified by vociferous criticism of commercial policies linked with forestry management, cattle ranching and agricultural development.[6] However, the agenda has been extended and applied throughout the continent, from national park policies in Costa Rica to woodchip operations in southern Chile.

In terms of international profile, it is the Green Agenda that has raised environmental consciousness. It was the extent of Brazil's tropical and temperate forest depletion, and the losses of habitat and biodiversity associated with it, that brought Brazil to centre stage in global environmental affairs. The situation also enabled Brazil to host the UN Conference on Environment and Development (UNCED) 'Earth Summit' in 1992. The issues discussed at the summit were essentially global in focus, such as the framework conventions on biodiversity and climate change, and the Statement on Forest Principles, although the Agenda 21 agreement sought to address the local opportunities for positive environmental change. Whilst global environmental changes such as climate modification mobilised international opinion, Agenda 21 confronted more immediate concerns, those of environmental health, well-being and the quality of life within communities.

From the 1960s in most Latin American republics, rising rates of urbanisation led to the creation of burgeoning metropoli. A range of 'push and pull' factors induced human migration, such as increased capitalisation of agricultural activities and industrial employment opportunities in urban areas. The outcome was the rapid expansion of intermediate and large cities. National and city planning resources did not match this expansion, leading to spontaneous settlements on the fringes of urban areas, often in geographically precarious sites, for example, the *favelas* (slums) on Rio de Janeiro's steep hillsides. Urbanisation – of people and economic activities – brought with it a range of environmental consequences. This urban environmental agenda has been termed the 'Brown Agenda'.

The Brown Agenda relates to potable water and sanitation issues, air quality and solid waste management. As such, it encompasses housing, transport and industrial policies, amongst other things.[7] The double burden of social pressures and industrial activities on inadequate urban infrastructure and long-term degradation creates strategic problems for planners and urban managers, and far more serious problems for urban residents, especially those living in low-income, marginalised locations: that is, the majority of Latin America's urban population.[8] Alongside the Green and Brown Agendas, it is also possible to include environmental concerns relating to mining despoliation, fisheries depletion, and infrastructural developments such as hydroelectric dams and gas and oil pipelines. What links this range of issues – or these agendas – is that they have impacts in terms of human health and livelihoods, natural resource sustainability (that is, wider long-term environmental degradation such as groundwater quality), and future land-use and other economic options (such as fisheries exploitation).

The various agendas are not mutually exclusive, nor resolvable in isolation. In order to confront the difficulties associated with each it is necessary to address the agents and agencies involved. What should be made clear is that the gravity of Latin America's environmental condition is a reaction to human-induced change. Whilst the El Niño phenomenon, devastating periodic drought (such as in north-east brazil's 'drought polygon'), earthquakes, flooding and mudslides are environmental catastrophes with severe human impacts, these impacts can only be partially planned for due to a range of uncertainties of scale and extent. In contrast, the opportunities for reducing impacts and environmental risks are far greater for industrial activities, agricultural practices, urban development and natural-resource exploitation, which can be forecast, witnessed and stopped if necessary. In both these cases, the political economy of environmental management becomes the key to reducing negative environmental impacts (atmospheric pollution, land degradation, water contamination) and also to promoting positive environmental impacts (cleaner technology, land remediation, more sustainable practices).

Towards 'greener' globalisation: trade, investment and regionalism

Numerous authors, such as Eduardo Galeano in *Open Veins of Latin America*, have written about the metaphorical 'rape' of Latin America by the Iberian colonisers and the European and US merchants and businessmen of the post-independence period. The continent has experienced centuries of social exploitation by external agents and this has most often been the focus within the literature, for example, Indian genocide and labour exploitation. Despite the social dimension of colonial and neocolonial exploitation, the environmental dimension is equally important and valid since the 'rape' of the environment (in terms of the introduction of inappropriate agricultural practices and intensive mining and extraction of natural resources) generated tremendous indirect social impacts. While conflict and labour conditions provide direct examples of exploitation, other factors, such as land expropriation and forced migration, may have had more widespread repercussions in terms of mortality and changes in livelihoods. One may make a strong argument that this process remains in place today as small-scale farmers and indigenous groups continue to be forced off their land, giving up sustainable practices, to make way for large-scale agribusiness, which attempts to disguise the unsustainability of their operations via the intensive use of short-term panacea such as fertilisers and pesticides.

Latin American history reveals that environmental exploitation and degradation were strong features of the colonial period, and the environment was effectively 'internationalised' from this point. At the end of the millennium, discourses revolve around globalisation rather than internationalisation, but the fundamentals remain remarkably similar. While the exploited commodities and modes of capital accumulation may have changed, that is, from slave labour to multinational portfolio investment, one can accurately talk of an export of natural resource capital that has intensified environmental degradation and increased obstacles to sustainability.[9]

Opponents of this perspective argue on several fronts: the absorptive and restorative capacity of the environment, including the price mechanism whereby resource scarcity is matched by changing values; the economic values generated from resource exploitation that are fed back into Latin American economies; the need to exploit naturally occurring comparative advantages;

the existence of new 'frontier' regions (including Antarctica) that may be exploited once others become unviable; potential new energy and minerals finds; and the lack of evidence regarding long-term impacts of activities and the 'carrying' capacities of particular environments. This last point refers to the lack of unanimity amongst the scientific community regarding causes and effects. Most problems revolve around the complex nature of environmental systems, with their range of inputs and influencing factors over time. Examples include the contribution of industrial versus transport and domestic heating and cooking emissions to atmospheric emissions in urban areas, and the contributions to river sedimentation of forestry versus agricultural activities within a catchment area.

These arguments support the neoliberal paradigm in Latin America and the continuing exploitation of natural resource capital. The process of globalisation, and its integral components of trade and investment, have deepened this historical legacy. Investment in Latin America has a long tradition dating back to independence and loans to Simón Bolívar. During the nineteenth century, it was concentrated in agricultural and mineral resource activities – that is, British investment in Chilean nitrate and Argentine cattle ranching, and US investment in Mexican oil and Central American fruit. These and other investments led to direct resource exports with little or no value-added processing, and considerable environmental adaptation and degradation such as forest clearing for plantation agriculture, and the soil erosion and sedimentation associated with it.

The question that must now be posed is whether investment in projects and ventures that lead to long-term environmental deterioration should be sanctioned by the state in order to pursue an agenda of shorter-term national and regional economic objectives. Due to Latin America's turbulent economic and financial history of boom and bust cycles, it has most often been natural resource capital that has been exploited for short-term restabilisation via new capital inflows. Traditionally this strategy remained largely unquestioned, but now the paradox of long-term depletion and degradation for short-term gain is being challenged. Notions such as producer responsibility and company environmental management on the one hand, and eco-labelling and 'green consumerism' on the other are slowly bringing pressure to bear on firms and are thus slowly beginning to influence investment decision-making. Having said this, there are wide variations between countries, sectors and firms in terms of commitment to environmental sustainability.

While more often than not companies argue that it is not in their best interests to maintain environmentally unsustainable practices (hence they should regulate themselves and adopt voluntary approaches to environmental management), there is evidence that challenges this assumption. In terms of investment, it should be remembered that much of it is footloose and not committed to long-term development. Investors seek returns, and if the sustainable yield falls below the economic yield, the capital is likely to flow away. A similar argument is that of the 'low-hanging fruits', which suggests that once companies have made the easiest profits from an operation they may be unlikely to invest in the more complicated future phases of development, preferring higher, short-term returns elsewhere.

The marine fisheries of Peru and Chile provide excellent examples of the problems associated with sustainable yields. Currently there are grave concerns regarding the stock levels of various Pacific coast fisheries as a result of over-fishing since the introduction of large-capacity, intensive factory-fishing in the 1970s. In terms of 'low-hanging fruits', the cattle-ranching operations in Brazil and Central America reveal the persistent territorial expansion of ranches with little investment in the management of existing pastures. As long as it is cheaper to exploit new land rather than manage old land, the problems will persist. An analogy may also be drawn with manufacturing industry, whereby a company may decide that investment in environmental technology would provide a sufficient burden for it to pursue an alternative investment strategy. Instead of investment in technology or a management strategy that is capital-intensive and involves a long-term financial commitment, the option of a less regulated sector with easier returns may prove more attractive. Another option might be closing a process in the plant and outsourcing.

In the same way that investment can have both beneficial – such as the environment industry – and detrimental – such as 'pollution intensive' industries – effects, trade can also be ambiguous in terms of environmental impacts.[10] To oversimplify Latin American trade is not difficult. Commodities and low value-added goods are traded for higher value-added goods.[11] The trade relationship is historically grounded and, although it is changing, it remains unpromising for the republics. Although some countries have sought to overcome certain trading obstacles, such as Brazil with its technology policy, most countries remain dependent on a limited range of products. Chile, hailed as the neoliberal economic miracle of Latin America and a model for all emerging markets, generates over 40 per cent of its export earnings from copper and its derivatives. Venezuela depends on oil; Guatemala and El Salvador on agribusiness.

In a movement away from traditional commodity and agricultural production, the 1980s and 1990s have been characterised by the promotion of non-traditional activities and products.[12] The aim was for diversification, new opportunities in international markets and less vulnerability to price fluctuations in traditional goods. The range of non-traditional activities has been extensive and many impact directly on the environment. Although Mexico's *maquiladoras* mostly process electrical goods and textiles, and therefore may appear to be less environmentally demanding than, for example, mangrove destruction for shrimp production in Ecuador, there are significant solid waste management and water discharge impacts. Many non-traditional activities may be on a par with traditional environmentally degrading activities; in other cases the rate and type of degradation are worse than traditional activities.

In southern Chile, a severe decline in catches in marine fisheries, especially for artisanal fishers, has led to the rapid expansion of salmon aquaculture since the early 1980s. Whilst it was thought that aquaculture would relieve pressure on marine ecosystems, it poses its own environmental problems such as chemical inputs to counter fish disease, the interbreeding of native and exotic fish species (with gene-pool ramifications), and seabed decay and eutrophication resulting from excessive feed inputs.[13] Another example is that of Chile's fruit and viticulture industries, which maintain high chemical inputs (i.e. pesticides) to maximise quality and output.[14] The long-term impacts of these inputs on workers and the natural environment have been questioned, but such practices are increasingly widespread, as in the non-traditional fruit and flower industries of Central America. Rather than resolving old problems, new ones have been created and have yet to be managed effectively by firms and controlled by the state.

The most common example of non-traditional activity on the Green Agenda is commercialised forestry and wood products.[15] Many Latin American republics have regional economies which are highly dependent on forest-resource exploitation, from tropical hardwoods to temperate evergreen and montane species. While traditionally, forest products served as a fuel resource and for domestic use such as housing and furniture, non-traditional forestry has focused on pulp and paper, and cellulose and woodchip production, largely for export markets. It is the scale of production, the intensity of forest use and the introduction of exotic species (with negative potential impacts on local and regional ecosystems) that have led to criticism and concern in this sector, not only in the countries in question but world-wide. Tropical hardwood exploitation in Amazonian Brazil has been the focus of international debate, but subtropical and temperate exploitation in Mexico, Chile and south-east Brazil is also worthy of attention.

With all non-traditional activities, the new job opportunities created are often used as a counterweight to any possible environmental impacts. Often introduced into downward transitional regional economies, the new activities take up employment lost in other, traditional operations. However, these new activities also displace existing activities. The name Chico Mendes symbolises the struggle for Latin American environmental protection and livelihood protection. This Brazilian rubber tapper, who opposed armed landowners to protect the common property traditions of forest-dwellers, was murdered in 1988. What he was able to achieve was to highlight the carrying capacity of forests and the recognition that sustainable forestry activities are small-scale and diverse rather than large-scale and single-use. In many ways this is a reflection of indigenous knowledge regarding forest use, which contrasts with the shorter time-horizon of export-oriented economic actors who are in pursuit of swift investment returns and profit maximisation.

What is evident from the Chico Mendes murder is that the political underpinnings of environmental resource management are critical. Until the state is decisive about environmental strategies – which must include the value of indigenous versus contemporary knowledge and approaches, sustainable rates of exploitation, and acceptable activities and practices – it is economic power and even violence which will determine environmental development and protection in Latin America.

Increasingly, international trade and investment patterns are being shaped by regional agreements (see Chapter 4). In Latin America, regionalism has historical traditions dating back to Gran Colombia and the United Provinces of Central America, but the late twentieth-century concept is based less on politics and more on commercial opportunities. Although the attempts to construct regional groupings from the early 1960s – the Latin American Free Trade Area (LAFTA), the Central American Common Market (CACM) and the Andean Pact – have been largely unsuccessful, the more recent return to regionalism has more far-reaching environmental impacts. Rather than the FTAA initiative, the Asia-Pacific Economic Cooperation Conference (APEC) or the Mercosur, it was the inclusion of Mexico within the NAFTA that has raised most environmental opposition and debate.[16] Opponents argue that, apart from the advantageous labour dimension, Mexico's inclusion takes advantage of weaker environmental policies. This is not only apparent in terms of occupational health but also in terms of toxic waste, air and water emissions and discharges. They argue that US firms may outsource the 'dirtier' components of their process across the border, or even establish subsidiaries or joint ventures to avoid potential difficulties or added costs at home. There is also the issue that is common to all ecological linkages across boundaries, whereby activities on either side may lead to altered environmental dynamics and species distribution patterns.[17]

The basis of the argument is that over the long term, environmentally degrading activities have flowed across the border and that US firms may now profit at the expense of Mexico's environmental quality. These same considerations have been extended to other countries desiring entry into the NAFTA, such as Chile, and also in terms of what the role of Latin American republics is within the new regional groupings.[18] In the context of agreements within and amongst the Americas, or with the EU or Asia-Pacific economies, it is clear that lowering tariff barriers between partners will ensure the pursuit of traditional activities and the export-oriented non-traditional activities which are, for the most part, environmentally demanding. For example, Mexico is unlikely to break into research and development-intensive technology whilst trading freely with the United States and Canada. Within the Mercosur, it is unlikely that Chile will generate a manufacturing industry base whilst trading freely with Brazil and Argentina. The FTAA initiative is likely to compound these obstacles, reinforcing the traditional characteristics of the republics as commodity and natural resource-intensive exporters. It is unclear whether those economies which sought alternative development paths, such as Cuba and Nicaragua under the Sandinistas, were able to reduce the environmental impacts of production. Nicaragua remained a war economy for the most part, whilst Cuba exchanged Western sugar markets for Council for Mutual Economic Assistance (COMECON) ones.

Across the issues connected with the current globalisation of Latin America's economies, the simplification is a trade-off between short-term export earnings potential and inward investment flows, and sustainable development[19] (socio-economic and environmental) that 'meets the needs of the present without compromising the ability of future generations to meet their own needs'. This is the essence of the sustainability concept proposed by Gro Harlem Brundt-land's report on *Our Common Future* for the World Commission on Environment and Development in 1987. While sustainability has entered the discourses of governments and policy-makers throughout the continent, the realities of how sustainability can be introduced to economies and societies are more complex. Discussions relating to the sustainability concept will increasingly revolve around the responsibilities and accountability of a range of actors and agencies.

Actors, agencies and accountability

The principal actors in environmental degradation and protection are spread across the three spheres of the private sector, the public sector (state involvement) and civil society. Such a sub-division is crude, but necessary in order to point to those individuals and institutions responsible for widespread degradation, and those who are actively engaged in protection and control. Since environmental degradation is nothing new, as advanced in the 'pristine myth' notion of Latin American environmental history,[20] this section will focus in particular on the post-1960 period of rapid industrialisation, agricultural change, and resource exploitation strategies.

The business sector, both private-and-public sector economic operations, must shoulder the lion's share of responsibility for environmental degradation in Latin America.[21] In terms of both sectors, their activities and resulting environmental impacts have been wedded to economic policies of import substitution, then neoliberalism. In this respect, the failure of business to accommodate environmental change in economic strategy can be placed at the door of governments – mostly authoritarian or technocratic – blinded by the exigencies of economic growth.

Non-Latin American firms were active in the various republics from independence, and provided the commercial and capital expertise to generate production and trade based initially on mineral, raw-material and agricultural opportunities. European and US manufacturing firms followed behind, locating in the continent from the early twentieth century. For this reason, it is difficult to make a separation between Latin American and non-Latin American degradation of the environments in question. From the 1960s, the influx of multinational manufacturing corporations (MNCs) gave rise to industrial concentration and a concomitant increase in air and water contamination and solid waste generation. The internationalisation of production that led MNCs to Central and South America gave rise to criticism that they located there to escape stricter regulations at home, but this 'pollution haven' theory is not substantiated by the available data.[22] Indeed, the throng of smaller and medium enterprises that were established by the multiplier effect of these larger MNCs, also other domestic manufacturing firms, were the major contributors to increases in pollution levels.

From the 1960s there has been a shift in economic ownership within the majority of republics, away from the model of the inter-war period and the promotion of import-substitution industrialisation when most strategic industries and utilities were in state hands. There has been a slow movement to private ownership, a process which has accelerated from the early 1980s. There is little doubt that state-owned enterprises have contributed massively to environmental degradation during the second half of the twentieth century. With few checks on emissions and discharges, and economic growth to the fore, the state was a poor self-regulator, despite the evidence of impacts on the environment and human health. With the most 'pollution-intensive' industries, such as chemicals and ferrous and non-ferrous metals industries under state control, accumulated impacts were severe. Brazil's 'Valley of Death', the city of Cubatão and its environs, provides the most well-known example of the impacts of industrial concentration and poor environmental protection.[23]

In the 1990s, it is only the jewels in the crown of the economy that remain in state hands, such as CODELCO (Corporación del Cobre) in Chile (copper) and PEMEX (Petróleos de Mexico) in Mexico (oil), although in the majority of cases the state remains in control of municipal services, such as water supply and sanitation.[24] The ascendancy of private ownership under neoliberalism has established a new balance of power regarding the political economy of the environment. Currently, the situation is that the state performs the role of regulator of private economic operations. The division of functions is clearer, and there are fewer conflicts of interest apart from the overriding one of economic growth and development.

The difficulties that are being faced at present in terms of effective environmental protection and control at the state level – national, provincial and municipal – revolve around the prioritisation of growth and the business interest groups that remain so powerful under neoliberalism. With the centrality of the private sector in neoliberal economic restructuring, and with private interests engaged in a full range of economic activities from mining and forestry to agriculture and manufacturing (often with investments across many sectors), the ability of the state to impose environmental regulations has been seen to be lacking in many instances. The same is true for those activities that remain in state hands.

The reasons for this are the weaknesses in the nascent environmental agencies that have been set up since the 1980s. They are weak in terms of their position in government and state circles vis-à-vis other departments and ministries, and also in terms of their resources, information systems and legal powers.[25] These agencies are regarded by governments as a necessary evil, but an evil that may penalise firms and lead to business opposition to other government policies. As such, they lack political power within a state apparatus that is oriented towards economic growth.

The 'win–win' theory, put forward by Porter and van der Linde, that investment in environmental protection may establish competitive advantages in terms of technological development and future regulatory and trade advantages, is not taken seriously or applied.[26] For this reason, Latin American republics continue to import environmental-control technologies, in spite of the high cost of such equipment and the supporting services.[27] Joseph Karliner observes that there have been three phases of environmental development in Latin America: first the arrival of polluting MNCs; second, the arrival of environmental regulations; and third, the arrival of environmental technology to service the regulatory demands.[28] He describes this flow as having a negative effect within Latin America, since the environmental agenda is being controlled from outside and linked to broader processes of capital accumulation and economic opportunities.

Beyond the issues of commercial pollution, although linked to them to an important degree, is what Paul Harrison defines as the 'ecology of poverty'.[29] The social impacts of contamination are felt most amongst the poorest groups of society.[30] Although air pollution is a great leveller, the health impacts of water access, water quality and solid waste disposal fall upon those with least resources to manage them. Living in precarious housing with little or no sanitation or waste-management facilities, millions of Latin Americans suffer the environmental consequences of their poverty, such as the rapid spread of disease (with poor health-care facilities) and higher morbidity and mortality rates. Whilst businesses contemplate environmental contamination in terms of economic values – fines paid, waste-disposal expenses saved – for Latin America's poor the price is valued in terms of illness and death. For this reason there is a stark difference in ideological starting points with respect to the environment between civil society movements and businesses, ranging from moral and ethical considerations to economic value considerations.

During the 1970s and 1980s, most social movements struggled for human rights, better living conditions and economic opportunities. However, from the late 1980s, the emergence of environmental NGOs (ENGOs) heightened the environmental dimension of these debates. In the late 1990s, ENGOs are widespread and are confronting businesses and bringing pressure to bear on the state on a broad front of issues from Green to Brown. In this respect they reflect the greater awareness and concern within civil society in terms of the connections made between health and environmental quality, and livelihoods and environmental change.[31] It is in Brazil that most ENGOs have become established due to the high profile of the country in global environmental affairs and the subsequent involvement and support of international environmental agencies.[32] Latin American ENGOs may be subdivided into particular groups: those operating as branches of international organisations; those operating as a national pressure group campaigning on a wide number of issues; and those with a single-issue, often local, agenda. The funding for these different groups is varied, often with an international contribution,[33] but generally speaking they all struggle to generate sufficient funds to resource their activities; in this respect, they are little different from human rights and other campaigning NGOs.

The non-governmental element of the environment movement is in many ways a response to two issues: the lack of state support and the lack of party-political support for those confronting environmental degradation. As regards the former, environment agencies are expected to make the links between the state, business and civil society, and balance the demands for economic growth against *patrimonio nacional* (national heritage), environmental sustainability and human health. This balance is rarely achieved due to the limited political power and resources of the agencies. In terms of 'green' political parties, Latin American politics is characterised by their absence or their small scale. There are many valid reasons why this should be the case in view of the strong party-political dimension of the authoritarian and transition periods in most countries in the past decade. However, as transitional governments become more embedded, there may be greater opportunities for green political parties to develop and put pressure on other parties to incorporate environmental awareness and green issues into their policy options. As urban atmospheric pollution, for example, leads to transport policies affecting the wealthier social groups, it is likely that the health dimension of environmental policy may lead to greater cross-society support for integrated, 'greener' approaches to urban management and 'greener' national economic development. The World Bank is already working on this second idea within a concept of 'Green GNP'. This indicator seeks to factor in environmental change within macroeconomic performance.

The promotion of sustainable management

For sustainable management of environments, societies and economies to become a reality, a range of policy initiatives must be implemented and inter-linked. However, to reach the stage of policy development, the condition of the nation's environments must be ascertained and objectives for environmental quality set. A major difficulty with environmental assessment in Latin America, as elsewhere, is the lack of comparable data and rigorous methodologies for tracing changes over time. Without these basic tools, it is even difficult to whether there is say an ecological crisis or not.[34] What we currently have is a broad range of local narratives and dislocated data that describe contamination and health and livelihood impacts. These are not well collated and tested by government agencies, giving those involved in contaminating activities a strong defence. The burden of proof is on the victims of environmental degradation.

There is a similar problem at the global level as there is still a disagreement within the climate change scientific community, providing business organisations a defence lifeline. Until causal relationships can be drawn between polluters and impacts, it is those who pollute and degrade environments who will remain in the driving seat.[35] It is the role of the state to protect the national environment and national health, but when economic development is prioritised above all else by government technocrats, environmental analysis, legislation and enforcement remain underfunded and underemphasised. This is the case across Latin America.

Despite the difficulties associated with assessing the extent of historical and current environmental degradation, (the capacity of the environment to recover as opposed to human intervention for positive environmental change), there is general acceptance that environment protection is an integral part of the development process. The government agencies and ENGOs established in the 1980s and 1990s, the increased reporting on environmental impacts by multilateral institutions such as the World Bank and IDB, and business and civic awareness, all contribute to this situation.

The mechanisms and instruments for promoting environmental protection and building it into development strategies are numerous, but the overarching conceptual theme is that of sustainable development. By taking this simple concept and working it into policies and programmes of social and economic change, it will be possible to reduce negative environmental impacts and promote a degree of environmental protection, and even remedy past environmental degradation. Sustainable development requires a range of policy responses and collaboration among numerous actors. The thrust must come from the state to enable private interests and civil society actors to make the necessary changes in their activities. Inevitably, this requires resources of capital and knowledge, but the trade-off in terms of cost and benefits of environmental responses and action by interest groups is still under-researched. Since neoliberalism is shaping the continent at present, until environmental and ecological economists establish systems for the valuation of a broad range of environmental factors and impacts, the science of economic assessment of environmental change will remain inadequate. Since this is the current state of affairs, evidence for environmental policy initiatives is often piecemeal. Nevertheless, this case-specific evidence should suffice in terms of stressing the need for action.

The problems raised relate to the generation of a comprehensive national environmental strategy based on guiding principles, effective inspection and monitoring, and consistent enforcement. Since particular ecosystems and geographical settings create widely varying environmental impacts from similar activities, the state has to be universally consistent and specifically flexible. This may generate opposition from firms or communities who feel that they are being treated unfairly relative to competitors or similar groups. To overcome this obstacle, there are two simple priorities for environmental agencies: the first prerequisite is that of 'environmental transparency' in terms of information, agenda-setting, and enforcement; the second is a clear link between environmental degradation and penalty systems (requiring stronger environmental awareness and action within the judiciary). Until there is an understanding that environmental degradation is a legal offence, and the issue is taken seriously via penalties that force firms to adopt sustainable practices, cleaner technologies and environmental management systems, it is unlikely that current levels of environmental degradation will be assuaged.

Conclusion: the environment as a development indicator

Since the Stockholm conference most of Latin America has suffered from strict authoritarianism, civil and guerrilla warfare, and crises of debt. The severity of these situations led to environmentalism being marginalised within government policy and also within civil society (more concerned with human rights and food security). The 1990s has created a new space within Latin American political economy. The transitions to democracy and the rise of neoliberalism have established a degree of political and economic stability that has allowed the environmental debates to be aired and contested.[36] The legislation and regulations imposed by fledgling agencies provide a state response, therefore recognition, of the environmental obstacles inherent within development strategies. While neither democratic transition nor neoliberalism are, in themselves, environmentally positive, what is important is that information regarding environmental change is increasingly (albeit slowly) available. With this basic information, civil-society groups and those contesting the environmental impacts of current economic activities and state service provision are able to present a more powerful case. Links across national boundaries also provide strength for these groups and organisations seeking change.

Political economy has traditionally preoccupied itself with macroeconomic indicators and the role of the state and the private sector in shaping economic policy and political stability. The emergence of the Human Development Index, to measure development, contests the static notion that 'the national condition' can best be measured by economic and political indicators alone. A stage further from the introduction of social indicators of development is the inclusion of environment indicators. Since people and environments are integral to macroeconomic indicators in the first instance – that is, agricultural output, marine fisheries, and raw materials and energy inputs into industry – the inclusion of indicators provides a more explicit recognition of environmental change as a concomitant of economic change and development policy.

Currently the integration of environment and economy is conducted along the lines of valuing the environment and the introduction of price mechanisms. Emissions charges and water-consumption charges provide examples of how, under neoliberalism, the resolution of environmental problems is being led by an attempt to extend the market to cover environmental criteria. The 'tragedy of the commons' and overexploitation of natural resources beyond sustainable levels leads critics to suggest that the market is not the best tool for environmental management. Clearly there are ethical dimensions to the environment debate, regarding *patrimonio nacional* and rights of access to potable water and clean air, for example. Latin America's marginal settlements provide examples of the failure of the market to deliver formal employment to millions of rural and urban workers. The application of the same principles to the environment is likely to lead to more large tracts of exhausted land, deteriorating water and air quality, and livelihood and health consequences for the majority of Latin Americans. Since the market consistently fails to value the environment beyond the short term, responsibility must be assumed by the state.[37] The state has the powers to dictate what is environmentally acceptable within its territorial limits, and is constitutionally bound to defend the interests and rights of the nation's citizens, including rights to a healthy environment.

What is the trade-off between private activities and state control and protection? Under the present state of affairs in Latin America, with the predominance of neoliberalism and the faith in market mechanisms to resolve economic and social development dilemmas, the environment will continue to be undervalued and overtraded. In the short term, ecological economists must place values on the environment that truly reflect intergenerational impacts and the demands for sustainability. In the medium term, business, the state and civil society must reach agreements on how the environment can be best integrated into national development policy – a balance somewhere between preservation, conservation and exploitation. In the longer term, fundamental issues of how the environment has been exploited in the pursuit of capital accumulation, how environmental equity and environmental rights should be constructed, and how the environment can both provide for existing and future generations within a context of globalising processes, have to be addressed and answered. There is an environmental imperative in Latin America that has been masked and hidden for at least half a millennium. It is high time that governments and societies gave it full recognition and placed themselves within the environmental change scenarios rather than outside them.

Notes

1 These debates are traced in Susan Place's review essay, 'Recent Trends in the Study of Latin American Environments', *Latin American Research Review*, 33:2 (1998), whilst Peter Furley provides an overview of the wide range of issues that have emerged from these transformations: 'Environmental Issues and the Impact of Development', in D. Preston (ed.), *Latin American Development: Geographical Perspectives* (Harlow, Longman, 1996).
2 Noted in A. Van Rooy, 'The Frontiers of Influence: NGO Lobbying at the 1974 World Food Conference, the 1992 Earth Summit and Beyond', *World Development*, 25:1 (1997).
3 Michael Redclift makes the important point of recognising the historical construction of the environment and the links between sustainability and the development of capitalism 'Development and the Environment: Managing the Contradictions?', in L. Sklair (ed.), *Capitalism and Development* (London, Routledge, 1994).
4 Many authors have addressed the complexity of this issue. Peter Utting, for example, makes the case for increased coherency of environmental planning with development strategies within Central America: 'Social and Political Dimensions of Environmental Protection in Central America', *Development and Change*, 25:1 (1994).

5 Two texts provide an overview of this type of approach across the South: W. Adams, *Green Development: Environment and Sustainability in the Third World* (London, Routledge, 1990), and R. Bryant and S. Bailey, *Third World Political Ecology* (London, Routledge, 1997).

6 Discussed in D. Cleary, 'The Greening of the Amazon', in D. Goodman and M. Redclift (eds), *Environment and Development in Latin America: The Politics of Sustainability* (Manchester: Manchester University Press, 1991). The most influential books in terms of raising awareness of Amazon development are R. Goodland and H. Irwin's *Amazon Jungle: Green Hell or Red Desert?* (Amsterdam, Elsevier, 1975), and S. Hecht and A. Cockburn's *The Fate of the Forest* (New York, Harper Collins, 1990).

7 An overview is provided in J. Leitmann, C. Bartone and J. Bernstein, 'Environmental Management and Urban Development: Issues and Options for Third World Cities', *Environment and Urbanisation*, 4:2 (1992).

8 Poor environmental quality is responsible for approximately 25 per cent of all preventable ill health (particularly diarrhoeal disease and acute respiratory infection. Whereas infant mortality rates (per 1,000 live births) in Scandinavia average 5, in Haiti they reach 84, Ecuador 46, Peru 46, Nicaragua 45, Brazil 43 and Guatemala 41. World Health Organization (WHO), *The World Health Organisation Report* (Geneva, WHO, 1998), p. 221.

9 Ecological economists are working towards estimations of natural capital losses. See, for example, R. Serôa da Motta, 'Estimativas de depreciação de capital natural no Brasil', in P. May (ed.), *Economia ecológica: aplicações no Brasil* (Rio de Janeiro, Editora Campus, 1995). The author calculates losses in the areas of water resources, mineral resources and vegetation and estimates natural capital depreciation for 1985 to a maximum of 28.62 per cent of GDP.

10 There are numerous ongoing debates regarding the ways in which trade can assist in environmental protection, and the ways in which it leads to environmental degradation. See H. Hoffman, 'Trade and Environment: Green Light or Red Light?', *CEPAL Review*, 62 (August 1997), and A. Batabyal, 'Development, Trade, and the Environment: Which Way Now?' *Ecological Economics*, 13 (1995).

11 Agricultural products constitute 24.8 per cent of total Latin American exports, with 23.0 per cent mining products. Although 51.4 per cent of exports are manufactures, 75.6 per cent of all imports are also manufactures, often with greater value-added and higher research and development inputs. World Trade Organization (WTO), *Annual Report*, Volume II (Geneva, 1997), p. 33.

12 See B. Barham *et al.*, 'Nontraditional Agricultural Exports in Latin America', *Latin American Research Review*, 27:2 (1992).

13 See J. Barton, 'Revolución azul?: El impacto regional de la acuicultura del salmón en Chile', *Revista Latinoamericana de Estudios Urbano Regionales (EURE)*, 22:68 (1997), and J. Barton, 'Environment, Sustainability and Regulation in Commercial Aquaculture: the Case of Chilean Salmonid Pproduction', *Geoforum*, 28:3–4 (1998).

14 The range of Chilean non-traditional sectors and environmental impacts are discussed in I. Scholz, 'Foreign Trade and the Environment: Experiences in Three Chilean Export Sectors', *CEPAL Review*, 58 (April 1996), R. Quiroga Martínez (ed.), *El tigre sin selva: Consecuencias ambientales de la transformación económica de Chile, 1974-1993* (Santiago, Instituto de Ecología Política, 1994), J. Collins and J. Lear, *Chile's Free-Market Miracle: A Second Look* (Oakland, Institute for Food and Development Policy, 1995), and R. Clapp, 'Waiting for the Forest Law: Resource-led Development and Environmental Politics in Chile', *Latin American Research Review*, 33:2 (1998).

15 For a discussion of the differing approaches to deforestation in the literature, see John Browder's review essay, 'Deforestation and the Environmental Crisis in Latin America', *Latin American Research Review*, 30:3 (1995).

16 See, for example, A. Nadal Egea, 'Technology, Trade and NAFTA's Environmental Regime', *United Nations University* (UNU/INTECH) Working Paper 15 (1995), and K. Griffith, 'NAFTA, Sustainable Development, and the Environment: Mexico's Approach', *Journal of Environment and Development*, 2:1 (1993). The pre-NAFTA situation is documented by S.

Mumme, C. Bath and V. Assetto, 'Political Development and Environmental Policy in Mexico', *Latin American Research Review*, 23:1 (1988), and D. Goldrich and D. Carruthers, 'Sustainable Development in Mexico? The International Politics of Crisis or Opportunity', *Latin American Perspectives*, 19:1 (1992). For a critical appraisal see J. Simon, *Endangered Mexico: An Environment on the Edge* (London, Latin America Bureau, 1998).

17 Cuauhtémoc Leon and Marina Robles use the examples of fire-control policies, forestry projects and agricultural uses that have influenced biological convergence between California and Baja California: 'Myths and Realities of Transborder Pollution between California and Baja California', in P. Girot (ed.), *World Boundaries: Volume 4: The Americas* (London, Routledge, 1994).

18 For the potential impacts, see H. Muñoz, 'Free Trade and Environmental Policies: Chile, Mexico and Venezuela', in G. MacDonald, D. Nielson and M. Stern (eds), *Latin American Environmental Policy in International Perspective* (Boulder, Westview, 1997).

19 The term is fraught with differing perceptions. See S. Lele, 'Sustainable Development: A Critical Review', *World Development*, 19:6 (1991). Lele stresses that the 'fuzziness' surrounding the concept should be replaced with precision in the conceptual underpinnings and a flexibility and diversity of approaches in developing strategies.

20 Rather than a linear process of degradation, there have been many periods of ecological rehabilitation in response to human impact changes. See W. Denevan, 'The Pristine Myth: The Landscape of the Americas in 1492', *Annals of the Association of American Geographers*, 82:3 (1992).

21 I support the assertion that most degradation is carried out by the poorest groups, i.e. wood-burning stoves, farming on unsuitable marginal land, untreated waste water and solid waste disposal into waterways. My argument is that it is business – agribusiness and manufacturing – and state development strategies that have forced people into these practices via concentrated landownership and eviction, lack of formal-sector employment, low wages, and little or no welfare or infrastructural support. Rather than focusing on activities *per se*, it is necessary to review the political ecology of the context of the activities.

22 One has to consider the outsourcing and subcontracting of elements of the production process in order to establish the pollution loads and responsibilities of foreign versus domestic manufacturers. The argument that companies moved to Latin America for environmental reasons is not supported by the evidence; however, it is the subtleties that may provide more interesting information regarding environmental responsibilities and culpability. See N. Birdsall and D. Wheeler, 'Trade Policy and Industrial Pollution in Latin America: Where are the Pollution Havens?', *Journal of Environment and Development*, 2:1 (1993), and J. Barton, 'To What Extent Do Environmental Regulations Lead to Changes in Competitiveness and Investment Patterns?', in D. Brack (ed.), *Trade and Environment: Conflict and Compatibility?* (London, Royal Institute for International Affairs (RIIA), 1998).

23 Jutta Gutberlet provides an excellent analysis of the political ecology of the city: *Cubatão: Desenvolvimento, exclusão social, degradacão ambiental* (São Paulo, Editora da Universidade de São Paulo, 1996).

24 Of Latin America's urban population, 91.4 per cent have water provision and 79.8 per cent, sanitation. However, there are wide international and rural–urban variations, and a critical issue is that only 10 per cent of total sewage collected is treated. World Resources Institute, *World Resources: A Guide to the Global Environment 1996–97* (Oxford, Oxford University Press, 1996), p. 22, and WHO, World Health Report, p. 172.

25 S. Mumme and E. Korzetz, 'Democratization, Politics and Environmental Reform in Latin America', in MacDonald, Nielson and Stern (eds), *Latin American Environmental Policy*. Note that by 1995 only Argentina, the Dominican Republic, Guatemala, Guyana, Panama, Paraguay and Peru lacked a cabinet-level environment agency. The resourcing and legal issues facing the new agencies are outlined by R. Neder, 'O problema da regulação pública ambiental no Brasil: três casos', in L. da Costa Ferreira and E. Viola (eds), *Incertezas de sustentabilidad na globalização* (Campinas, Unicamp, 1996), and M. Faure, 'Enforcement Issues for Environmental

Legislation in Developing Countries', *United Nations University (UNU/INTECH) Working Paper* 19 (1995).

26 M. Porter and C. Van der Linde, 'Towards a New Conception of the Environment-Competitiveness Relationship', *Journal of Economic Perspectives*, 9:4 (1995).

27 The scale of environmental equipment imports depends on research and development capabilities. In 1992, 19 per cent of Brazil's environment industry market was supplied by imports, whereas Venezuela imported 97 per cent and Chile 89 per cent. US Agency for International Development (USAID) figures cited in J. Barton, 'The North–South Dimension of the Development of the Environment Industry and the Spread of Cleaner Technologies', *CEPAL Review*, 64, 1998. The environment industry is expected to double from $300 billion (1990) to $600 billion (2000), and Latin America will account for much of this growth, as a region of demand. International Finance Corporation (IFC), *Investing in the Environment: Business Opportunities in Developing Countries* (Washington, DC, IFC Environment Unit, 1992).

28 J. Karliner, 'The Environment Industry: Profiting from Pollution', *The Ecologist*, 24:2 (1994). Mumme, Bath and Assetto, 'Political Development and Environmental Policy', describe this process as the 'demonstration effect'.

29 P. Harrison, *Inside the Third World* (London, Penguin, 1993).

30 Data from, IDB, *Latin America after a Decade of Reforms* (Washington, DC, Johns Hopkins University Press, 1997), p. 41. See also Harrison, *Inside the Third World*; also J. Hardoy and D. Satterthwaite, *Squatter Citizen: Life in the Urban Third World* (London, Earthscan, 1989), and J. Hardoy, S. Cairncross and D. Satterthwaite, *The Poor Die Young: Housing and Health in Third World Cities* (London, Earthscan, 1990).

31 With the recognition of interconnections there is a growing emphasis on information exchange, which Sheldon Annis terms 'informational empowerment': 'Evolving Connectedness among Environmental Groups and Grassroots Organisations in Protected Areas of Central America', *World Development*, 20:2 (1992).

32 A survey of participants at the First International Meeting of NGOs and UN System Agencies identified ecology as the most important theme for the 1990s, surpassing democratisation, civil society and economic development. R. Cesar Fernandes and L. Piquet Carneiro, 'Brazilian NGOs in the 1990s: a Survey', in C. Reilly (ed.), *New Paths to Democratic Development in Latin America: the Rise of NGO–municipal Collaboration* (Boulder, Lynne Rienner, 1995).

33 This North–South feature of NGO activity in many way mirrors the internationalisation of production that preceded it, with the evolution of BINGOs (big NGOs), GONGOs (government-organised NGOs) and DONGOs (donor-organised NGOs). See C. Meyer, 'Opportunism and NGOs: Entrepreneurship and Green North–South Transfers', *World Development*, 23:8 (1995). Marc Williams notes that within the North–South construction of the environment debates there may be a new focus for Southern coalitions such as G77: 'Re-articulating the Third World Coalition: The Role of the Environmental Agenda', *Third World Quarterly*, 14:1 (1993).

34 Many authors argue that a critical stage has already been reached, with ecology constructed as a feature of the socio-economic crisis of capitalist development. See D. Faber, 'The Ecological Crisis of Latin America', *Latin American Perspectives*, 19:1 (1992), J. Carriere, 'The Crisis in Costa Rica: An Ecological Perspective', in D. Goodman and M. Redclift (eds), *Environment and Development in Latin America: The Politics of Sustainability* (Manchester, Manchester University Press, 1991), E. Dore, 'Capitalism and Ecological Crisis: Legacy of the 1980s', in H. Collinson (ed.), *Green Guerillas: Environmental Conflicts and Initiatives in Latin America and the Caribbean* (London, Latin America Bureau, 1996).

35 An important dimension are the North–South contributions to pollution loads. Ranking the highest CO_2 industrial emissions economies in the world, Mexico ranks only 13, and Brazil 22. The 'developed world' is the high-consumption and intensive-polluting region. A further example is that of solid waste, where Washington, DC's population generates 1,246 kg per capita per year (1994) against only 352 for São Paulo (1991:), World Resources Institute, *World Resources*, p. 70.

36 Political liberalisation has enabled environmental pressure groups in some ways, but it has also

posed new challenges, as discussed in Mumme and Korzetz, 'Democratization'.
37 The limits of the market are briefly outlined by M. Redclift, 'A Framework for Improving Environmental Management: Beyond the Market Mechanism', *World Development*, 20:2 (1992), and A. Markandya, 'Is Free Trade Compatible with Sustainable Development?', *UNCTAD Review* (1994).

Appendix: Virtual Latin America

This section offers a guide to the various Web sites relevant to issues and subjects discussed in this book and the sister volume, *Case Studies in Latin American Political Economy*. Whilst clearly it would be impossible to be comprehensive in our listing, we hope to provide a general guide to some of the most important sites, to either complement Web sites already used by those studying the region or as a means of encouraging any remaining 'webphobes'. Given the paucity of attention Latin America receives in the British media, the Internet has become an invaluable source of information on the region and should be viewed as a critical tool of research. Whilst many of the country-specific Web sites are in Portugese and Spanish, there are also English sites which can be accessed. The addresses given were correct at the time of going to print and address changes should be taken as inevitable.

Perhaps the most useful and informative Web site for any Latin Americanist is the University of Texas LANIC page. This provides access to extensive links on a variety of Latin America-specific topics, which are broken down in a user-friendly manner either by country or subject. For a specific country, insert the name at the end of the address. So, for example, for Peru this would be:

www.lanic.utexas.edu/la/peru/

As an example of a search by topic, the human rights page, which provides links to international organisations and country-specific human rights groups, can be found at:

http://info.lanic.utexas.edu/la/region/hrights/

From this site you can access Amnesty International, Human Rights Watch, the Peacenet Directory of Human Rights resources, the US Department of State Country Report on Human Rights Practices and the DIANA international human rights database:

http://www.law.uc.edu:81/Diana/index.html.

The country-specific human rights pages are also extensive. See, for example, the Argentine human rights page, the Vanished Gallery, at:

http://www.yendor.com/vanished/

or the Colombian support network:

http://www.igc.apc.org/csn/index.html

For those interested in following up gender issues, we recommend you consult:

http://info.lanic.utexas.edu/la/region/women/

On the military, see:

http://info.lanic.utexas.edu/la/region/military/

On the environment:

http://info.lanic.utexas.edu/la/region/environment/

On indigenous groups, go to:

http://info.lanic.utexas.edu/la/region/indigenous/

And for access to the pages of financial and economic institutions see:

http://info.lanic.utexas.edu/la/region/economic/

In the government and political science section (which can be accessed directly at http://info.lanic.utexas.edu/la/region/government/) there is an extensive list of country resources. With links from this page to detailed sites on constitutions, political parties, Congress, government departments and the presidency, it is an invaluble site. As an example, the Argentine Constitution can be accessed through this site, or directly at:

http://reality.sgi.com/employees/.../argentina/Constitucion/ctoc.html

The Brazilian Constitution at:

http://www.rede-brasil.com/normas.html

For the Chilean Constitution, go to:

http://www.georgetown.edu/LatAmer...al/Constitutions/Chile/chile.html

For Peru, access:

http://www.georgetown.edu/LatAmer...al/Constitutions/Peru/peru.html

and for Uruguay:

http://www.georgetown.edu/LatAmer...al/Constitutions/Uruguay/uruguay.html

The government and political science page also provides links to recent election results in Latin America, a directory of all parties in the various countries and links to their home pages. The sites also provide information on public-opinion polling, pressure groups and laws governing political parties. See, for example:

wysiwyg://146/http://www.agora.stm.it/elections/election/argentina.htm
wysiwyg://157/http://www.agora.stm.it/elections/election/brazil.htm
wysiwyg://37/http://www.agora.stm.it/elections/election/chile.htm
wysiwyg://64/http://www.agora.stm.it/elections/election/colombia.htm
wysiwyg://81/http://www.agora.stm.it/elections/election/mexico.htm
wysiwyg://101/http://www.agora.stm.it/elections/election/peru.htm
wysiwyg://120/http://www.agora.stm.it/elections/election/uruguay.htm
wysiwyg://149/http://www.agora.stm.it/elections/election/venezuela.htm

If you require detailed psephological and political information, the above sites are complemented by the excellent Political Database of the Americas and the Lijphart Election Archive, the latter providing election results from the 1940s. The Political Database of the Americas can be found at:

http://www.georgetown.edu/pdba/

and the various country archives on the Lijphart site can be located at:

http://dodgson.ucsd.edu/lij/argn.html   for Argentina

http://dodgson.ucsd.edu/lij/chle.html   for Chile
http://dodgson.ucsd.edu/lij/clba.html   for Colombia
http://dodgson.ucsd.edu/lij/mxco.html   for Mexico
http://dodgson.ucsd.edu/lij/peru.html   for Peru

All Latin American countries covered in this book have developed their own 'virtual tours' of Congress and the presidency. These visually impressive Web sites provide detailed information on the relationship between the separate branches of the state, review forthcoming legislation, give historical information for visitors and provide graphs to demonstrate the breakdown of political power in the Legislative Assembly. Tour the Chilean, Colombian, Mexican and Peruvian Congresses at:

http//www.congreso.cl/camara/camara.html explanation of parl
http://www.camara-de-representantes.gov.co/
http://www.senado.gob.mx/
http://www.congreso.gob.pe/index.htm

The Venezuelan congresssional Web site, SAIL, allows surfers to request specific pieces of legislation:

http://www.internet.ve/sail/sv/home.html

In addition to congressional Web sites, there is extensive provision of government Web sites which give access to detailed information on government departments, legislation and budgets. A good example is the Peruvian government Web site at:

http://ekeko.rcp.net.pe/rcp/rcp-gob.shtml

For information on Latin American political personalities, we recommend a visit to the Cable News Network (CNN) profile page. Information on a specific president or politician can be accessed through the addition of the name at the end of the address. So, for example, information on Argentine President Carlos Menem can be found at:

http://cnn.com/resources/newsmakers/world/samerica/menem.html

The *Washington Post* has an extensive archive of back issues covering Latin American-related topics and news. This can be accessed at the following address, with the relevant country name inserted at the end of the address (here using Mexico as an example):

http://www/washingtonpost.com/wp-srv/inatl/longterm/wordlref/country/mexico.htm

The site also has links to back copies of Associated Press reports on Latin America, the CIA World Factbook and US State Department Notes. These latter two sites are particularly recommended as they provide detailed political, historical, geographic, social and economic information on all Latin American countries. For direct access to the CIA factbook page, use the following address with the relevant country abbreviation at the end, so for Peru, go to:

www.odci.gov/cia/publications/factbook/pe.html

For details of Latin American research centres and for access to exhaustive research findings on a broad range of topics and a variety of publications, visit the Consejo Latinoamericano de Ciencias Sociales (CLACSO, Latin American Council for the Social Sciences) at:

gopher://lanic.utexas.edu:70/00/la/region/clacso/about

and for the Centro Latinoamericano de Administración para el Desarrollo (CLAD, Latin American Administration Centre for Development) public-sector modernisation project go to:

gopher://lanic.utexas.edu:70/00/la/region/clad/about

CEPAL, the UN Economic Commission for Latin America and the Caribbean, is located at:

http://www.eclac.cl/

with this site providing access to CEPAL reports and archives.

In terms of the core political and economic international actors in Latin America, we can recommend the following sites for information on projects in the region and the role of the relevant external agent. For the Inter American Development Bank (IDB):

http://www/iadb.org/exr/english/index_english.htmv

or access the country directory at:

http://database.iadb.org/INT/_BRPTNET/brptpubframe.htm

The IDB site also has a site called 'Links to the Americas', which gives access to all sorts of relevant information:

http://iadb.org/common/links/links_americas.htm

The World Bank and International Monetary Fund (IMF) can be found at:

http://www.wordlbank.org/ and http://www.imf.org/

The UN Economic Commission for Latin America (ECLAC) has a really good site, with papers available for downloading:

http://www.eclac.cl

Information on the major trading blocs is abundant. For the NAFTA, go through LANIC to Mexico in the country index and access the section entitled 'NAFTA Resources'. The Mexican Embassy in London also has a site with a good range of links: http://www.demon.co.uk/mexuk

For the Mercosur, try:

http://www.geocities.com/WallStreet/Floor/2089/Mercosurhome.html

as well as the country pages from LANIC.
For documents on the Summit of the Americas, go to:

http://www.miami.edu/nsc/summit/summit.htm

One of the great benefits of the Internet is that the daily newspapers in Latin America can be accessed and read on the day of publication. Whilst clearly the majority of these are in the domestic language, there are a number of excellent English language newspapers. For example, read the *Colombia Post* at:

http:/www.colombiapost.com/

The Argentine English Language daily the *Buenos Aires Herald* can be found at:

http://www.buenosairesherald.com/

and the Chilean English newspaper

http://www.chip.cl/

The main Colombian dailies *El Mundo*, *El País* and *El Tiempo* can be accessed at:

http://www.elmundo.com/
http://www.elpais-cali.com/actual/dia/diario.htm
http://www.eureka.com.co/noticias/

The Peruvian dailies *El Comercio* and *Expresso* are at:

http://www.elcomercioperu.com.pe/
http://www.expresso.com/pe/

The Mexican financial journal *Economista* and the daily *Excelsior* are at:

http://www.economista.com.mx/
http://www.excelsior.com.mx/

For the main Argentine dailies, see *Clarín* and *La Nación*:

http://www.clarin.com/
http://www.lanacion.com.ar/

and for Chile, *El Mercurio* and *La Epoca* are located at:

http://www.mercurio.cl/
http://www.laepoca.cl

The best method of accessing magazine and newspaper information for all Latin American countries is to use Yahoo, with the regional country page providing access to all publications. Yahoo country pages can be located at:

http://www.yahoo.com/Regional/countries/colombia
http://www.yahoo.com/Regional/countries/peru

etc.

The country pages also provide links to a range of sites such as universities, travel, social indices and government Web sites. Military Web sites can also be accessed from the country pages. These provide detailed organisational, expenditure and 'mission' information. See, for example, the Venezuelan navy and armed forces at:

http://www.armada.mil.ve/
http//ejercito.ven.net/

For information on military expenditure in the region, or for a discussion of 'military themes', visit:

http://www.sipri.se/projects/milex/introduction.html
http://info.lanic.utexas.edu/la/region/military/
http://www.geocities.com.capitolhill/7109/carlos.html

Search engines like Yahoo are also helpful in terms of tracking down relatively obscure pages such as those of guerrilla groups. For detailed information on the Mexican Zapatista movement, the Zapatista Net of Autonomy and Liberation is an informative, comprehensive Web site, with links to a range of Zapatista-related topics:

http://www.actlabe.utexas.edu/~zapatistas/guide.html

and

wysiwyg://89/http://spin.com.mx/~floresu/FZLN/

The EZLN web page can be found at:

http://www.ezln.org/

and for information on the Colombian FARC, visit:

http://www.constrast.org/mirrors/farc/

Extensive information on travel, social sciences, humanities and social indices can be accessed via Yahoo, and the country pages are also another method of accessing congressional and presidential Web pages, as well as information on the military, NGOs and human rights.

Another useful resource is the Stanford Virtual Library at:

http://vlib.stanford.edu//Overview.html

Select bibliography

The neoliberal economic model

Agosín, M. R. and R. Ffrench-Davis, 'Trade Liberalization and Growth: Recent Experiences in Latin America', *Journal of Interamerican Studies and World Affairs*, 37:3 (1995).

Cardoso, E. and A. Helwege, *Latin America's Economy: Diversity, Trends and Conflicts*, Cambridge, MA, MIT Press, 1992.

Chalmers, D. A. *et al.*, *The New Politics of Inequality in Latin America: Rethinking Participation and Representation*, Oxford, Oxford University Press, 1996.

CEPAL, *Estudio económico de América Latina y El Caribe*, Santiago, CEPAL, annual.

CEPAL, *Panorama económico de América Latina*, Santiago, CEPAL, annual.

CEPAL, *The Social Summit: A View from Latin America and the Caribbean*, Santiago, CEPAL, 1994.

Comisión Económica para América Latina (CEPAL), *Balance preliminar de la economía de América Latina y el Caribe*, Santiago, CEPAL, annual.

Devlin, R., 'Privatisations and Social Welfare', *CEPAL Review*, 49 (1993).

Edwards, S., *Crisis and Reform in Latin America: From Despair to Hope*, Washington, DC, World Bank, 1995.

Ffrench-Davis, R. and M. Agosín, 'Liberalización comercial y desarrollo en América Latina', *Nueva Sociedad* (September/October 1994).

Green, D., *Silent Revolution: The Rise of Market Economics in Latin America*, London, Cassell, 1995.

Hojman, D., 'The Political Economy of Recent Conversions to Market Economics in Latin America', *Journal of Latin American Studies*, 26:1 (1994).

IDB, *Socio-economic Reform in Latin America: The Social Agenda Study*, Washington, DC, IDB, 28 April 1993.

Inter-American Development Bank (IDB), *Economic and Social Progress in Latin America*, Washington, DC, IDB, annual.

Madeley, J., D. Sullivan and J. Woodroffe, *Who Runs the World?*, London, Christian Aid, 1994.

Oxford Analytica, *Latin America in Perspective*, Boston, MA, Oxford Analytica, 1991.

Philip, G., 'The New Economic Liberalism in Latin America: Friends or Enemies?', *Third World Quarterly*, 14:3 (1993).

Philip, G., 'The New Economic Liberalism and Democracy in Spanish America', *Government and Opposition*, 29:3 (1994).

Psacharopoulos, G. *et al.*, *Poverty and Income Distribution in Latin America: The Story of the 1980s*, Washington, DC, World Bank, December 1992.

Roxborough, I., 'Neo-Liberalism in Latin America: Limits and Alternatives', *Third World Quarterly*, 13:3 (1992).

Van der Hoeven, R. and F. Stewart, *Social Development during Periods of Structural Adjustment in Latin America*, Geneva, International Labour Organization, 1994.

Veltmeyer, H., J. Petras and S. Vieux, *Neoliberalism and Class Conflict in Latin America: A Comparative Perspective on the Political Economy of Structural Adjustment*, Basingstoke, Macmillan, 1997.

Welch, J., 'The New Face of Latin America: Financial Flows, Markets and Institutions in the 1990s', *Journal of Latin American Studies*, 25:1 (1993).

Institutions and democracy

Ducatenzeiler, G. and P. Oxhorn, 'Democracia, autoritarismo y el problema de la gobernabilidad en América Latina', *Desarrollo Económico*, 34:133 (1994).

Gargarella, R., 'Recientes reformas constitucionales en América Latina: Una primera aproximación', *Desarrollo Económico*, 36:144 (1997).

Knight, A., 'Populism and Neo-Populism in Latin America, Especially Mexico', *Journal of Latin American Studies*, 30 (1998).

Linz, J., 'Presidential or Parliamentary Democracy: Does It Make a Difference?', in J. Linz and A. Valenzuela (eds), *The Failure of Presidential Democracy: The Case of Latin America*, Baltimore, Johns Hopkins University Press, 1994.

Linz, J. and A. Stepan, *Problems of Democratic Transition and Consolidation: Southern Europe, South America and Post-Communist Europe*, Baltimore, Johns Hopkins University Press, 1996.

Linz, J. and A. Valenzuela (eds), *The Failure of Presidential Democracy: The Case of Latin America*, Baltimore, Johns Hopkins University Press, 1994.

Little, W. and E. Posada-Carbo, *Political Corruption in Europe and Latin America*, Basingstoke, Macmillan, 1996.

Mainwaring, S., G. O'Donnell and A. Valenzuela, *Issues in Democratic Consolidation: The New South American Democracies in Comparative Perspective*, Notre Dame, University of Notre Dame Press, 1992.

Mainwaring, S. and M. Soberg Shugart, *Presidentialism and Democracy in Latin America*, Cambridge, Cambridge University Press, 1997.

Manzetti, L. and C. H. Blake, 'Market Reforms and Corruption in Latin America', *Review of International Political Economy*, 3:4 (1996).

North, D., *Institutional Change and Economic Performance*, Cambridge, Cambridge University Press, 1990.

O'Donnell, G., *Modernization and Bureaucratic–Authoritarianism: Studies in South American Politics*, Berkeley, University of California Press, 1973.

O'Donnell, G., 'Delegative Democracy', *Journal of Democracy*, 5:1 (1994).

Philip, G., 'Democratic Institutions in South America: Comparative and Historical Perspectives', *Third World Quarterly*, 17:4 (1996).

Philip, G., 'The New Populism in Spanish South America', *Government and Opposition*, 33:1 (1998).

Przeworski, A., *Democracy and the Market: Political and Economic Reforms in Eastern Europe and Latin America*, Cambridge, Cambridge University Press, 1991.

Rueschemeyer, D., E. Stevens and J. Stevens, *Capitalist Development and Democracy*, London, Polity, 1992.

Electoral and party politics

Castañeda, J., *Utopia Disarmed: The Latin American Left after the Cold War*, New York, Knopf, 1993.

Chalmers, D. A., M. do Carmo Campello de Souza and A. A. Borón (eds), *The Right and*

Democracy in Latin America, New York, Praeger 1992.

Chilcote, R. (ed.), 'Post-Marxism, the Left, and Democracy', edition of *Latin American Perspectives*, 17 (Spring 1990).

Conaghan, C. M., 'Troubling Questions: Looking Back at Peru's Election', *Latin American Studies Association (LASA) Forum*, 26 (Summer 1995).

Coppedge, M., *Strong Parties and Lame Ducks: Presidential Partyarchy and Factionalism in Venezuela*, Stanford, Stanford University Press, 1994.

Domínguez, J. (ed.), *Technopols: Freeing Politics and Markets in Latin America in the 1990s*, University Park, Pennsylvania State University Press, 1997.

Gibson, E. L., *Class and Conservative Parties: Argentina in Comparative Perspective*, Baltimore, Johns Hopkins University Press, 1996.

Hellinger, D., 'The *Causa R* and the *Nuevo Sindicalismo* in Venezuela', *Latin American Perspectives*, 23 (Summer 1996).

Jones, M. P., 'Evaluating Argentina's Presidential Democracy', in S. Mainwaring and M. Soberg Shugart (eds), *Presidentialism and Democracy in Latin America*, Cambridge, Cambridge University Press, 1997.

Keck, M., *The Workers' Party and Democratisation in Brazil*, New Haven, Yale University Press, 1992.

Lynch, E. A., *Latin America's Christian Democratic Parties: A Political Economy*, Westport, Praeger, 1993.

Mainwaring, S., 'Brazil: Weak Parties, Feckless Democracy', in S. Mainwaring and T. Scully (eds), *Building Democratic Institutions: Party Systems in Latin America*, Stanford, Stanford University Press, 1995.

Mainwaring, S. and T. Scully (eds), *Building Democratic Institutions: Party Systems in Latin America*, Stanford, Stanford University Press, 1995.

Mainwaring, S. and M. Soberg Shugart (eds), *Presidentialism and Democracy in Latin America*, Cambridge, Cambridge University Press, 1997.

Partidos y clase política en América Latina, San José, Costa Rica, Instituto Interamericano de Derechos Humanos, 1995.

Riquelme, M. A., 'Negotiating Democratic Corridors in Paraguay', *LASA Forum*, 24 (Winter 1994).

Rubin, J. W., 'Elections, Repression, and Limited Reform: Update on Southern Mexico', *LASA Forum*, 18 (Summer 1967).

Vilas, C., 'What Future for Socialism?', *NACLA Report on the Americas*, 25 (May 1992).

Global and regional linkages

Atkins, G. P., *Latin America in the International Political System*, third edition, Boulder, Westview, 1995.

Bernal-Meza, R., *América Latina en la economía política mundial*, Buenos Aires, Grupo Editor Latinoamericano, 1994.

Bouzas, R. 'Mercosur and Preferential Trade Liberalisation in South America: Record, Issues and Prospects', Serie de Documentos e Informes de Investigación no. 176, FLACSO, Buenos Aires, February 1995.

Bouzas, R., 'La agenda económica del Mercosur: Desafíos de política a corto y mediano plazo', *Integración & Comercio* BID/INTAL, January–April 1996.

Bouzas, R. and N. Lustig (eds), *Liberalización comercial e integración regional: De*

NAFTA a Mercosur, Buenos Aires, FLACSO and Grupo Editor Latinoamericano, 1992.

Calvert, P., *The International Politics of Latin America*, Manchester, Manchester University Press, 1994.

Chudnovsky, D. and F. Porta, 'On Argentine-Brazilian Economic Integration', *CEPAL Review*, 39 (December 1989).

ECLAC, *América Latina frente a la iniciativa Bush*, Santiago, 1990.

ECLAC, *Policies to Improve Linkages with the Global Economy*, Santiago, 1995.

Ferrer, A. 'Mercosur: Trayectoria, situación actual y perspectivas', *Desarrollo Económico*, 35:140 (1996).

Fontana, A., 'Argentina and the Politics of International Security', mimeo, Buenos Aires, 1997.

Fuentes, J., 'Reconciling Subregional and Hemispheric Integration', *CEPAL Review*, 45 (December 1991).

Fuentes, J., 'El regionalismo abierto y la integración económica', *CEPAL Review*, 53 (August 1994).

Gitli, R., 'Latin American Integration and the Enterprise for the Americas Initiative', *Journal of World Trade*, 20:4 (1992).

Grugel, J., 'Latin America and the Remaking of the Americas', in A. Gamble and A. Payne (eds), *Regionalism and World Order*, Basingstoke, Macmillan, 1996.

Hirst, M., 'Mercosur and the New Circumstances for its Integration', *CEPAL Review*, 46 (April 1992)

Hirst, M., 'La dimensión política del Mercosur: Actores, politización e ideología', Serie de Documentos e Informes de Investigación no. 198, FLACSO, Buenos Aires, November 1995.

Hirst, M., 'The Obstacles to Regional Governance in the Western Hemisphere: Old Regionalism in a New World Order', Serie de Documentos e Informes de Investigación no. 180, FLACSO, Buenos Aires, May 1995.

Hufbauer, G. C. and J. J. Schott, *Western Hemisphere Economic Integration*, Washington, DC, Institute for International Economics, 1994.

Hurrell, A., 'Latin America in the New World Order: A Regional Bloc of the Americas?', *International Affairs*, 68:1 (1992).

Hurrell, A., 'Explaining the Resurgence of Regionalism in World Politics', *Review of International Studies*, 21:4 (1995).

Hurrell, A., 'Regionalism in the Americas', in L. Fawcett and A. Hurrell (eds), *Regionalism in World Politics: Regional Organization and World Order*, Oxford, Oxford University Press, 1995.

Inter-American Development Bank/Institute for the Integration of Latin America and the Caribbean (IDB/INTAL), *Informe Mercosur*, various issues.

Latin American Special Reports, 'Latin American Trading Blocs: The State of Play' April 1995.

Lavagna, R., 'Coordinación macroeconómica, la profundización de la interdependencia y derivaciones para el Mercosur: Notas sobre la oferta y demanda de coordinación', *Desarrollo Económico*, 36:142 (1996).

Lowenthal, A. F. and G. F. Treverton (eds), *Latin America in a New World*, Boulder, Westview, 1994.

Lucángeli, J., 'La integración de la Argentina en el Mercosur: Revisión de antecedentes y evaluación del desarrollo y perspectivas del acuerdo regional', CECE Centro de

Estudios para el Cambio Estructural CECE Serie de Estudios no. 26, Buenos Aires, April 1998.

Mace, G., L. Bélanger and J. P. Thérien, 'Regionalism in the Americas and the Hierarchy of Power', *Journal of Interamerican Studies and World Affairs*, 35:2 (1993).

Manzetti, L., 'Argentine–Brazilian Economic Integration: An Early Appraisal', *Latin American Research Review*, 25:3 (1990).

Manzetti, L., 'The Political Economy of Mercosur', *Journal of Interamerican Studies and World Affairs*, 35:4 (1993–94).

Muñoz, H., 'A New OAS for the New Times', in A. F. Lowenthal and G. F. Treverton (eds), *Latin America in a New World*, Boulder, Westview, 1994.

Norden, D., 'Keeping the Peace, Outside and In: Argentina's United Nations Missions', *International Peacekeeping*, 2:3 (1995).

Pastor, R., 'The Bush Administration and Latin America: The Pragmatic Style and the Regionalist Option', *Journal of Interamerican Studies and World Affairs*, 33:3 (1991).

Payne, A., 'The United States and its Enterprise for the Americas', in A. Gamble and A. Payne (eds), *Regionalism and World Order*, Basingstoke, Macmillan, 1996.

Phillips, N., 'The Future Political Economy of Latin America', in R. Stubbs and G. R. D. Underhill, *Political Economy and the Changing Global Order*, second edition, Oxford University Press, forthcoming.

Porter, R., 'The Enterprise for the Americas Initiative: A New Approach to Economic Growth', *Journal of Interamerican Studies and World Affairs*, 32:4 (1990).

Rojas Aravena, F., *América Latina y la iniciativa para las Américas*, Buenos Aires, FLACSO, 1993.

Rosenthal, G., 'Regional Integration in the 1990s', *CEPAL Review*, 50 (August 1993).

Salgado, G., 'Latin American Integration and External Openness', *CEPAL Review*, 42 (December 1990).

Springer, G. L. and J. L. Molina, 'The Mexican Financial Crisis: Genesis, Impact and Implications', *Journal of Interamerican Studies and World Affairs*, 37:2 (1995).

Tussie, D., 'In the Whirlwind of Globalization and Multilateralism: The Case of Emerging Regionalism in Latin America', in W. D. Coleman and G. R. D. Underhill (eds), *Regionalism and Global Economic Integration: Europe, Asia and the Americas*, London and New York, Routledge, 1998.

Weintraub, S., 'The New US Economic Initiative Toward Latin America', *Journal of Interamerican Studies and World Affairs*, 33:1 (1991).

Weintraub, S. (ed.), *Integrating the Americas: Shaping Future Trade Policy*, New Brunswick, Transaction, 1994.

Whalley, J., 'CUSTA and NAFTA: Can a WHFTA be far behind?', *Journal of Common Market Studies*, 30 (1992).

Wiarda, H. J., 'After Miami: The Summit, the Peso Crisis, and the Future of US–Latin American Relations', *Journal of Interamerican Studies and World Affairs*, 37:1 (1995).

Wrobel, P. S., 'A Free Trade Area of the Americas in 2005?', *International Affairs*, 74:3 (1998).

The Military

Agüero, F., *Soldiers, Civilians, and Democracy: Post-Franco Spain in Comparative Perspective*, Baltimore, Johns Hopkins University Press, 1995.

Aguilera, G., 'Fuerzas armadas, redefinición de seguridad y democracia en América Latina', *Estudios Internacionales*, 9:1–6 (1994).

Arceneaux, C. L., 'Democratic Consolidation or Deconsolidation?: Military Doctrine and the 1992 Military Unrest in Venezuela', *Journal of Political and Military Sociology*, 24:1 (1996).

Arriagada, G. H., *El pensamiento político de los militares*, Santiago, Centro de Investigaciones Socioeconómicas, 1981.

Bagley, B. M. and W. O. Walker III (eds), *Drug Trafficking in the Americas*, Coral Gables and New Brunswick, University of Miami, North–South Center and Transaction, 1994.

Baloyra, E., *Comparing New Democracies: Transition and Consolidation in Mediterranean Europe and the Southern Cone*, Boulder, Westview, 1987.

Blaiser, C., *The Hovering Giant: U.S. Responses to Revolutionary Change in Latin America, 1910–1985*, Pittsburgh, University of Pittsburgh Press, 1985.

Bryan, A. T., 'The New Clinton Administration and the Caribbean: Trade, Security, and Regional Politics', *Journal of Interamerican Studies and World Affairs*, 39:1 (1997).

Comblin, J., *The Church and the National Security State*, New York, Orbin Books, 1979.

Conca, K., 'Technology, the Military, and Democracy in Brazil', *Journal of Interamerican Studies and World Affairs*, 34:1 (1992).

Farcau, B. W., *The Transition to Democracy in Latin America: The Role of the Military*, Westport, Praeger, 1996.

Finer, S. E., *The Man on Horseback: The Role Of the Military in Politics*, New York, Praeger, 1962, 1988.

Fitch, J. S., 'Military Professionalism, National Security and Democracy: Lessons from the Latin American Experience', *Pacific Focus*, 4:2 (1989).

Franko, P., 'De Facto Demilitarization: Budget-Driven Downsizing in Latin America', *Journal of Interamerican Studies and World Affairs*, 36:1 (1994).

Hakim, P., 'The OAS: Putting Principles into Practice', *Journal of Democracy*, 4 (July 1993).

Hens, M. and J. A. Sanahuja, 'Seguridad, conflictos y reconversión militar en América Latina', *Nueva Sociedad*, 138 (1995).

Horowitz, I. L., 'Militarism and Civil–Military Relationships in Latin America: Implications for the Third World', *Research in Political Sociology*, 1 (1985).

Hunter, W., *State and Soldier in Latin America: Redefining the Military's Role in Argentina, Brazil, and Chile*, Washington, DC, United States Institute of Peace, 1996.

Hunter, W., 'Civil–Military Relations in Argentina, Chile, and Peru', *Political Science Quarterly*, 112:3 (1997).

Hunter, W., *Eroding Military Influence in Brazil: Politicians Against Soldiers*, Chapel Hill, University of North Carolina Press, 1997.

Huntington, S. P., *The Soldier and the State: The Theory and Politics of Civil–Military Relations*, Cambridge, MA, Belknap Press of Harvard University Press, 1957.

International Institute for Strategic Studies, *The Military Balance*, London, Oxford University Press, annual.

Johnson, J., *The Military and Society in Latin America*, Palo Alto, Stanford University Press, 1964.

Joyce, E. and C. Malamud, *Latin America and the International Drug Trade*, New York, St Martin's Press, 1998.

Leonard, T. M., *Central America and the United States: The Search for Stability*, Athens,

University of Georgia Press, 1991.

McFadyen, D., 'Consorting with Tyrants', *NACLA Report on the Americas*, 30:1 (1996).

Malamud Goti, J., 'Los militares y la guerra contra las drogas', *Nueva Sociedad*, 130 (March–April 1994).

Maldifassi, J. O. and P. A. Abetti, *Defense Industries in Latin American Countries*, Westport, Praeger, 1994.

Malloy, J. M. and M. A. Seligson (eds), *Authoritarians and Democrats: Regime Transition in Latin America*, Pittsburgh, University of Pittsburgh Press, 1987.

Mares, D., 'Nuevas tendencias en la seguridad hemisférica: El aporte norteamericano', in *Cambios globales y América Latina: Algunos temas de la transición estratégica*, Santiago, CLADDE-FLASCO, 1993.

Nun, J., 'The Middle-Class Military Coup', in C. Veliz (ed.), *The Politics of Conformity in Latin America*, London, Oxford University Press, 1967.

O'Donnell, G., *Modernization and Bureaucratic Authoritarianism: Studies in South American Politics*, Berkeley, University of California Press, 1973.

Pala, A. L., 'The Increased Role of Latin American Armed Forces in UN Peacekeeping: Opportunities and Challenges', *Air Power Journal* (1995 special edition).

Palmer, D. S., 'Peru–Ecuador Border Conflict: Missed Opportunities, Misplaced Nationalism, and Multilateral Peacekeeping', *Journal of Interamerican Studies and World Affairs*, 39:3 (1997).

Pasqualucci, J., 'The Whole Truth and Nothing but the Truth: Truth Commissions, Impunity and the Inter-American System', *Boston University International Law Journal*, 12:2 (1994).

Perelli, C., 'El nuevo ethos militar en América Latina: Las crisis existenciales de las fuerzas armadas de la region en los 90s', PIETHO Working Paper no. 80, Montevideo, PIETHO, 1991.

Pion-Berlin, D., 'Latin American National Security Doctrines: Hard- and Softline Themes', *Armed Forces and Society*, 15:3 (1989).

Pion-Berlin, D., 'Military Autonomy and Emerging Democracies in South America', *Comparative Politics*, 25 (1992).

Pion-Berlin, D., 'The Armed Forces in Politics: Gains and Snares in Recent Scholarship', *Latin American Research Review*, 30:1 (1995).

Pion-Berlin, D., *Through Corridors of Power: Institutions and Civil–Military Relations in Argentina*, University Park, Pennsylvania State University Press, 1997.

Remmer, K., *Military Rule in Latin America*, Boston, Unwin Hyman, 1989.

Richani, N., 'The Political Economy of Violence: The War System in Colombia', *Journal of Interamerican Studies and World Affairs*, 39:2 (1997).

Rojas Aravena, F., 'Procesos de decisiones en el gasto militar latinoamericano', *Fuerzas Armadas y Sociedad*, 9:3 (1994).

Romero, A., *América Latina: Militares, integración, y democracia*, Caracas, Instituto de Altos Estudios de América Latina, Universidad Simón Bolívar, 1989.

Rouquié, A. *The Military and the State in Latin America*, Berkeley, University of California Press, 1987.

Scheetz, T., 'The Evolution of Public Sector Expenditures: Changing Political Priorities in Argentina, Chile, Paraguay, and Peru', *Journal of Peace Research*, 29:2 (1991).

Scheetz, T., 'La necesaria reforma militar argentina', *Nueva Sociedad*, 138 (July–August 1995).

Sharpe, K. E., 'The Military, the Drug War and Democracy in Latin America: What

Would Clausewitz Tell Us?', in G. Marcella (ed.), *Warriors in Peacetime: The Military and Democracy in Latin America*, Portland, Frank Cass, 1994.

Simpson, J., *In the Forests of the Night: Encounters in Peru with Terrorism, Drug-Running and Military Oppression*, New York, Random House, 1994.

Stepan, A., 'The New Professionalism of Internal Warfare and Military Role Expansion', in A. Lowenthal and J. S. Fitch (eds), *Armies and Politics in Latin America*, New York, Holmes and Meier, 1986.

Stepan, A., *Rethinking Military Politics: Brazil and the Southern Cone*, Princeton, Princeton University Press, 1988.

United States Arms Control and Disarmament Agency (USACDA), *World Military Expenditures and Arms Transfers*, Washington, DC, USACDA, annual.

US Department of State (Bureau of Democracy, Human Rights, and Labor), *Reports on Human Rights Practices for 1997 – Latin America and the Caribbean*, Washington, DC, US Department of State, 30 January 1998.

Valenzuela, A., 'Paraguay: The Coup that Didn't Happen', *Journal of Democracy*, 8:1 (1997).

Varas, A., 'Military Autonomy and Democracy in Latin America', in A. Varas (ed.), *Democracy Under Siege: New Military Power in Latin America*, New York, Greenwood, 1989.

Welch, Jr, C. E. (ed.), *Civilian Control of the Military: Theory and Cases from Developing Countries*, Albany, State University of New York Press, 1976.

Zirnite, P., 'The Militarization of the Drug War in Latin America', *Current History*, 97:618 (1998).

Guerrilla Movements

Alvarez, F., 'Peasant Movements in Chiapas', *Bulletin of Latin American Research*, 7:2 (1988).

Balfour, S., *Castro*, London, Longman, 1992.

Bradford Burns, E., *At War in Nicaragua: The Reagan Doctrine and the Politics of Nostalgia*, New York, Harper and Row, 1987.

Calvert, P., *A Study of Revolution*, Oxford, Clarendon Press, 1970.

Calvert, P., *Revolution and International Politics*, second edition, London, Pinter, 1996.

Crawley, E., *Dictators Never Die: A Portrait of Nicaragua and the Somozas*, London, Hurst, 1979.

Debray, R., *Revolution in the Revolution?*, Harmondsworth, Penguin, 1969.

Debray, R., *Strategy for Revolution*, ed. R. Blackburn, London, Jonathan Cape, 1970.

Fluharty, V. L., *Dance of the Millions: Military Rule and the Social Revolution in Colombia, 1930–1956*, Pittsburgh, Pittsburgh University Press, 1957.

González, M., 'The Culture of the Heroic Guerrilla: The Impact of Cuba in the Sixties', *Bulletin of Latin American Research*, 3:2 (1984).

González, M., *Nicaragua – What Went Wrong?*, London, Bookmarks, 1990.

Gott, R., *Guerrilla Movements in Latin America*, London, Nelson, 1970.

Guevara, E. Che, *Guerrilla Warfare*, New York, Monthly Review Press, 1967.

Guevara, E. Che, *The Complete Bolivian Diaries of Che Guevara and Other Captured Documents*, ed. D. James, New York, Stein and Day, 1968.

Guevara, E. Che, *Reminiscences of the Cuban Revolutionary War*, London, Allen and Unwin and Monthly Review Press, 1968.

Hales, C. R., *Resistance and Contradiction: Miskitu Indians and the Nicaraguan State, 1894–1987*, Stanford, Stanford University Press, 1994.

Harris, R. L., *Death of a Revolutionary: Che Guevara's Last Mission*, New York, Norton, 1970.

Howard, P. and T. Homer-Dixon, *Environmental Scarcity and Violent Conflict: the Case of Chiapas, Mexico*, Toronto, University of Toronto Press, 1995.

Kampwirth, K., 'Creating Space in Chiapas: An Analysis of the Strategies of the Zapatista Army and the Rebel Government in Transition', *Bulletin of Latin American Research*, 15:2 (1996).

Kapcia, A., 'What Went Wrong? The Sandinista Revolution', *Bulletin of Latin American Research*, 13:3 (1994).

Mercier Vega, L., *Guerrillas in Latin America: The Techniques of the Counter-State*, London, Pall Mall, 1969.

Montgomery, T. S., 'Cross and Rifle: Revolution and the Church in El Salvador and Nicaragua', *Journal of International Affairs*, 36 (1982).

Palmer, D. S. (ed.), *The Shining Path of Peru*, London, Hurst, 1992.

Poole, D. and G. Rénique, 'The New Chroniclers of Peru: US Scholars and the "Shining Path" of Peasant Rebellion', *Bulletin of Latin American Research*, 10:2 (1991).

Poole, D. and G. Rénique, *Peru: Time of Fear*, London, Latin America Bureau, 1992.

Schoultz, L., *National Security and United States Policy Toward Latin America*, Princeton, Princeton University Press, 1987.

Smith, H., 'The Conservative Approach: Sandinista Nicaragua's Foreign Policy', in S. Chan and A. J. Williams (eds), *Renegade States: The Evolution of Revolutionary Foreign Policy*, Manchester, Manchester University Press, 1994.

Taylor, L., 'Counter-Insurgency Strategy, the PCP–Sendero Luminoso and the Civil War in Peru, 1980–1996', *Bulletin of Latin American Research*, 17:1 (1998).

NGOs and the state

Bebbington, A. and G. Thiele, *Non-Governmental Organizations and the State in Latin America*, London and New York, Routledge, 1993.

Bennett, J. (ed.), *Meeting Needs: NGO Coordination in Practice*, London, Earthscan, 1995.

Bosch, M., 'NGOs and Development in Brazil: Roles and Responsibilities in a "New World Order"', in D. Hulme and M. Edwards (eds), *NGOs, States and Donors: Too Close for Comfort?*, London, Macmillan and Save the Children, 1997.

Burge, A., 'Central America: NGO Coordination in El Salvador and Guatemala, 1980–1994', in J. Bennett, *Meeting Needs: NGO Coordination in Practice*, London: Earthscan, 1995.

Dawson, E., 'Mobilisation and Advocacy in the Health Sector in Peru', in M. Edwards and D. Hulme (eds), *Making a Difference*, London: Earthscan, 1993.

Edwards, M. and D. Hulme, 'NGO Performance and Accountability in the Post-Cold War World', *Journal of International Development*, 7:6 (1995).

Edwards, M. and D. Hulme (eds), *Making a Difference*, London, Earthscan, 1993.

Friedmann, J., *Empowerment: The Politics of Alternative Development*, Oxford, Basil Blackwell, 1992.

Hulme, D. and M. Edwards (eds), *NGOs, States and Donors: Too Close for Comfort?*, London, Macmillan and Save the Children, 1997.

Kakabadse, Y. and S. Burns, 'Movers and Shapers: NGOs in International Affairs', World Resources Institute Working Paper, Washington, DC, World Resources Institute, 1994.

Macdonald, L., *Supporting Civil Society*, London, Macmillan, 1997.

Nelson, P., *The World Bank and Non-Governmental Organizations*, London, Macmillan, 1997.

Pearce, J., 'Between Co-option and Irrelevance? Latin American NGOs in the 1990s', in D. Hulme and M. Edwards (eds), *NGOs, States and Donors: Too Close for Comfort?*, London, Macmillan and Save the Children, 1997.

Piester, K., 'Targeting the Poor: The Politics of Social Policy Reforms in Mexico', in D. A. Chalmers *et al.*, *The New Politics of Inequality in Latin America: Rethinking Participation and Representation*, Oxford, Oxford University Press, 1997.

Randel, J. and T. German, *The Reality of Aid 1996*, London, Earthscan, 1996.

Reilly, C. (ed.), *New Paths to Democratic Development in Latin America*, Boulder, Lynne Rienner, 1995.

Robinson, M., 'Governance, Democracy and Conditionality: NGOs and the New Policy Agenda', in A. Clayton (ed.), *Governance, Democracy and Conditionality: What Role for NGOs?*, London, Intract, 1993.

Segarra, M., 'Redefining the Public/Private Mix: NGOs and the Emergency Social Investment Fund in Ecuador', in D. Chalmers *et al.*, *The New Politics of Inequality in Latin America*, Oxford, Oxford University Press, 1997.

Turner, M. and D. Hulme, *Governance, Administration and Sevelopment*, London, Macmillan, 1997.

Wood, E., 'The Uses and Abuses of "Civil Society"', *Socialist Register* (1990).

Wood, G., 'States Without Citizens: The Problem of the Franchise State', in D. Hulme and M. Edwards (eds), *NGOs, States and Donors. Too Close for Comfort?*, London, Macmillan and Save the Children, 1997.

Human rights

Acuña, C. *et al.* (eds), *Juicio, castigos y memorias: Derechos humanos y justicia en la política argentina*, Buenos Aires, Ediciones Nueva Visión, 1995.

Albó, X., 'From Kataristas to MNRistas? The Surprising Alliance between Aymaras and Neoliberals in Bolivia', in D. Van Cott (ed.), *Indigenous Peoples and Democracy in Latin America*, Washington, DC, Inter-American Dialogue, 1994.

Angell, A., 'La cooperación internacional en apoyo de la democracia política en América Latina: El caso de Chile', *Foro Internacional*, 20 (1989)

Angell, A. and Carstairs, S., 'The Exile Question in Chilean Politics', *Third World Quarterly*, 9 (1987).

Aptekar, L., *Street Children of Cali*, Durham, Duke University Press, 1988.

Avirama, J. and Márquez, R., 'The Indigenous Movement in Colombia', in D. van Cott (ed.), *Indigenous Peoples and Democracy in Latin America*, Washington, DC, Inter-American Dialogue, 1994.

Baehr, P. L. Sadiwa and J. Smith (eds), *Human Rights in Developing Countries Yearbook 1996*, Oslo, Nordic Human Rights Publications, 1996.

Barahona de Brito, A., *Human Rights and Democratization in Latin America: Uruguay and Chile*, New York and Oxford, Oxford University Press, 1997.

Barsh, R., 'Indigenous Peoples and the UN Commission on Human Rights: A Case of the Immovable Object and the Irresistible Force', *Human Rights Quarterly*, 18 (1996).

Béjar, H. and P. Oakley, 'From Accountability to Shared Responsibility: NGO Evaluation in Latin America', in M. Edwards and D. Hulme (eds), *Beyond the Magic Bullet: NGO Performance and Accountability in the Post-Cold War World*, West Hartford, Kumarian, 1996.

Berryman, P., *Liberation Theology: The Essential Facts About the Revolutionary Movement in Latin America and Beyond*, New York, Pantheon, 1987.

Bowen, J., 'The Myth of Global Ethnic Conflict', *Journal of Democracy*, 7 (1996).

Brett, S., *Chile, A Time of Reckoning: Human Rights and the Judiciary*, Geneva, International Commission of Jurists, 1992.

Brysk, A., 'From Above and From Below: Social Movement, the International System, and Human Rights in Argentina', *Comparative Political Studies*, 26 (1993).

Brysk, A., 'Acting Globally: Indian Rights and International Politics in Latin America', in D. van Cott (ed.), *Indigenous Peoples and Democracy in Latin America*, Washington, DC, Inter-American Dialogue, 1994.

Brysk, A., *The Politics of Human Rights in Argentina*, Stanford, Stanford University Press, 1995.

Caldeira, T., 'Crime and Individual Rights: Reframing the Question of Violence in Latin America', in E. Jelin and E. Hirshberg (eds), *Constructing Democracy: Human Rights, Citizenship, and Society in Latin America*, Boulder, Westview, 1996.

Cleary, E. L., *The Struggle for Human Rights in Latin America*, Westport, Praeger, 1997.

Cleary, E. L. and H. Stewart-Gambino (eds), *Conflict and Competition: The Latin American Church in a Changing Environment*, Boulder, Lynne Rienner, 1993.

Cohen, S., 'Government Responses to Human Rights Reports: Claims, Denials and Counterclaims', *Human Rights Quarterly*, 18 (1996).

Comisión Nacional Sobre la Desaparición de Personas, *Nunca más Argentina: Informe sobre la desaparición forzada de personas*, Buenos Aires, Eudeba, 1984.

Comisión Nacional de Verdad y Reconciliación, *Informe de la Comisión Nacional de Verdad y Reconciliación*, Santiago, Talleres de la Nación, 1991.

Correa, J., 'Dealing with Past Human Rights Violations: The Chilean Case After Dictatorship', *Notre Dame Law Review*, 67 (1992).

Del Huerto Amarillo, M. and Sabella Serrentino, A., *Movimiento de derechos humanos en el Uruguay*, Montevideo, IELSUR, 1986.

Dimenstein, G., *Brazil: War on Children*, London: Latin American Bureau, 1991.

Donnelly, J., *International Human Rights: Dilemmas in World Politics*, Boulder, Westview, 1993.

Farer, T., 'The Rise of the Inter-American Human Rights Regime: No Longer a Unicorn, Not Yet an Ox', *Human Rights Quarterly*, 19 (1997).

Farer, T. (ed.), *Beyond Sovereignty: Collectively Defending Democracy in the Americas*, Baltimore, Johns Hopkins University Press, 1996.

Forsythe, D., *Human Rights and US Foreign Policy: Congress Reconsidered*, Gainsville, University of Florida Press, 1988.

Frühling, H., *Represión política y defensa de los derechos humanos*, Santiago, Ediciones Chile América, 1986.

Garretón, M. A., 'Human Rights and Processes of Democratisation', *Journal of Latin American Studies*, 26 (1994).

Garretón, M. A., 'Human Rights in Democratisation Processes', in E. Jelin and E. Hirshberg (eds), *Constructing Democracy: Human Rights, Citizenship, and Society in Latin America*, Boulder, Westview, 1996.

Gledhill, J., 'Liberalism, Socio-Economic Rights and the Politics of Identity: From Moral Economy to Indigenous Rights', in R. Wilson (ed.), *Human Rights, Culture and Context: Anthropological Perspectives*, London, Pluto, 1997.

Guest, I., *Behind the Disappearances: Argentina's Dirty War Against Human Rights and the United Nations*, Philadelphia, University of Pennsylvania Press, 1990.

Harvey, N., 'Rebellion in Chiapas: Rural Reforms and Popular Struggle', *Third World Quarterly*, 16 (1995).

Jelin, E. and E. Hirshberg (eds), *Constructing Democracy: Human Rights, Citizenship, and Society in Latin America*, Boulder, Westview, 1996.

Keck, M., 'Social Equity and Environmental Politics in Brazil: Lessons for the Rubber Tappers of Acre', *Comparative Politics*, 27 (1995).

Keck, M. and K. Sikkink, *Activists Beyond Borders: Advocacy Networks in International Politics*, Ithaca, Cornell University Press, 1998.

Marés de Sousa, C., 'On Brazil and its Indians', in D. van Cott (ed.), *Indigenous Peoples and Democracy in Latin America*, Washington, DC, Inter-American Dialogue, 1994.

Martin, L. and K. Sikkink., 'US Policy and Human Rights in Argentina and Guatemala, 1973–1980', in P. B. Evans, H. K. Jacobson and R. D. Putnam (eds), *Double-Edged Diplomacy: International Bargaining and Domestic Politics*, Berkeley, University of California Press, 1993.

Orellana, P. and E. Quay Hutchinson (eds), *El movimiento de derechos humanos en Chile, 1973–1990*, Santiago, Centro de Estudios Políticos Latinoamericanos Simón Bolívar, 1991.

Otto, D., 'Non-Governmental Organizations in the UN System: The Emerging Role of International Civil Society', *Human Rights Quarterly*, 18 (1996).

Panizza, F., 'Human Rights: Global Culture and Social Fragmentation', *Bulletin of Latin American Research*, 12 (1993).

Panizza, F., 'Human Rights in the Process of Transition and Consolidation of Democracy in Latin America', *Political Studies*, XLIII (1995).

Panizza, F. and A. Barahona de Brito, 'The Politics of Human Rights in Democratic Brazil: A Lei nâo pega', *Democratisation*, December 1998.

Perelli, C., 'Settling Accounts with Blood Memory: The Case of Argentina', *Social Research*, 59 (1992).

Pinheiro, P. S. and P. de Mesquita Neto, 'O Programa Nacional de Direitos Humanos: Avaliação do primeiro ano e perspectivas', *Estudos Avançados*, 11 (1997).

Roniger, L. and M. Sznajder, 'The Legacy of Human Rights Violations in the Southern Cone: Argentina, Chile and Uruguay', Jerusalem, mimeo, 1997.

Sanders, D., 'Getting Lesbian and Gay Issues on the International Human Rights Agenda', *Human Rights Quarterly*, 18 (1996).

Schoultz, L., *Human Rights and United States Policy Towards Latin America*, Princeton, Princeton University Press, 1981.

Servicio de Paz y Justicia (SERPAJ), *Uruguay nunca más: Informe sobre la violación a los derechos humanos, 1972–1985*, Montevideo, SERPAJ, 1989.

Sieder, R. (ed.), *Impunity in Latin America*, London, Institute of Latin American Studies, 1995.

Sikkink, K., 'The Emergence, Evolution, and Effectiveness of the Latin American Human Rights Network', in E. Jelin and E. Hirshberg (eds), *Constructing Democ-*

racy: Human Rights, Citizenship, and Society in Latin America, Boulder, Westview, 1996.

Smith, J., 'Transnational Political Processes and the Human Rights Movement', in M. Dobkowski *et al.* (eds), *Research in Social Movements, Conflicts, and Change*, Greenwich, JAI Press, 1995.

Van Cott, D. (ed.), *Indigenous Peoples and Democracy in Latin America*, Washington, DC, Inter-American Dialogue, 1994.

Weissbrodt, D. and M. Bartolomei, 'The Effectiveness of International Human Rights Pressures: The Case of Argentina', *Minnesota Law Review*, 7 (1991).

Weissbrodt, D. and P. W. Fraser, 'National Commission on Truth and Reconciliation: Report of the Chilean Commission on Truth and Reconciliation', *Human Rights Quarterly*, 14 (1992)

Weschler, L., *A Miracle, a Universe: Settling Accounts with Past Torturers*, New York, Pantheon, 1990.

Willetts, J. D., 'International Human Rights Law and Sexual Orientation', *18 Hastings International and Comparative Law Review*, 1 (1994).

Wilson, R. (ed.), *Human Rights Culture and Context: Anthropological Perspectives*, London, Pluto, 1997.

Wiseberg, L. and Scobie, H. (eds), *Human Rights Directory: Latin America, Africa and Asia*, Washington, DC, Human Rights Internet, 1981.

Women

Acosta-Belén, E. and C. Bose (eds), *Researching Women in Latin America and the Caribbean*, Boulder, Westview, 1993.

Afshar, H. (ed.), *Women and the Empowerment: Illustrations from the Third World*, Basingstoke, Macmillan, 1998.

Alvarez, S. E., *Engendering Democracy in Brazil: Women's Movements in Transition Politics*, Princeton, Princeton University Press, 1990.

Alvarez, S. E., 'The (Trans)formation of Feminism(s) and Gender Politics in Democratizing Brazil', in J. Jaquette (ed.), *The Women's Movement in Latin America: Participation and Democracy*, Boulder, Westview, 1994.

Americas Watch, *Criminal Injustice: Violence against Women in Brazil*, New York, Human Rights Watch, 1991.

Angel, A. and F. Macintosh, *The Tiger's Milk: Women of Nicaragua*, London, Virago, 1987.

Benjamin, M. (ed.), *Don't be Afraid, Gringo: A Honduran Woman Speaks from the Heart: The Story of Elvia Alvarado*, San Francisco, Institute for Food and Development Policy, 1987.

Bergman, E. L. (ed.), *Women, Culture and Politics in Latin America: Seminar on Feminism and Culture in Latin America*, Berkeley, University of California Press, 1990.

Chaney, E., *Supermadre: Women in Politics in Latin America*, Austin, Texas, Institute of Latin American Studies, University of Texas at Austin, 1979.

Chinchilla, N. S., 'Revolutionary Popular Feminism in Nicaragua: Articulating Class, Gender and National Sovereignty', *Gender and Society*, 4:3 (1990).

Chuchryck, P. 'From Dictatorship to Democracy: The Women's Movement in Chile', in J. Jaquette (ed.), *The Women's Movement in Latin America: Participation and Democracy*, Boulder, Westview, 1994.

Collinson, H. *et al.* (eds), *Women and Revolution in Nicaragua*, London, Zed, 1990.

Corcoran-Nantes, Y., 'Women and Popular Urban Social Movements in São Paulo, Brazil', *Bulletin of Latin American Research*, 9:2 (1990).

Corcoran-Nantes, Y., 'Female Consciousness or Feminist Consciousness? Women's Consciousness-Raising in Community-based Struggles in Brazil', in S. A. Radcliffe and S. Westwood (eds), *'Viva': Women and Popular Protest in Latin America*, London, Routledge, 1993.

Craske, N., 'Women's Political Participation in the Colonias Populares in Guadalajara, Mexico', in S. A. Radcliffe and S. Westwood (eds), *'Viva': Women and Popular Protest in Latin America*, London, Routledge, 1993.

Craske, N., 'Women and Regime Politics in Guadalajara's Low-Income Neighbourhoods', *Bulletin of Latin American Research*, 13:1 (1994).

Deighton, J. *et al.*, *Sweet Ramparts: Women in Revolutionary Nicaragua*, London, War on Want and Nicaragua Solidarity Campaign, 1983.

Dwyer, A., *On the Line: Life on the US–Mexican Border*, London, Latin America Bureau, 1994.

Eckstein, S. (ed.), *Power and Popular Protest: Latin American Social Movements*, Berkeley, University of California Press, 1989.

Escobar, A. and S. Alvarez (eds), *The Making of Social Movements in Latin America: Identity, Strategy and Democracy*, Boulder, Westview, 1992.

Fisher, J. *Mothers of the Disappeared*, London, Zed, 1989.

Fisher, J., *Out of the Shadows: Women, Resistance and Politics in South America*, London, Latin America Bureau, 1993.

Franco, J., 'The Gender Wars', *NACLA Report on the Americas*, XXIX:4 (1996).

Goetz, A. M., *The Politics of Integrating Gender to State Development Processes: Trends, Opportunities and Constraints in Bangladesh, Chile, Jamaica, Mali, Morocco and Uganda*, Geneva, UNRISD/UNDP Occasional Series for the Fourth World Conference on Women no. 2, 1995.

Hahner, J. E., 'Feminism, Women's Rights and the Suffrage Movement in Brazil 1850–1932', *Latin American Research Review*, 15:1 (1980)

Hahner, J. E., *Emancipating the Female Sex: The Struggle for Women's Rights in Brazil*, Durham, NC, Duke University Press, 1990.

Heise, L. L., A. Germaine and J. Pitanguy, *Violence Against Women: The Hidden Health Burden*, Washington, DC, World Bank, 1994.

Inter-American Development Bank (IDB), *Women in the Americas: Bridging the Gender Gap*, Washington, DC, IDB, 1995.

Jaquette, J. (ed.), *The Women's Movement in Latin America: Participation and Democracy*, Boulder, Westview, 1994.

Jelin, E. (ed.), *Women and Social Change in Latin America*, London and Geneva, Zed and UNRISD, 1990.

Jones, K. B. and A. G. Jónasdóttir (eds), *The Political Interests of Gender: Developing Theory and Research with a Feminist Face*, London, Sage, 1988.

Küppers, G. (ed.), *Compañeras: Voices from the Latin American Women's Movements*, London, Latin America Bureau, 1994.

McGee Deutsch, S., 'Gender and Sociopolitical Change in Twentieth-century Latin America', *Hispanic American Historical Review*, 71:2 (1991).

Macias, A., *Against All Odds: The Feminist Movement in Mexico to 1940*, Westport, Greenwood, 1982.

Marchand, M., 'Gender and the New Regionalism in Latin America: Inclusion/Exclusion', *Third World Quarterly*, 15:1 (1994).

Menchú, R., *I, Rigoberta Menchú: An Indian Woman in Guatemala*, ed. E. Burgos-Debray, London, Verso, 1984.

Miller, F., 'Latin American Feminism and the Transnational Arena', in E. L. Bergman (ed.), *Women, Culture and Politics in Latin America: Seminar on Feminism and Culture in Latin America*, Berkeley, University of California Press, 1990.

Miller, F., *Latin American Women and the Search for Social Justice*, Hanover, University Press of New England, 1991.

Molyneux, M., 'Mobilisation Without Emancipation? Women's Interests, the State and Revolution in Nicaragua', *Feminist Studies*, 11:2 (1985).

Momsen, J. and V. Kinnaird (eds), *Different Places, Different Voices: Gender and Development in Africa, Asia and Latin America*, London, Routledge, 1993.

Nash, J. and H. I. Safa (eds), *Women and Change in Latin America*, South Hadley, Bergin and Garvey, 1986.

Radcliffe, S. A. and S. Westwood (eds), *'Viva': Women and Popular Protest in Latin America*, London, Routledge, 1993.

Randall, M., *Sandino's Daughters*, Zed, London, 1981.

Randall, M., *Sandino's Daughters Revisited*, New Brunswick, Rutgers University Press, 1994.

Safa, H. I., 'Women's Social Movements in Latin America', *Gender and Society*, 4:3 (1990).

Sternbach, N. S. *et al.*, 'Feminisms in Latin America: From Bogotá to San Bernardo' *Signs* 17:2 (1992), reprinted in A. Escobar and S. Alvarez (eds), *The Making of Social Movements in Latin America: Identity, Strategy and Democracy*, Boulder, Westview, 1992.

Stoner, K. L., *From the House to the Streets: The Cuban Women's Movement for Legal Reform 1898–1940*, Durham, NC, Duke University Press, 1991.

Thomson, M., *Women of El Salvador: The Price of Freedom*, London, Zed, 1986.

Valdés, T., *Mujeres que sueñan: Las organizaciones de pobladoras en Chile: 1973–1989*, Santiago, FLACSO, 1993.

Valdés, T. and E. Gómariz (eds), *Latin American Women: Compared Figures*, Santiago, CEPAL and Madrid, FLACSO and Instituto de la Mujer, 1995.

Waylen, G., 'Rethinking Women's Political Participation and Protest: Chile 1970–1990', *Political Studies*, 40:2 (1992).

Waylen, G., 'Women's Movements and Democratisation in Latin America', *Third World Quarterly*, 14:3 (1993).

Waylen, G., 'Women's Movements, the State and Democratization in Chile', *Institute of Development Studies (IDS) Bulletin*, 26:3 (1995).

The Environmental Agenda

Adams, W., *Green Development: Environment and Sustainability in the Third World*, London, Routledge, 1990.

Ames, B. and M. E. Keck, 'The Politics of Sustainable Development: Environmental Policy-Making in Four Brazilian States', *Journal of Interamerican Studies and World Affairs*, 39 (Winter 1997–98).

Annis, S., 'Evolving Connectedness among Environmental Groups and Grassroots

Organisations in Protected Areas of Central America', *World Development*, 20:2 (1992).

Balvin, D., J. L. López and M. Hordijk, 'Innovative Urban Environmental Management in Ilo, Peru', *Environment and Urbanization*, 8:1 (1996).

Barham, B. *et al.*, 'Nontraditional Agricultural Exports in Latin America', *Latin American Research Review*, 27:2 (1992).

Barton, J., 'Revolución azul?: El impacto regional de la acuicultura del salmón en Chile', *Revista Latinoamericana de Estudios Urbano Regionales (EURE)*, 22:68 (1997).

Barton, J., 'Environment, Sustainability and Regulation in Commercial Aquaculture: The Case of Chilean Salmonid Production', *Geoforum*, 28:3–4 (1998).

Barton, J., 'The North–South Dimension of the Development of the Environment Industry and the Spread of Cleaner Technologies', *CEPAL Review*, 64 (1998).

Barton, J., 'To What Extent Do Environmental Regulations Lead to Changes in Competitiveness and Investment Patterns?', in D. Brack (ed.), *Trade and Environment: Conflict and Compatibility?*, London, Roual Institue for International Affairs (RIIA), 1998.

Batabyal, A., 'Development, Trade, and the Environment: Which Way Now?', *Ecological Economics*, 13 (1995).

Birdsall, N. and D. Wheeler, 'Trade Policy and Industrial Pollution in Latin America: Where are the Pollution Havens?', *Journal of Environment and Development*, 2:1 (1993).

Brack, D. (ed.), *Trade and Environment: Conflict and Compatibility?*, London, RIIA, 1998.

Browder, J., 'Deforestation and the Environmental Crisis in Latin America', *Latin American Research Review*, 30:3 (1995).

Bryant, R. and S. Bailey, *Third World Political Ecology*, London, Routledge, 1997.

Carriere, J., 'The Crisis in Costa Rica: An Ecological Perspective', in D. Goodman and M. Redclift (eds), *Environment and Development in Latin America: The Politics of Sustainability*, Manchester, Manchester University Press, 1991.

Clapp, R., 'Waiting for the Forest Law: Resource-led Development and Environmental Politics in Chile', *Latin American Research Review*, 33:2 (1998).

Cleary, D., 'The "greening" of the Amazon', in D. Goodman and M. Redclift (eds), *Environment and Development in Latin America: the Politics of Sustainability*, Manchester: Manchester University Press, 1991.

Collins, J. and J. Lear, *Chile's Free-Market Miracle: A Second Look*, Oakland, Institute for Food and Development Policy, 1995.

Collinson, H. (ed.), *Green Guerrillas: Environmental Conflicts and Initiatives in Latin America and the Caribbean*, London, Latin America Bureau, 1996.

Denevan, W., 'The Pristine Myth: The Landscape of the Americas in 1492', *Annals of the Association of American Geographers*, 82:3 (1992).

Dore, E., 'Capitalism and Ecological Crisis: Legacy of the 1980s', in H. Collinson (ed.), *Green Guerrillas: Environmental Conflicts and Initiatives in Latin America and the Caribbean*, London, Latin America Bureau, 1996.

Faber, D., 'The Ecological Crisis of Latin America', *Latin American Perspectives* 19:1 (1992).

Furley, P., 'Environmental Issues and the Impact of Development', in D. Preston (ed.), *Latin American Development: Geographical Perspectives*, Harlow, Longman, 1996.

Galeano, E., *Open Views of Latin America: Five Centures of the Pillage of a Continent*,

New York, Monthly Review Press (1973, 1997).

Goldrich, D. and D. Carruthers, 'Sustainable Development in Mexico? The International Politics of Crisis or Opportunity', *Latin American Perspectives*, 19:1 (1992).

Goodland, R. and H. Irwin, *Amazon Jungle: Green Hell or Red Desert?*, Amsterdam, Elsevier, 1975.

Goodman, D. and M. Redclift (eds), *Environment and Development in Latin America: The Politics of Sustainability*, Manchester: Manchester University Press, 1991.

Griffith, K., 'NAFTA, Sustainable Development, and the Environment: Mexico's Approach', *Journal of Environment and Development*, 2:1 (1993).

Hardoy, J. and D. Satterthwaite, *Squatter Citizen: Life in the Urban Third World*, London, Earthscan, 1989.

Hardoy, J., S. Cairncross and D. Satterthwaite, *The Poor Die Young: Housing and Health in Third World Cities*, London, Earthscan, 1990.

Harrison, P., *Inside the Third World*, London, Penguin, 1993.

Hecht, S. and A. Cockburn, *The Fate of the Forest*, New York, Harper Collins, 1990.

Hoffman, H., 'Trade and Environment: Green Light or Red Light?', *CEPAL Review*, 62 (August 1997).

International Finance Corporation (IFC), *Investing in the Environment: Business Opportunities in Developing Countries*, Washington, DC, IFC Environment Unit, 1992.

Karliner, J., 'The Environment Industry: Profiting from Pollution', *The Ecologist*, 24:2 (1994).

Keck, M., 'Social Equity and Environmental Politics in Brazil: Lessons for the Rubber Tappers of Acre', *Comparative Politics*, 27 (1995).

Leitmann, J., C. Bartone and J. Bernstein, 'Environmental Management and Urban Development: Issues and Options for Third World Cities', *Environment and Urbanisation*, 4:2 (1992).

Lele, S., 'Sustainable Development: A Critical Review', *World Development*, 19:6 (1991).

Leon, C. And M. Robles, 'Myths and Realities of Transborder Pollution between California and Baja California', in P. Girot (ed.), *World Boundaries, Volume 4: The Americas*, London, Routledge, 1994.

MacDonald, G., D. Nielson and M. Stern (eds), *Latin American Environmental Policy in International Perspective*, Boulder, Westview, 1997.

Markandya, A., 'Is Free Trade Compatible with Sustainable Development?', *UNCTAD Review* (1994).

May, P. (ed.), *Economia ecológica: Aplicações no Brasil*, Rio de Janeiro, Editora Campus, 1995.

Meyer, C., 'Opportunism and NGOs: Entrepreneurship and Green North–South Transfers', *World Development*, 23:8 (1995).

Mumme, S., C. Bath and V. Assetto, 'Political Development and Environmental Policy in Mexico', *Latin American Research Review*, 23:1 (1988).

Mumme, S. and E. Korzetz, 'Democratization, Politics and Environmental Reform in Latin America', in G. MacDonald, D. Nielson and M. Stern (eds), *Latin American Environmental Policy in International Perspective*, Boulder, Westview, 1997.

Muñoz, J., 'Free Trade and Environmental Policies: Chile, Mexico and Venezuela', in G. MacDonald, D. Nielson and M. Stern (eds), *Latin American Environmental Policy in International Perspective*, Boulder, Westview, 1997.

Place, S., 'Recent Trends in the Study of Latin American Environments', *Latin American Research Review*, 33:2 (1998).

Porter, M. and C. Van der Linde, 'Towards a New Conception of the Environment–Competitiveness Relationship', *Journal of Economic Perspectives*, 9:4 (1995).

Quiroga Martínez, R. (ed.), *El tigre sin selva: Consecuencias ambientales de la transformación económica de Chile, 1974–1993*, Santiago, Instituto de Ecología Política, 1994.

Redclift, M., 'A Framework for Improving Environmental Management: Beyond the Market Mechanism', *World Development*, 20:2 (1992).

Redclift, M., 'Development and the Environment: managing the contradictions?', in L. Sklair (ed.), *Capitalism and Development*, London, Routledge, 1994.

Scholz, I., 'Foreign Trade and the Environment: Experiences in Three Chilean Export Sectors', *CEPAL Review*, 58 (April 1996).

Silva, E., 'The Politics of Sustainable Development: Native Forest Policy in Chile, Venezuela, Costa Rica and Mexico', *Journal of Latin American Studies*, 30 (May 1998).

Simon, J. , *Endangered Mexico: An Environment on the Edge*, London, Latin America Bureau, 1998.

Tulchin, J. S. and A. I. Rudman (eds), *Economic Development and Environmental Protection in Latin America*, Boulder and London, Lynne Rienner, 1991.

Utting, P., 'Social and Political Dimensions of Environmental Protection in Central America', *Development and Change*, 25:1 (1994).

Van Rooy, A., 'The Frontiers of Influence: NGO Lobbying at the 1974 World Food Conference, the 1992 Earth Summit and Beyond', *World Development*, 25:1 (1997).

Williams, M., 'Re-articulating the Third World Coalition: The Role of the Environmental Agenda', *Third World Quarterly*, 14:1 (1993).

World Health Organization (WHO), *The World Health Organisation Report* (Geneva, WHO, 1998).

World Resources Institute (WRI), *World Resources: A Guide to the Global Environment 1996–97*, Oxford, Oxford University Press, 1996.

Index

abortion 39
Academia de Humanismo Cristiano en Chile 147
Academy of Christian Humanism in Chile *see* Academia de Humanismo Cristiano en Chile
Acción Democrática 57, 59, 61
Acción Popular 123
accountability 39, 42, 86, 134, 138, 152, 154, 163, 164
AD *see* Acción Democrática
adjustment loans 139
adjustment process 78
Africa 22, 94
aid 118, 153
aid agencies 138
Alemán, Miguel 63
Alfonsín, Raúl 39, 102
Alianza Democrática 119
Alianza Nacional Popular 116–17
Alianza Popular Revolucionaria Americana 57, 65, 120–1
Alianza Republicana Nacional 63, 64
Allende, Salvador 59, 64
Amazonia 187
American Popular Revolutionary Alliance *see* Alianza Popular Revolucionaria Americana
amnesties 96
Amnesty International 122, 123, 148, 159
Annan, Kofi 158
ANAPO *see* Alianza Nacional Popular
Andean community, Andean Pact, Andean Group 22, 79, 82, 88, 193
anti-clericalism 63
anti-statist 68
anti-party politics 61
Apparel Industrial Partnership 160
APRA *see* Alianza Popular Revolucionaria Americana
ARENA *see* Alianza Republicana Nacional
Argentina 2, 3, 15, 16, 17, 19, 20, 21, 22, 24, 25 (taxes), 35, 39, 42, 45, 51, 53, 56, 57, 58, 59, 60, 66, 67, 72, 73, 75, 76, 79, 80, 81, 84–5, 94, 96, 98–9, 102, 105–7, 147, 154, 156–9, 169, 172, 175, 177, 179, 190, 193
Argentine Homosexual Community 159
armed forces 73, 94
arms trade 105
Artisans du Monde 160
Aruba 104
Asia 22, 45, 76, 94
Asian crisis 75
Asia–Pacific Economic Cooperation Conference 193
Asociación de Mujeres Nicaraguenses Luisa Amanda Espinoza 174, 179
Aspe, Pedro 66
Association of Honduran Homosexuals against AIDS 159
Australasia 94
Austral Plan 16
authoritaranism 37, 54, 135
Autonomous University of Mexico 147
Ayacucho 122

Bahamas 104
bail-out 19, 20
bancada femenina 177
Bandera Roja 120
Barco, Virgilio 118
barrio dwellers 53, 54, 59, 169
Batista, Fulgencio 62
Beijing Conference *see* UN Conference on Women
Beijing Platform of Action 181
Bermudez, Enrique Adolfo 115
Betancur, Belisario 117
binominal system 176
biodiversity 188
blacks 61, 178 (women)
Blanco Party 58
Blancos 56
Bolívar, Simón 190
Bolivia 35, 39, 45, 46, 57, 79, 96, 98,

103–4, 106, 114, 136, 137, 141, 151,
154, 156, 168, 176
bond issues 19
Brady, Nicholas 17
"Brady Plan" 17, 123
Brazil 15, 16, 17, 18 (privatisation), 19,
20, 22, 24, 25, 26 (state services), 35,
39, 41, 42, 44, 51, 53, 56, 57, 59, 60,
61, 66, 67, 76, 78, 79, 80, 82, 83, 84,
85, 93, 96, 97, 98, 105, 106, 107, 136,
137, 147, 150, 154, 155, 156, 157,
170, 174, 175, 176, 177, 178, 179,
181, 182, 183, 187, 188, 191, 192,
193, 193, 195, 196
Brazilian Democratic Movement Party see
Partido do Movimento Democratico
Brasileiro
Brazilian Workers' Party see Partido dos
Trabalhadores Brasileiros
Britain 24, 37, 63, 160, 190
Brown agenda 188, 196
Brundtland, Gro Harlem 194
Bucaram, Assad 39, 53
bureaucracy (state, weberian) 41, 42
"bureaucratic authoritarian" 42
Bush, George 82, 118
business community 67
business organisations 50, 98, 159
business oriented neoliberals 60
business oriented parties 63

Cabañas, Lucio 127
Caciques 67
Caldera, Rafael 2, 53
Cali Cartel 119
Camacho Solis, Manuel 125
Cambio 90 party 52, 122
Canada 21, 149, 193
capital flight 76
capitalism 34, 132
Cárdenas, Cuauhtémoc 60, 67
Cardoso, Fernando Henrique 17, 19, 37,
66
Caribbean 79, 83, 104
"carpa blanca" (white tent) 3
Carter, James 149
Castellanos Dominguez, Absalón 125
Castro, Fidel 63, 113–44

Catch-all parties 58–60
Catholic Church 40, 47, 56, 58, 135,
147, 170
Catholic Fund for Overseas Development
23
Caudillo, caudillismo 56, 63, 67, 97
Causa R 52, 60, 61
Cavallo, Domingo 66, 76, 78, 190–2,
194
CEAS see Comisión Episcopal de Acción
Social
Central America 7, 53, 57, 63, 94, 98,
104, 147, 154, 170, 181, 190–2,
194
Central America Common Market 79,
193
Central Intelligence Agency 50
Central Unica do Trabalhadores 175
Centre for Victims of Torture in
Minneapolis 154
centre left parties 175
centrist parties 64
CEPAL see Comisión Económica para
América Latina
Cerpa Cartolini, Néstor 124, 125
certification 103, 104
Chaco War 96
Chamorro, Violeta 27, 62
Chávez, Hugo 62
Chiapas 3, 55, 60, 125, 126, 128
Chicago Boys 13, 64
Chico Mendes 192
child labour 155, 160
Chile 13, 15, 22, 24, 25 (tax), 27 (state
services), 29, 42, 43, 44, 45, 51, 54,
56, 58, 59, 61, 64, 65, 66, 76, 79, 94,
96, 97, 98, 104, 105, 106, 136, 147,
148, 154, 156, 158, 159, 169, 172,
174, 175, 176, 177, 179, 182, 187,
190, 191, 192
Christian Aid 23
Christian democratic parties 58
Christian democrats 63, 64, 66, 68, 147,
174, 175
CIA see Central Intelligence Agency
citizenship 131, 136, 142, 151, 153, 161,
162, 171
civil–military studies 101, 103

civil society 4, 54, 60, 86, 131, 133, 134,
    135, 137, 138, 139, 140, 142, 153,
    169, 172, 174, 180, 186, 194, 196,
    197, 198, 199, 200
civil war 56, 63
class conflict 34
clientelistic, clientelism, clientelist 37, 41,
    42, 43, 68, 164
climate change 188
Clinton, Bill (William) 22
coalitions 2
coca, cocaine 36, 104, 118, 120
cold war 73, 96, 98, 103, 104, 105, 108,
    134
collectivist ideas 40
Collor de Mello, Fernando 35, 39, 40, 67
Colombia 3, 7, 15, 20, 25 (tax), 36, 46,
    47, 52, 53, 55, 56, 58, 59, 62, 67, 93,
    94, 95, 97, 98, 99, 103, 104, 105, 113,
    116–30, 147, 150, 151, 154–8, 160,
    177, 180
Colombian Communist Party see Fuerzas
    Armadas Revolucionarias de Colombia
Colorado Party 52, 53
Colorados 58
Comando Rodrigo Franco 122
COMECON see Council for Mutual
    Economic Assistance
Comisión Andina de Juristas 147
Comisión Económica para América
    Latina y el Caribe 18, 20, 22, 23, 24,
    25, 26, 75
Comisión Episcopal de Acción Social 147
Comité de Organización Política Electoral
    58
Common External Tariff 79, 80, 81
communism 50, 57, 62, 103, 104, 105,
    112, 134
Communist Parties 51, 56, 58, 116
Communist Party of Cuba see Partido
    Comunista de Cuba
CONAVIGUA see Coordinadora
    Nacional de Viudas de Guatemala
Concertación coalition 61, 169, 172, 177
conditionality 34
Congress 39, 43, 59, 65, 178
Consejo Nacional Protestante 147
conservative organisations 56, 64

Conservative Party (Colombia) 65, 115
conservatives 56, 58, 63, 66, 118
"consolidation" phase 2, 171, 180
consulting firms 152
consumer groups 54, 152
Continental Meeting for Humanity and
    Against Neoliberalism 127
contras 115
convertibility 76, 86
Coordinación de Mujeres del Paraguay
    181
Coordinadora Nacional de Viudas de
    Guatemala 170, 178
Coordinación Nacional de Viudas de la
    Violencia Política 170, 178
COPEI see Comité de Organización
    Política Electoral
Corporación del Cobre – CODELCO
    195
corruption 3, 34, 37, 38, 39, 43, 45, 55,
    63, 65, 68, 93, 97, 152
Costa Rica 23, 29, 55, 56, 57, 58, 59, 97,
    99, 115, 151, 155, 157, 158, 159, 176,
    187
Council for Mutual Economic Assistance
    193
coup 51, 55, 56, 57, 59, 64, 68, 93, 100
credit 25
crime 36
cross-conditionality 139
Cruzado Plan 16
Cuba 1, 7, 49, 51, 58, 62, 63, 69, 82, 94,
    97, 98, 99, 112, 113, 115, 130, 159,
    174, 193
Cuban revolution 50, 60
cultural relativism 151
Customs Unions 79

Da Silva, Benedita 176
Da Silva, José Ignacio 61, 67, 76
Da Silva, Marina 176
death squads 52
debt 30 t.1.1.
debt crisis 13, 16, 26, 29, 46, 73, 133
debt service 14, 15
Declaration on the Elimination of
    Violence Against Women 158
De la Madrid, Miguel 72

"delegative democracy" 54
demobilisation (societal) 2
democracy 35, 44, 50, 51, 53, 74, 132, 133, 136, 142, 147, 149, 154, 174
democracy (participatory) 3
democracy (neoliberal) 3
"democraduras" ("democratorships") 2
Democratic Action see Acción Democrática
democratic breakdown 39
democratic governance 150
democratic institutions 40
Democratic Revolutionary Party see Partido de la Revolución Democrática
democratic transition 35, 101
democratisation 33, 83, 85, 103, 104, 107, 112, 134, 135, 137, 138, 142, 146, 167, 150, 161, 164, 183
deregulation 15, 19, 21, 46, 77, 133
desegregation 39
De Soto, Hernando 65
Dianderas, Fernando 125
dictatorships 50, 51
domestic demand 14
domestic industries 57
domestic political stability 46
domestic violence 183
Dominican Republic 51
donors 139
drainage 27
drugs 34, 46, 47, 67, 104, 116, 118, 128, 156
dual legitimation 38
Dutch Clean Clothes 160
Duvalier, Jean Claude 97
Duverguer, Maurice 42

Earth Summit of Rio de Janeiro 187
East Asia 34, 141; see also Asia
Eastern Europe 16
ecology of poverty 196
Economic and Social Council 159
economic crisis 35
economic planning 42
Ecuador 27, 39, 53, 94, 96, 97, 101, 105, 106, 151, 154, 156, 158, 159, 176, 183, 191

education 26, 38, 49, 63, 136, 138, 140, 141, 142, 161, 177
Ejército de Liberación Nacional 95, 116, 117, 118, 119
Ejército Popular Revolucionario 127
Ejército Zapatista de Liberación Nacional 3, 60, 62, 87, 125
elections 49, 54, 55, 62, 63, 68, 69, 124
electoral democracy 50
electoral movement 60, 69
electoral politics 66, 68
electoral system 52, 171, 175
elite 40, 46, 65
ELN see Ejército de Liberación Nacional
El Salvador 52, 55, 57, 96, 98, 115, 116, 135, 150, 154, 155, 159, 160, 170, 174, 177, 179, 182, 191
"emerging markets" 19, 131
empowerment 33
Enterprise for the Americas Initiative 82
"Entre Amigos" 159
environment 186–200
environmental groups 152
environmental non-governmental organisations 196, 198
environmental policies 61
EPR see Ejército Popular Revolucionario
equality 49
Ernst and Young 160
Europe 20, 34, 41, 53, 59, 69, 78, 148, 149, 189, 194
European Commission 78, 149
European Parliament 159, 160
European Union 35
evangelical groups 106
Executive, Executive power 39, 40, 43
Excelsior 128
exchange rate 21, 133
external debt 15, 72
external shocks 20
external trade 72
export competitiveness 19
Exporters Manufacture's Association 160
export-led growth 14
exports 30 t.1.1

factionalism 57
Faith and Joy see Fé y Alegría

Falklands War 74
family 27
Farabundo Martí Front for National
  Liberation *see* Frente Farabundo Martí
  de Liberación Nacional
FARC *see* Fuerzas Armadas
  Revolucionarias de Colombia
fascism 34, 40, 58
fascist ideology 57
"fast-track" procedure 22
favelas 188
Fayad, Alvaro 117
FDI *see* foreign direct investment
FDN *see* Fuerza Democrática
  Nicaraguense
Fé y Alegría 136, 141
federal constitutional structure 57
federalism 56
feminisation of poverty 182
feminism 169, 174, 176–8, 183
fidelistas 62
financial markets 21
First Amendment 39
flexibilisation 27, 182
FMLN *see* Frente Farabundo Martí de
  Liberación Nacional
Ford Foundation 148
foreign debt 18, 68
foreign direct investment 16, 17, 75, 81
foreign economic policy 72, 73
foreign intervention 55
foreign investors 65
Foxley, Alejandro 66
France 38, 127
free market economy 37, 38, 45, 100
free market reforms 45
free trade agreements 21, 22
Free Trade Area of the Americas (FTAA)
  7, 22, 82, 83, 84, 193
Frente Amplio 60
Frente Farabundo Martí de Liberación
  Nacional 55, 57, 62, 64, 135, 174
Frente Grande 60
Frente para el País Solidario 74
Frente Sandinista de Liberación Nacional
  55, 57, 113, 170, 174, 177, 179
FREPASO *see* Frente para el País
  Solidario

FSLN *see* Frente Sandinista de Liberación
  Nacional
FTAA *see* Free Trade Area of the
  Americas
FTAs *see* free trade agreements
Fuerza Democrática Nicaraguense 115
Fuerzas Armadas Revolucionarias de
  Colombia 95, 116, 117, 119, 156
Fujimori, Alberto 2, 35, 37, 40, 52, 53,
  65, 67, 72, 86, 107, 122, 123, 124,
  128, 150
Fujimorización 53
Fukuyama, Francis 49
Fundación Mediterránea 66

Galán Sarmiento, Luis Carlos 117, 118
Galeano, Eduardo 189
García Pérez, Alan 65, 121, 122
García Torres, Cístero 124
Gaviria Trujillo, César 119
gay and lesbian rights 158
GDP *see* gross domestic product
gender 8, 136, 157, 158, 169, 174, 175
Generalised System of Preferences 83
Gilded Age 37
global capital markets 40
global economy 19
globalisation 1, 3, 4, 5, 33, 34, 46, 72,
  74, 75, 77, 78, 85, 87, 103, 106, 108,
  151, 153, 157, 168, 182, 194
Gonzales Mosquera, Guillermo 119
good government 40, 43, 152
Goulart, Joao 57, 59
governance 33
government bonds 17
government controls 15
Gramsci, Antonio 65
grassroots organisations 54, 134, 174, 178
Great Depression 56
green agenda 187, 192, 196
gross domestic investment 16
gross domestic product 18, 22, 30 t.1.1,
  35, 37, 116
growth 17, 44
Guatemala 3, 51, 53, 63, 94–8, 107, 114,
  115, 116, 135, 146, 150, 154, 155,
  156, 157, 160, 170, 171, 172, 178,
  180, 191

Guayaquil 27
guerrilla movements 55, 61, 104,
    112–30, 173, 199
Guevara, Che 114, 129
gulf war 73
Guyana 93, 98, 154
Guzmán, Abimael 120, 122, 123
Guzmán, Jaime 64

Haiti 97, 104, 107, 150, 157
Hayek, Frederick 64
health 26, 27, 49, 135, 136, 138, 140,
    142, 171, 177, 179, 186, 188, 196
"heterodox" stabilisation programmes 16,
    26
high tech exports 20
Homeland for All see Patria para Todos
homosexuals, homosexuality 47, 139
Honduras 56, 96–8, 151, 154, 159, 172
Human Development Index 199
human rights 3, 36, 47, 50, 55, 65, 74,
    96–8, 102, 104–5, 118, 126, 135–7,
    146–67, 177–8, 180, 186, 196–7, 199
Human Rights Committee 158
Human Rights Watch 148, 159, 160
Huntington, Samuel 100
hyperinflation 25, 45, 67, 178

IDB see Interamerican Development Bank
illegal drugs see drugs
IMF see International Monetary Fund
impeachment 39
import liberalisation 20, 28, 133
imports 30 t.1.1
import substitution industrialisation 13,
    44, 45, 59, 60, 68, 72, 100, 195
import tariffs 20
impunity 154
income distribution 46, 132–4, 140,
    142
income tax 25
Independent Democratic Union see Unión
    Democrática Independiente
Independent Electoral Committee of the
    People see Comité de Organización
    Política Electoral
Independent Liberal Party see Partido
    Liberal Independiente

Indians 56, 126, 127, 189
indigenous peoples, groups 61, 178, 189,
    192
Indio Guayas 28
individual rights see human rights
inequality 22, 69
infant mortality 26
inflation 14, 37, 38, 106
inflationary expectations 16
"informal sector" 28
infrastructure 18
institution-building 43, 46, 47
institutional reform 45
Institutional Revolutionary Party see
    Partido Revolucionario Institucional
insurgent groups 36
insurgent violence 47
intellectual property rights 83
Interamerican Commission on Human
    Rights 159
Interamerican Commission on Women 179
Interamerican Development Bank 16, 50
interamerican relations 82
Interamerican Treaty of Reciprocal
    Assistance 96
internal politics 33
International Commission of Jurists 148
International Covenant of Civil and
    Political Rights 158
International Decade of the World's
    Indigenous Populations 157
international financial institutions 20, 34,
    37, 75, 76
International Lesbian and Gay
    Association 159
International Monetary Fund 3, 14, 15,
    16, 17 (Stand–by Arrangement), 26,
    34, 37, 45, 50
international non-governmental
    organisations 148–50, 159–60
Inti Plan 16
investor confidence 17
Irán–contra scandal 116
Israel 127

Jamaica 26, 51, 53, 99, 104, 154
Jaramillo, Bernardo 118
judicial power 39

judicial reform 3
judicial system 38
justicialismo 58

Keynesianism 13, 132, 142

"Labour behind the Label" 160
labour (flexibilisation) 2, 24, 75, 171
labour movement 61
labour parties 59
laissez-faire philosophy 60
landowner 34
land reform 114, 136
Latin America and Caribbean Network
  Against Domestic and Sexual Violence
  157
Latin America Free Trade Area 193
"La Violencia" 116
law enforcement 39
law of repentance 123
Layers Committee for Human Rights 148
left-leaning presidents 42
left organisations 56
left parties 60, 64
left-wing 44
legal institutions 34
Lenin 58, 60
lesbian rights see gay and lesbian rights
Les Magasins du Monde 160
ley de cupos see quota system, quota law
liberalisation 44, 78, 85, 150
Liberal Party (Colombia) 64
liberals 56
Liberty and Democracy Institute 65
Linz, Juan 38
"Living Earth" see Tierra Viva
living standards 38
London 19
long-term capital 46
López Michelsen, Alfonso 117
López Portillo, José 45
"lost decade" 35
low-tech goods 20
Luis Amanda Espinoza Association of
  Nicaraguan Women 174
"Lula" see Da Silva, José Ignacio

M-19 see Movimiento 19 de abril

machismo 64, 67
"Mamá Maquín" 171
maoist 115
Mao Zedong 122
Manley, Michael 51
Maquiladoras, maquilas 20, 158, 160,
  182, 191
marginalisation (of participatory
  democracy) 3
marianismo 64
Mariátegui, José Carlos 120
market-led approach 16
market-oriented economic reforms 35,
  37, 45, 51, 66
Martí, José 51, 58, 113
Marulanda, Manuel 116
marxism 58
marxist–leninist 115
MAS see Movimiento al Socialismo
mass-based parties 57
mass organisations 62
media 44, 65, 66, 67, 69
Mediterranean Foundation see Fundación
  Mediterránea
Meeting of American Armies 104
Menchú, Rigoberta 146
Menem, Carlos 2, 18, 19, 35, 37, 57, 58,
  59, 66, 67, 72, 81, 86, 180
Mercado Común del Sur 5, 20, 22, 78,
  79, 80, 81, 82, 84, 86, 193
MERCOSUR see Mercado Común del
  Sur
meritocracy 42
mestizo 65
Mexico 3, 13 (default), 15, 16, 17
  (crash), 17, 18 (privatisation), 19
  (crash), 20, 21, 24, 25 (tax system), 29,
  34, 37, 39, 44, 45, 52, 54, 55, 56, 60,
  61, 62, 63, 67, 72 (default), 73, 74, 75,
  76, 77, 80, 82, 83, 87, 87–99, 103–4,
  113–44, 125–9, 137, 147, 150, 154,
  156, 158, 168, 180, 190, 192
Middle East 94
migration 186
military 7, 34, 36, 41, 47, 51, 52, 56, 59,
  60, 93–103, 133, 135, 146, 149.
military aid 105
military doctrine 100

military governments 52
MINUGUA *see* UN verification mission in Guatemala
miskito 115
Miterrand, Francois 14
MNC's *see* Multinational Manufacturing Corporations
MNMMR *see* Movimiento Nacional de Meninos e Meninas da Rua
MNR *see* Movimiento Nacional Revolucionario
mobilisation 35
monarchy 57
Monterrey 63
Montesinos, Vladimiro 123
Morote, Osmán 121
Moscow 59
Mothers of the Plaza de Mayo 146, 169
movement parties 61
Movement 26 July 113, 114
Movement towards socialism *see* Movimiento al Socialismo
Movimiento 19 de abril 55, 62, 117, 118, 119, 156
Movimiento al Socialismo 59
Movimiento Nacional de Meninos e Meninas da Rua 155
Movimiento Nacional Revolucionario 57
Movimiento Revolucionario Túpac Amaru 124, 125–7, 156
MRTA *see* Movimiento Revolucionario Túpac Amaru
Multinational Manufacturing Corporations 194–6
multi-party systems 51
municipalities 56

NAFTA *see* North American Free Trade Agreement
narcotics *see* drugs
National Action Party *see* Partido para Acción Nacional
National Coalition of Women 176
National Coordination of Guatemalan Widows of Political Violence *see* Coordinación Nacional de Viudas de la Violencia Política
National Development Plan 135

National Endowment for Democracy 50, 69
nationalisation 65
nationalism 65, 118
Nationalist Party *see* Partido Nacionalista
Nationalist Renovation *see* Renovación Nacional
National Labour Committee and the Press for Change and Global Exchange 160
National Liberation Army *see* Ejército de Liberación Nacional
national liberation movements 112
National Opposition Union *see* Unión Nacional Opositora
national-populist parties 57
National Protestant Council *see* Consejo Nacional Protestante
National Republican Alliance *see* Alianza Republicana Nacional
National Revolutionary Movement *see* Movimiento Nacional Revolucionario
National Rifle Association 104
national security doctrine 101, 103
National Street Children's Movement *see* Movimiento Nacional de Meninos e Meninas de Rua
National Women's Forum 171, 180
NATO *see* North Atlantic Treaty Organisation
NED *see* National Endowment for Democracy
neighbourhood organisations 61
NEM *see* New Economic Model
neoliberal agenda 54, 58, 75, 77, 132, 133, 136–7
neoliberal democracy 3, 86
neoliberal economic reforms 49, 63, 73, 82, 112
neoliberal intellectuals 64
neoliberalism 2, 4, 16, 25, 38, 51, 52, 53, 57, 58, 59, 60, 64, 69, 74, 76, 85, 135, 139, 142, 190, 194–5, 198–200
neo-nationalism 106
neopopulist 2
nepotism 62
Netherlands Antilles 104
Network of Women Against Violence 176

New Economic Model 134
New International Economic Order 73
"new left" 56, 60, 62
new liberals 117
new right 56, 64, 66
New York 20
NGO's *see* non governmental
  organisations
Nicaragua 27, 50, 51, 55, 56, 57, 58, 63,
  97, 98, 99, 113, 114–16, 151, 154–6,
  159, 170, 172, 174, 176, 178, 182,
  193
Nicaraguan Democratic Force 115
non-commissioned officers 42, 97
non-governmental organisations (NGO's)
  4, 8, 9, 34, 50, 131–45, 197
non-state actors 7
North American Free Trade Agreement 5,
  21, 29, 52, 63, 74, 79, 125, 150, 193
North Atlantic Treaty Organisation 94
North Douglass 33, 41
Northern non governmental
  organisations 134–5
North–South relations 134, 140
NSD *see* national security doctrine
nuclear non-proliferation 78

OAS *see* Organisation of American States
Oaxaca 55, 126, 128
OECD *see* Organisation for Economic
  Cooperation and Development
oil 38, 43, 45, 68, 118, 156, 190
oligarchy, oligarchs 63, 68, 115
ombudsmen 150, 177
open regionalism 77, 78
Optional Protocol of the Convention
  against Torture 147
Organisation of American States 73, 74,
  107, 148, 150, 153, 179
Organisation for Economic Cooperacion
  and Development 134, 138
organisations of debtors 54
Ortega Saavedra, Daniel 115, 170
outsider 67
Oviedo, Lino 54, 107

PAN *see* Partido para Acción Nacional
Panama 63, 97, 155, 150, 151, 154–6

Paraguay 22, 52, 53, 56, 58, 79–80,
  84–5, 96–8, 154, 156, 168, 176
Paraguayan Women's Coordination *see*
  Coordinadora de Mujeres del
  Paraguaya
Paramilitary groups 127–8
Paris Club 123
parliamentary system 38
participatory democracy 3
Partido Comunista de Cuba 55, 62, 63
Partido Comunista del Perú – Bandera
  Roja 120
Partido de la Revolución Democrática 60,
  61
Partido do Movimiento Democratico
  Brasileiro 170
Partido dos Trabalhadores 57, 60, 61,
  67
Partido dos Trabalhadores Brasileiros 57
Partido Liberal Independiente 58, 63
Partido Liberal Rádical Auténtico 176
Partido Nacionalista 64
Partido para Acción Nacional 61, 63, 76
Partido para la Democracia 60, 61, 175
Partido Peronista Femenino 174, 175
Partido Revolucionario de los
  Trabajadores 119
Partido Revolucionario Institucional 54,
  55, 57, 60, 61, 63, 66, 125, 176
Partido Socialista 59, 61, 175
Partido Socialista Revolucionario 124
"partyarchy" 61
Party for Democracy *see* Partido para la
  Democracia
party organisations 54
party system 40, 41, 179
Pastora, Edén 116
Patria para Todos 60, 62
patrimonialism 37
Patriotic Union *see* Unión Patriótica
patriotism 64
patronage 55, 57, 59, 162–4
PCC *see* Partido Comunista de Cuba
PdVSA *see* Petróleos de Venezuela
peasants 28, 53
peasants associations, organisations 54,
  68, 154
PEMEX *see* Petróleos de México

Peoples' Liberation Army *see* Ejército de Liberación Nacional
Peoples' United Front 117
per capita income 46
Perez, Carlos Andrés 39, 45, 53, 59, 93
Perez, Manuel 118
Perón, Juan 57, 172
Peronist Party 59, 66, 67
peronists 57
Peronist Women Party *see* Partido Peronista Femenino
Peru 2, 3, 7, 16, 20, 24, 35, 37, 43, 45, 52, 53, 57, 64, 65, 67, 72, 79, 77, 79, 95, 96, 97, 98, 103, 107, 113, 120–5, 127–8, 147, 150–1, 154, 156–8, 168, 191
Petróleos de México 195
Petróleos de Venezuela 38, 42, 44
Pinochet, Augusto 13, 15, 27, 43, 54, 64, 172
"pistoleros" 126
Pizarro León Gómez, Carlos 118
PLI *see* Partido Liberal Independiente
PMDB *see* Partido do Movimiento Democratico Brasileiro
PN *see* Partido Nacionalista
polarisation 35
Polay Campos, Víctor 124
police 49
political authority 34, 39
political culture 40
"political ecology" 187
political institutions 33, 35, 40
political liberalisation 73
political parties 42, 43, 50, 51, 55, 66, 86, 98, 137, 169, 172, 174
political prisoners 51, 147
political systems 33, 177
political violence 36
"polyarchy" 50
Popular Action Party *see* Acción Popular
popular democracy 50
popular mobilisation 3
popular movements 61, 62
Popular National Alliance 116
populist, populism 37, 40, 45, 52, 55, 57, 58, 59, 60, 64, 66, 100, 132
populist parties 56, 68

post-transition period 5
post-war period 134
poverty 22, 25, 112, 133
"power gap" 9
PPD *see* Partido para la Democracia
PPE *see* Partido Peronista Femenino
PPT *see* Patria para Todos
praetorianism 100
PRD *see* Partido de la Revolución Democrática
pre-military era 55
"Presidente Gonzalo" *see* Guzmán, Abimael
presidential government 53
presidentialism 38, 39, 40, 43
PRI *see* Partido Revolucionario Institucional
privatisation 17, 18, 19, 37, 77, 81, 123, 133, 139, 140
property rights 141, 156
proportional system 67, 176
prostitution 63, 157
protectionism 37
PRT *see* Partido Revolucionario de los Trabajadores
PS *see* Partido Socialista
PSR *see* Partido Socialista Revolucionario
PT *see* Partido dos Trabajadores
PTB *see* Partido dos Trabalhadores Brasileiros
public services 140
Puerto Rico 157
Punto Fijo pact 43

quasi-authoritarian 2
quota system, quota law 175–6

Rabanal, Jorge 121
Radical Cause *see* Causa R
Radical Party *see* Unión Cívica Radical
Radicals 56
Ramirez Durand Oscar 123
Reagan, Ronald 13, 36, 112, 115
Real plan 17, 25
real wages 24
Reboredo Iparraguirre, Elena 123
Red Flag *see* Partido Comunista del Perú–Bandera Roja

re-election 59
reform of the state 3
regional integration 21, 77, 84, 85, 106
regionalism, regionalisation 5, 72, 77–8, 84
regional trade blocs 72
Rehabilitation and Research Centre for Torture Victims 154
religious organisations 50
Renovación Nacional 65
"repoliticisation" 2, 3
repression 34
reproductive rights 171, 179, 183
republicans 63
revolution 51, 62, 168
Revolutionary Armed Forces of Colombia see Fuerzas Armadas Revolucionarias de Colombia
revolutionary parties 52
revolutionary regimes 51
Revolutionary Workers' Party see Partido Revolucionario de los Trabajadores
Río Group 150
Río Pact see Interamerican Treaty of Reciprocal Assistance
RN see Renovación Nacional
Rojas Pinilla, Gustavo 117
Roldán Betancurt, Antoni 118
Ruíz, Samuel 125
rule by decree 39
rule of law 49
rural poor 23; rural society, rural movements 23, 44, 178

Saez, Irene 62
SAFTA see South American Free Trade Area
sales tax 25
Salinas de Gortari, Carlos 52, 125, 137
Samper, Ernesto 119
San Cristobal de Huamanga 120
San Cristobal de las Casas 125, 127
Sandinista Front for National Liberation see Frente Sandinista de Liberación Nacional
Sandinistas 51, 58, 115, 174, 193
Sandino, Augusto César 51

sanitation 49
Saucedo Sanchez, César 124
second generation (of structural reforms) 2, 3
Secretaría de la Mujer 181
security forces 36; see also military
self-determination 155–156
semi-parliamentary 43
semi-presidential system 38
Sendero Luminoso 7, 65, 95, 120–2
SERNAM see Servicio Nacional de la Mujer
SERPAJ see Servicio de Paz y Justicia
Serrano, Jorge 53, 150
Servicio de Paz y Justicia 147
Servicio Nacional de la Mujer 177, 179–81
sexual discrimination 181
sexual minorities 47
Shining Path see Sendero Luminoso
short-term capital 46
Sierra Maestra 114
"silent revolution" 13, 17, 19
Siles Suazo, Hernán 39
Simón Bolívar Guerrilla Coordinating Board 119
SL see Sendero Luminoso
social consensus 46
"social debt" 16
social democratic parties 59
social forces 40
socialism 40, 64
socialist 56, 174
socialist parties 58–9
Socialist Party see Partido Socialista
Socialist Revolutionary Party see Partido Socialista Revolucionario
social modernisation 47
social movements 54, 60, 69, 86, 174, 176, 178
social revolution 162
social scientists 34
social security 54, 134, 182
social transformation 34
societal authoritarianism 43, 47
Somalia 73
Somoza, Anastasio 115
soup kitchen 169, 178

South American Free Trade Area 82–3
Southern Common Market *see* Mercado
  Común del Sur
Southern Cone Network Against
  Domestic and Sexual Violence 157
Southern Europe 35; *see also* Europe
southern non-governmental organisations
  114–15
sovereignty 150
Soviet Union 49, 58, 162
Spain 113, 181
stabilisation 18, 19
state autonomy 34
state banks 25
state enterprises 15
state institutions 35, 41
Statement on Foreign Principles 188
state planning 37
statism 57
Stockholm Conference on the Human
  Environment 186, 189
stock markets 19
Stroessner, Alfredo 53, 58, 97, 181
structural adjustment 14, 23, 28, 29, 52,
  53, 59, 133, 139, 142
structural reforms 2
structural rigidities 14
Sub Comandante Marcos 126
subsidies 26, 54
Summit of the Americas, summitry of the
  americas 74, 82, 104
Supreme Court 40, 117
sustainable development 194
sustainable management 197–9

tariff reductions 77
Tax(es), taxation 25, 37, 46, 62, 97, 106,
  133
tax system 25, 37
technocrats 45, 66, 85, 198
"technopols" 66
"Tequila effect" 19
"terceristas" 115
terrorist, terrorism 113, 124, 127
Thatcher, Margaret 13, 36
theory of the "foco" 114
think-tanks 64–6
Third World 55, 73

Tierra Viva 179
"tirofijo" *see* Marulanda, Manuel
"tonton macoute" 97
Torres Restrepo, Camilo 117
trade and environment 78, 81, 133, 156
trade (balance) 15
trade (deficit) 19
trade (deregulation) 14
trade (intraregional) 20, 22
trade (surplus) 14, 15
trade unions 24, 43, 50, 54, 57, 61, 98,
  154, 182
transnational capital 44
"transition" phase 2, 52, 162
Treaty of Asunción 79
"trickle down effect" 6, 29
Túpac Amaru Revolutionary Movement
  see Movimiento Revolucionario Túpac
  Amaru
Tzotzil 127

UCR *see* Unión Cívica Radical
UDI *see* Unión Democrática
  Independiente
"underemployment" 22
unemployment 22, 134, 142
Unidad Revolucionaria Nacional de
  Guatemala 96
Unión Cívica Radical 58
Unión Democrática Independiente 64
Unión Nacional Opositora 116
Unión Patriótica 117–18
unions *see* trade unions
United Nations (UN) 73, 116, 163, 155,
  158, 170
UN Committee on the Elimination of
  Discrimination Against Women 169
UN Conference on Human Rights 149
UN Conference on Environment and
  Development 188
UN Conference on Women 149, 171,
  175, 179
UN Declaration on the Rights of
  Indigenous Peoples 157
UN Economic Commission for Latin
  America and the Caribbean *see*
  Comisión Económica para América
  Latina y el Caribe

UN Human Rights Commission 169
UN International Fund for Agricultural
Development 22
UN International Non-Governmental
Organisation Conference on
Discrimination Against Indigenous
Populations in the Americas 157
UN peace-keeping missions 73
UN verification mission in Guatemala
171
UN Working Group on Indigenous
Populations 157
United Provinces of Central America
193
United States 20, 21, 28, 36, 39, 40, 41,
47, 49, 51, 53, 62, 63, 66, 69, 72, 73,
79, 82, 83, 96, 98, 103, 104, 105, 108,
112, 115, 116, 120, 127, 148, 149,
160, 194
US Catholic Conference 148
US Maritime and Overflight Agreement
104
US military intervention 51, 69
UNO see Unión Nacional Opositora
UP see Unión Patriótica
urban society 44
URNG see Unidad Revolucionaria
Nacional de Guatemala
Uruguay 22, 43, 51, 56, 58, 59, 60,
79–80, 84, 94, 96–8, 106–7, 147, 154,
155, 172, 176, 178
Uruguay Round 83

value added tax 14
vanguardist parties 69
Vargas, José 57, 183
Vargas Llosa, Mario 65, 67
Vásquez Castaño, Fabio 117
VAT see value added tax
Velasco Alvarado, Juan 120
Velásquez Andrés 61, 62
Venezuela 2, 15, 17, 20, 23, 35, 37, 38,

39, 42, 43, 44, 45, 52, 53, 54, 55, 56,
58, 59, 60, 61, 68, 75, 79, 93, 97, 99,
102, 118, 147, 151, 156, 191
Vicaría de la Solidaridad 147
Videla, General 178
vigilante justice 49
Vienna Conference see UN Conference
on Human Rights
violence against street children 155
violence against women 179, 182, 183

Washington 19, 50
"Washington Consensus" 15, 49, 52, 59,
72, 133
Washington Office on Latin America 148
Wasmosy, Juan Carlos 53, 107
water supply 27
Weberian democracy 47
welfare 24, 132, 141, 177
Wolfenson, James 158
women 27, 28, 50, 54 (groups), 61, 155,
157, 168–85
women's police stations 182
Workers' Pary see Partido dos
Trabalhadores
working class 56, 57
World Bank 23, 26, 27, 37, 45, 139, 141,
158, 179, 197, 198
World Commission on Environmental
Development 194
World Council of Churches 147
World Development Report 23, 141
World Health Organisation 24
World Trade Organisation 83

"young officers' movement" 42

Zamora, Rubén 62
Zapatista National Liberation Army see
Ejército Zapatista de Liberación
Nacional
Zedillo, Ernesto 60, 127, 128